T0075724

Digital Agricultural Ecosystem

Revolutionary Advancements in Agriculture

Edited by

Kuldeep Singh

School of Management, Gati Shakti Vishwavidyalaya, Vadodara, India

and

Prasanna Kolar

School of Humanities and Social Sciences, Jain (Deemed-to-be University), Bengaluru, India

Scrivener
Publishing

WILEY

This edition first published 2024 by John Wiley & Sons, Inc., 111 River Street, Hoboken, NJ 07030, USA and Scrivener Publishing LLC, 100 Cummings Center, Suite 541J, Beverly, MA 01915, USA
© 2024 Scrivener Publishing LLC
For more information about Scrivener publications please visit www.scrivenerpublishing.com.

All rights reserved. No part of this publication may be reproduced, stored in a retrieval system, or transmitted, in any form or by any means, electronic, mechanical, photocopying, recording, or otherwise, except as permitted by law. Advice on how to obtain permission to reuse material from this title is available at http://www.wiley.com/go/permissions.

Wiley Global Headquarters
111 River Street, Hoboken, NJ 07030, USA

For details of our global editorial offices, customer services, and more information about Wiley products visit us at www. wiley.com.

Limit of Liability/Disclaimer of Warranty
While the publisher and authors have used their best efforts in preparing this work, they make no representations or warranties with respect to the accuracy or completeness of the contents of this work and specifically disclaim all warranties, including without limitation any implied warranties of merchant-ability or fitness for a particular purpose. No warranty may be created or extended by sales representatives, written sales materials, or promotional statements for this work. The fact that an organization, website, or product is referred to in this work as a citation and/or potential source of further information does not mean that the publisher and authors endorse the information or services the organization, website, or product may provide or recommendations it may make. This work is sold with the understanding that the publisher is not engaged in rendering professional services. The advice and strategies contained herein may not be suitable for your situation. You should consult with a specialist where appropriate. Neither the publisher nor authors shall be liable for any loss of profit or any other commercial damages, including but not limited to special, incidental, consequential, or other damages. Further, readers should be aware that websites listed in this work may have changed or disappeared between when this work was written and when it is read.

Library of Congress Cataloging-in-Publication Data

ISBN 978-1-394-24293-1

Cover image: Pixabay.Com
Cover design by Russell Richardson

Set in size of 11pt and Minion Pro by Manila Typesetting Company, Makati, Philippines

Printed in the USA

10 9 8 7 6 5 4 3 2 1

Dedication

We humbly dedicate this edited book, 'Digital Agricultural Ecosystem,' to the cherished memories of those whose invaluable influence and unwavering support have shaped our lives and inspired the pursuit of knowledge in the field of agriculture. We pay homage to *Shri Harishchandra Master Ji*, the grandfather of Dr. Kuldeep Singh, whose profound wisdom as a science teacher in Jhunjhunu, Rajasthan, continues to resonate in our hearts. After his honorable retirement, he imparted invaluable insights about agriculture, its challenges, and its significance at the grassroots level. In loving memory of *Late Fauji Ravinder Singh*, the father of Dr. Kuldeep Singh, who devoted his entire career to serving in the Indian Army. His dedication, discipline, and selflessness have been a guiding light, inspiring us to strive for excellence in our endeavors. With boundless love and gratitude, we acknowledge *Mrs. Suresh Devi*, the mother of Dr. Kuldeep Singh, whose genuine affection for the soil and profound knowledge of agricultural practices has been a wellspring of motivation. Her insights into the realities of rural agriculture in Northern India have been a driving force behind our efforts. To the parents of Dr. Prasanna Kolar, *Mr. Ashok Kolar, and Mother Shakuntala Kolar*, we extend our heartfelt appreciation. Their unyielding support and encouragement have nurtured the seeds of curiosity and dedication, enabling us to explore the depths of Agricultural Economics. In remembrance of those who have come before us and in appreciation of those who walk alongside us, this book stands as a testament to the enduring legacy of knowledge and the collective pursuit of a sustainable and thriving agricultural ecosystem.

With utmost gratitude and reverence,
Dr. Kuldeep Singh and Dr. Prasanna Kolar
January 2024

Contents

Preface xvii

Part 1: Knowledge Sharing in the Digital Agricultural Ecosystem 1

1 Digital Agricultural Ecosystem: An Introduction 3
   Kuldeep Singh, Prasanna Kolar and Rebecca Abraham
   1.1 Introduction 3
   1.2 Digital Agricultural Ecosystem 4
   1.3 Definition 5
   1.4 Entities 6
        1.4.1 Role of Farmers in Digital Agricultural Ecosystem 6
        1.4.2 Role of Technology Providers in Digital Agricultural Ecosystem 7
   1.5 Role of Researchers in Digital Agricultural Ecosystem 8
        1.5.1 Role of Policymakers in the Digital Agricultural Ecosystem 8
        1.5.2 Role of Customers in the Digital Agricultural Ecosystem 9
   1.6 Elements 10
        1.6.1 Hardware 10
        1.6.2 Software 11
        1.6.3 Data 11
        1.6.4 Human Capital 12
        1.6.5 Efficiency, Sustainability, and Profitability of Agricultural Operations 13
        Conclusion 14
        References 14

2 Smart and Sustainable Agriculture: Systematic Literature Review
   and Bibliometric Analysis 17
   Madhavi Shamkuwar, Vidya Kadam, Pratik Arte and Pandurang Patil
   2.1 Introduction 17
   2.2 Systematic Literature Review 19
        2.2.1 PRISMA Protocol 19
        2.2.2 Visual Literature Review 20
   2.3 Bibliometric Analysis 21
        2.3.1 Research Database 21
        2.3.2 Search Strategy 22
        2.3.3 Advance Search 23
   2.4 Related Study 28
        2.4.1 Climate-Related Literature 28

2.4.2 Technology-Related Literature 29
2.5 Conclusion 30
References 30

3 **Agriculturist Engagement and Knowledge Sharing in Digital Ecosystem: Insights from Social Media** 35
Jitendra Yadav, Nripendra P. Rana, Pankaj Kumar Singh and Ramendra Pratap Singh
3.1 Introduction 35
3.2 State of Literature 37
3.2.1 Agriculture Digital Transformation 37
3.2.2 Significance of YouTube in Fostering Engagement and Knowledge Sharing 38
3.3 Methodology 39
3.3.1 Data Description 39
3.3.2 Algorithmic Evaluation 39
3.4 Findings 43
3.4.1 Content Analysis 43
3.4.2 Sentiment Analysis 44
3.5 Discussion 48
3.6 Limitations and Future Scope 49
3.7 Conclusions 49
References 50

Part 2: Adoption and Impact of Digital Technologies in Agriculture 55

4 **Electronic National Agriculture Market (e-NAM) so Far…! A Gestation Period Analysis** 57
Mohit Kumar and Kuldeep Singh
4.1 Introduction 57
4.2 The Importance of Agriculture Marketing 58
4.3 APMC Allahabad (Prayagraj) as a Case Organization 59
4.4 Objectives of the Study 59
4.5 Study Area: APMC Allahabad 60
4.6 Methodology 60
4.7 Auction and Transaction Process 61
4.8 Process Review 61
4.9 General Assessment of Causes 61
4.10 Discussion 63
4.11 Development during the COVID Period 64
4.12 Conclusion 64
References 65
Appendix 1 66
Appendix 2 68

5   **Development of Ecologically Safe Production: Digital Trends
    in the Agri-Food Sector**   **71**
    *Zamlynskyi Viktor, Diachenko Oleksii, Halytskyi Oleksandr,
    Levina-Kostiuk Mariia and Yurii Vitkovskyi*
    5.1   Introduction   71
    5.2   Legislative Support for the Functioning of Ecologically Safe Production   72
    5.3   Market Analysis of Environmentally Sound Goods   75
    5.4   Strategic Directions for Ensuring the Growth of Ecologically Safe
          Production in the Agri-Food Complex   81
    5.5   Digital Optimization of Ecologically Safe Production   81
    5.6   Conclusions   87
          References   89

6   **Adoption and Impact of Blockchain Technology on the Silk Industry's
    Supply Chain**   **91**
    G.S. Vijaya, Lakshmi Sevukamoorthy and Divakar Rajamani
    6.1   Introduction   91
    6.2   Mulberry—The Fodder   92
          6.2.1   Plantation Technique   93
    6.3   Embryogenesis of the Silkworm   97
    6.4   Silk Rearing—An Art by Itself   97
          6.4.1   The Procedural Outlay   98
          6.4.2   Diseases and Predators of Silkworms   107
                  6.4.2.1   Diseases   107
                  6.4.2.2   Predators   110
    6.5   Blockchain Technology   111
          6.5.1   Blockchain Categories   112
          6.5.2   Blockchain Framework   112
          6.5.3   Blockchain Concept   112
          6.5.4   Blockchain Technology Features   113
    6.6   BCT and the Supply Chain   114
    6.7   The Proposed Model: VL-SS-23   115
    6.8   Conclusion   116
          References   117

7   **Transforming Indian Agriculture: Unleashing the Potential of Digital
    Agriculture Using Efficiency Analysis**   **123**
    Neetu Mishra, Anil Vashisht and Sandeep Raghuwanshi
    7.1   Introduction—The Role of Agriculture as the Foundation of All Industries   123
    7.2   Analysis of the Agriculture Sector in India   124
          7.2.1   Brief Background   124
          7.2.2   Preserving Biodiversity and Agricultural Practices   125
          7.2.3   Traditional Agricultural Practices and Challenges   125
          7.2.4   Impact of Globalization on Indian Agriculture   127
          7.2.5   Data Envelopment Analysis (DEA)   127
          7.2.6   Implementation of ICT (Information and Communication
                  Technology) in Rural Tribal Farming Communities   128

7.2.7	Data Management	129
	7.2.7.1 Variable Rate Treatment (VRT)	129
	7.2.7.2 Geographic Information System (GIS)	130
7.2.8	Data Utilization	130
	7.2.8.1 Internet of Things (IoT)	130
	7.2.8.2 Robotics	130
	7.2.8.3 Global Positioning System (GPS) and Geographic Information System (GIS)	131
	7.2.8.4 Drones	131
	7.2.8.5 Radio Frequency Identification (RFID)	131
7.2.9	Data Acquisition	131
	7.2.9.1 Remote Sensing	131
	7.2.9.2 Close-Range Sensing	131
	7.2.9.3 Chemical-Specific Sensors	132
	7.2.9.4 Global Positioning System and Differential Global Positioning (GPS-DGPS)	132
7.2.10	Analysis of Imports and Exports	132
	7.2.10.1 Increasing Trend	134
	7.2.10.2 Import–Export Gap	134
	7.2.10.3 Trade Balance	134
	7.2.10.4 Steady Export Growth	134
	7.2.10.5 Potential for Export Expansion	134
7.3	Methodology	134
7.3.1	Production	135
7.3.2	Area	136
7.3.3	Poverty Levels	136
7.3.4	Government Expenditure	136
7.3.5	Regional Disparities	136
7.3.6	Data for 2018–2019 of the Top 17 States Based on Agricultural Land	136
7.4	Discussion	137
7.4.1	Analysis of DEA Results	137
7.5	Implications	138
7.5.1	Managerial Implications of the Study	138
	7.5.1.1 Performance Benchmarking	138
	7.5.1.2 Resource Allocation	138
	7.5.1.3 Best Practice Sharing	138
	7.5.1.4 Policy Formulation	139
	7.5.1.5 Poverty Alleviation	139
	7.5.1.6 Government Expenditure Analysis	139
7.5.2	Theoretical Implications	139
	7.5.2.1 Efficiency Rankings	139
	7.5.2.2 Resource Utilization	139
	7.5.2.3 Input and Output Orientations	140
	7.5.2.4 Policy and Decision-Making	140
	7.5.2.5 Poverty Alleviation and Sustainable Agriculture	140

7.6   Limitations and Future Directions   140
7.7   Conclusion   140
       References   141

8 **Digital Agriculture: Transforming Farming Practices and Food Systems
   for a Sustainable Future**   **145**
   D. Pushpa Gowri and Anitha Ramachander
   8.1   Introduction   145
   8.2   Need for Digital Agriculture and Food Security   146
   8.3   Role of Digital Agriculture in Economic Transformation   147
   8.4   Digital Value Chain and Food Systems   148
   8.5   Innovation in Agriculture   149
          8.5.1   Innovative Techniques in Agriculture   150
          8.5.2   Transition to Agriculture 5.0   151
   8.6   Benefits and Limitations of Digital Agriculture   151
          8.6.1   Benefits   151
          8.6.2   Limitations   152
   8.7   Digital Agriculture in India   152
          8.7.1   Measures Taken by the Government of India to Improve Digital
                   Agriculture   153
   8.8   Future of Digital Agriculture   155
          Conclusion   156
          References   157

9 **Exploring the Impact of Artificial Intelligence on Agriculture - A Study
   on Farmers' Level of Awareness**   **161**
   Shrinivas Patil, Premalatha K. P. and Iqbal Thonse Hawaldar
   9.1   Introduction   161
   9.2   Review of Literature   163
   9.3   Research Design   164
   9.4   Analysis   165
          9.4.1   Descriptive Statistics—Farmers' Demographic Profile   165
          9.4.2   Awareness of Artificial Technology   166
          9.4.3   Inferential Analysis   168
   9.5   Discussion   171
   9.6   Implications   172
   9.7   Limitations and Scope for Future Research   172
   9.8   Conclusion   172
          References   173

10 **Precision Technologies and Digital Solutions: Catalyzing Agricultural
   Transformation in Soil Health Management**   **175**
   *Anandkumar Naorem, Abhishek Patel, Sujan Adak, Puja Singh
   and Shiva Kumar Udayana*
   10.1   Introduction   175
   10.2   Importance of Soil Health Management   176
   10.3   Soil Health Monitoring and Assessment   177

	10.3.1	Soil Sensors and Internet of Things (IoT) Devices	177
	10.3.2	Remote Sensing and Imaging Techniques	179
	10.3.3	Data Analytics and Modeling for Soil Health Assessment	181
10.4	Precision Irrigation Management		182
	10.4.1	Components of Precision Irrigation System	183
	10.4.2	Precision and Automation in Irrigation: Sensors and IoT	185
10.5	AI-Based Models and Irrigation Scheduling		185
10.6	Conclusions		186
	References		187

Part 3: Smart Farming and Sustainable Agriculture   **191**

11 Blockchain Technology—Adoption, Opportunities, and Challenges for a Sustainable Agricultural Ecosystem   **193**

Sweta Kumari and Vimal Kumar Agarwal

11.1	Introduction		193
	11.1.1	What is Blockchain?	194
	11.1.2	Recent Developments and Investments in Indian Agriculture and Food Industry	196
11.2	Blockchain in the Agriculture Ecosystem		198
	11.2.1	Cases of Blockchain Use in Agriculture	199
	11.2.2	Management of Supply Chains	199
	11.2.3	Smart Contracts and Agriculture	200
	11.2.4	Agricultural Finance	201
	11.2.5	Controlling the Weather Crisis	202
	11.2.6	Agricultural Insurance	203
	11.2.7	Mitigation of Food Fraud	204
	11.2.8	Maintaining the Quality of Raw Materials	204
	11.2.9	Decentralized Smaller Organizations	205
	11.2.10	The Quality Controls	205
	11.2.11	Sustainable Water Management	206
11.3	Cases of Blockchain in Agriculture		206
11.4	Challenges and Future Implications		207
	References		208

12 Fostering Agriculture Ecosystem for Sustainability   **211**

Batani Raghavendra Rao, Anusha R. Batni and Preeti Shrivastava

12.1	Introduction		211
12.2	Agriculture Ecosystem and Agriculture Value Chain		212
	12.2.1	Agricultural Ecosystem	212
	12.2.2	Agriculture Value Chain	212
12.3	Growth Drivers for Sustainable Agriculture		214
	12.3.1	Growth Drivers	214
12.4	Role of the Government and Policy Interventions		215
12.5	Technology Initiatives of Corporates and Start-Ups		217
	12.5.1	Role of Incumbent Corporates	217
	12.5.2	Role of Start-Ups	218

12.6 Agritech Investment 219
12.7 Global Outlook 219
12.8 Conclusion 222
References 225

13 Design of Smart Digital Crop Harvester Monitoring Cluster 229
Aditi Oak, Ishwari Patil, Aarya Phansalkar, Ashwini M. Deshpande
and Shounak Sharangpani

13.1 Introduction 229
13.2 Literature Survey 230
13.3 Methodology 231
13.3.1 Working 231
13.3.2 Design of Fuel Level Measurement Circuit 232
13.3.3 Design of the Temperature Measurement Circuit 234
13.3.4 Design of the Battery-Level Measurement Circuit 235
13.3.5 Design of the Oil Pressure Measurement Circuit 237
13.3.6 Design of the RPM Measurement Circuit 238
13.3.7 Design for the Threshing RPM Measurement Circuit 240
13.3.8 Design of the Power Supply 240
13.3.9 Design of Reverse Polarity Circuit 241
13.3.10 Microcontrollers 242
13.3.11 ESP32 243
13.3.12 API—Application Programming Interface 244
13.3.13 TouchGFX Designer 245
13.3.14 STM32CubeMX and STM32CubeIDE 247
13.4 Results and Discussion 250
13.4.1 Temperature Sensing Results 250
13.4.2 Battery Voltage Measurement Results 252
13.4.3 Fuel Level Sensing Results 253
13.4.4 Pressure Level Results 253
13.4.5 Engine Running Hours Sensing Results 254
13.4.6 RPM and Indicator Results 254
13.5 Conclusion 256
References 257

14 Exploring the Prospects and Challenges of Digital Agriculture for Food Security—A Case Study of the "Hands Free Hectare" Digital Farm in the UK 259
Arnab Chatterjee

14.1 Introduction 259
14.1.1 The Need for Smart Farms 260
14.1.2 The Case of the Hands-Free Farm in the UK 263
14.1.3 The Challenges 264
14.1.4 The Key People 264
14.1.5 Appraisal of the Hands-Free Farm 266
14.2 Conclusion 266
References 267

15 Smart Farming—A Case Study from India   **269**
Vedantam Seetha Ram, Kuldeep Singh and Bivek Sreshta
15.1   Introduction   269
    15.1.1   Types of Farming   270
       15.1.1.1   Subsistence Farming   270
       15.1.1.2   Dryland Farming   270
       15.1.1.3   Arable Land Farming   271
       15.1.1.4   Aquaculture   271
       15.1.1.5   Dairy Farming   271
15.2   Technology in Farming   275
    15.2.1   Laser Land Leveling Technology   276
    15.2.2   Watershed Technology   276
    15.2.3   Internet of Things   277
    15.2.4   Machine Navigation and Robotics   278
    15.2.5   Drone Technology   278
    15.2.6   Data Analytics   279
    15.2.7   Government Schemes in Smart Farming   279
15.3   Discussion   281
    15.3.1   India's Agriculture Journey from 2001–2002 to 2020–2021   281
15.4   Conclusion   284
    References   285

16 Frugal Innovation in Developing a Fertilizer Sprayer—A Case of an Ingenious Design in Maharashtra   **291**
Madhavi R., Urmila Itam, Harold Andrew Patrick, Ravindran Balakrishnan, Chaya Bagrecha, Shalini R. and V. Y. John
16.1   Introduction   291
16.2   Fertilizers and Their Usage   292
16.3   Role of Technology in Agriculture   293
16.4   Research Gap and Objective   294
16.5   Research Design   294
16.6   Jugadu Kamlesh—The Inventor-Farmer Turned Agripreneur and His Fertilizer Sprayer   295
16.7   The Design Journey   296
16.8   The Shark Tank: India Experience   296
16.9   Design Thinking   303
16.10   The Path Ahead   304
16.11   Conclusion   304
    Conflict of Interest   305
    Acknowledgments   305
    References   305

17 For Sustainable Farming in India: A Data Analytics Perspective   **307**
Shanta Pragyan Dash and K. G. Priyashantha
17.1   Introduction   307

17.1.1   Current Status of the Farming Industry in India   308
17.1.2   Data Analytics and Its Applied Methods in Current Farming
         Practices   310
17.1.3   Capacity Building through Data Analytics in the Farming Industry   311
17.1.4   Future Scope of India with Data Analytics in the Farming Industry   313
17.1.5   Urge Toward Adapting Data Analytics for Rural Areas in India   314
17.1.6   Mapping the Future of Data Analytics in Farming and Linking
         to SDGs   315
17.2   Conclusion   316
       References   316

Part 4: Modeling and Analysis of Agricultural Systems   319

18   Modeling Barriers to Access Credit from Institutional Sources in Rural Areas
     Using the ISM Approach   321
     Priyanka Yadav, Bhartrihari Pandiya and Alok Kumar Sharma
18.1   Introduction   321
18.2   Literature Review   322
18.3   Data and Research Methodology   324
       18.3.1   Data   324
       18.3.2   Research Methodology   326
                18.3.2.1   Building the Structural Self-Interaction Matrix (SSIM)   326
                18.3.2.2   Reachability Matrix   327
                18.3.2.3   Level Partitioning   327
                18.3.2.4   Development of the ISM Model   331
                18.3.2.5   MICMAC Analysis   331
18.4   Results and Discussion   333
18.5   Implications of the Research   334
18.6   Conclusions   334
       References   335

19   Modeling the Water Consumption Process with the Linear Model and a Local
     Interpolation Cubic Spline   339
     Varlamova Lyudmila P., Seytov Aybek J., Bahromov Sayfiddin A.,
     Berdiyorov Shokhjakhon Sh. and Mirzaolimov Akhmadjon K.
19.1   Background   339
       19.1.1   Application of Correlation and Regression Methods
                to Analyze Patterns of Changes in Water Consumption
                and Water Use in the Republic of Uzbekistan   342
19.2   Establishment of the Patterns of Formation of Volumes of Water
       Resources in Areas of Their Usage   350
19.3   Forecasting Water Use Based on Mathematical Models of Water
       Management of Distributed Irrigation Systems   360
       19.3.1   Based on the Given Information, See the Model
                of Water Distribution Based on the Least Square Method   360

19.3.2   Building a Model Using a Local Cubic Spline   364
Conclusion   366
References   366

20 The Role of Electric Vehicles in the Agriculture Industry Using IoT: Turning Electricity into Food   369
Parul Asati, Sandeep Raghuwanshi, Arif Hasan and Aadil Zeffer
20.1   Introduction   369
20.1.1   Electric Vehicles in Agriculture   370
20.1.2   Smart Agriculture and Smart Farming Using IoT Technology   370
20.1.3   Off-Road Vehicle Technology   371
20.2   Department of Energy   371
20.2.1   Unmanned Ground Vehicles (UGVs) for Agriculture   372
20.2.2   India a Growing Market for Tractors   372
20.2.3   Electric Tractors   372
20.2.4   Green Technology for Agricultural Vehicles   373
20.2.5   Agriculture Tractors Electrification   373
20.2.6   Multipurpose Electric Vehicle for Farmers   373
20.2.7   Organic Farming with Electric Vehicles   374
20.3   Electric Vehicles and Robots in the Agricultural Sector   374
20.3.1   Internet of Things (IoT) for a Sustainable Future   374
20.3.2   IoT Technology for Smart Agriculture and Farming   375
20.3.3   Electric Robotics and Machines in Agriculture   375
20.4   Blockchain-Based IoT Systems   375
20.4.1   Turning Electricity into Food   375
Conclusion   376
References   376

Index   381

Preface

Agriculture has historically been the foundation of human civilization. Its provision of sustenance and resources benefits communities all around the world. Agriculture has been practiced from the dawn of time, when our ancestors worked the land and had a close relationship with nature. Agriculture has a creative, adaptable, and innovative history, and as the digital age draws closer, agriculture is once again poised for change.

This book demonstrates the combined efforts of all the authors and co-authors involved, and will stand as a vital resource for academics and professionals who work in the sectors of agricultural and digital technologies.

The twenty chapters herein explore the connection between agricultural and technological advancements, which suggests a diversified environment. Each chapter delves into diverse tracks on four key areas.

Part 1 covers knowledge sharing in the digital agricultural ecosystem. In the context of modern agriculture, the materials here underline the importance of information flow. Through comprehensive reviews of literature and assessments of farmer participation on social media platforms, these chapters illustrate the value of information sharing for sustainable agriculture.

Part 2 explores the adoption and impact of digital technologies in agriculture. The use of cutting-edge digital technologies in agriculture is examined thoroughly in this section. The chapters included here outline how precision, artificial intelligence, and blockchain technology have the potential to transform methods of agriculture and improve food systems.

Part 3 addresses smart farming and sustainable agriculture. This section focuses on sustainability and offers details on eco-friendly production methods, the significance of smart farming in many nations, including India and the UK, and cost-effective fertilizer sprayer technologies.

Part 4 examines modelling and analysis of Agricultural systems. The last section explores how mathematical modelling and data analytics are used in agricultural systems, with insights on everything from the study of credit access constraints in rural regions to water resource management in irrigation systems.

The editors have greatly valued the contributions of each author. The information collected in this volume is largely inspired by their academic work and research experience. We would also like to express our gratitude to the co-authors whose dedication and hard work have enriched this publication. Finally, we have greatly appreciated the dedicated support and valuable assistance rendered by Martin Scrivener and the Scrivener Publishing team during the publication of this book.

Dr. Kuldeep Singh
Dr. Prasanna Kolar
January 2024

Part 1

KNOWLEDGE SHARING IN THE DIGITAL AGRICULTURAL ECOSYSTEM

Digital Agricultural Ecosystem: An Introduction

Kuldeep Singh[1]*, Prasanna Kolar[2] and Rebecca Abraham[3]

[1]School of Management, Gati Shakti Vishwavidyalaya, Vadodara, India
[2]School of Humanities and Social Sciences, Jain (Deemed-to-be University), Bengaluru, India
[3]Huizenga College of Business and Entrepreneurship, Nova Southeastern University, Fort Lauderdale, Florida, USA

Abstract

The primary goal of this chapter is to offer a comprehensive examination of digital agriculture from a critical perspective with a specific emphasis on forming an ecosystem that highlights the linkages between agriculture and technology. This chapter examines various definitions of digital agriculture and explores the theoretical foundation that supports this concept and emphasizes the essential elements required for establishing this ecosystem. The present chapter also discusses how technology has affected the development of agriculture, with a focus on the potential benefits of digital agriculture for productivity, sustainability, and profitability. Such an objective should be a top priority for government stakeholders and decision-makers due to the possible policy consequences. The research also emphasizes the necessity for the adoption of clear ethical and regulatory rules in order to secure the long-term viability of digital technologies in agriculture for the benefit of all stakeholders.

Keywords: Digital, agriculture, ecosystem, sustainability

1.1 Introduction

The agriculture sector is an important pillar of the global economy and also contributes significantly to food security, economic growth, and the livelihoods of millions of people around the world. On one side, traditional agricultural methods face several challenges, such as rising costs, lower profitability, and higher demand for sustainable and environmentally friendly agro-practices. On the other side, digital agriculture has emerged as a capable solution to the abovementioned challenges with the potential to transform agro-industry through the integration of modern technology such as blockchain, artificial intelligence, big data, and the Internet of Things (IoT).

One of the most widely used definitions of digital agriculture is based on the integration of technology and data into farm practices to increase efficiency, sustainability, and profitability [1–3]. Basically, this definition encompasses various technologies such as precision agriculture, remote sensing, and decision support systems. However, this definition is still

**Corresponding author*: kuldeepsinghcsr@gmail.com, ORCID: https://orcid.org/0000-0002-8180-4646

Kuldeep Singh and Prasanna Kolar (eds.) Digital Agricultural Ecosystem: Revolutionary Advancements in Agriculture, (3–16) © 2024 Scrivener Publishing LLC

open to interpretation and lacks specificity in terms of the types of technologies and practices that fall under the digital agriculture umbrella.

If we look at the recent research on digital agriculture, success depends on several factors like access to technology, adoption of innovative tools by farmers, and the ability to integrate digital tools into existing agricultural systems. Despite the growing interest and investment in digital agriculture, there are several issues and controversies surrounding its use. One of the primary concerns is the digital divide where farmers in low-income countries may lack access to the necessary technology and infrastructure. Additionally, there are other concerns such as data privacy, the potential for technology to exacerbate existing inequalities, and the need for clear regulations and standards to ensure the ethical use of digital tools in agriculture.

Xie *et al.* [4] mentioned in their study that the role of technology in rural agricultural development is critical. Digital agriculture has the potential to transform farm practices and improve the livelihoods of farmers through increased yields, cost reduction, and better market access. While it is pertinent to recognize the unequal distribution of benefits in digital agriculture, there is a potential risk of exacerbating the existing digital divide due to insufficient emphasis on prioritizing technology access, particularly in low-income countries.

This article aims to provide a critical review of the available literature on the digital agriculture ecosystem with a focus on defining the relationship between agriculture and technology. The study further aims to investigate diverse interpretations and past advancements in digital agriculture. Moreover, it intends to scrutinize the fundamental components and constituents that constitute a digital agriculture ecosystem.

1.2   Digital Agricultural Ecosystem

The history of digital agriculture can be traced back to the 1970s when the first computerized decision support systems were developed to optimize agricultural practices [5]. Since then, digital agriculture has evolved significantly mainly with the integration of various technologies and the emergence of new business models and practices [6].

Upon examining the latest technological advancements in agriculture, it is evident that the digital agriculture ecosystem is a multifaceted framework that encompasses a multitude of technological constituents and participants who collaborate with each other to enhance agricultural processes. Such digital agriculture ecosystem encompasses the capacity to utilize technology and data to augment the effectiveness, sustainability, and profitability of agricultural operations. However, there is still a lack of clarity around what digital agriculture entails and how it should be defined. Therefore, by taking into consideration most of the entities and elements, we construct an ecosystem that enables us to better understand the association between technology and agriculture.

Based on the available literature on digital agriculture, it is evident that the digital agricultural ecosystem comprises a variety of entities and elements that interact with each other to optimize agricultural practices (see Figure 1.1). The entities section includes *farmers*, *technology providers*, *researchers*, *policymakers*, and *customers*. The technology providers mainly include firms that provide hardware, software, and data services for agriculture,

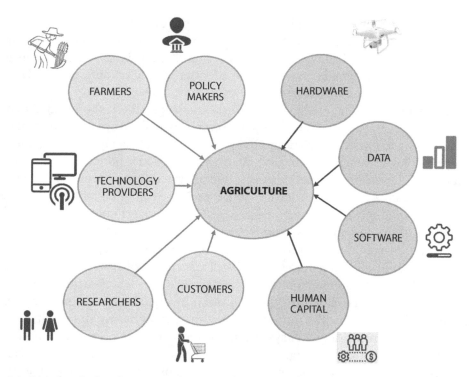

Figure 1.1 Digital agricultural ecosystem (source: authors' own).

while researchers develop new technologies and practices to improve agricultural practices. The regulatory framework that governs the adoption and implementation of digital technologies in agriculture is significantly impacted by policymakers, while customers influence the demand for sustainably produced food.

On the other side, the different elements that form the digital agricultural ecosystem include *hardware, software, data*, and *human capital.* Hardware includes sensors, drones, and other devices that collect data from the field. Software includes tools for data analysis, modeling, and visualization. Data include various types of information such as weather data, soil data, and market data. Human capital includes the skills and knowledge required to develop, deploy, and use digital agriculture technologies effectively.

The complete network of the digital agriculture ecosystem functions as a collaborative network of interdependent entities and constituents working toward shared objectives (see Figure 1.1). These objectives include improvement in the efficiency, sustainability, and profitability of farm practices; reduced environmental impact; and enhanced food security. The digital agriculture ecosystem can propose novel business prospects and value chains that are advantageous to farmers, technology providers, and consumers.

1.3 Definition

According to a FAO report [7], "digital technologies have the potential to enhance agricultural productivity and sustainability, particularly in developing countries. It highlights the role of mobile phones, drones, satellite imagery, and other digital tools in improving access to information, markets, and financial services for smallholder farmers. It also emphasizes the need to address challenges related to digital literacy, infrastructure, and policy frameworks to ensure equitable and inclusive adoption of digital agriculture." However, the digitalization of agriculture also faces challenges such as cybersecurity, data protection, labor replacement, and digital divide. Despite these challenges, FAO is committed to bridge multidisciplinary digital divides to ensure that everyone benefits from the emergent digital society. According to the United Nations Global Compact, "digital agriculture is the use of advanced technologies integrated into a system to improve food production for farmers and stakeholders [8]. Unlike traditional methods, digital agriculture systems gather data frequently and accurately, often with external sources such as weather information [8]." As per this statement, digital agriculture integrates new and advanced technologies to enable farmers to make informed decisions based on frequent and accurate data leading to improved food production through the use of robotics and advanced machinery.

Mark Shepherd [9] mentioned how digital agriculture can offer social advantages that satisfy the needs and requirements of different stakeholders such as farmers, processors, regulators, and consumers. Based on the utilization of digital technologies, agricultural production can be boosted while minimizing environmental harm. The result is a more efficient transportation and logistics system, improved work conditions for workers, and timely delivery of products that align with consumer needs. Digital agriculture can also address consumer demands for responsible and sustainable production as well as provide evidence of socio-ethical factors and product origin. As per Hackfort [10], digital agriculture refers to digitization that involves the transformation of analog information into digital data, and digitalization is the social process of accepting computer technologies.

Sawant *et al.* [11] mentioned that data science and machine learning are crucial for agricultural data analysis and decision processes in digital farm, noting that data mining, analytics, and data science have significantly benefited digital agriculture. Studies conducted on various agricultural elements have derived models and optimized resource usage and facilitated data-driven analysis for forecasts, resource optimization, and understanding of agricultural processes.

1.4 Entities

1.4.1 Role of Farmers in Digital Agricultural Ecosystem

Digital agriculture has brought significant changes in the way farmers collect and analyze data to improve agricultural production and reduce waste. For digital agriculture to be successful, the active participation of farmers is crucial. Farmers play an essential role in the adoption and implementation of digital technologies, and their feedback and expertise are vital to enhance the effectiveness and efficiency of digital tools and practices.

Farmers play a vital role in the usage of digital tools and techniques as they are often the first entity to try new technology. In this way, farmers can identify any issues or areas for improvement for further enhancement and upgradation [12].

However, farmers also play a proactive role in the construction of digital tools and procedures. By having a close interaction with technology developers, farmers can make sure that digital solutions are easy to use and meet the needs of the agricultural industry.

At the usage level, farmers are responsible for the implementation of digital technologies and practices. It is needed to understand the technology and to modify farmers' current agricultural methods to allow them to use the tools provided by technology developers effectively.

Farmers play a significant role in the collection and analyses of data in the digital agriculture ecosystem. With the use of digital technology, farmers can collect and use vast amounts of data about their farms in order to optimize their farm practices and make data-driven decisions.

However, to use data efficiently in the context of digital agriculture, farmers need specialized knowledge and skills to gather and analyze data. In a rural context, farmers may consider the specific needs of their farm operation, too.

Farmers play a vital role in the development and implementation of sustainable and resilient agricultural practices. The integration of digital technology has the potential to significantly enhance productivity and efficiency in agricultural operations. It is incumbent upon farmers to acknowledge their responsibility in adopting practices that are environmentally sustainable and socially responsible, thereby avoiding any adverse effects on the environment and ensuring the well-being of communities.

1.4.2 Role of Technology Providers in Digital Agricultural Ecosystem

The integration of digital technologies with age-old agricultural practices has given birth to a remarkable era in agriculture, commonly known as digital agriculture. This paradigm shift equips farmers with a diverse range of tools and resources to unlock the full potential of their land, optimizing agricultural productivity, bolstering efficiency, and minimizing the ecological footprint. Within this evolving landscape, technology providers assume a paramount role, leading the charge in developing, designing, and implementing cutting-edge digital solutions tailored to empower farmers and refine their age-old methods [13].

At the heart of the digital agriculture ecosystem lies the crucial responsibility of technology providers: to create and offer a host of digital tools and technologies that seamlessly integrate with farmers' practices, enabling them to unleash the full potential of their agricultural endeavors. Precision agriculture, smart irrigation systems, enhanced crop management systems, and sophisticated data analytics tools are a few of the most noteworthy examples of these disruptive technologies. These revolutionary breakthroughs can assist farmers in making informed decisions that result in improved productivity, efficiency, and sustainable agricultural practices.

Farmers can develop complex maps that allow them to change their agricultural practices with remarkable precision and perfectly address the unique requirements of each crop, by carefully gathering important information on soil conditions, crop growth patterns, and a variety of environmental elements. With the exact application of fertilizers, herbicides, and water supplies made possible by this method, waste is decreased, while yields increase to levels that were previously unattainable.

Empowered by this wealth of information, farmers can effortlessly optimize their irrigation practices, ensuring that water resources are utilized with the utmost efficiency and efficacy.

The implementation of such smart irrigation systems not only contributes to water conservation efforts but also assists farmers in reducing costs while maximizing agricultural yields. Additionally, these solutions prove instrumental in reducing costs while simultaneously bolstering agricultural yields.

Data analytics tools are also instrumental in the digital agriculture ecosystem. Technologies empower farmers to collect and analyze data from various sources, including soil sensors, weather stations, and crop sensors. With this, farmers can build sophisticated models that forecast crop yields, identify potential issues, and receive tailored recommendations on enhancing their agricultural practices.

1.5   Role of Researchers in Digital Agricultural Ecosystem

The role of researchers in the digital agricultural ecosystem is to generate new knowledge and insights that can be applied to improve agricultural practices and productivity. This is related to the development of new digital technologies and the examination and refinement of existing technologies. On the other hand, it is also related to conducting research on the social, economic, and environmental impacts of digital agriculture. Basically, researchers help to ensure that digital technologies are deployed in a responsible and effective way that benefits all the stakeholders related to agriculture.

The researchers' responsibilities include the design and testing of innovative tools such as sensors, drones, machine learning algorithms, and other devices that enable the collection and analysis of data crops, soils, weather patterns, and environmental factors. The utilization of such insights results in improved yields and enhanced profitability for farmers.

Also, researchers have a crucial responsibility to test and refine present digital technologies to ensure their effectiveness across diverse agricultural contexts. In addition to their involvement in the development of digital technologies, researchers also undertake research on the social, economic, and environmental impacts of digital agriculture.

For researchers to excel in their roles, they must possess a profound comprehension of the needs and priorities of farmers and other stakeholders within the digital agricultural ecosystem. Such engagement in terms of dialogue with stakeholders allows researchers to ensure that their research will be utilized to inform decision processes and practical implementation in the agricultural domain.

1.5.1   Role of Policymakers in the Digital Agricultural Ecosystem

Policymakers' unwavering commitment encompasses the formulation of robust regulations that not only foster the widespread adoption of groundbreaking technologies but also guarantee the utmost safety, reliability, and accessibility for farmers.

Policymakers play a crucial role in advancing the evolution of digital infrastructure, encompassing the development and enhancement of essential policies such as financial inclusion, availability of resources, price determination, and community welfare.

In terms of association, policymakers collaborate closely with farmers, academics, and technology suppliers, coalescing their expertise to design inclusive policies that prioritize digital data privacy and security within the agricultural realm. Through stakeholders' active involvement, policymakers contribute to the establishment of a robust legal framework that safeguards sensitive agricultural data, fostering a conducive environment for innovation and exponential growth in the realm of digital agriculture.

One effective approach involves providing financial support for the development of training programs and instructional materials that equip farmers with the proficiency to effectively navigate the intricacies of digital technologies. Moreover, policymakers may implement a range of financial incentives, including tax breaks and subsidies, as effective motivators to encourage the widespread adoption of digital tools and solutions within agricultural operations [12].

Furthermore, in order to drive transformative change, policymakers forge partnerships with esteemed international organizations such as the United Nations. It helps to harness collective wisdom to foster the utilization of digital technology in agriculture. Collaboratively, policymakers direct stakeholders regarding resources and allocate funds toward cutting-edge research and development initiatives. Such worldwide cooperation aims to spark a significant revolution in the industry, boosting food security and advancement in the socioeconomic growth of countries attempting to overcome agricultural issues.

1.5.2   Role of Customers in the Digital Agricultural Ecosystem

Digital agriculture has opened up new avenues for customer engagement and connectivity with agriculture. Customers encompass individuals and organizations alike who procure agricultural products or services for personal or commercial purposes. Customers as an entity play an integral role in the complex web structure that forms the digital agriculture ecosystem. Their significance lies in their capacity to shape the demand for products and services, thereby exerting influence over the intricate web of the supply chain and the overall functionality of the agriculture sector.

This digital framework facilitates customers' active involvement in various aspects, encompassing investment in agricultural operations, provision of capital for production, acquisition of agricultural produce, and even sharing in the ensuing profits.

Customers further contribute to the agricultural landscape by providing invaluable feedback to farmers and other stakeholders. Leveraging the capabilities offered by digital technologies, farmers can seamlessly collect and meticulously analyze customer feedback. This overall feedback loop provides farmers with an advantageous position in planning their production and pricing strategies, boosting their overall performance and enhancing overall customer satisfaction.

Additionally, digital technologies have acted as a catalyst for direct-to-consumer (DTC) marketing channels, eliminating the need for middlemen and enabling farmers to connect directly with their customers. The prevalence of online platforms and social media also acts as powerful enablers, which allow farmers to sell their produce at competitive rates and also assure that they get a fair and equitable share of the earnings. This innovative approach has found huge success in the digital age as consumers gravitate toward locally sourced, high-quality food products [14].

Customers can influence public policy by promoting environmentally and socially responsible farming practices. Customers can effect change by strongly supporting policy changes that put an emphasis on sustainability and ethical behavior. They can do this by applying significant pressure to lawmakers to enact rules and incentives that would accelerate the general adoption of sustainable agriculture practices. Customers and legislators working together in harmony have a revolutionary effect that affects the entire agriculture industry and ushers in a new era of progress.

1.6 Elements

1.6.1 Hardware

Hardware encompasses a diverse array of devices, including sensors, drones, robots, GPS receivers, and cameras. These instrumental tools are the main players in terms of efficiency and optimization in agricultural production and in gathering, transferring, and interpreting data.

The hardware's vital role within the digital agricultural ecosystem can be demonstrated by considering its extensive participation in the three key areas of data collection, transmission, and analysis. One instance of how hardware is essential to data collection is the usage of sensors. These cutting-edge instruments are adept at gathering crucial data on nutrient concentrations, temperature swings, and soil moisture levels. Whether they are discretely affixed to plants or deeply submerged in the soil, these sensors operate in real time, flawlessly delivering a continuous stream of valuable information. Drones, which are essential hardware elements for data collection, support this endeavor. Drones use their flying capabilities to acquire high-resolution photographs of crops, enabling thorough crop growth monitoring, disease or pest identification, and evaluation of overall crop health. Additionally, the installation of GPS receivers makes it possible to get exact information about the movement and placement of equipment, providing opportunities for the field operations' optimization.

The hardware plays a crucial part in enabling the data's flawless transmission to the cloud for in-depth analysis after it has been carefully collected. The landscape of digital agriculture attests to the necessity of technology in the field of data transfer. Wireless sensors become crucial partners, transferring the cautiously gathered data across cellular or internet networks, guiding it toward the vast world of the cloud. Additionally, by utilizing their wireless capabilities, drones and robots allow the quick transmission of data to the cloud, significantly increasing the effectiveness of the entire system. In the meantime, GPS receivers accurately communicate location data, making it possible to optimize field operations and hence improve agricultural practices broadly.

The importance of hardware in maximizing the potential of massive datasets has been directly observed in the field of data analysis. High-performance computers and servers diligently analyze vast data, including satellite images and meteorological information, as necessary. In order to help people make well-informed decisions, these computing giants carefully unearth invaluable data regarding crop health and growth trends. GPUs, which serve as accelerators and improve the system's capabilities, greatly speed up the analysis process and ensure quicker, more accurate findings. Hardware accelerators like field-programmable gate arrays (FPGAs), which speed up the processing of certain algorithms like those used in machine learning models, also play a significant role. By overcoming traditional computational limitations, these accelerators shift the paradigm and increase the speed and accuracy of data processing.

Hardware has an impact on visualization, enabling farmers to understand and use the revelations brought about by data analysis. In this area, displays and monitors take the front stage, giving farmers the tools they need to visualize data in a useful and natural way. This promotes agricultural practices based on a deep grasp of the underlying facts by enabling quick comprehension and well-informed decision-making. Additionally, cutting-edge innovations like virtual reality (VR) and augmented reality (AR) are powerful tools that give farmers access to immersive experiences that enable the visualization and interactive exploration of data in unique and revolutionary ways.

1.6.2   Software

A rise in agricultural productivity has been required as a result of the expanding world population and a remarkable increase in food consumption. The use of contemporary technology must be integrated in order to accomplish this ambitious objective. Software emerges as one of the key elements in the field of digital agriculture, providing the ability to gather, analyze, and interpret data, thus allowing informed decision-making and boosting production effectiveness.

Software technologies shape the landscape of digital agriculture by allowing farmers to collect, store, and evaluate massive volumes of data from many sources. Information regarding weather patterns, soil quality, crop health, and animals are just a few of the numerous rich data sources that software applications can access. By filtering and analyzing the collected data, these cutting-edge technologies offer priceless insights into trends and patterns that serve as indicators that guide farmers in the direction of prudent decisions. Using data-driven insights, farmers may increase crop yields, minimize losses, and manage resources effectively.

The importance of software applications is demonstrated by precision agriculture, which enables the careful monitoring and management of crop health, soil moisture, and other elements that affect crop growth. Real-time information about crop growth and environmental conditions is provided by software applications, which act as channels for data collection from sensors and other sources. The farmers are advised by this invaluable data to optimize irrigation, fertilization, and other inputs, reducing waste and increasing production.

Applications of software also play a significant role in the management of the agricultural supply chain. These tools carefully monitor crop quality, storage, and transportation to ensure the prompt and effective delivery of commodities to the market. Farmers can make sure that their harvests arrive in markets in perfect shape by utilizing these applications. Farmers can employ supply chain management software to track their products and keep an eye on prices, giving them the information they need to make wise decisions about when and where to sell their crops.

1.6.3   Data

Data, a catalyst that provides farmers with the information they need to make well-informed choices at every stage of the agricultural cycle, from planting and fertilizing to harvesting and selling their crops, are at the center of the digital agricultural ecosystem.

Digital agriculture's cornerstone, precision agriculture, is built on a solid database. Digital agriculture is being recognized more and more as an effective tool for improving the productivity, sustainability, and profitability of agricultural firms. Farmers can gather and study enormous volumes of data containing critical elements like crop status, soil quality, weather patterns, and more thanks to this innovative approach. This vast amount of data is obtained by utilizing cutting-edge technologies like sensors, drones, satellites, and other data collection mechanisms and is then rigorously analyzed using cutting-edge algorithms and machine learning approaches. Farmers can optimize their planting tactics, fertilization routines, irrigation techniques, and harvesting strategies, thanks to the insights that come as a result.

Data-driven agriculture offers a number of advantages, including the ability to make precise, focused decisions that save a lot of water, which is important in areas where there is a water shortage. Additionally, the position of data in the digital agricultural location is crucial since it allows for the tracking of crop trajectories from farm to market and gives farmers invaluable insights into consumer trends. Farmers are better equipped to decide on price, distribution, and market timing based on this intelligence, ensuring that their goods are delivered to customers quickly and effectively.

In addition to its immediate implications on supply chain management and precision agriculture, data have immense promise for assuring the sustainability of agricultural output. With the newfound understanding, farmers are better able to safeguard the long-term financial success of their farms while reducing the environmental effect of their agricultural operations.

Several initiatives have evolved to encourage data exchange throughout the sector in order to foster a data-driven strategy in agriculture. The Global Open Data for Agriculture and Nutrition (GODAN) initiative serves as a noteworthy example. It promotes the dissemination of open data to improve food security worldwide. It functions as a vital network. GODAN facilitates the transmission of agricultural data on a worldwide scale by establishing connections between data suppliers, users, and policymakers [15].

The European Union-backed SmartAgriHubs project, which seeks to create a network of digital innovation hubs, is another important aspect [16]. To promote precision agriculture technologies, these hubs act as collaborative platforms that bring together farmers, academics, and technology vendors.

1.6.4   Human Capital

In the digital agricultural ecosystem, human capital—which consists of the skills and knowledge of professionals like software engineers, data scientists, agronomists, and agricultural experts—plays a crucial role. These experts use their expertise to construct user-friendly interfaces, assess data, and offer suggestions for enhanced agricultural practices. They also make vital contributions to the design, development, and maintenance of technology and data systems. They are involved in more than just the beginning stages; they are also involved in the deployment and adoption of these technologies, assuring their efficient use through in-depth instruction and training. Their knowledge is crucial to the continued upkeep and development of technology and data systems, and their involvement actively promotes stakeholder collaboration and aids in the creation of policies that support the sustainability and prosperity of the ecosystem. Given the importance of their position, it is crucial that farmers and agricultural workers receive thorough training on how to use these systems effectively and efficiently. This calls for the presence of trainers and educators who are knowledgeable about both technology and agricultural practices.

Human capital is also necessary for the ongoing maintenance and improvement of technology and information systems. As technology advances and new data are received, adjustments and enhancements are needed to guarantee the continued transmission of accurate and important information.

The growth and viability of the digital agricultural ecosystem depend on the active participation and involvement of farmers and agricultural workers. They provide additional evidence of their significant contributions to the ecosystem's human capital through their perceptive observations on the usability and effectiveness of technical and data systems.

Additional areas where human capital is essential include relationship-building and maintenance as well as encouraging effective stakeholder participation. Communication and teamwork experts establish a climate that supports the expansion and development of the digital agriculture ecosystem.

Additionally, human capital is essential for the creation and application of laws and rules that support and advance the digital agriculture environment.

1.6.5 Efficiency, Sustainability, and Profitability of Agricultural Operations

Digital agriculture has gained industry adoption and is now a powerful instrument for enhancing the effectiveness, sustainability, and profitability of agricultural operations. Using digital technologies, farmers can gain access to vast amounts of information regarding crucial factors that affect agricultural productivity, such as crops, soils, and weather patterns. The abundance of information available to farmers allows them to make well-informed decisions that maximize their use of resources like water, fertilizers, and pesticides while minimizing waste. This approach is best demonstrated by the use of precision irrigation systems, which allow farmers to provide each plant with the exact amount of water that it needs. By carefully controlling water use, considerable consumption decreases and increased crop yields are achieved, highlighting the potential of digital agriculture to maximize output and optimize resource use (see Figure 1.2).

Additionally, digital agriculture gives farmers advanced monitoring tools that let them keep a close eye on their crops and quickly spot any potential problems at an early stage. Farmers are able to minimize crop loss, decrease the severity of problems, and take rapid corrective action thanks to this early detection capacity.

Digital agriculture has a big influence beyond efficiency gains. This optimization helps to decrease the impact of conventional farming practices on the environment by

Figure 1.2 Efficiency, sustainability, and profitability (source: authors' own).

minimizing runoff and contamination of water sources. The implementation of resource- and energy-efficient and ethical farming practices is also supported by digital agriculture.

In addition to promoting sustainability, digital agriculture helps agricultural businesses become more profitable. It first offers farmers the chance to make the most of their inputs, reduce costs, enhance yields, and ultimately increase profitability. By adopting digital technologies for close crop monitoring, farmers can immediately identify and address issues, effectively prevent crop loss, and optimize returns on investment. Digital agriculture has also given farmers new ways to enter untapped markets and diversify their revenue streams.

Conclusion

This chapter provides the first-of-its-kind introduction to the digital agriculture ecosystem with references to several key components and stakeholders. The study also emphasizes waste reduction, the promotion of ecological practices, and increasing agricultural output. The roles of significant players, including farmers, technology providers, researchers, policymakers, customers, and human capital, are thoroughly discussed. This study also underlined the importance of cooperation between stakeholders and other elements in order to achieve common objectives. It is acknowledged that hardware and software are crucial components for efficient data collection and processing. This study is not without limitations. The study mostly relies on earlier research, publications, and records from organizations that influence policy choices, which may not exactly reflect the state of technology at the moment. We propose that future studies should draw inspiration from this work and conduct qualitative or quantitative analyses to better understand the elements of the digital agricultural ecosystem.

References

1. Fountas, S., Espejo-Garcia, B., Kasimati, A., Mylonas, N., Darra, N., The future of digital agriculture: technologies and opportunities. *IT Prof.*, 22, 1, 24–28, 2020.
2. Klerkx, L., Jakku, E., Labarthe, P., A review of social science on digital agriculture, smart farming and agriculture 4.0: New contributions and a future research agenda. *NJAS Wagening. J. Life Sci.*, 90, 100315, 2019.
3. Ozdogan, B., Gacar, A., Aktas, H., Digital agriculture practices in the context of agriculture 4.0. *Journal of Economics, Finance and Accounting (JEFA)*, 4, 2, 186–193, 2017.
4. Xie, L., Luo, B., Zhong, W., How are smallholder farmers involved in digital agriculture in developing countries: A case study from China. *Land*, 10, 3, 245, 2021.
5. Liu, J. and Sengers, P., Legibility and the legacy of racialized dispossession in digital agriculture. *Proc. ACM Hum.-Comput. Interact.*, 5, CSCW2, 1–21, 2021.
6. Degila, J., Tognisse, I.S., Honfoga, A.C., Houetohossou, S.C.A., Sodedji, F.A.K., Avakoudjo, H.G.G., Assogbadjo, A.E., A survey on digital agriculture in five West African countries. *Agriculture*, 13, 5, 1067, 2023.
7. FAO, *The Future of Food and Agriculture—Trends and Challenges*, Food and Agriculture Organization, Italy, 2017, https://www.fao.org/3/i6583e/I6583E.pdf.

8. UN Global Compact, *Digital Agriculture: feeding the future*, UNglobalcompact. New York, NY 2017, Retrieved on June 12, 2023 from http://breakthrough.unglobalcompact.org/disruptive-technologies/digital-agriculture/.

9. Shepherd, M., Turner, J.A., Small, B., Wheeler, D., Priorities for science to overcome hurdles thwarting the full promise of the 'digital agriculture' revolution. *J. Sci. Food Agric.*, 100, 14, 5083–5092, 2020.

10. Hackfort, S., Patterns of inequalities in digital agriculture: A systematic literature review. *Sustainability*, 13, 22, 12345, 2021.

11. Sawant, S., Sarangi, S., Pappula, S., AgSkyNet: Harnessing the power of sky and earth for precision agriculture, in: *Precision Agriculture: Modelling*, pp. 251–261, Springer International Publishing, Cham, 2023.

12. Abdulai, A.R., Kc, K.B., Fraser, E., What factors influence the likelihood of rural farmer participation in digital agricultural services? Experience from smallholder digitalization in Northern Ghana. *Outlook Agric.*, 52, 1, 57–66, 2023.

13. Balasundram, S.K., Shamshiri, R.R., Sridhara, S., Rizan, N., The role of digital agriculture in mitigating climate change and ensuring food security: An overview. *Sustainability*, 15, 6, 5325, 2023.

14. Mancuso, I., Petruzzelli, A.M., Panniello, U., Innovating agri-food business models after the Covid-19 pandemic: The impact of digital technologies on the value creation and value capture mechanisms. *Technol. Forecast. Soc. Change*, 190, 122404, 2023.

15. Han, D., Big data analytics, data science, ML&AI for connected, data-driven precision agriculture and smart farming systems: Challenges and future directions, in: *Proceedings of Cyber-Physical Systems and Internet of Things Week 2023*, pp. 378–384, 2023.

16. Feurich, M., Kourilova, J., Pelucha, M., Kasabov, E., Bridging the urban-rural digital divide: Taxonomy of the best practice and critical reflection of the EU countries' approach. *Eur. Plan. Stud.*, 32, 3, 1–23, 2023.

Smart and Sustainable Agriculture: Systematic Literature Review and Bibliometric Analysis

Madhavi Shamkuwar[1]*, Vidya Kadam[2], Pratik Arte[3] and Pandurang Patil[4]

[1]Zeal Institute of Business Administration, Computer Application & Research, Pune, India
[2]Rajarambapu Institute of Technology Rajaramnagar Affiliated to Shivaji University, Kolhapur, India
[3]Department of Entrepreneurship, Innovation, and Strategy, Newcastle Business School,
Newcastle-upon-Tyne, United Kingdom
[4]Zeal Institute of Business Administration, Computer Application & Research, Pune, India

Abstract

The digital farming ecosystem involves multiple stakeholders including farmers, customers, vendors, consumers, retail malls, and a third party. The system involves multiple processes including farming, the use of pesticides, food security, buying, lending, and auction. The system is highly complex in nature involving data sources in heterogeneous formats involving multiple stakeholders and processes that are crucial. In recent times, terms like smart agriculture, sustainable agriculture, and precision agriculture have started gaining momentum. The technology is the "cure" or "curse." The cure lies in the implementation of multiple technologies such as blockchain, the Internet of Things, big data analytics, machine learning, artificial intelligence, and soft computing. Also, it may become a curse for maintaining the agricultural ecosystem related to privacy concerns, security issues, data leakage, etc. It has become very crucial to design robust technology strategies to solve agriculture problems and even to predict the problems that may arise in the future. The current agriculture system has to look beyond the horizon so that the door to new problems and solutions is opened to give a wide spectrum to the agriculture system worldwide. The chapters provide multiple dimensions of agriculture with technology at heart.

Keywords: Smart agriculture, sustainable agriculture, PRISMA, bibliometric analysis, VOSviewer

2.1 Introduction

In India, agriculture is the backbone of the agrarian economy, and most of the rural population of the country depends on it as it is a hereditary occupation; the urban population is also influenced by zero residual, zero waste, and organic agricultural products. In the twenty-first century, technology has the supremacy to bring "dawn" or "dusk" to multiple sectors, which are currently in the spawning or mature stage of their growth. On the planet, every sector is witnessing digital transformations due to the gigantic nature of IT to solve

---

*Corresponding author: madhavi.sh@gmail.com

Kuldeep Singh and Prasanna Kolar (eds.) Digital Agricultural Ecosystem: Revolutionary Advancements in Agriculture, (17–34) © 2024 Scrivener Publishing LLC

multiple problems associated with various sectors. In India, 70% of the earning population depends on the agricultural sector directly or indirectly. Across the globe, India's agriculture has made a significant contribution to the country's GDP. Fifty percent of labor is generated by agriculture and related functions, making it the dominant source of income for many in rural and urban communities. Thus, it contributes significantly to the global economy and is responsible for the well-being of people depending directly or indirectly on agriculture. Agriculture is the primary source of farm-generated products such as food grains, vegetables, and fruits [1]. A country's economic growth is greatly impacted by its agricultural sector. It is the main source of income and is vital to enhancing the country's economic status [2]. Additionally, agriculture accounts for a sizeable portion of India's exports, which greatly boosts the nation's benefits in foreign cash [3]. India has a long history that dates back thousands of years. Early texts like the Arthashastra and Vedas, which chronicle the existence of ingrained farming practices throughout the Indian subcontinent, are evidence of this rich legacy [4]. In recent years, India has observed numerous innovative technologies and practices that have transformed the agricultural sector. These innovations have been expected to enhance profitability, productivity, and sustainability for farmers while ensuring food security for the growing population. Due to ignorance and the lack of access to local experts, farmers have historically been unable to identify the majority of problems. The integration of Internet technologies and future-oriented technologies for usage as smart objects is the most fundamental prerequisite for the growth of agriculture [5–9]. Applying data-driven agriculture management can help solve production problems, but for better results, competent data analysis is required. As experts rethink agricultural practices, robots are positioned to be a key player in the evolution of agriculture [10].

Technology advancements promote the growth of agriculture [11, 12]. Increased agricultural output strength results from the use of cutting-edge technology like geographic information systems (GIS), unmanned aerial vehicles (UAVs), image processing, land management, and precision agriculture. Farmers may obtain crucial crop and market information using digital agriculture, which uses information and communication technology [13]. Agriculture revolves around the principles of productivity, control, and delivering optimal outcomes. However, the challenge lies in automating all agricultural activities using machines and robots. This necessitates the development of new technological innovations to achieve a seamless agriculture industry [14]. Smart agriculture, as the name suggests, embodies the qualities of cleverness, perception, and intelligence [15]. Smart agriculture is a highly automated and systematic method of farming. It involves the continuous monitoring of multiple aspects within the farm environment, including climate conditions, water availability, humidity levels, livestock health, and crop growth. By doing so, the system generates intelligent decisions and valuable insights, either to guide human intervention or autonomously optimize farming processes [16]. These advanced technologies enable the visualization of the collected information and the performance of in-depth analysis to extract meaningful insights. With the aid of these technologies, farmers may gain a full understanding of the conditions on their farms and use data analysis to inform their actions [17]. Smart agriculture makes use of cutting-edge technologies like big data, cloud computing, and the Internet of Things (IoT) to automate and expedite multiple farming activities. It enables the recognition, automation, and exploration of diverse farm operations. This involves leveraging hardware and software technologies such as sensor nodes, control systems, robotics, satellite imaging and positioning, data storage and analysis, alert systems,

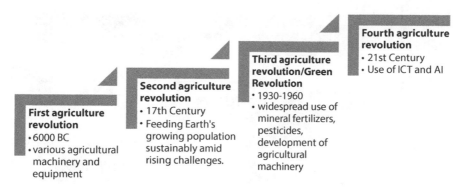

Figure 2.1 Agricultural revolution phases.

drones, and robots [18]. The leading goal of smart agriculture is to enhance the agricultural sector by promoting efficiency, sustainability, and superior quality throughout the entire farming cycle while addressing the specific needs of the farmers. Figure 2.1 indicates the progressive agriculture revolution phases in India and use of ICT and AI for its betterment.

The next section describes the systematic literature review comprised of two subsections: first, the PRISMA method was used to short-list the research articles for the review purpose. Furthermore, a visual literature review is provided so that the various associated terms with the given topic are visualized well in advance.

2.2   Systematic Literature Review

A thorough and methodical technique to examine the body of literature on a particular subject or research issue is known as a systematic literature review. It entails a methodical and organized process of locating, picking, assessing, and synthesizing pertinent research in order to present an objective and thorough overview of the state of knowledge of a certain topic. The objective of a literature review is to provide openness in the selection and assessment of research while minimizing bias.

2.2.1   PRISMA Protocol

For a solid and robust literature review, content analysis as part of the meta-analysis has to be conducted [19]. The quantitative method of analysis was chosen as suggested by previous studies [20, 21]. PRISMA, which stands for Preferred Reporting Items for Systematic Reviews and Meta-Analyses, is a universally designed set of guidelines [22] helpful to conduct systematic reviews and meta-analyses. The PRISMA protocol as previously mentioned consists of a checklist [23] item and a research flow diagram which clarifies the purpose of systematic reviews and meta-analyses so that the entire process is visualized with transparency to the stakeholders. The checklist consists of crucial components such as the title, abstract, methods, results, discussion, and funding. These components are very much helpful for applying search strategy, filter strategy, data collection, data extraction and analysis, and interpretation of the results.

The PRISMA flow diagram is a four-phase pictorial representation of a process—identification, screening, eligibility, and inclusion of research articles as shown in Figure 2.2.

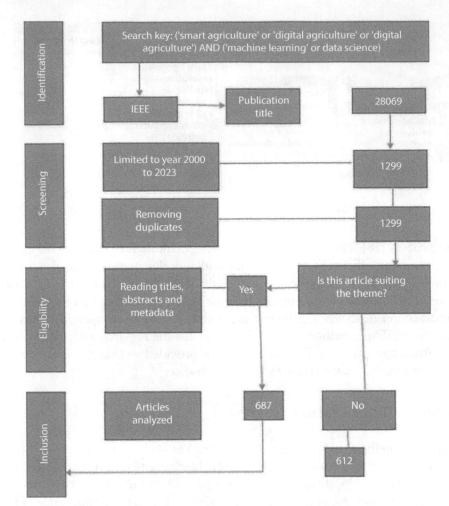

Figure 2.2 Application of PRISMA for literature review.

2.2.2   Visual Literature Review

The research subtopics are being noted by performing a literature review using various research tools that create the image for the review at a glance. The tools used are Carrot2, Open Knowledge Maps, and Citation Gecko. Carrot2 is an open-source engine [24] that creates clusters of documents and represents them pictorially. It supports five different languages, namely, English, French, German, Italian, and Spanish, and supports documents from eight countries, i.e., Austria, France, Germany, Great Britain, Lichtenstein, Italy, Spain, and Switzerland. A visual representation as indicated in Figure 2.3 was generated when the search keyword "smart agriculture" was used. Figure 2.4 depicts the sunburst chart generated from Carrot website with keyword 'smart agriculture', thus elaborating major concerns of the related.

Citation Gecko is a graphical user interface [25] exclusively created to find the association between various papers for the related keyword(s). A visual representation was generated when using the search keyword "smart agriculture," and all the papers were considered to be "seed papers." As a result, two visualizations were created: a list of seed papers and clusters of seed papers and related papers. The visualizations are given below:

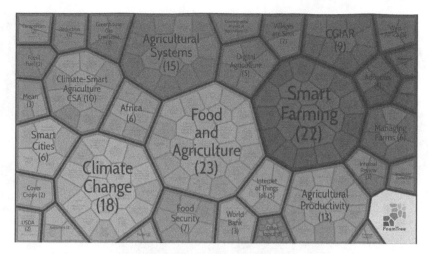

Figure 2.3 Tree map generated with the keyword "smart agriculture" from Carrot2.

As shown in Figure 2.5, the center of the cluster is the seed paper and the others are the papers citing the seed paper shown in yellow color. It can be noted that the seed papers are surrounded by many other papers in most of the cases; however, in some cases, the seed papers are in isolation.

After a sound understanding of the systematic literature review and visualizing various dimensions of the given topic, bibliometric analysis is performed. Bibliometric analysis is used to quantify the research article data to know the impact of various research articles.

2.3   Bibliometric Analysis

The effect and visibility of research articles within a particular subject or discipline are assessed using bibliometric analysis, a sort of quantitative data analysis. Bibliometric analysis [26], a type of quantitative data analysis, is used to evaluate the impact and visibility of research articles within a given subject or discipline [27, 28].

2.3.1   Research Database

To initiate a bibliometric study, the initial step involves determining a suitable database from which to retrieve relevant documents. A bibliometric analysis was performed utilizing IEEE Xplore (Institute of Electrical and Electronics Engineers), a research database providing a collection of various research articles in the field of electrical engineering, electronics, computer science, and concerned domains [29, 30]. It consists of four million documents comprised of research articles, conference proceedings, standards, books [31], and other publications. IEEE Xplore considers data in various formats: .ris, .bib, and .csv. IEEE Xplore performs basic and advanced search to apply the foundation queries or filter methods respectively. Moreover, the platform offers data with multiple dimensions, including article type, publication year, author, affiliation, publication title, publisher, conference location, standard status, standard type, and publication topics. This enables users to search for terms within titles, titles/abstracts, journal names, author names, or affiliations, facilitating

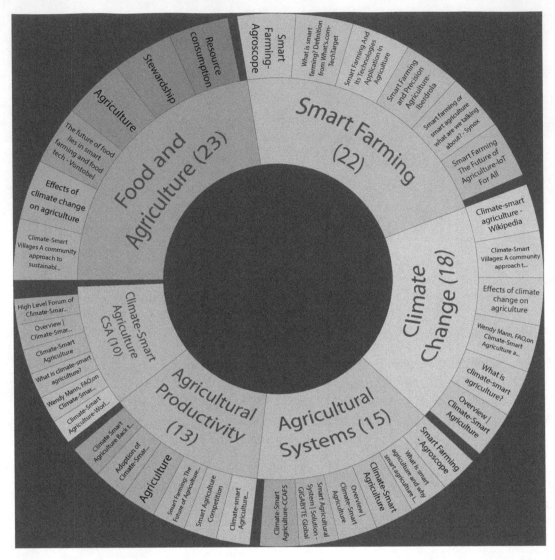

Figure 2.4 Sunburst chart generated with the keyword "smart agriculture" from Carrot2.

precise and targeted searches within the database. Data from about 2,000 research articles have been selected and downloaded in .csv format.

2.3.2 Search Strategy

Another challenge in bibliometric studies is constructing a valid search query that strikes a balance between retrieving a significant number of relevant documents while minimizing the presence of irrelevant (false-positive) results. This challenge is particularly relevant in the field of agriculture, where numerous technologies are augmenting research endeavors. The technologies include big data, artificial intelligence, and machine learning. However, in the current study, since machine learning is one of the disruptive technologies, the authors reviewed multiple articles on the said technology. As depicted in Table 2.1, the search query term "smart agriculture" and "machine learning" were searched for "full text

Table 2.1 Cluster of seed papers generated with the keyword "smart agriculture" from Citation Gecko.

Sr. no.	Theme	Description
1.	The motor themes	The field of research structuring themes is highly significant and well-developed. These themes hold a prominent position on the strategic map, specifically in the upper right quadrant.
2.	The niche themes	The themes within this domain are characterized by their specialized nature and peripheral position. These themes are situated in the upper left quadrant of the strategic map.
3.	The emerging or declining themes	Themes with low density and low centrality on the strategic map represent emerging or declining topics. These themes are located in the lower left quadrant, indicating their potential for growth or the possibility of diminishing importance.
4.	The basic themes	The themes located in the lower right quadrant are significant and hold potential although they are not yet well-developed in the research field. These themes are fundamental, encompassing general concepts that cut across various areas within the research field. They are considered transversal, providing a foundation for further exploration and advancement.

and metadata," and this was done to gain more dimensions about the query terms. The year of search selected was from 2001 to 2023. A metric known as centrality measures how much a network of keywords interacts with other keyword networks. It gauges the degree to which various networks are interconnected. Contrarily, density measures a network's internal cohesiveness or strength by examining how closely and intricately interwoven its words are. We may divide the themes into four different groups based on their varied levels of centrality and density by taking both centrality and density into account [32]. As depicted in Figures 2.5 and 2.6, the cluster of research paper generated from the search term termed as 'seed term', in this case 'smart agriculture' is searched at citation gecko website. As a result a linear and cluster of research papers related to the seed papers are being generated and are depicted in Figures 2.5 and 2.6. Citation gecko is a search engine website to generate a relationships among various research papers.

2.3.3   Advance Search

("Document Title":agriculture) OR ("Document Title":farming) AND ("Document Title":big data) AND ("Author Keywords":climate) OR ("Author Keywords":environment, global warming) OR ("Author Keywords":temperature, hot, heat, season, wind, air, rain).

Data were exported from the obtained literature into Microsoft Excel. The data that were exported contained information on the yearly increases in publications, document types, languages, nations, authors, institutions, journals, citations, and funding organizations. In order to construct network visualization maps, the acquired literature was also exported to

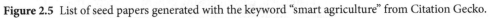

Figure 2.5 List of seed papers generated with the keyword "smart agriculture" from Citation Gecko.

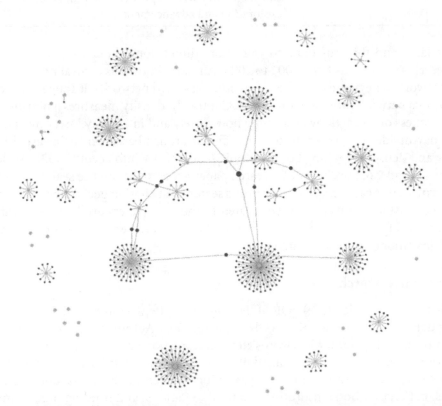

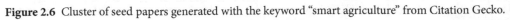

Figure 2.6 Cluster of seed papers generated with the keyword "smart agriculture" from Citation Gecko.

the VOSviewer. The VOSviewer software possesses the ability to establish networks among concepts, terms, and keywords. Utilizing the Visualization of Similarity (VOS) algorithm, VOSviewer generates maps that visually represent these networks. The distances between pairs of objects on the map accurately depict their similarity with high mathematical precision [33]. We utilize a feature that enables the creation of co-occurrence networks using keywords. In these networks, keywords utilized by authors are represented as nodes. The size of each node reflects the frequency of occurrence of the respective keyword. Additionally, the links between nodes are proportional to the degree of co-occurrence between the associated words [34].

To showcase the strength of international research collaboration, we utilized the total link strength (TLS) metric, which is automatically generated by VOSviewer when mapping the research activities of selected nations. The TLS metric serves as an indicator of the extent and intensity of collaborative ties between countries in the research domain, providing valuable insights into the level of cooperation and knowledge exchange among nations. The degree of international research collaboration is inversely correlated with the TLS, with a higher TLS value indicating more collaboration. During that period, the primary research focused on the advancement of digital agriculture encompassing several key areas. These included the establishment of comprehensive databases, the formulation of metadata standards, the innovation of monitoring systems, the design of decision-making forecasting systems, and the implementation of information dissemination systems. These research endeavors aimed to lay the foundation for the progress and development of digital agriculture [35, 36]. However, in the subsequent years, there was a scarcity of publications focusing on these subjects. For the study, the quality journals were considered with high citations and h-index [37]. The top 10 active bibliometric indicators were displayed. Tableau was utilized to depict the annual growth of publications.

In the present study, the authors devised an extensive and inclusive search query with the aim of retrieving all relevant documents pertaining to different aspects of agriculture.

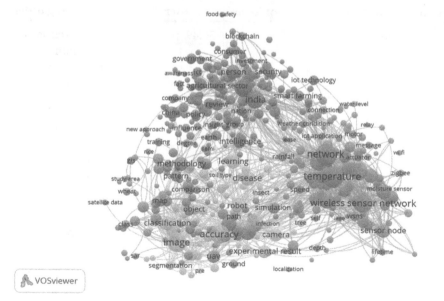

Figure 2.7 Binary counting 409/845.

The search query was meticulously constructed, primarily focusing on both the full document and metadata, ensuring that the retrieved documents were clearly and directly related to the subject of interest. The documents obtained from the search query specifically targeting climate change were referred to as "climate-related literature."

Documents related to various technologies and related to agriculture such as wireless sensor network, artificial intelligence, and blockchain along with the various issues and concerns such as privacy, security, scalability, and reliability were obtained. The documents retrieved for technology were called "technology-related literature."

Documents related to agriculture and related dimensions such as global warming, farming, vegetation, disease, food safety, food security, smart farming, and traditional farming were obtained. The documents retrieved for technology were called "agriculture-related literature."

As shown in Figure 2.7, the three clusters thus formed provide a list of items (see also Table 2.2).

As part of the visual representation of the literature review, it was decided to find article citation and patent citation number. As a result, the following visualization "viz" to be precise was created using Tableau Desktop. It was found that article citation count gradually increased; it was more significant in the years 2017, 2018, and 2019, and then it declined. However, for the patent citation number, we can find a sudden hike in the form of "spikes" for the years 2005, 2007, 2012, and 2018. The article citation and patent citation numbers from 2001 to 2022 are shown in Figure 2.8. Furthermore, Figure 2.9 depicts the exponential rise in the article and reference count is given in Figure 2.9.

Table 2.2 Types of cluster, cluster color, and the related significant words.

Cluster no.	Cluster color	No. of items	Percentage of items in the cluster (%)	Name of items arranged in ascending order
1	Red	177	36.49	Agricultural sector, communication sector, population, India, smart farming
2	Green	133	27.42	Network, communication, humidity, temperature, soil moisture, wireless sensor network, irrigation system
3	Blue	100	20.61	Experiment, index, mapping, imagery classification, UAV, season, measurement
4	Yellowish green	75	15.46	Accuracy, camera, image, disease, deep learning, robot

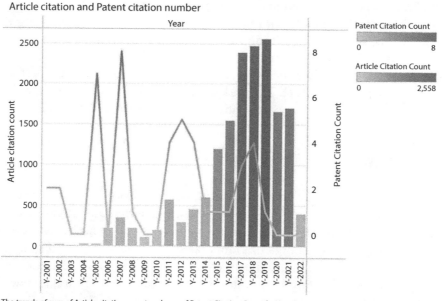

Article citation and Patent citation number

The trends of sum of Article citation count and sum of Patent Citation Count for Year. For pane Sum of Article citation count: Color shows sum of Article citation count. For pane Sum of Patent Citation Count: Color shows sum of Patent Citation Count.

Figure 2.8 Article and patent citation count from 2001 to 2022.

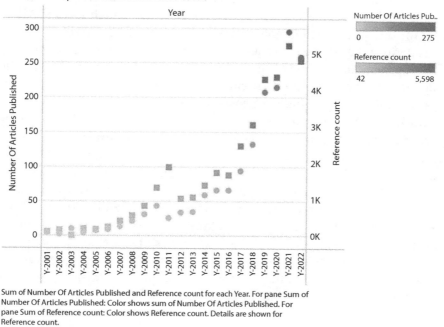

No. of article published and Reference count

Sum of Number Of Articles Published and Reference count for each Year. For pane Sum of Number Of Articles Published: Color shows sum of Number Of Articles Published. For pane Sum of Reference count: Color shows Reference count. Details are shown for Reference count.

Figure 2.9 Article published and reference count from 2001 to 2022.

As part of the visual representation of the literature review, it was decided to explore the number of articles published and their reference count. As a result, the following visualization "viz" to be precise was created using Tableau Desktop. It was found that the reference count growth is proportional to the number of articles published.

The subsequent section describes the study of various technologies performed for smarter and sustainable agriculture. The work conducted so far gives an idea about various agriculture functions and technology utilization for effective implementation.

2.4   Related Study

After performing the systematic literature review, three types of reviews were conducted: climate literature review, technology literature review, and agriculture literature review. The climate-related literature review comprises the rain prediction model, climate-oriented agricultural activities, paperless organization strategy to reduce paper consumption, use of decision support tools, greenhouse effects, etc. The agriculture-related literature consists of technology; thus, the following section specifies the techno-agricultural review claiming the entire section as smart agriculture.

2.4.1   Climate-Related Literature

Weather conditions are highly unpredictable leading to loss of agriculture yield, negatively impacting its quality and yield stability. More focus has been placed on shifting climatic circumstances as a result of scholars' growing interest in the study of weather and how it affects agriculture. Climate conditions are largely associated with rainfall frequency and quantity in terms of water level. Hence as per [38], a long short-term memory (LSTM) system is required for the rainfall prediction model, which is built on the deep learning framework, to produce a superior prediction performance. The climatic conditions are highly unpredictable, and farm production is dependent on the behavior of the respective climate location. Optimizing the impact of weather on agriculture involves employing a range of techniques, including correlation analysis, multidimensional modeling, k-means clustering, artificial neural networks (ANNs), support vector machines (SVMs), knowledge graph classification (KG classification), partitioning around medoids (PAM), clustering large applications (CLARA), and density-based spatial clustering of applications with noise (DBSCAN) [39]. There is a need to develop a tool that takes into account the conventional farmers' crop calendars created by years of farming experience and has strong relevance and adaptability to the changing climate conditions and predictions of agricultural activities. The CCAFS research program on Climate Change, Agriculture and Food Security [9] is interested in connecting its research findings with open data sources, software developers, and problems in Latin America, and they held a hackathon in Lima in 2014 to create innovative applications that assist farmers in basing their decisions on scientific evidence. The demand and supply relation prevails: if the demand increases, supply also increases, and vice versa. In this case, the more the amount of pages used in any organization, the more impact it has on global warming. When we concentrate on the studies, we found that deforestation caused by the growing demand for paper has a negative impact on our planet [40]. The massive clearing of trees has a negative impact on the earth's climate impacting global pollution.

To support agricultural decisions, decision support tools (DSTs) are used by NASA for the following uses/cases: a) GISS GCM and other GCMs consider the synoptic of the region than just designing a scenario product to understand how fluctuations in climate affect major climate variability systems and their Central American teleconnections; b) the use of DST-GISS GCM, other GCMs, and RCMs to analyze extreme climate changes such as heat waves, droughts, and floods; and c) TRMM, GPCP, PERSIANN, and CMORPH to develop probable scenarios which cater the various climate changes that could occur in the future [41]. The climatic quantitative data such as temperature, humidity, and direction of the wind can be measured by cloud-based and lab stations to simulate farm scenarios [42]. Agricultural activity impacted by greenhouse effects is significantly affected by global warming. This study examines the economic impacts of global warming on agriculture using a worldwide CGE-GTAP model [43].

2.4.2   Technology-Related Literature

Modern technology is used in "smart agriculture," often referred to as "precision agriculture" or "digital farming," to optimize agricultural practices, increase output, and use as few resources as possible. This literature review examines the most recent advancements in smart agriculture, concentrating on the tools and software used in this field. The paper emphasizes how smart agriculture affects a variety of factors, including agricultural productivity, resource efficiency, environmental sustainability, and economic viability. This review seeks to provide light on the state of smart agriculture now and suggest areas for future research by looking at a variety of studies. By carefully monitoring and managing numerous elements including irrigation, fertilization, and pest control, farmers can increase crop yields, enhance crop quality, and reduce input wastage by utilizing smart agricultural techniques. Maximizing agricultural productivity helps to ensure global food security while simultaneously increasing farmer profitability. Additionally, essential in encouraging sustainable farming methods is smart agriculture. Farmers may effectively manage their water resources, use less chemicals, and embrace eco-friendly pest management methods by utilizing sensor networks, satellite images, and predictive analytics. This helps to lessen the negative consequences of climate change, conserve natural resources, and lessen the impact of agriculture on the environment. Additionally, smart agriculture improves decision-making by giving farmers access to real-time data and insights. By examining a lot of data, farmers may make informed decisions about crop planning, market trends, and resource allocation. Farmers now have the chance to boost the output, efficiency, and overall profitability of their farms. Although smart agriculture offers a lot of potential, some issues still need to be resolved before it can be employed extensively. The main obstacles are issues with data security and privacy, poor connectivity in rural areas, and the requirement for specific solutions for small-scale farmers. Additionally, frameworks for policy and regulation need to be created to encourage the use of smart agriculture techniques and guarantee that all farmers have equitable access to technology.

The research article outlines the key metrics that need to be tracked in order to maximize the automation system's efficiency. In MATLAB, a mathematical model was created using the measured precipitation, perturbations, and soil humidity as input and output variables [44]. The prototype thus designed is termed the DesignWare ARC EM Starter Kit [45]. The Synopsys ARC EM family of embedded CPU cores is used to monitor plant development.

This is accomplished by keeping an eye on a number of characteristics, including soil moisture, nutrients, pH, temperature, soil texture, weather, and light, utilizing a network of sensors. Actuators are also used by the system to maintain and modify these settings as needed. This paper presents a unique technique that incorporates information from vineyard 3D point cloud models, thermal imaging, and multispectral pictures to reliably measure the variability of canopy states within row plan vineyards. The proposed approach seeks to analyze and combine these many data sources to offer a thorough insight into the health and growth trends of the grapevine. In [46], the authors make use of spectral and spatial data collected using remote sensing methods. For precision agriculture, the ATmega328P microcontroller in Arduino Uno was used to sense the soil moisture, turn on the sprinklers, generate an alarm signal in case of external agents, and monitor in real time agriculture fields with good efficiency [47]. In [48], a new approach for processing and combining data from a vineyard 3D point cloud model, thermal imagery, and multispectral imagery was presented, with the goal of accurately representing the canopy state fluctuation among row layout vineyards.

2.5   Conclusion

In conclusion, smart agriculture has enormous potential to revolutionize conventional farming methods and solve farmer problems, hence transforming the agricultural industry. Smart agriculture has given the road map for the future economy across the nation and worldwide and has given directions for the current and forthcoming agriculture systems to witness changes in the economy using smart agriculture. The technologies are disruptive in nature and overpromising and provide multifaceted and one-click solutions. The present chapter discusses about various technology frontiers to devise the smart ecosystem for the agricultural ecosystem.

The book chapter discusses the emerging research trend using PRISMA to filter research articles in a systematic and structured manner. The visual literature review is an unconventional method used to leverage the utilization of artificial intelligence tools to facilitate the research processes. The systematic literature review augmented by various graphs and images makes the review much stronger and lays an impact on the depth of smart agriculture coupled with the implementation of tools. The impact of climate change on socioeconomic life and more precisely on traditional and modern agriculture is crucial, which is also highlighted in this research.

References

1. Vishwanatth, K., Performance of Indian agriculture and rural development: Need for reforms, 7, 03, 2022. DOI: 10.33564/IJEAST.2022.v07i03.010.
2. Abate, G.T., Bernard, T., de Brauw, A., Minot, N. The impact of the use of new technologies on farmers' wheat yield in Ethiopia: Evidence from a randomized control trial. *Agric. Econ (United Kingdom)*, 49, 409–421, 2018.

3. Usama, M., A review on achievement of financial security in agrarian economy through sustainable livelihoods options in Rural India, in: *The Changing Scenario of Management*, Aargon Press, New Delhi, 2022, doi: DOI: 10.11114/smc.v11i2.5932.

4. Bhuvaneswari, R., Editorial: Indian literature: Past, present and future. *Stud. Media Communication*, 11, 2, 1, 2023. availiable at research gate.net/publication/368721746 DOI: 10.11114/smc.v11i2.5932.

5. Keller, M., Rosenberg, M., Brettel, M., Friederichsen, N., How virtualization, decentralization-and network building change the manufacturing landscape: An industry 4.0 perspective. *Int. J. Mechanical, Aerospace, Ind. Mechatronic Manufacturing Eng.*, 8, 37–44, 2014.

6. Lasi, H., Fettke, P., Kemper, H.G., Feld, T., Hoffmann, M., Industry 4.0. *Bus. Inf. Syst. Eng.*, 6, 239–242, 2014.

7. Liao, Y., Deschamps, F., E.d., F.R., Ramos, L.F.P., Past, present and future of industry 4.0—A systematic literature review and research agenda proposal. *Int. J. Prod. Res.*, 55, 3609–3629, 2017.

8. Maynard, A.D., Navigating the fourth industrial revolution. *Nat. Nanotechnol.*, 10, 1005–1006, 2015.

9. Pivoto, D., Waquil, P.D., Talamini, E., Finocchio, C.P.S., Dalla Corte, V.F., deVargas Mores, G., Scientific development of smart farming technologies and their application in Brazil. *Inf. Process. Agric.*, 5, 21–32, 2018.

10. Saiz-Rubio, V. and Rovira-Más, F., From smart farming towards agriculture 5.0: A review on crop data management. *Agronomy*, 10, 1–11, 2020.

11. Kapur, R., Usage of technology in the agricultural sector. *Acta Sci. Agric.*, 2, 78–84, 2018.

12. Rehman, A. and Hussain, I., Modern agricultural technology adoption its importance, role and usage for the improvement of agriculture. *Am.-Eurasian J. Agric. Environ. Sci.*, 16, 2, 284–288, 2016.

13. Costa, C., Antonucci, F., Pallottino, F., Aguzzi, J., Sun, D.W., Menesatti, P., Shape analysis of agricultural products: A review of recent research advances and potential application to computer vision. *Food Bioprocess Technol.*, 4, 673–692, 2011.

14. Klerkxi, A review of social science on digital agriculture, smart farming and agriculture 4.0: New contributions and a future research agenda. *NJAS: Wageningen Journal of Life Sciences*, 90–91, 100315, 2019.

15. van ersum, M.K., Integrated assessment of agricultural systems –a component-based framework for the European Union (SEAMLESS). *Agric. Syst.*, 96, 1–3, 150–165, March 2008.

16. Garg, D. and Alam, M., Smart agriculture: A literature review. *J. Manage. Anal.*, 10, 2, 359–415, 2023, doi: DOI: 10.1080/23270012.2023.2207184.

17. Bacco, M., Barsocchi, P., Ferro, E., Gotta, A., Ruggeri, M., The digitisation of agriculture: A survey of research activities on smart farming, array, vol. 3–4, 2019, 100009, ISSN 2590-0056, https://doi.org/10.1016/j.array.2019.100009.

18. Sarfraz, S., Ali, F., Hameed, A., Ahmad, Z., Riaz, K., Sustainable agriculture through technological innovations. *Sustainable Agriculture in the Era of OMICs Revolution*, pp. 223–239, Springer, Cham., 2023. doi: 10.1007/978-3-031-15568-0_10.

19. Kraus, S., Breier, M., Dasí-Rodríguez, S., The art of crafting a systematic literature review in entrepreneurship research. *Int. Entrep. Manage. J.*, 16, 1023–1042, 2020.

20. Haddow, G., *Bibliometric research Methods: Information, Systems, and Contexts*, Second ed, pp. 241–266, Chandos Publishing, an imprint of Elsevier, Cambridge, MA, United States, 20182018.

21. Navrotsky, Y. and Patsei, N., Zipf's distribution caching application in named data networks, in: *2021 IEEE Open Conference of Electrical, Electronic and Information Sciences, eStream 2021-Proceedings*, 2021, 2021.

22. Galvão, T.F., de S.A, T., Harrad, D., Principais itens para relatar Revisões sistemáticas e Meta-análises: A recomendação PRISMA. *Epidemiol. Serv. Saúde*, 24, 335–342, 2015.

23. Hilmi, M.F. and Mustapha, Y., E-learning research in the middle east: a bibliometric analysis. *2020 Sixth International Conference on e-Learning (econf)*, Sakheer, Bahrain, pp. 243–248, 2020, doi: 10.1109/econf51404.2020.9385513.

24. https://search.carrot2.org/#/search/web

25. https://www.citationgecko.com/

26. Sweileh, W.M., Wickramage, K., Pottie, K., Hui, C., Roberts, B., Sawalha, A.F., Zyoud, S.H., Bibliometric analysis of global migration health research in peer-reviewed literature (2000-2016). *BMC Public Health*, 18, 1, 1–8, 2018.

27. Aria, M. and Cuccurullo, C., bibliometrix: An R-tool for comprehensive science mapping analysis. *J. Informetr.*, 11959-975, 2017, 2017.

28. Van Eck, N.J. and Waltman, L., *VOSviewer Manual*, Version 1.6.13, Universiteit Leiden, 2019, 2019, https://www.vosviewer.com/documentation/Manual_ VOSviewer_1.6.13.pdf.

29. Durniak, A., Welcome to IEEE Xplore. *IEEE Power Eng. Rev.*, 20, 11, 12, Nov. 2000, doi: 10.1109/39.883281.

30. Sinha, S., Lacquet, B., Maharaj, B.T.J., IEEE Xplore digital library indexes the Transactions of the SAIEE, 1909 to date. *SAIEE Afr. Res. J.*, 112, 4, 158–159, Dec. 2021.

31. Cobo, M.J., Martínez, M.A., Gutiérrez-Salcedo, M., Fujita, H., HerreraViedma, E., 25 years at knowledge-based systems: A bibliometric analysis. *Knowl.-Based Syst.*, 80, 3–13, 2015.

32. Van Eck, N.J. and Waltman, L., Visualizing bibliometric networks, in: *Measuring Scholarly Impact*, Y. Ding, R. Rousseau, D. Wolfram (Eds.), pp. 285–320, Springer International Publisher, Cham, 2014.

33. Tang, S., Zhu, Q., Zhou, X., Liu, S., Wu, M., Aconception of digital agriculture, in: *International Geoscience and Remote Sensing Symposium (IGARSS)*, Toronto, Ontario, 2002, pp. 3026–3028, 2002.

34. Yong, L., Xiushan, L., Degui, Z., Fu, L., The main content, technical support and enforcement strategy of digital agriculture. *Geo Spat. Inf. Sci.*, 5, 68–73, 2002.

35. Hirsch, J.E., An index to quantify an individual's scientific research output. *Proc. Natl. Acad. Sci.*, 102, 46, 16569–16572, 2005, doi: 10.1073/pnas.0507655102.

36. Oswalt, M.S. and Ananth, J.P., MapReduce and optimized deep network for rainfall prediction in agriculture. *Compu. J.*, 63, 1, 900–912, Jan. 2020, doi: 10.1093/ comjnl/bxz164.

37. Yadav, S.A., Sahoo, B.M., Sharma, S., Das, L., An analysis of data mining techniques to analyze the effect of weather on agriculture. *2020 International Conference on Intelligent Engineering and Management (ICIEM)*, London, UK, pp. 29–32, 2020, doi: 10.1109/ ICIEM48762.2020.9160110.

38. Pajarito Grajales, D.F., Mejia, F., Jhoana Asprilla Mosquera, G., Piedrahita, L.C., Basurto, C., Crop-planning, making smarter agriculture with climate data. *2015 Fourth International Conference on Agro-Geoinformatics (Agro-geoinformatics)*, Istanbul, Turkey, pp. 240–244, 2015, doi: 10.1109/Agro-Geoinformatics.2015.7248124.

39. Nayyar, N. and Arora, S., Paperless technology–a solution to global warming. *2019 2nd International Conference on Power Energy, Environment and Intelligent Control (PEEIC)*, Greater Noida, India, pp. 486–488, 2019, doi: 10.1109/PEEIC47157.2019.8976599.

40. Rosenzweig, C. and Horton, R., Application of NASA climate models and missions to agriculture DSS: The solutions network approach. *IGARSS 2008-2008 IEEE International Geoscience and Remote Sensing Symposium*, Boston, MA, USA, pp. IV–463-IV-466, 2008, doi: 10.1109/ IGARSS.2008.4779758.

41. Tenzin, S., Siyang, S., Pobkrut, T., Kerdcharoen, T., Low cost weather station for climate-smart agriculture. *2017 9th International Conference on Knowledge and Smart Technology (KST)*, Chonburi, Thailand, pp. 172–177, 2017, doi: 10.1109/KST.2017.7886085.

42. Jie, X., Greenhouse effects on the world agriculture—Based on computable general equilibrium model analysis. *2010 International Conference on Mechanic Automation and Control Engineering*, Wuhan, China, pp. 2082–2085, 2010, doi: 10.1109/MACE.2010.5536266.

43. Suciu, G., Marcu, I., Balaceanu, C., Dobrea, M., Botezat, E., Efficient IoT system for precision agriculture. *2019 15th International Conference on Engineering of Modern Electric Systems (EMES)*, Oradea, Romania, pp. 173–176, 2019, doi: 10.1109/EMES.2019.8795102.

44. Grimblatt, V., Ferré, G., Rivet, F., Jego, C., Vergara, N., Precision agriculture for small to medium size farmers—An IoT approach. *2019 IEEE International Symposium on Circuits and Systems (ISCAS)Sapporo, Japan*, pp. 1–5, 2019, doi: 10.1109/ISCAS.2019.8702563.

45. Comba, L., Biglia, A., Aimonino, D.R., Barge, P., Tortia, C., Gay, P., 2D and 3D data fusion for crop monitoring in precision agriculture. *2019 IEEE International Workshop on Metrology for Agriculture and Forestry (MetroAgriFor)*, Portici, Italy, pp. 62–67, 2019, doi: 10.1109/MetroAgriFor.2019.8909219.

46. Liao, Z., Dai, S., Shen, C., Precision agriculture monitoring system based on wireless sensor networks. *IET International Conference on Wireless Communications and Applications (ICWCA 2012)*, Kuala Lumpur, pp. 1–5, 2012, doi: 10.1049/cp.2012.2107.

47. Comba, L., Biglia, A., Aimonino, D.R., Barge, P., Tortia, C., Gay, P., 2D and 3D data fusion for crop monitoring in precision agriculture. *2019 IEEE International Workshop on Metrology for Agriculture and Forestry (MetroAgriFor)*, Portici, Italy, pp. 62–67, 2019, doi: 10.1109/MetroAgriFor.2019.8909219.

48. Nishant, P.S., Sai Venkat, P., Avinash, B.L., Jabber, B., Crop yield prediction based on Indian agriculture using machine learning. *2020 International Conference for Emerging Technology (INCET)*, pp. 1–4, Belgaum, India, 2020, doi: 10.1109/INCET49848.2020.9154036.

Agriculturist Engagement and Knowledge Sharing in Digital Ecosystem: Insights from Social Media

Jitendra Yadav[1]*, Nripendra P. Rana[2], Pankaj Kumar Singh[1] and Ramendra Pratap Singh[3]

1Department of Marketing & Strategy, ICFAI Business School, Hyderabad, A Constituent of IFHE (Deemed to be University), Hyderabad, India
2Department of Management and Marketing, College of Business and Economics, Qatar University, Doha, Qatar
3Department of Marketing, Indian Institute of Management–Tiruchirappalli, Sooriyur, Tamil Nadu, India

Abstract

The agricultural industry has been impacted by the recent surge in the utilization of social media. The aforementioned phenomenon could potentially be elucidated by the convenience afforded to users by social media platforms in disseminating and proliferating information and various forms of content among themselves. The present study aims to investigate the involvement of agricultural producers, organizations, and governments in the dissemination of information within virtual communities. This study employs different methodologies, including content analysis, word co-occurrence analysis, and sentiment analysis, to conduct a comprehensive analysis of YouTube data. The analysis of user-generated videos on YouTube has provided insights into the discourse surrounding the utilization of technology in the agricultural sector. The research reveals that social media platforms play a significant role in facilitating communication and information exchange within the farming community. Additionally, the study indicates that the utilization of analytics on YouTube yields significant outcomes regarding the characteristics and inclinations of engagement and dissemination of information in the digital realm. Furthermore, the study highlights various constraints and impediments pertaining to YouTube analytics and proposes potential avenues for future research.

Keywords: Agriculture, digital ecosystem, engagement, knowledge sharing, social media analytics, YouTube

3.1 Introduction

The significance of agriculture in furnishing sustenance and economic opportunities to individuals worldwide is crucial for the advancement of human society. The viability of conventional farming is threatened by various factors such as population expansion, climate change, limited resources, and the necessity for sustainable practices [1]. The emergence

Corresponding author: yadavjitendra.phd@gmail.com

Kuldeep Singh and Prasanna Kolar (eds.) Digital Agricultural Ecosystem: Revolutionary Advancements in Agriculture, (35–54) © 2024 Scrivener Publishing LLC

of digital technologies has become a powerful influence in the agricultural sector, offering innovative solutions to longstanding challenges. The ubiquitous adoption of digital technology has facilitated the emergence of precision agriculture, which constitutes a notable deviation from conventional agricultural methodologies. The implementation of advanced technologies such as GPS, GIS, and remote sensing has facilitated farmers in conducting meticulous evaluations of soil conditions, environmental patterns, and agricultural productivity [2, 3]. The utilization of a data-driven approach may enable farmers and other agriculturalists to enhance resource allocation efficiency, thereby reducing their environmental impact [4]. Research has demonstrated that the utilization of precision farming equipment can enhance productivity, reduce expenses, and improve operational efficiency [5]. The integration of sensors and other Internet of Things (IoT) devices has facilitated the attainment of real-time monitoring and data collection in the domain of agriculture. The function of sensors, as indicated by several authors [6, 7], is to gather and relay information from embedded devices situated in different environments. The compiled data pertain to a diverse array of subjects, encompassing soil moisture levels, nutrient composition, insect infestations, and the well-being of animals. Farmers have the ability to remotely monitor their agricultural operations and make necessary modifications through the utilization of data gathered by technological devices. The integration of IoT devices leads to enhanced productivity and minimized losses through the automation of repetitive tasks, timely identification of potential issues, and the ability to take proactive measures.

Social networking platforms have demonstrated their efficacy as instruments for enabling communication, augmenting information dissemination, fostering collaboration, and cultivating ingenuity [8, 9]. The pervasive existence of social media platforms, including Facebook, Twitter, and Instagram, has become an essential component of modern-day existence. The advent of these platforms has brought about a significant transformation in the realm of communication by enabling cooperation and coordination among users, specialists, and enthusiasts [10–13]. The forum provides a platform for individuals who are interested in a domain (such as digitization of agriculture) to gather and share their viewpoints, findings, and expertise. Users are inclined to engage in communal gatherings, participate in discourse pertaining to their experiences with the incorporation of digital tools, and gain knowledge from their fellow peers [9, 14]. Facilitating discussions among individuals about their experiences with digitalization can promote the establishment of a support network, facilitate the generation of innovative ideas, and aid in the resolution of challenges.

YouTube, the largest global platform for sharing videos, has revolutionized the way in which we obtain and distribute information [15]. Within the framework of the knowledge sharing platforms, YouTube has emerged as a platform of great value for the facilitation of visual learning and the dissemination of information. The YouTube platform is utilized by agricultural experts, farmers, and organizations to disseminate valuable resources to the general public [16]. The utilization of visual format in YouTube videos enhances the effectiveness of comprehending concepts, enables the observation of practical applications, and encourages the envisioning of potential transformations in the agricultural sector due to digitization [17, 18].

At present, individuals involved in agriculture, including farmers and enthusiasts, enjoy unimpeded access to contemporary practices, equipment, and technology without any physical barriers. Moreover, YouTube enables the interchange of concepts and discourse among its users via the functionality that permits direct commenting on videos. Although YouTube is a strong platform for information exchange, relatively limited research has been conducted to investigate its potential in the agricultural sector [19, 20]. The existing literature either provides methods of disseminating agricultural information via organizational YouTube handles [20] or focuses on a single section of the category such as in the study of Clark *et al.* [21]. Motivated by the increased integration of digital technologies in various aspects of agriculture, as well as the lack of literature on knowledge sharing methodologies via highly engaging social media platforms, this study aims to analyze the communication ecology related to agriculture's digital environment, as well as to address the following research questions:

RQ1: Which type of videos are being posted over YouTube concerning the agriculture digital ecosystem?
RQ2: How are the viewers responding to the videos posted on YouTube?

The organization of the paper is as follows. Section 3.2 introduces the related work. Section 3.3 describes the data collection and analysis methodology adopted in our study, and Section 3.4 presents the findings of the algorithmic evaluation of YouTube content. The implications of our findings are further discussed in Section 3.5. Section 3.6 highlights the limitations of this research along with suggestions for future researchers. Finally, Section 3.7 concludes the paper.

3.2 State of Literature

3.2.1 Agriculture Digital Transformation

The agricultural sector holds a significant and enduring role in human civilization, dating back to ancient times. Its responsibility encompasses the provision of sustenance, apparel, and other fundamental goods to the global populace. Throughout time, agriculture has undergone various changes, ranging from the implementation of novel crop strains to the utilization of contemporary equipment [22]. Digital transformation is currently regarded as one of the most notable changes that the agricultural sector is undergoing [23].

The integration of sophisticated technology in diverse agricultural activities, including but not limited to crop cultivation, animal husbandry, and soil administration, characterizes the digitalization of agriculture [24–26]. The objective is to optimize the efficacy and output of agricultural practices while mitigating the ecological footprint of farming. Precision agriculture has emerged as a prominent feature of the digital transformation in agriculture. Precision agriculture is an agricultural approach that utilizes advanced technology and techniques to manage and enhance crop growth and yield [27, 28]. It enables farmers to make informed decisions by utilizing up-to-date data on factors such as soil moisture, temperature, and nutrient levels [29, 30]. Farmers who utilize this information can enhance crop yields and mitigate wasteful practices by adjusting their current methods to conform to new information.

The livestock farming industry is among the sectors that are capitalizing on digital transformation. The utilization of digital technology has enabled farmers to effectively oversee and regulate the welfare, nourishment, and yield of their livestock, thereby facilitating a rise in their economic gains [31, 32]. Wearable devices have the potential to be utilized by farmers to monitor the physiological attributes and movement behaviors of their livestock. This facilitates the prompt detection of potential health issues in livestock by farmers [33]. Moreover, the utilization of digital technology possesses the potential to enhance feeding schedules and facilitate the surveillance of livestock growth and welfare, ultimately fostering optimal animal health and productivity [34].

The adoption of digital transformation in agriculture yields noteworthy advantages. The utilization of digital technology holds promise in augmenting the efficiency and productivity of agricultural operations while concurrently mitigating inefficiencies and minimizing the environmental footprint of farmers. The implementation of digital technology has the potential to enhance farmers' risk management strategies, including those aimed at safeguarding crops against adverse weather conditions, pest invasions, and disease epidemics [35, 36]. The utilization of real-time data can reduce farmers' dependence on intuition and conjecture.

3.2.2 Significance of YouTube in Fostering Engagement and Knowledge Sharing

The widespread adoption of digital media platforms in recent times has resulted in significant transformations across various industries, including agriculture. The utilization of YouTube, the largest video-sharing platform globally, has emerged as a potent mechanism for disseminating knowledge and revolutionizing the agriculture sector [20]. The extensive collection of readily available videos has provided farmers with a plethora of pragmatic knowledge, techniques, and remedies that can be customized to suit their requirements. Crop cultivation, livestock management, irrigation systems, and farm equipment are just a few of the areas in which professionals and seasoned farmers use YouTube to share their knowledge with the world [37–39]. Moreover, academic institutions, agricultural associations, and governmental establishments employ YouTube as a platform to disseminate research outcomes, optimal methodologies, and regulatory revisions, thereby guaranteeing the dissemination of significant knowledge to a wider spectrum of viewers.

YouTube has facilitated the development of a dynamic worldwide community comprised of farmers, agricultural enthusiasts, and industry experts. The interactive functionalities of the platform, including comments, likes, and shares, serve to enhance user engagement and foster collaborative efforts [19]. Farmers hailing from diverse geographical locations and socioeconomic backgrounds can engage in knowledge sharing, seek consultation, and extend mutual assistance to each other. The virtual community functions as a significant source of support, particularly for smallholder farmers who may encounter difficulties in accessing local networks [40]. In addition, the algorithmic recommendations on YouTube facilitate the exploration of novel channels, thereby augmenting one's knowledge in a specific domain and fostering global connections with individuals who share similar interests [41].

Although YouTube has brought about significant changes in the field of agriculture, certain challenges and considerations need to be taken into account. The veracity and dependability of information disseminated on the platform may fluctuate, necessitating users to exercise discernment in assessing sources and corroborating data [42, 43]. Moreover, the presence of the digital divide and the absence of Internet connectivity in remote areas could potentially curtail the extent and efficacy of YouTube's influence on farmers in certain localities. It is imperative to undertake measures to narrow this divide and guarantee equitable access to the knowledge-sharing capabilities of the platform for all farmers.

3.3   Methodology

The extensive assortment of video content, recommendation algorithm, comments section, user-generated content, and advertising platform render YouTube a distinctive platform for knowledge sharing and interaction [44]. Through an examination of these facets of the platform, scholars can acquire a significant understanding of user conduct, inclinations, and affinities [45, 46]. Given the growing significance of data in contemporary society, YouTube represents a valuable repository of data that can be leveraged for scholarly investigation and scrutiny. In contrast to conventional text-based platforms, YouTube's principal mode of communication is video, which has facilitated the emergence of a vibrant community of content producers and consumers. This renders it a suitable platform for investigating social dynamics and the power of influence. This study through YouTube data mining and analytics identifies prominent channels streaming in the community, identifies clusters of interest, and monitors the dissemination of trends and viral content.

3.3.1   Data Description

The study by using the keyword "agriculture digital transformation" scrapes the related videos on YouTube through the Tuber package available in RStudio software (Version 2023.03.1+446) [47] on 10 May 2023. The dataset contains 592 videos posted on the topic of digital integration in the various facets of crop management, livestock management, and the digitalization of agriculture. Table 3.1 presents a sample of 10 videos from the dataset on agriculture digital transformation with the date of video publication on YouTube, the channel that hosted the video, the title of the video, description of the video, title of the channel, and publication time stamp along with views, likes, favorites, and comments received by each video.

3.3.2   Algorithmic Evaluation

Initial descriptive statistics have been calculated based on the video publication date and the views, likes, favorites, and comments received by each video. Furthermore, the researchers were interested in exploring the reactions of the users on the posts of videos concentrating on five themes, i.e., 1) farm—general videos related to the digitalization of farming; 2) smart—the use of smart technologies in agriculture activities extending to data recording and monitoring; 3) economy—videos relating to agriculture economy digitalization, financial inclusion, and enhancing farm income; 4) industry—videos on agriculture section through Industry 4.0 applications; and 5) technology—videos on technology integration in farming machinery, precision farming, data security and privacy, and efficient connectivity. The words with a high correlation with the five themes (farm, smart, economy, industry,

Table 3.1 Sample of the dataset.

Video ID	Published at	Channel ID	Title	Description	Channel title	View count	Like count	Favorite count	Comment count
tQ5jAD0DAs	44271	UCE9mrcoX-oE-2f1BL-iPPoQ	Digital agriculture new frontiers food system	What is the value of evolving digital technologies to the agrifood system? Our agrifood system does more than keep people fed, …	World Bank	11,176	175	0	5
g8tHedBgrRA	43628	UCIm75cHMxkp6uM1hZ0TVfOg	Digitalization agriculture	Meet Sonya. She is a new generation of digital farmer. The power to increase production and transform smallholder farming is in …	CTA	24,627	298	0	6
MQaRqZpkQxk	43110	UCsT0YIqwnpJCM-mx7-gSA4Q	Digital agriculture transforming farmers lives Michael Robertson Tedxuwa	Digital technologies have enormous power to change the way farmers will grow food in the future. In Africa, where farmers …	TEDx Talks	34,878	570	0	11
C4W0qSQ6A8U	43216	UChHKVJ3slPNkI1jcqIIV8vg	Innovating agribusiness EY Microsoft		EY Global	47,127	663	0	NA

(Continued)

Table 3.1 Sample of the dataset. (*Continued*)

Video ID	Published at	Channel ID	Title	Description	Channel title	View count	Like count	Favorite count	Comment count
T33dmV5Biso	43742	UCXscwCVOk653HlNY9wwES_w	Digital transforming farming cognizant	AquaTEK™, a brand of Monsanto Corporation, envisioned the need for an easy-to-use digital application to help farmers monitor …	Cognizant	1,955	14	0	0
aChi0hFtrIQ	44456	UCafpueX9hFLJs24ed6UddEQ	Digital agriculture point Drishti IAS English	Recently, the Ministry of Agriculture and Farmers Welfare signed five Memorandums of Understanding (MOUs) with private …	Drishti IAS: English	17,111	707	0	52
TTf_VXparLY	43601	UCQ0Fi352poXD2b7kSj6ZktQ	Digital agriculture	Abe Stroock of the Cornell College of Engineering explains technological innovations that could save water, minimize the use of …	Cornell Research	2,916	22	0	2

(*Continued*)

Table 3.1 Sample of the dataset. (*Continued*)

Video ID	Published at	Channel ID	Title	Description	Channel title	View count	Like count	Favorite count	Comment count
DsFmzYdCq8w	44042	UCFjb52dVb1QEvgabyLwA2-g	Role digital technologies agricultural transformation	With the increasing global population, Industry 4.0 applications throughout agrifood value chains can help achieve food security.	Asian Productivity Organization	995	21	0	3
Ee5Dv0RZtMw	44170	UC3g8Ulf6iWD5fjCQ_YDeTlg	Digital transformation agriculture	With featured guest, Professor Lesly Goh, former Chief Technology Officer at the World Bank Group, Ranveer Chandra, Chief ...	Empowering Asian Women at Columbia University	262	8	0	1
NtuGLB0z-1A	44216	UChFY7E48saxGiDsDXewl1lg	Digital transformation agriculture Agritech	The use of technology even in the most manpower-based industries like agriculture is not unknown to people for a decade. But ...	NetBramha Studios	143	0	0	0

and technology) have been identified to understand the prominent domains on which the major focus has been invested by the content creators on YouTube.

Furthermore, the comments on the videos falling into the five themes have been collected to explore the trend of posting comments and the emotions displayed by the users in their comments. Prior to semantic analysis, the collected comments are pre-processed thus eliminating non-ASCII characters, emoticons, URLs, stop words, mentions, and unnecessary breaks and spaces. After pre-processing, sentiment analysis of the comments has been conducted using the NRC Word-Emotion Association Lexicon repository that classifies the words used in the comments into two semantic polarities, namely, positive and negative, and eight emotions, namely, anger, anticipation, disgust, fear, joy, sadness, surprise, and trust.

3.4 Findings

3.4.1 Content Analysis

The data presented in Figure 3.1 display the frequency of videos pertaining to the topic of "agriculture digital transformation" that were published starting from the year 2013. The visual representation illustrates a noticeable rise in the number of YouTube videos pertaining to the topic of "agriculture digital transformation" subsequent to the year 2016.

Upon conducting a comprehensive examination of the videos that have been posted over the years, it is evident that the video pertaining to the adoption of technological advancements, specifically blockchain, in the year 2018, garnered a significant amount of attention. Moreover, the videos that have been shared over the years have portrayed the utilization of technology to augment agricultural productivity, thereby serving as a significant information resource for individuals involved in the field of agriculture (as illustrated in Figure 3.2).

Furthermore, the videos emphasizing the digitalization of agriculture gained substantial viewership. However, it is noteworthy that the majority of such videos have been disseminated by institutional bodies (e.g., the Food and Agriculture Organization), technology

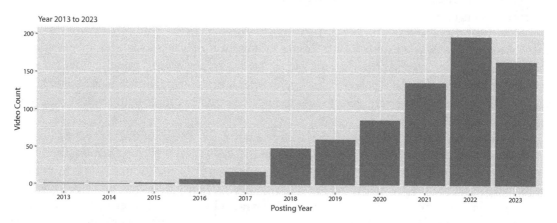

Figure 3.1 Year-wise frequency of video posting.

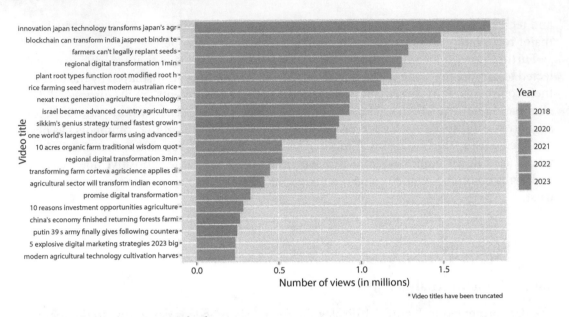

Figure 3.2 The top 20 most viewed videos.

enthusiasts (e.g., Keith Sherringham), and forums dedicated to knowledge exchange (e.g., TEDx Talks). Figure 3.3 illustrates that a combination of diverse organizational and non-organizational entities has contributed to the average amount of video postings pertaining to agriculture digital transformation.

3.4.2   Sentiment Analysis

The aforementioned depiction offers valuable understanding regarding the contemporary focus of information prosumers on the digital advancements transpiring within the agricultural industry. This is achieved through the identification of the most viewed videos and prominent channels responsible for their dissemination on the YouTube platform. While descriptive statistics offer a general understanding of the research setting, it is imperative to comprehend the response of the public and users to technological innovations that affect diverse aspects of agriculture.

The videos contained within the data corpus have been categorized into one of five distinct themes: economy, farm, industry, smart, and technology. These groupings have been created in order to facilitate further analysis of the videos' emotional content. The titles of videos pertaining to the aforementioned five themes were subjected to a word correlation algorithm in order to ascertain additional significant terms in the video titles and topics of interest (refer to Figure 3.4).

After a careful inspection of the correlation visualization depicted in Figure 3.4, a comprehensive range of terms that have been utilized in association with the theme's key terms (namely, economy, farm, industry, smart, and technology) is revealed. The examination of user comments on videos featuring the designated keyword revealed that the topics of economy, farming, and smart agriculture have attracted significant interest from viewers over an extended period (see Figure 3.5). Conversations pertaining to agriculture from an

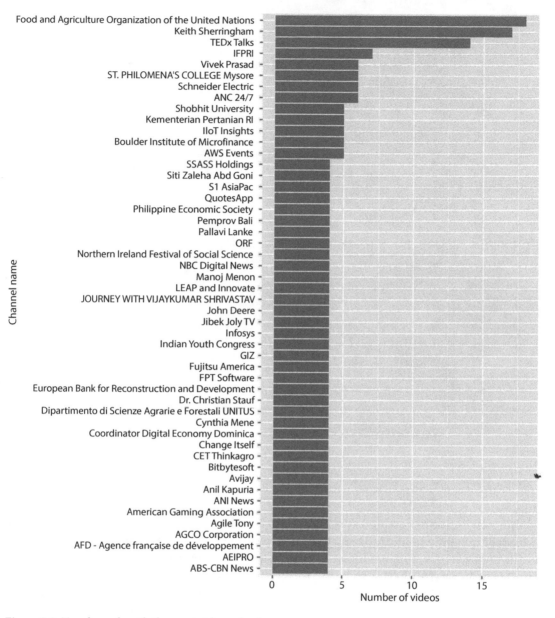

Figure 3.3 Top channels with the most video uploads.

industrial standpoint and the integration of advanced technology have generated recent interest yet have elicited a relatively limited user response in the form of comments.

The comments pertaining to each topic were analyzed using sentiment analysis to ascertain the emotions conveyed by the users through their comments on the videos classified under each category. The distribution of two semantic polarities, namely, positive and negative, and eight emotions, namely, anger, anticipation, disgust, fear, joy, sorrow, surprise, and trust, in the comments provided by the users is depicted in Figure 3.6.

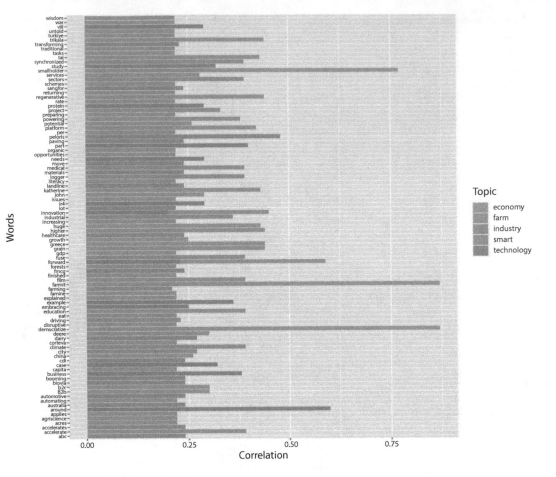

Figure 3.4 Topic-wise word correlation.

The visualization presented above indicates that the comments posted across all themes are predominantly characterized by positive sentiment. The prevalent emotion observed in the comments section of videos pertaining to the economy and farming is anticipation. However, surprise and trust are also prominent emotions expressed in the context of the economy and smart. Further in-depth investigation into the distribution of sentiments has been carried out in order to further corroborate the conclusion represented in Figure 3.6 by separating the emotions as indicated in Figure 3.7.

Figure 3.7 depicts the segregated distribution of emotions exhibited by users in their comments over the years on videos categorized under each theme. Based on a comprehensive analysis of the visualization, it can be asserted that while there are certain points in the timeline where a surge in the prevalence of negative emotions is evident, conversely, positive emotions are dominant throughout the timeline across all themes. The findings depicted in Figures 3.6 and 3.7 indicate a prevalence of positive emotions, leading to the inference that users exhibit an inclination toward embracing novel technological advancements within the agricultural industry.

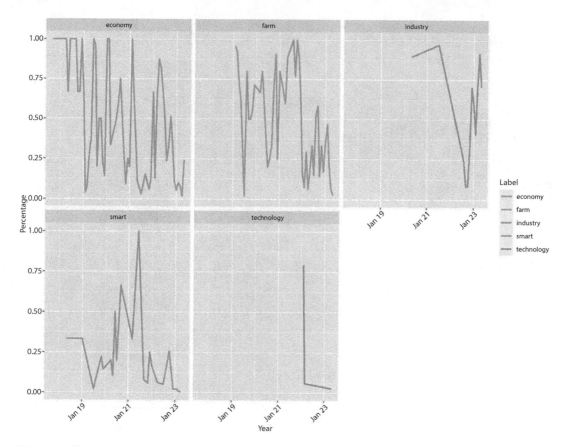

Figure 3.5 Year-wise frequency of comments.

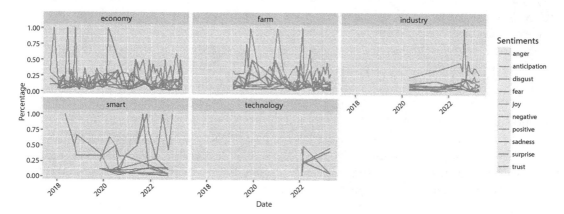

Figure 3.6 Sentiments trending over time.

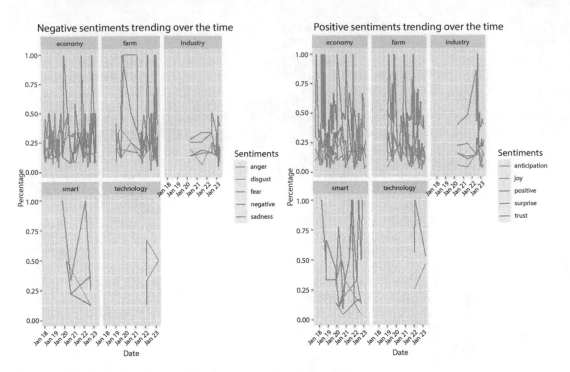

Figure 3.7 In-depth distribution of sentiments over the years.

3.5 Discussion

The present study investigated the potential of YouTube as a digital platform for facilitating participation and exchange of information among agriculturists. The findings of this study suggest that individuals employed in the profession of agriculture may utilize the platform of YouTube as a means of establishing connections with other professionals who share similar interests and disseminating their knowledge and skills to a broader audience. Following data collection and analysis, we identified numerous recurring themes about agriculture in the videos posted to YouTube. Conversations focused on exchanging knowledge, providing examples from real-world situations, addressing common challenges, establishing new professional contacts, and interacting with people who share similar interests. The primary objective of this study was to assess the viability of YouTube as a platform for disseminating knowledge related to agriculture. The findings of the study indicate that YouTube offers a plethora of informative videos pertaining to diverse agricultural subjects, including but not limited to crop management and animal welfare. The utilization of YouTube as a resource for individuals involved in the field of agriculture is highly advantageous due to the extensive range of content available and the convenience of accessibility. This suggests that YouTube has the potential to facilitate the dissemination of agricultural knowledge to a wider audience, thereby mitigating the existing information disparity.

This study placed emphasis on the utilization of YouTube as a medium for showcasing agricultural demonstrations and facilitating experiential learning. According to the study, numerous YouTube channels are dedicated to instructing farmers on various agricultural practices such as seed planting, pest control, and irrigation system enhancement. The videos not only facilitate the enhancement of farmers' theoretical comprehension but also equip them with practical skills that can be readily applied. The conventional approach to agricultural education is enhanced by the distinctive pedagogical opportunity afforded by visual observation and emulation of agricultural practices through YouTube videos. Furthermore, this research aimed to investigate the potential of YouTube as a platform for fostering discussions on addressing agricultural challenges. The findings indicate that farmers utilize YouTube as a platform to discuss issues pertaining to their crops and agricultural practices. Agricultural professionals may engage in online discourse through comment sections and forums associated with YouTube videos to solicit guidance, share insights, and obtain resolutions to prevalent concerns. Through collaborative efforts aimed at problem solving, the agricultural sector collectively progresses by leveraging the specialized knowledge and expertise of its constituent members.

3.6   Limitations and Future Scope

YouTube presents a multitude of opportunities; however, it is also accompanied by specific limitations and challenges. The study briefly touches on the knowledge being disseminated over YouTube concerning digital transformation in agriculture; however, there may be challenges related to topics of bias, content credibility, and the imperative need for quality assurance. These challenges underscore the necessity of employing discerning analysis and verifying data from trustworthy sources, given their potential impact on agricultural methodologies and means of subsistence. The findings of this study provide a foundation for novel endeavors aimed at enhancing the involvement of farmers in agriculture-related online forums and facilitating the exchange of information among them. In order to authenticate agricultural information disseminated through YouTube, forthcoming research endeavors may primarily focus on devising mechanisms and protocols for capturing misleading information. Ensuring that agriculturists are provided with current and accurate information would serve as a means of mitigating the possibility of misinformation.

The potential of YouTube to enhance information sharing and collaboration among farmers warrants further investigation to optimize its efficacy. Acquiring knowledge of efficacious techniques for establishing thriving virtual communities of practice would be advantageous. YouTube can be utilized by governmental bodies and agricultural extension agencies as a means of disseminating resources and information to farmers. The effectiveness of these interventions can be evaluated by analyzing the outcomes of the study.

3.7   Conclusions

The study provides novel insights into how digital platforms, such as YouTube, foster engagement and knowledge sharing within the agricultural community. The findings of the study emphasize the significance of YouTube as an appealing platform for agricultural professionals to distribute information and promote innovative agricultural techniques. The platform provides a plethora of resources, encompassing instructional manuals, visual illustrations, and comprehensive analyses, for individuals engaged in the realm of agriculture. Farmers can enhance their decision-making abilities, optimize their techniques, and effectively address regional challenges by conveniently obtaining this information.

Furthermore, the study underscores the collaborative ethos of the YouTube community, wherein farmers exchange expertise, engage in discussion on pertinent subjects, and offer and receive constructive feedback. Individuals who engage in an online community are inclined to experience a sense of belonging, establish novel relationships, and exchange acquired knowledge. Furthermore, it provides a platform for farmers to showcase their achievements, potentially fostering motivation and inspiration among their peers in the agricultural community. Although YouTube offers numerous advantages, this study acknowledges the challenges that farmers encounter in the contemporary digital era. Obstacles to effective participation and dissemination of knowledge encompass an excess of information, issues with the credibility of content, linguistic barriers, and limited access to the Internet in geographically isolated areas. In order to surmount these challenges, it is imperative that multiple stakeholders, such as regulatory bodies, content creators, and digital platform providers, collaborate in order to ensure equitable accessibility, top-notch content, and user-friendly interfaces.

References

1. Liu, J., Oita, A., Hayashi, K., Matsubae, K., Sustainability of vertical farming in comparison with conventional farming: A case study in Miyagi Prefecture, Japan, on nitrogen and phosphorus footprint. *Sustainability*, 14, 2, 1042, Jan. 2022, doi: 10.3390/su14021042.
2. Pandey, P.C. and Pandey, M., Highlighting the role of agriculture and geospatial technology in food security and sustainable development goals. *Sustain. Dev.*, 31, 5, 3175–3195, May 2023, https://doi.org/10.1002/sd.2600.
3. Yadav, J., Misra, M., Goundar, S., An overview of food supply chain virtualisation and granular traceability using blockchain technology. *Int. J. Blockchains Cryptocurrencies*, 1, 2, 154, 2020, doi: 10.1504/IJBC.2020.108997.
4. Moso, J.C., Cormier, S., de Runz, C., Fouchal, H., Wandeto, J.M., Anomaly detection on data streams for smart agriculture. *Agriculture*, 11, 11, 1083, Nov. 2021, doi: 10.3390/agriculture11111083.
5. Liu, Q. *et al.*, The experiences of health-care providers during the COVID-19 crisis in China: A qualitative study. *Lancet Glob. Health*, 8, 6, e790–e798, 2020, doi: 10.1016/S2214-109X(20)30204-7.
6. Ramli, M.R., Daely, P.T., Kim, D.-S., Lee, J.M., IoT-based adaptive network mechanism for reliable smart farm system. *Comput. Electron. Agric.*, 170, 105287, Mar. 2020, doi: 10.1016/j.compag.2020.105287.
7. Shaik Mazhar, S.A. and Akila, D., Machine learning and sensor roles for improving livestock farming using big data, in: *Cyber Technologies and Emerging Sciences*, pp. 181–190, 2023.
8. Chatterjee, S., Rana, N.P., Dwivedi, Y.K., Social media as a tool of knowledge sharing in academia: an empirical study using valance, instrumentality and expectancy (VIE) approach. *J. Knowl. Manage.*, 24, 10, 2531–2552, Sep. 2020, doi: 10.1108/JKM-04-2020-0252.
9. Yadav, J., Yadav, A., Misra, M., Rana, N.P., Zhou, J., Role of social media in technology adoption for sustainable agriculture practices: Evidence from twitter analytics. *Commun. Assoc. Inf. Syst.*, ahead-of-p, no. ahead-of-print, 52, 833–851. https://doi.org/10.17705/1CAIS.05240 2023. [Online]. Available: https://aisel.aisnet.org/cais/vol52/iss1/35.

10. Yadav, J., Misra, M., Rana, N.P., Singh, K., Exploring the synergy between nano-influencers and sports community: Behavior mapping through machine learning. *Inf. Technol. People*, 35, 7, 1829–1854, Dec. 2022, doi: 10.1108/ITP-03-2021-0219.

11. Yadav, J., Misra, M., Singh, K., Sensitizing Netizen's behavior through influencer intervention enabled by crowdsourcing–a case of reddit. *Behav. Inf. Technol.*, 41, 6, 1286–1297, Apr. 2022, doi: 10.1080/0144929X.2021.1872705.

12. Yadav, J., Misra, M., Rana, N.P., Singh, K., Goundar, S., Netizens' behavior towards a blockchain-based esports framework: A TPB and machine learning integrated approach. *Int. J. Sports Mark. Spons.*, 23, 4, 665–683, Aug. 2022, doi: 10.1108/IJSMS-06-2021-0130.

13. Yadav, J., Misra, M., Kumar, S., Do you feel me? Exploring reception of advertising emotions by consumers, in: *2021 12th International Conference on Computing Communication and Networking Technologies (ICCCNT)*, pp. 1–5, Jul. 2021, doi: 10.1109/ ICCCNT51525.2021.9579658.

14. Yadav, J., Misra, M., Rana, N.P., Singh, K., Goundar, S., Blockchain's potential to rescue sports: A social media perspective, in: *Distributed Computing to Blockchain*, Rajiv Pandey, Sam Goundar, and Shahnaz Fatima (eds.), 405–414. Cambridge, Massachusetts: Academic Press, 2023. https://doi.org/10.1016/B978-0-323-96146-2.00025-5.

15. Pires, F., Masanet, M.-J., Scolari, C.A., What are teens doing with YouTube? Practices, uses and metaphors of the most popular audio-visual platform. *Inf. Commun. Soc.*, 24, 9, 1175–1191, Jul. 2021, doi: 10.1080/1369118X.2019.1672766.

16. Holt-Day, J., Curren, L., Irlbeck, E., USDA agricultural checkoff programs' YouTube presence and video quality. *J. Agric. Educ.*, 6, 1, 190–202, 2020, doi: 10.5032/ jae.2020.01190.

17. Davidson, J. *et al.*, The YouTube video recommendation system, in: *Proceedings of the Fourth ACM Conference on Recommender Systems*, pp. 293–296, Sep. 2010, doi: 10.1145/1864708.1864770.

18. Chtouki, Y., Harroud, H., Khalidi, M., Bennani, S., The impact of YouTube videos on the student's learning, in: *2012 International Conference on Information Technology Based Higher Education and Training (ITHET)*, pp. 1–4, Jun. 2012, doi: 10.1109/ITHET.2012.6246045.

19. Chakma, K., Ruba, U.B., Das Riya, S., YouTube as an information source of floating agriculture: analysis of Bengali language contents quality and viewers' interaction. *Heliyon*, 8, 9, e10719, Sep. 2022, doi: 10.1016/j.heliyon.2022.e10719.

20. Wickman, A., Duysen, E., Cheyney, M., Pennington, W., Mazur, J., Yoder, A., Development of an educational YouTube channel: A collaboration between U.S. agricultural safety and health centers. *J. Agromedicine*, 26, 1, 75–84, Jan. 2021, doi: 10.1080/1059924X.2020.1845269.

21. Clark, J.R., Miller, F.L., Jecmen, A.C., YouTube videos provide expansion of information of fruit cultivars. *Hortscience*, 50, 9, S258, 2015.

22. Chakrabarty, A. and Mudang, T., Smart and sustainable agriculture through IoT interventions: Improvisation, innovation and implementation—an exploratory study, in: *IoT and Analytics for Agriculture*, Pattnaik, P.K., Kumar, R., Pal, S., Panda, S.N. (Eds.), pp. 229–240, 2020.

23. Cook, S., Jackson, E.L., Fisher, M.J., Baker, D., Diepeveen, D., Embedding digital agriculture into sustainable Australian food systems: Pathways and pitfalls to value creation. *Int. J. Agric. Sustain.*, 20, 3, 346–367, May 2022, doi: 10.1080/14735903.2021.1937881.

24. DeClercq, M., Vats, A., Biel, A., Agriculture 4.0: The future of farming technology, in: *The future of farming technology. Proceedings of the World Government Summit*, pp. 11–13, 2018.

25. Eastwood, C.R., Edwards, J.P., Turner, J.A., Review: Anticipating alternative trajectories for responsible Agriculture 4.0 innovation in livestock systems. *Animal*, 15, 100296, Dec. 2021, doi: 10.1016/j.animal.2021.100296.

26. Jakku, E., Fleming, A., Espig, M., Fielke, S., Finlay-Smits, S.C., Turner, J.A., Disruption disrupted? Reflecting on the relationship between responsible innovation and digital agriculture research and development at multiple levels in Australia and Aotearoa New Zealand. *Agric. Syst.*, 204, 103555, Jan. 2023, doi: 10.1016/j.agsy.2022.103555.

27. Mondal, P. and Basu, M., Adoption of precision agriculture technologies in India and in some developing countries: Scope, present status and strategies. *Prog. Nat. Sci.*, 19, 6, 659–666, Jun. 2009, doi: 10.1016/j.pnsc.2008.07.020.

28. Carrer, M.J., de S. Filho, H.M., M. de M. B. Vinholis, Mozambani, C., II, Precision agriculture adoption and technical efficiency: An analysis of sugarcane farms in Brazil. *Technol. Forecast. Soc. Change*, 177, 121510, Apr. 2022, doi: 10.1016/j.techfore.2022.121510.

29. Saiz-Rubio, V. and Rovira-Más, F., From smart farming towards agriculture 5.0: A review on crop data management. *Agronomy*, 10, 2, 207, Feb. 2020, doi: 10.3390/ agronomy10020207.

30. Srbinovska, M., Gavrovski, C., Dimcev, V., Krkoleva, A., Borozan, V., Environmental parameters monitoring in precision agriculture using wireless sensor networks. *J. Clean. Prod.*, 88, 297–307, Feb. 2015, doi: 10.1016/j.jclepro.2014.04.036.

31. Alonso, R.S., Sittón-Candanedo, I., García, Ó., Prieto, J., Rodríguez-González, S., An intelligent Edge-IoT platform for monitoring livestock and crops in a dairy farming scenario. *Ad Hoc Netw.*, 98, 102047, Mar. 2020, doi: 10.1016/j.adhoc.2019.102047.

32. Berckmans, D., Precision livestock farming technologies for welfare management in intensive livestock systems. *OIE Rev. Sci. Tech.*, 33, 1, 189–196, 2014, https://doi.org/10.20506/rst.33.1.2273.

33. Neethirajan, S., Tuteja, S.K., Huang, S.-T., Kelton, D., Recent advancement in biosensors technology for animal and livestock health management. *Biosens. Bioelectron.*, 98, 398–407, Dec. 2017, doi: 10.1016/j.bios.2017.07.015.

34. González-Briones, A., Casado-Vara, R., Márquez, S., Prieto, J., Corchado, J.M., Intelligent livestock feeding system by means of silos with IoT technology, in: *Distributed Computing and Artificial Intelligence, Special Sessions II, 15th International Conference*, pp. 38–48, 2020.

35. da Silveira, F., Lermen, F.H., Amaral, F.G., An overview of agriculture 4.0 development: Systematic review of descriptions, technologies, barriers, advantages, and disadvantages. *Comput. Electron. Agric.*, 189, 106405, Oct. 2021, doi: 10.1016/j.compag.2021.106405.

36. Grieve, B.D. *et al.*, The challenges posed by global broadacre crops in delivering smart agri-robotic solutions: A fundamental rethink is required. *Glob. Food Sec.*, 23, 116–124, Dec. 2019, doi: 10.1016/j.gfs.2019.04.011.

37. Thakur, D. and Chander, M., Use of social media in agricultural extention: Some evidences from India. *Int. J. Sci. Environ. Technol.*, 7, 4, 1334–1346, 2018.

38. Rodan, D. and Mummery, J., The 'make it possible' multimedia campaign: Generating a new 'everyday' in animal welfare. *Media Int. Aust.*, 153, 1, 78–87, Nov. 2014, doi: 10.1177/1329878X1415300110.

39. Seger, J., The new digital s[t]age: Barriers to the adoption and adaptation of new technologies to deliver extension programming and how to address them. *J. Ext.*, 49, 1, 1–6, 2011.

40. Irungu, K.R.G., Mbugua, D., Muia, J., Information and communication technologies (ICTs) attract youth into profitable agriculture in Kenya. *East Afr. Agric. For. J.*, 81, 1, 24–33, Jan. 2015, doi: 10.1080/00128325.2015.1040645.

41. O'Callaghan, D., Greene, D., Conway, M., Carthy, J., Cunningham, P., Down the (white) rabbit hole: The extreme right and online recommender systems. *Soc Sci. Comput. Rev.*, 33, 4, 459–478, Aug. 2015, doi: 10.1177/0894439314555329.

42. Cooley, D. and Parks-Yancy, R., The effect of social media on perceived information credibility and decision making. *J. Internet Commer.*, 18, 3, 249–269, Jul. 2019, doi: 10.1080/15332861.2019.1595362.

43. Xiao, M., Engaging in dialogues: The impact of comment valence and influencer-viewer interaction on the effectiveness of YouTube influencer marketing. *J. Interact. Advert.*, 23, 2, 166–186, Jan. 2023, https://doi.org/10.1080/15252019.2023.2167501.

44. Arthurs, J., Drakopoulou, S., Gandini, A., Researching YouTube. *Convergence-The Int. J. Res. into New Media Technol.*, 24, 1, 3–15, Feb. 2018, doi: 10.1177/1354856517737222.

45. Kušen, E., Strembeck, M., Conti, M., Emotional valence shifts and user behavior on Twitter, Facebook, and YouTube BT-influence and behavior analysis in social networks and social media, in: *Influence and Behavior Analysis in Social Networks and Social Media. ASONAM 2018. Lecture Notes in Social Networks*, Springer International Publishing, Cham, pp. 63–83, doi: 10.1007/978-3-030-02592-2_4.

46. Lindgren, S., It took me about half an hour, but I did it!' Media circuits and affinity spaces around how-to videos on YouTube. *Eur. J. Commun.*, 27, 2, 152–170, Jun. 2012, doi: 10.1177/0267323112443461.

47. Sood, G., Lyons, K., Muschelli, J., *Package 'tuber'.*, pp. 1–41, CRAN, 2022, [Online]. Available: http://github.com/soodoku/tuber.

Part 2

ADOPTION AND IMPACT OF DIGITAL TECHNOLOGIES IN AGRICULTURE

Electronic National Agriculture Market (e-NAM) so Far…! A Gestation Period Analysis

Mohit Kumar[1]* and Kuldeep Singh[2]

[1]United Institute of Management, Prayagraj, India
[2]School of Management, Gati Shakti Vishwavidyalaya, Vadodara, India

Abstract

This chapter is dedicated to agriculture marketing in India with the introduction of technological tools, methods, and equipment, and the current scenario of agriculture marketing is evaluated. The initiative Electronic National Agriculture Market (e-NAM) was taken by the government in order to strengthen nationwide agri-products marketing, distribution, and selling through an electronic medium. The success of e-NAM is dependent on the awareness and adoption of a technical system by stakeholders especially the farmers who are less educated in most parts of India, as well as on the infrastructure requirement for the system to function properly. This chapter deals with a thorough analysis of how the e-NAM works as a system and its current status compared with its inception in terms of adoption, integration, revenue generation to the government, and farmers' well-being.

Keywords: Agriculture marketing, e-NAM, case study

4.1 Introduction

It has been more than 6 years since the inception of the electronic National Agriculture Market (e-NAM) which was initiated in 2016, and as of 2023, the project has completed a significant journey in creating a system of transparent and time-efficient marketing of agri-products throughout India. This study attempts to make a review of the gestation period of e-NAM from its initial progress to its current status. A case study on the initial periods (2017–2018) of the implementation of e-NAM and a secondary data analysis of its current progress were taken into consideration for a comprehensive review [7, 8].

As of 2022–2023, the trading of agricultural produce through e-NAM has increased up to 41%, i.e., 18.6 million tons as compared with the past year's 13.2 million tons. In monetary value terms, the e-NAM platform has generated Rs. 74,656 crore which is a 32% rise from the past year's Rs. 56,497 crore. The trading between interstate Agricultural Produce Marketing Committees (APMCs) also increased by 36% from 2,36,140 metric tons in 2022–2023 as compared with 1,74,268 in the previous financial year 2021–2022, which is a 117% increase in monetary value [9].

Corresponding author: mk03018@gmail.com
Kuldeep Singh: ORCID https://orcid.org/0000-0002-8180-4646

Kuldeep Singh and Prasanna Kolar (eds.) Digital Agricultural Ecosystem: Revolutionary Advancements in Agriculture, (57–70) © 2024 Scrivener Publishing LLC

A total of 1,361 APMCs or mandis have been integrated with the e-NAM project from 23 states and 4 union territories of India. More than 17.5 million farmers and 0.243 million traders have registered on the e-NAM platform (as of 31 March 2023). In recent developments, innovative products that are not traditionally traded in mandis across India such as silk cocoons, saffron, and bamboo have now started to be sold on the platform [2].

The government plays a significant role in the development of the e-NAM infrastructure and provides financial assistance of up to 7.5 million to each APMC for its infrastructural development in processes like cleaning, sorting, grading, and packaging.

Essentially, the government has taken a tremendous initiative in introducing transparency in agriculture product marketing and ensuring better prices for small farmers and sellers. Despite this, it has been observed in the initial phases of the implementation of the e-NAM project that there were serious concerns such as adoption rate, fair prices, lack of infrastructure, and awareness. According to a study conducted in the Karnataka region, only selected commodities on some selected days are sold through e-NAM. Another study presented different concerns like commission agents registered as traders and the existence of several commissions and charges. Marginal farmers are reluctant to go for grading and other quality parameters, but the e-NAM project has saved the time and efforts of small and marginal farmers. Also, a study specified that there is a lack of unification of the APMC market, which leads to difficulty in standardized processes.

4.2   The Importance of Agriculture Marketing

The regulation of agriculture marketing in India is rooted in the Royal Commission of Agriculture (1928) in which a recommendation for market legislation has been made. Establishing common standards for measuring the quality of agricultural produce and restricting malpractices and to deliver better returns to the farmers, the said commission for agriculture has provisions. The Directorate of Marketing and Inspection (DMI) was set up in the year 1935, under the Ministry of Agriculture, which was responsible for the development of marketing activities dedicated to agriculture and allied produce in the country in an integrated manner [1]. The DMI was set up with the objective to safeguard the interests of farmers/producers (sellers) as well as the end consumers.

Under the DMI, there are several schemes and subschemes formulated and implemented in the timeline. Likewise, the agriculture marketing infrastructure (AMI) scheme is subsumed with the agriculture marketing infrastructure, grading, and standardization (AMIGS) scheme, which is actually a scheme implementing the provisions of Grading and Marketing, Act 1937 as amended in 1986. Later on, this scheme paved the way for the extension of the Agmarknet portal [1]. On the lines of integrated development of agriculture produce marketing, the National Agriculture Market (NAM), a project of the government of India, launched in March 2016, enhances the transparency in the transaction of agriculture commodities.

Agriculture marketing activities strengthen the system of procurement, marketing, and selling of agricultural produce and contribute to the Indian economy [3, 4]. However, over the past few decades, the manufacturing and services sectors have contributed more than the agriculture sector in India, and its GDP contribution has reduced to 15.4% (at constant prices) and 17.5% (at current prices) in 2015–2016 as compared with 50% in the 1950s [5].

The reason for the reduced contribution to GDP could be the efficient growth of the manufacturing and industrial sectors and the lesser effectiveness of the agriculture sector.

4.3   APMC Allahabad (Prayagraj) as a Case Organization

Agriculture is a state subject in India, and various states have their wholesale agriculture markets regulated through the Agricultural Produce Marketing Act of 1963 [6, 7]. The Act authorizes the state governments to specify places for the agriculture market to set up and notify commodities that could be traded there. The APMCs are tasked with such specified marketplace and operations related to commodity trading as provided in the Act [10].

In this study, an APMC of Allahabad district in the state of Uttar Pradesh is selected as the pilot study to have a glimpse of the trading and transaction process of APMCs [12–14]. A Model Act was passed in 2006 that allows amendments to APMA 1963, but the state of Uttar Pradesh has not yet adopted this Model Act, so the provisions of APMA 1963 are taken into consideration.

The basic objective of APMCs is to provide a platform for underprivileged producers to trade and ensure the best prices to deliver to them above than MSP set for a commodity [13, 14]. An open auction or e-auction process is adopted for better prices to be delivered to the farmers for their agricultural produce.

In fulfilling these basic objectives, APMCs try to make efforts in various areas of their operational domain like the following:

(i)   transparent bidding,
(ii)   quality grading,
(iii)   direct transfer of money, and
(iv)   restricting illegal or unauthorized wholesale trading.

The APMC Act provides that the first sale for the notified commodities can only be performed at the specified market. Licensed commission agents by paying fees and taxes can freely trade in the designated marketplace of APMCs [10]. No person or agency can trade in wholesale elsewhere if an area is specified or declared as a market area by the committee. A license to trade is issued by the state, and trading in wholesale can be done in such declared market areas or mandis [11].

4.4   Objectives of the Study

Taking into consideration the importance of agricultural produce and the market committee, the study has the following objectives:

(i)   To analyze the transaction process of major commodities traded at APMC Allahabad through the e-trading system (e-NAM) or offline mode.
(ii)   To examine the adoption rate of the e-NAM trading module by the local farmers.
(iii)   To explore the probable causes of low or high adoption rate among farmers.

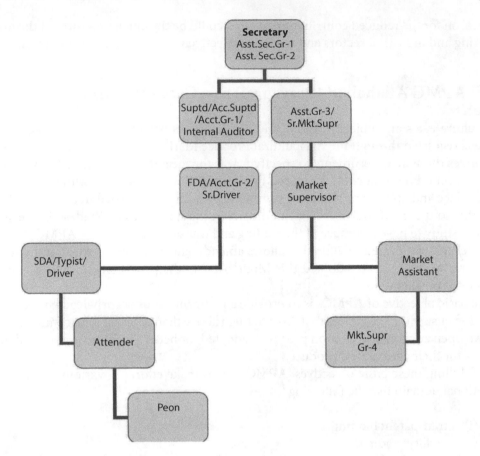

Figure 4.1 The general organisational structure of APMCs (Source: APMC, Mysuru).

4.5   Study Area: APMC Allahabad

A total of 510 APMCs (both primary and secondary) divided among the 70 districts of Uttar Pradesh are listed in the Directorate of Marketing & Inspection, India (agmarknet.nic.in). Among all the districts of Uttar Pradesh, Allahabad has the largest number of whole-sale agriculture markets (19) in nearby regions of Allahabad. This is also the reason why Allahabad APMC was selected as the pilot study to determine the functionality of trading. Allahabad APMC has four markets along with the Allahabad main wholesale market, and the other markets include Ajuha, Jasra, and Sirsa. The organizational structure at Allahabad is the same as the APMCs in other parts of India, headed by the Secretary along with other subordinates at a particular market area. APMC Allahabad is concerned with the trading of fruit and vegetable commodities only, and no food grains have been traded so far.

4.6   Methodology

The study is based on secondary data collected from APMC Allahabad uploaded on e-NAM and data from Allahabad APMC uploaded on Agmarknet, a project of the government of India (http://agmarknet.gov.in/). The primary data source includes open-ended interviews conducted with government officials and employees at APMC Allahabad. The arrival quantities and transaction or bidding price of three major commodities comprised of two vegetable items and one fruit item, i.e., potato, onion, and banana, respectively, were selected because of regular (throughout the year) arrival and selling at APMC Allahabad. Data regarding quantities and prices of the three commodities uploaded on both websites for APMC Allahabad are taken into consideration in making analysis and drawing conclusions.

4.7 Auction and Transaction Process

APMC Allahabad started the e-auctioning system under the National Agriculture Market (e-NAM) project of the government of India on 30 September 2016. Now, the selling of agricultural produce brought by farmers and marginal producers is auctioned and the optimum price is ensured for these products. Auctioning through e-NAM is done through the e-NAM portal where Allahabad APMCs are enrolled, and a login is provided to all its licensed members (traders, buyers) for taking part in the online auctioning process. The online system of auctioning and transaction starts from the bilti slip generation at the gate entry at mandi and ends with the issue of a sale agreement to the buyers and sellers each day after the sales were performed [14].

4.8 Process Review

In the process flow presented in Chart 4.1, the activities and entities involved in the auctioning and transaction process are shown. Reviewing the chart, it is clear that APMC Allahabad has some functional activities performed through the offline mode and some through the online mode using the e-NAM portal login. Members that are sellers and buyers can log in to the e-NAM portal and play for bid. The highest bid from a trader (buyer) wins the bid, and this result is made public by the APMC on the e-NAM portal to maintain transparency. However, farmers or producers (sellers) are free whether to auction or sell directly to the trader the produce they brought to the marketplace (APMC Allahabad). In the case of not opting for auctioning, sampling, or grading of their produce, the best prices could not be ensured for the sellers (farmers/producers). The role of the APMC in this case is only to record the quantities of what were sold to the traders so that specified fees, commission, etc. could be charged from them.

4.9 General Assessment of Causes

(i) Quantity Issue
Farmers are free to go through the auctioning process to sell their produce or sell directly to the traders or buyers licensed under Allahabad APMC [8]. Table 2 in Appendix 2 provides the quantities of three commodities in terms of arrival and sales at Allahabad APMC on

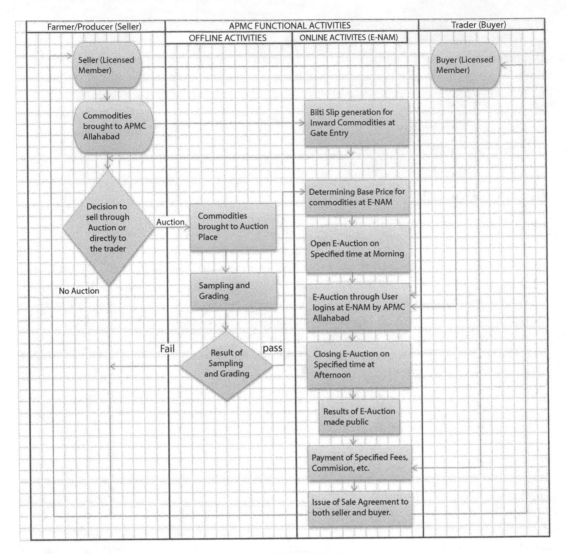

Chart 4.1 Auctioning and transaction system at APMC Allahabad.

a daily basis (see Chart 4.1). The data for 12 consecutive months were provided including those for 10 days (21 August 2017 to 30 August 2017), 25 days (from 1 September 2017 to 25 September 2017), 15 days (from 3 October 2017 to 18 October 2017), and all working days of the months (from November 2017 to August 2018) to understand the gap of quantities' arrival and sales through the online bidding process. Since farmers can voluntarily decide to go through the online bidding system, selling of agricultural produce through the e-auctioning process is quite less. The percentage of quantities (see Table 1 in Appendix 1) of the three selected commodities sold through the online auctioning and transaction system for the months of 2017–2018 helps in evaluating the efficiency of the online bidding system (e-NAM) and the adoption by the members of the APMC. The Table 4.1 shows the months' performance in terms of percentage sales through the e-NAM.

Table 4.1 Months' performance in terms of percentage sales through the e-NAM.

August, September, October, November, and December in the year 2017 and January, April, and May in the year 2018	Considered as low (>50% quantities of commodities to total arrival sold through e-NAM)
March and June in 2018	Considered as *moderate* (at least quantities of one out of three commodities cross the 50% sales through e-NAM)
July and August in the year 2018	Considered as *high* (at least quantities of one out of three commodities cross the 60% sales through e-NAM)
February in the year 2018	Considered as *excellent* (quantities of two out of three commodities cross the 80% sales through e-NAM)

Source: Author's own work.

(ii) Price Issue

Prices of the commodity traded in APMC Allahabad also have huge differences as shown in http://agmarknet.gov.in/ (Agmarknet project of the government of India) for APMC Allahabad itself, compared with the uploaded prices at the e-NAM portal from the personal login of APMC Allahabad. A study of the prices of three primarily traded commodities in APMC Allahabad for the 13-month period (taken as a sample for the quantity issue above) is mentioned (see Table 2 in Appendix 2) to understand the differences. However, the reason is unknown for such differences, and even officials at AMPC Allahabad who were interviewed were not able to give an explanation for such discrepancies in prices.

4.10   Discussion

Quantities of commodities sold through the online process are almost half (or less than half) of the total arrival for most part of the year (8 out of 13 months are marked with less than 50% of the sales through e-NAM). Four months are considered moderate and high, respectively, and only 1 month is considered excellent in terms of sales performed through the online bidding system, i.e., e-NAM. The rest of the quantities not sold through the online bidding system of e-NAM may include wastes and residuals, but that percentage certainly is not half of the total arrivals at APMC Allahabad. Quantities not sold through e-NAM may be sold by other modes, i.e., through open bidding (traditional-biased system), etc.

This indicates that both buyers and sellers are discouraged by the electronic system of trading. The e-NAM project is, however, quite transparent and beneficial for sellers especially the marginal farmers to get better prices for their produce at the wholesale market. The reasons behind this low interest or non-adopting a transparent system for ensuring good prices may be the lack of interest and awareness, lack of technical know-how among users, technical failures of the system like Internet unavailability, etc. The officials and employees of APMC also do not have any concrete explanation for this dispirited approach of the members toward a good system.

The price ranges shown (in Table 2 of Appendix 2) are for the same periods, i.e., a duration of 13 months at Agmarknet as well as at e-NAM. Huge differences can be observed in the minimum (min.) and maximum (max.) prices per quintal between both online platforms. Price uploading made by Allahabad APMC at e-NAM portal after online bidding (shown in the fourth column of Table 2 of Appendix 2) varies with the Agmarknet.gov. in website (shown in the third column of Table 2 of Appendix 2); however, the differences might be due to some faulty practices in the online bidding process or other reasons.

4.11   Development during the COVID Period

- During the COVID period, the trading module FPO (Farmer Producer Organization) was introduced as a mobile application on the e-NAM platform. This enables farmers not to be present physically with their produce at APMCs; they can sell their produce through the app at their collection center. About 2,575 FPOs are now onboard the e-NAM platform, and commodities traded in value terms of ₹ 2.50 lakh crore were recorded on the e-NAM platform. Trading through the warehouses is also encouraged with the trading module named e-NWR (Electronic Negotiable Warehouse Receipt) on the e-NAM platform.
- A remarkable development has been made recently in the year 2022 when the Platform of Platforms (POP) under the National Agriculture Market (e-NAM) was started in order to facilitate the farmers to sell their produce across state borders using the e-NAM platform. This service enables the farmers to access a wider market coverage with added features of transparency, safety, and time efficiency. Different service providers share the platform to deliver services like providing market intelligence, fintech services, warehousing services, transportation, quality checks, and trading.

4.12   Conclusion

APMCs are formed to strengthen the system of agricultural produce marketing in specified areas, resulting in farmers and producers getting good prices for their produce on one hand as well as retail prices to maintain a fair level on the other hand. In this case study, the transparent system (e-NAM) efficiency is evaluated, which is not up to the mark even after a period of 2 years of its launching as reflected in the case of APMC Allahabad which was conducted between 2017 and 2018. However, it is too early to assess the overall efficiency of the system or initiative that has been implemented at the pan-country level and when the initiative involves a huge number of stakeholders with technology adoption. The government has come up with such a system to develop a foolproof mechanism in agriculture marketing to ensure the overall development of the people indulged in agricultural production by delivering better prices for their produce and also to keep check and balances on significant price variations in retail markets so that the end consumers will also get benefitted. Such a system like e-NAM, which ensures transparency at both the buyers' and sellers' end, must be made efficient enough to restrict malpractices involved in the marketing of agricultural commodities, enabling the agricultural economy to flourish. As what has been observed in the recent developments even in the COVID times in the area of e-NAM implementation and execution in almost all the states of India, the advantages of using the platform in terms of adoption rate, inclusion of more commodities in trading, more transparency in auctioning, and fair price delivery can surely be assumed.

References

1. Annual Report, *Department of Agriculture, Cooperation & Farmers Welfare (DACFW)*, Ministry of Agriculture & Farmers Welfare, Government of India, 2016.
2. APEDA, Agricultural products trade via e-NAM surges 41% in FY23, Agricultural and Processed Food Products Export Development Authority, 2, 23, 1–8, 2023. https://agri exchange. apeda. gov.in/news/NewsSearch.aspx?newsid=50305.
3. Chatterjee, S. and Kapur, D., *Understanding Price Variation in Agricultural Commodities in India: MSP, Government Procurement, and Agriculture Markets*, India Policy Forum, National Council of Applied Economic Research, 2016.
4. Das, B.K., In-depth: Analysis of e-NAM portal impact on farmers and agriculture sector, ET Government, 7, 21, 1–3, 2021. https://government.economictimes.indiatimes.com/news/policy/in-depth-analysis-of-e-nam-portal-impact-on-farmers-and-agriculture-sector/81945532.
5. Deshpande, T., *State of Agriculture in India*, PRS Legislative, India, 2017.
6. Gupta, S., Priyadarshi, R., Singh, S., Role of IT in agricultural marketing in India: A case study. *International Conference on Recent Advances in Information Technology*, 2012.
7. IAMP., Indian Agricultural Markets Policy, *Challenges and Alternatives, Focus on the Global South*, Focus on the Global South, Rosa Luxemburg Stiftung-South Asia 2019, https://focusweb.org/wp-content/uploads/2020/03/Ag_Market_Report_Final.pdf.
8. Intodia, V., *Investment in Agricultural Marketing and Market Infrastructure–A Case Study of Bihar*, eSocialSciences, India, 2012.
9. Khan, N. and Khan, M.M., Marketing of agricultural crops in rural indian economy: A case study. *J. Econ. Sustain. Dev.*, 3, 2, 3–50, 2012.
10. Krishnamurthy, M. and Witsoe, J., *Understanding Mandis: Market Towns and The Dynamics of India's Rural and Urban Transformations*, International Growth Center, London School of Economics, 2014.
11. Lele, U., *A Case Study In Agricultural Marketing The Modern Rice Mill In India*, Occasional Paper No. 49 Department of Agricultural Economics, Cornell University, 1971.
12. Roy, R., Singh, S.D., Ahmad, H., *Impact of Emerging Marketing Channels in Agricultural Marketing in Uttar Pradesh*, Agro-Economic Research Centre, University of Allahabad, 2011.
13. Agricoop, *Salient Features of the Model Act on Agricultural Marketing*, 2019, https://agricoop.nic.in/sites/default/files/apmc.pdf. Ministry of Agriculture & Farmers' Welfare.
14. Vipra, T., *Demand for Grants 2023-24 Analysis Agriculture and Farmers Welfare*, PRS Legislative Research, India, 2023, https://prsindia.org/files/budget/budget_parliament/2023/Agriculture_DFG_2023-24.pd.

Appendix 1

Table 1 Arrival and sales of commodities at Agmarknet and APMC Allahabad.

Month	Commodity	Arrival (in tons)	Quantity sold (in tons) through online bidding (e-NAM)	Balance quantity (in tons) (sold through other modes)	Percentage of sales to total arrival through online bidding (e-NAM)
August, 2017	Potato	4,610.00	190.70	4,419.30	4.14
	Onion	2,450.00	201.60	2,248.40	8.23
	Banana	1,100.00	49.90	1,050.10	4.54
September, 2017	Potato	2,950.00	270.75	2,679.25	9.18
	Onion	1,435.00	297.91	2,248.40	20.76
	Banana	1,330.00	96.50	1,233.50	7.26
October, 2017	Potato	1,860.00	282.35	1,577.65	15.18
	Onion	780.00	212.15	567.50	27.20
	Banana	665.00	228.30	436.10	34.33
November, 2017	Potato	12,780.00	602.30	12,177.70	4.71
	Onion	1,975.00	542.17	1,432.83	27.45
	Banana	1,710.00	289.60	1,420.40	16.94
December, 2017	Potato	11,050.00	948.30	10,101.70	8.58
	Onion	1,235.00	703.45	531.55	56.96
	Banana	638.50	249.80	388.70	39.12
January, 2018	Potato	11,540.00	1,109.40	10,430.60	9.61
	Onion	2,704.00	1,053.27	1,650.73	38.95
	Banana	420.00	149.10	270.90	35.50

(*Continued*)

Table 1 Arrival and sales of commodities at Agmarknet and APMC Allahabad. (*Continued*)

Month	Commodity	Arrival (in tons)	Quantity sold (in tons) through online bidding (e-NAM)	Balance quantity (in tons) (sold through other modes)	Percentage of sales to total arrival through online bidding (e-NAM)
February, 2018	Potato	3,630.00	1,254.80	2,395.20	34.57
	Onion	2,030.00	1,833.08	196.92	90.30
	Banana	315.50	270.00	45.50	85.58
March, 2018	Potato	2,435.00	1,298.70	1,136.3	53.33
	Onion	1,670.00	788.02	881.98	47.19
	Banana	224.00	45.50	178.50	20.31
April, 2018	Potato	2,570.00	426.8	2,143.2	16.61
	Onion	2,940.00	1,076.25	40.5	36.61
	Banana	283.00	1,863.75	242.5	14.31
May, 2018	Potato	1,763.5	273.8	1,489.7	15.53
	Onion	2,160.00	891.8	1,268.2	41.29
	Banana	339.00	23.4	315.6	6.90
June, 2018	Potato	1,257.5	173.3	1,084.2	13.78
	Onion	1,570.00	857.75	712.25	54.63
	Banana	239.5	106.6	132.9	44.51
July, 2018	Potato	1,347.00	676.00	671	50.19
	Onion	1,378.00	952.11	425.9	69.09
	Banana	1,018.00	192.9	825.1	18.95
August, 2018	Potato	1,405.00	890.9	514.1	63.41
	Onion	1,104.5	464.5	639.5	42.06
	Banana	2,367.00	206.1	2,160.9	4.14

Note: Author's own analysis.
Source: Agmarknet.in and APMC Allahabad.

Appendix 2

Table 2 Price ranges of commodities at Agmarknet and APMC Allahabad.

Month	Commodity	Price range (per quintal) at Agmarknet		Price range (per quintal) of APMC Allahabad at e-NAM	
		Min (in Rs.)	Max (in Rs.)	Min (in Rs.)	Max (in Rs.)
August, 2017	Potato	450	650	490	1,170
	Onion	1,800	2,100	500	1,600
	Banana	1,700	1,900	500	818
September, 2017	Potato	450	655	410	575
	Onion	1,800	2,050	1,110	1,670
	Banana	1,700	1,900	710	800
October, 2017	Potato	480	630	480	530
	Onion	1,100	1,950	1,455	1,835
	Banana	1,500	1,800	710	810
November, 2017	Potato	460	655	486	523
	Onion	2,600	2,900	1,602	1,806
	Banana	1,500	1,800	433	810
December, 2017	Potato	400	600	475	498
	Onion	2,100	2,800	1,582	1,777
	Banana	1,400	2,000	510	711
January, 2018	Potato	300	580	433	498
	Onion	2,700	3,250	1,555	3,115
	Banana	1,600	1,800	510	825
February, 2018	Potato	400	590	452	499
	Onion	2,000	3,250	1,804	4,812
	Banana	1,675	1,850	658	858
March, 2018	Potato	500	840	452	725
	Onion	1,150	2,100	1,200	1,825
	Banana	1,500	1,800	705	712

(Continued)

Table 2 Price ranges of commodities at Agmarknet and APMC Allahabad. (*Continued*)

Month	Commodity	Price range (per quintal) at Agmarknet		Price range (per quintal) of APMC Allahabad at e-NAM	
		Min (in Rs.)	Max (in Rs.)	Min (in Rs.)	Max (in Rs.)
April, 2018	Potato	665	1,350	704	808
	Onion	800	1,380	700	1,425
	Banana	1,500	1,800	602	605
May, 2018	Potato	1100	1,300	823	1,554
	Onion	700	980	705	1,003
	Banana	1,700	1,900	658	706
June, 2018	Potato	1,150	1,380	957	1,403
	Onion	650	1,050	685	1,253
	Banana	1750	1985	704	758
July, 2018	Potato	1,250	1,550	1,084	1,410
	Onion	1,200	1,650	790	1,355
	Banana	1,750	2,100	602	1,000
August, 2018	Potato	1,100	1,500	1,010	1,255
	Onion	1,200	1,850	783	1,253
	Banana	1,400	2,200	702	1,305

Note: Author's own analysis.
Source: Agmarknet.in and APMC Allahabad.

Development of Ecologically Safe Production: Digital Trends in the Agri-Food Sector

Zamlynskyi Viktor[1]*, Diachenko Oleksii[2], Halytskyi Oleksandr[2], Levina-Kostiuk Mariia[2] and Yurii Vitkovskyi[3]

[1]National University of Technology, Odessa, Ukraine
[2]State Agrarian University, Odesa, Ukraine
[3]Faculty of Applied Science, WSB University, Krakow, Poland

Abstract

Environmental problems have reached a global scale, which became the basis for the quick expansion of the production of environmentally safe and organic products. Our research analyzes the situation of Ukrainian organic agriculture, and it was found that the country has a strong potential for its own production of ecologically safe products of the agri-food sector, their domestic consumption, and export. Highlighting the export of organic products separately, its significant growth was found. Strategic directions were determined thanks to the increase in the awareness of producers of goods in the agrarian sphere regarding the attractiveness and perspective of ecologically safe and organic food products for consumers of the domestic market and for export. Environmentally safe production, taking risks into account and publishing specific results regarding their leveling with the help of digital reporting, will have a positive impact on the company's growth strategy. The possibilities and technologies of digital optimization were analyzed, and recommendations were offered regarding the quality of environmental data analysis in real time. The active implementation of digital platforms will have a positive effect on optimizing utilization of the resources, reducing waste, and augmenting the effectiveness of risk management, corporate sustainability reporting, and investment attraction.

Keywords: Ecologically safe food production, digital platform, agri-food sector, organic agricultural product, quality management, corporate sustainability reporting, ecologically clean products

5.1 Introduction

The current state of evolution of the production of goods in the agrarian sector largely requires a strategically oriented plan for the organization of production and marketing of ecologically safe food products based on the global socioeconomic trends of the sufficiency of natural resources. The food that every inhabitant of the planet consumes every day is continuously produced, but sustainable global food systems are still lacking. Most of

---

*Corresponding author: zam.agrariy@gmail.com

Kuldeep Singh and Prasanna Kolar (eds.) Digital Agricultural Ecosystem: Revolutionary Advancements in Agriculture, (71–90) © 2024 Scrivener Publishing LLC

the world's food-supplying countries face serious environmental problems. Ensuring food safety is both necessary and complex, as it involves the entire supply chain, including growing, processing, storage, transportation, and trade. Pollution of water, air, and soil threatens human health every day through food consumption. The introduction of new technologies has not yet eliminated food shortages that have existed throughout human history. Modern digital solutions and technologies will positively affect strategic development through the transition to big data and artificial intelligence platforms for the agricultural sector.

The aim of the study is to provide a theoretical foundation for the aspects and provide practical guidelines regarding digital trends in the development of environmentally safe production within the agricultural and food sectors.

5.2   Legislative Support for the Functioning of Ecologically Safe Production

To develop the production of goods with organic status in Ukraine, the Law of Ukraine "On Basic Principles and Requirements for Organic Production, Circulation and Labeling of Organic Products," which was adopted on 10 July 2018 [1], which helps regulate activities in the field of environmentally safe products, represents a set of recommended substances that are allowed for use in the process of environmentally safe production and their permissible content and product certification procedures for acquiring the status of organic and assigning it a special label [2, 3].

The legislation of Ukraine identifies eight branches of ecologically safe production. They are clearly illustrated in Figure 5.1.

Therefore, organic products can be produced in all aspects of agricultural activity, which ensures the production of goods for the final consumer, or as a component for the production of such products; in addition, it is designed to contribute to increasing the pace of development of the organic world as a whole.

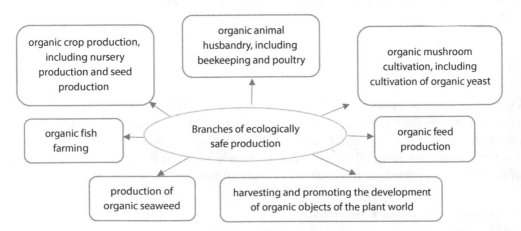

Figure 5.1 Classification of branches of ecologically safe production. Built by the authors based on reference [1].

The formation and functioning of the market for ecologically safe products in Ukraine takes place under the influence of external and internal factors.

Internal factors ensure an increase in the living standard of the country's population, popularization of a healthy lifestyle, and as a result, an increase in demand for healthy, high-quality, and safe products.

Table 5.1 Evolution of the market of ecologically safe products and its digital processes.

Name of the stage	Characteristic	Development in Ukraine
Individual (narrow)	Organization by producers and interested consumers of separate organizations for the sale and purchase of organic products	1994—Registration of the International Organization Information Center "Green Dossier" 1996—Registration of the first organic agricultural enterprise—private enterprise "Agroecology"
Sectoral	The growth of consumer demand for organic products and, as a result of the increase in producers, the formation of professional associations and the first regulatory and legal documents of the promotion of organic production as a separate branch of agriculture	1997—Signing of an international cooperation agreement at the level of the government of Switzerland and Ukraine regarding technical and financial cooperation in the context of promoting the growth of organic agriculture 2003—With the assistance of the "Green Dossier" center, the release of the debut Ukrainian documentary film about organic production 2004—The start of the work of the association of bioproduction participants "BIOLAN Ukraine"
Market	Significant growth of the market of environmentally safe products and its infrastructure, as well as the production, processing, and sale of these goods within the framework of the specified law	2005—The start of the work of the Federation of the Organic Movement of Ukraine 2007—Appearance of "Organic Standard"—Ukrainian certification body 2007—Appearance of domestically produced organic products in trade networks 2013—The Union of Certified Organic Products Producers "Organic Ukraine" begins 2014—Law "On Production and Circulation of Organic Agricultural Products and Raw Materials" 2014—For the first time, the regional budget envisages state support for ecologically safe production

(Continued)

Table 5.1 Evolution of the market of ecologically safe products and its digital processes. (*Continued*)

Name of the stage	Characteristic	Development in Ukraine
National	The priority of ecologically safe production at the state level. Significant support and stimulation of the development of ecologically safe production by the state both at the level of producers and promotion of formation in the minds of the public of consumers of the importance of using ecologically clean, safe products	2015—Launch of the organic portal OrganicInfo.ua 2015—Establishment of ecologically safe production as one of the strategic directions for gaining new positions in the level of agricultural efficiency 2019—Law of Ukraine "On Basic Principles and Requirements for Organic Production, Circulation and Labeling of Organic Products" 2019—Entry of Ukraine into the TOP-5 main suppliers of goods of such quality to the EU 2020—Creating an Organic Knowledge Platform 2020—Legislative support for ecologically safe producers 2021—The appearance of ecologically safe production in the National Economic Strategy of Ukraine 2022—Launch of the catalog of Ukrainian exporters of ecologically safe products 2022—Start of the Grant Program "Supporting the Organic Sector in Ukraine" 2023—The start of the registry at the state level of certification bodies, in terms of the production of environmentally safe products and the circulation of these products in Ukraine 2023—Start of digitalization of organic production

Built by the authors based on sources [1, 4, 5].

External factors are primarily caused by the dynamic growth of the European and global market for organic agricultural products and the significant interest of the international community in Ukraine as a promising, powerful producer of such products [4].

The rapid development of the world market of ecologically safe products has gone through four stages, which are the basis for the effective functioning of such a market in Ukraine (Table 5.1).

Among the important events in the progress of the national direction of ecologically safe production in Ukraine, measures at the state level that contribute to the development of ecologically safe production should be noted.

Notably, in 2020, specific measures were established in the amendments to the Law "On State Support of Agriculture of Ukraine" [6] on the areas of support at the state level for ecologically safe agricultural production:

1. Setting the level of reimbursement of certification costs—30% of the cost.
2. Establishment of the reimbursement level for the purchase of seeds, planting material of appropriate quality, permission for the use of fertilizers, and plant protection products—30% of the cost.
3. Allocation of state subsidies for land cultivation and livestock development [7].

Of particular importance for the export potential of the ecologically safe production sector in Ukraine was the decision of the EU to abolish import tariffs and customs duties on Ukrainian organic goods exported to the EU. In addition, the fact that Ukraine, for the first time since 2015, was excluded from the list of countries subject to additional control measures for ecologically safe products imported into the EU significantly simplified the process of exporting ecologically safe products. The result of this is a reduction in both time and material costs associated with sampling and analysis and additional inspection. Such measures opened an opportunity for the export of new goods and the growth of sales volumes of already existing ones [8].

In addition, in recognition of the increase in the number of organic enterprises, the Resolution "On the Approval of the National Economic Strategy for the Period Until 2030" states that one of the priority tasks of agriculture is to ensure that at least 3% of agricultural land is organically managed by 2030 [1].

So, organic production is a step into the future without forgetting the past. This is a combination of business management traditions with innovations and the latest scientific developments, the emphasis of which is not only to ensure high productivity but also to simultaneously contribute to the enhancement of the nature and to form optimal relationships in the field of "production—nature."

5.3   Market Analysis of Environmentally Sound Goods

The role of ecologically safe production is growing in all countries of the world, as evidenced by the data of the International Federation of Organic Agrarian Movement, which every year presents the results of the development of ecologically safe production in most countries of the world. If, in 2010, 3,704,1004 hectares were involved in ecologically safe production, which is 0.85% of the total area of agricultural land, then by 2021, the number has doubled and amounted to 7,6403,777 hectares, which is 1.6% of the total area agricultural lands [9, 10]. Ukraine, as a European country, supports international trends toward environmentally safe production and increases its organic activity. According to the results of the latest statistical studies, Ukraine is 21st in terms of the area of agricultural land involved in the general system of ecologically safe farming among 183 countries of the world (Figure 5.2).

Deepening the study of the role of Ukraine in the world organic market, it should be noted that among 45 European countries in 2021, the country ranks 13th in terms of the

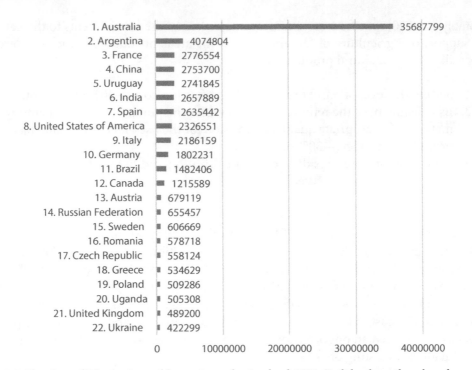

Figure 5.2 The place of Ukraine in world organic production land, 2021. Built by the authors based on statistical data [10].

number of organics (Figure 5.3). Examining the experience of European countries, it should be noted that a special emphasis on organic agriculture is highlighted in the economic development policy of France, which within a year moved from fifth to third place in terms of the area of ecologically safe agriculture, and Romania, which strengthened its position and from 20th place reached 16th place in 2021.

Organic lands in Ukraine occupy only 1% of the total agricultural land areas and have the potential for organic direction in the future. In turn, for France, which is in first place, organic land occupies 9.6% of all agricultural land; for Spain and Germany, it is 10.8%; and for Austria, it is 26.5%.

If, in the agricultural lands of Ukraine, the area of ecologically safe land occupied the same level as the leaders of Europe—10%, then their area would be 4,270,000 hectares, which would provide an opportunity to immediately occupy first place in Europe and second place in the world in terms of organic land area, after the undisputed leader of this industry—Australia.

The Resolution "On the Approval of the National Economic Strategy for the Period Until 2030" prescribes directions for achieving 3% of the area under organic production by 2030 [7]. This would ensure the availability of 128,100 hectares of such land and would give the opportunity to take a place in the top five producers of organic products in Europe. Such a strategy would provide a powerful result for the country's organic production and would significantly strengthen the state's image among the European community.

Studying the dynamics of the development of ecologically safe production in Ukraine, significant growth is observed in both the areas involved in organic farming and the enterprises participating in it (Figure 5.4).

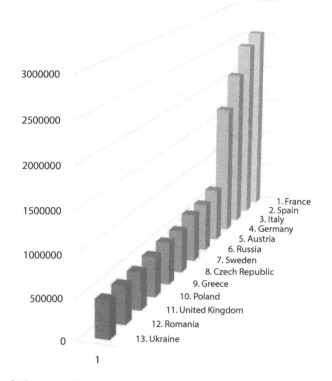

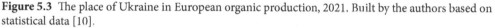

Figure 5.3 The place of Ukraine in European organic production, 2021. Built by the authors based on statistical data [10].

Within the study period from 2002 to 2021, the area under ecologically safe agriculture in Ukraine increased by more than 2.5 times and, in 2021, occupied 1% of all land for agricultural purposes. Such trends also exist in relation to the number of manufacturers involved in the production of ecologically safe products, which have increased 13 times. This shows that producers see an economic interest in the development of this type of production.

The land resources of Ukraine allow us to increase these areas, and the potentially large demand for such products in the world ensures the presence of potential consumers of organic products from Ukraine all over the world.

According to the information of the Ministry of Agrarian Policy of Ukraine, the export of ecologically safe products accounts for approximately 70% of all ecologically safe agricultural production. That is, at the moment, the level of consumer demand and prices for products abroad is potentially more attractive for product manufacturers [4].

Examining the production and sale of organic products in terms of physical and monetary aspects, it was found that in terms of dynamics, the largest volumes of sales of ecologically safe products fell in 2019, and the subsequent decrease in sales was largely caused by the external factors of the COVID-19 pandemic. This affected the level of export of products, and the large-scale armed conflict on Ukrainian territory had a negative impact on the future. Despite these negative factors, the volume of exports of organic products increased by 114,000 tons or 46.7% over the past 7 years (Figure 5.5).

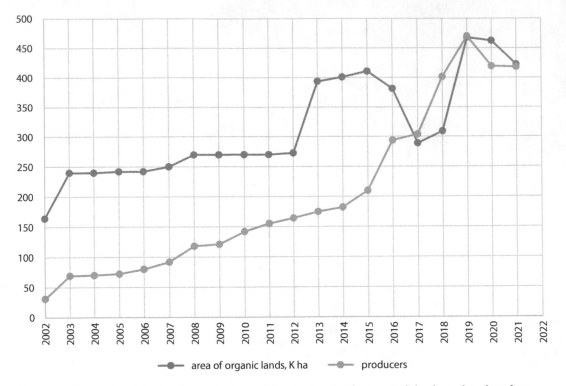

Figure 5.4 Dynamics of the development of organic production in Ukraine. Built by the authors based on statistical data [10].

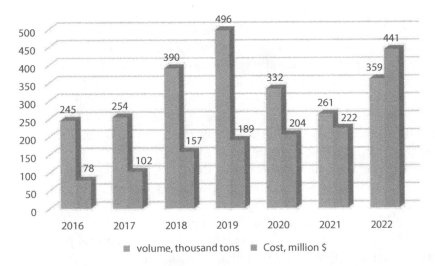

Figure 5.5 Export volumes of organic products. Built by the authors based on statistical data [11–13].

In the value expression of 2022 that marked the highest profitability for Ukraine in terms of ecologically safe production, the results indicate a significant increase in the profitability of this industry, and this is due primarily to the growth of organic processed products and semifinished products, which include frozen berries, apple juice, and sunflower oil. That is, there is an increase in the share of value-added goods in exports, thanks to which revenues from the organic goods industry increased by $363 million or 5.7 times [13].

It should be emphasized that despite the extremely difficult conditions for conducting economic activity in 2022–2023, the Ministry of Agrarian Policy (Ukraine) assured EU countries and the European Commission that the export obligations of domestic producers and exporters of organic products will be fulfilled. The results of 2022 have already shown that the agricultural complex works effectively, overcoming all obstacles, and it was able to export organic products more than in 2021 by 98,000 tons or 37.7%, which was reflected in the increase in income by $219 million or 2 times. To ensure sustainable exports in 2022, the emphasis on transportation was given to road transport, which accounted for 52.2% of the structure, 33.8% was provided by water transport, and 14.0% by rail transport [12, 14].

Examining the products that are the basis of the export of Ukrainian ecologically safe products (Figure 5.6), it was found that by 2021, the leading positions in world exports are occupied by the sale of organic corn (80,000 tons), soybeans (65,000 tons), and wheat, including spelt (29,000 tons). At the same time, researching the export of products to European countries (Figure 5.7), it was found that the world results were supported, and the leaders have similar products. At the same time, the general trends toward the growth of export volumes in the dynamics of 2 years are also reflected in the trends for individual products.

In addition to the mentioned crops, sunflower and its processed products are strengthening their positions (Figure 5.8). This product has the largest volumes of sales, while soy provides 26.7% of revenues from the organic products export. Despite the fact that sunflower oil is in sixth place in terms of sales volume, it brings 11.3% of revenues; in addition, wheat ranks third both in terms of volumes and revenues, providing 10% of revenues from the sale of ecologically safe products.

Studying the situation of environmentally sound manufacturing in Ukraine, it was found that the country has a strong potential for its own production of ecologically safe products of the agri-food sector, their domestic consumption, and export. Highlighting the export of organic products separately, its significant growth was found. Such perspectives were

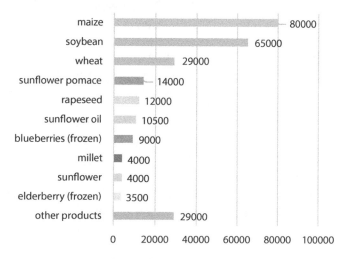

Figure 5.6 World export volumes—2021, thousand tons. Built by the authors based on statistical data [12, 15].

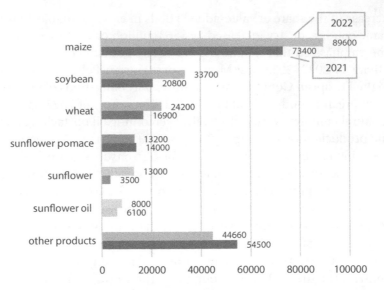

Figure 5.7 Export volumes to EU countries, 2021–2022. Built by the authors based on statistical data [12, 15].

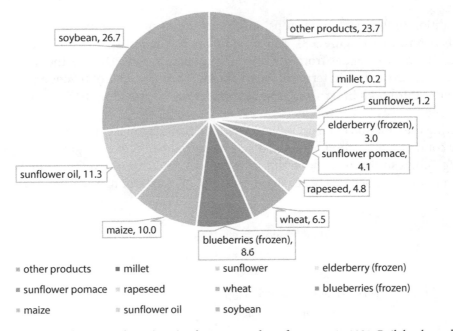

Figure 5.8 Structure of revenues from the sale of organic products for export in 2021. Built by the authors based on statistical data [15].

reflected at the state level, which approved the National Economic Strategy for the period up to 2030. The identified strategic directions can be implemented, thanks to the growing awareness of agricultural producers regarding the attractiveness and opportunities for environmentally friendly and healthy food products for consumers in the domestic market and for export.

5.4   Strategic Directions for Ensuring the Growth of Ecologically Safe Production in the Agri-Food Complex

The basis for the formation of strategic directions for the growth of opportunities for environmentally friendly and healthy food products of the agri-food sector is the Resolution "On the Approval of the National Economic Strategy for the Period Until 2030" [7]. It forms a nationwide strategic plan for the growth of the economy, including environmentally safe production.

Based on the activities of organizations in the field of ecologically safe production and based on the determined Resolution, we have highlighted promising directions for the growth of ecologically safe production (Figure 5.9).

So, the identified strategic directions can be implemented, thanks to the increase in the awareness of agricultural producers regarding the attractiveness and prospects of the production of ecologically safe and organic food products for domestic and export market consumers.

The basis for this should be the government's encouragement of the increase of such production in Ukraine. Special attention needs to be paid to the protection of the natural environment and the animal world; "climate-oriented" production of agricultural goods, promoting the expansion of methods used in organic farming; the use of the latest biotechnologies; and management of the use of natural resources, which involves not only their consumption but also the increase of their biodiversity. It is determined that the prospects for the development of ecologically safe production of agri-food goods in Ukraine are primarily based on significant state support for this important direction.

5.5   Digital Optimization of Ecologically Safe Production

Forecasts of the increase of digital technologies in agricultural activity foresee an increase in the role of automation of production processes, robotics, and the growth of new-generation information technologies by 2030.

The increase in information technologies involves the introduction of the following innovations:

- The use of such modern technologies as "Internet of Things" and "big data" in organic production. Thus, increasing the efficiency of processes in crop production can be ensured with the use of "big data," in the process of determining the optimal terms of technological processes, such as sowing, applying fertilizers, and watering.
- The introduction of artificial intelligence capabilities to find new scientific developments and solutions in the field of ecologically safe production [20].

Among the mechanization of the ecologically safe production process, the use of unmanned systems in production is of particular importance in crop production. Unmanned systems take pictures from above, monitor the growth of crops and the condition of fields, sow seeds and irrigate them, ensure the application of organic fertilizers,

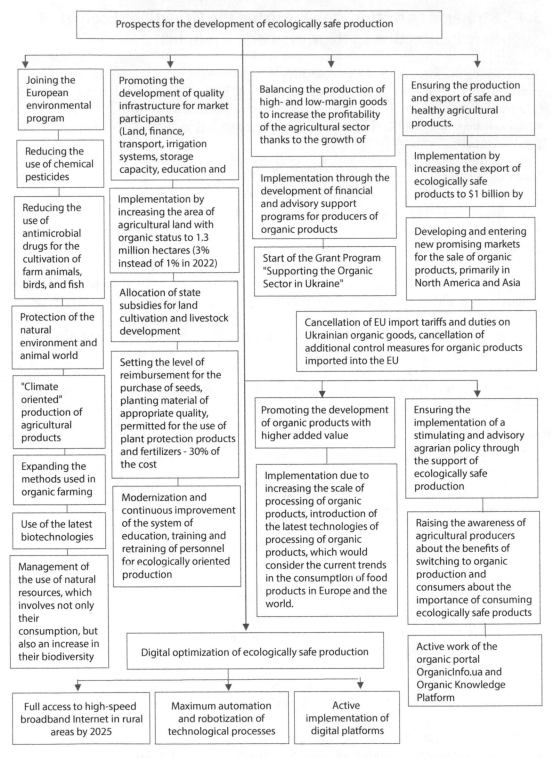

Figure 5.9 Strategic directions for the development of ecologically safe production. Built by the authors based on sources [1, 7, 13, 16–19].

provide 3D maps, and provide automation of control functions on commodity farms in the livestock industry (Table 5.2).

Unmanned systems ensure the reduction of human presence in the technological processes of the crop production industry, which is economically beneficial and saves time for entrepreneurs in the agricultural sector.

Modern unmanned systems can be used to solve the following tasks in the process of environmentally safe production:

1) assessment of quality characteristics of crops and timely detection of crop damage;
2) determination of the most accurate area of damaged crops;
3) determination of sowing defects and problem areas;
4) monitoring compliance of crop rotation structure and plans;

Table 5.2 Unmanned systems as an aid in the field of agriculture.

Function	Characteristic
Aerial photography	In the context of finding bald spots, crop failure after exposure to natural factors, and other defects that require timely elimination. Aerial photography with the help of unmanned systems is much better than satellite photography in terms of detail. The main reason for this is a sufficiently low flight height.
Video recording	In the context of surveying the condition of fields and crop growth. The productivity of the unmanned system in the process of work is 30 km in 1 h, and this performance is much higher than the equipment that can be used on the ground, not only in terms of time characteristics but also in terms of price.
3D modeling	Allows you to determine waterlogged or dry areas and soil excavation, competently create maps of soil, and plans moistening or drying, reclamation of areas, or land reclamation.
Planting seeds	Practiced relatively recently and is still at the stage of testing the feasibility of such use of unmanned systems. At the same time, agricultural innovators are trying this option when planting seeds.
Thermal imaging	Can have an important function in ecologically safe plant breeding, due to the determination of the terms of differentiation of growth points, which provides results that can be used to preserve important properties of plants and direct their productivity while preserving the hereditary potential of the variety.
Laser scanning	Used for terrain analysis in hard-to-reach or inaccessible areas. This method provides accurate results with detailed modeling of the terrain and can be used with a significant density of plantings.

Built by the authors based on sources [20–22].

5) analysis of the results of the implementation of actions aimed at protecting plants in organic production;
6) detection of violations and deviations in the process of carrying out technical work in organic production;
7) conducting relief analysis and, based on it, forming a map of vegetation indices (PVI, NDVI);
8) taking part in the construction of reclamation systems;
9) monitoring of the storage conditions of the harvested crops;
10) creation of maps for differentiated application of organic fertilizers;
11) audit and land inventory; and
12) counting seedlings and biological productivity [20–22].

Precision agriculture using the latest developments is especially important in the growth of organic agriculture, which requires more effort while simultaneously observing the ecological safety of products and minimal ecological effects from the production process of such products. That is why, the widespread introduction of the latest technologies will provide the opportunity to expand the size of organic land and ensure the growth of the efficiency of such production under conditions of limited resources that meet organic quality standards.

Noteworthy is the reality that the development of organic farming acquires significant prospects with the existing development of scientific technologies in the fields of mechanization, robotics, and information automation and wide access to new technologies and databases that can be used in this process.

Global socioeconomic trends of natural resource sufficiency and agri-production as a food-producing industry require the development of an appropriate digital platform because no inhabitant of the planet will be able to exist without daily consumption of natural resources and food. Modern digital solutions should have a positive impact on productivity on a global scale. Increasing the share of ecological products, reducing waste, and increasing the effectiveness of risk management when attracting investments under the conditions of transparent management of an agricultural enterprise should lead to a positive result. The progressive shift from manufacturing standalone products to adopting a service-focused approach using cloud technologies, incorporating augmented reality, managing and analyzing data through accounting and web analytics, harnessing the power of the Internet of Things, utilizing advanced networking tools, and employing AI-driven marketing techniques to enhance the marketing and sales of products and services signifies a comprehensive set of actions that accompany the process of adapting information and communication technologies to meet management requirements [23].

Management of the life cycle of plants and animals is more difficult than such tasks as the development and management of any inanimate object. For example, the algorithm for growing wheat is based on the interaction of natural and climatic conditions, soil fertility, seed material, fertilizers, anthropogenic factors, and compliance with the technological map of the growing season. The surplus or lack of water and sun, the influence of pests and diseases, cataclysms, and military actions, which are quite difficult to predict and cannot be postponed, "conserved," or compensated for, only shorten the period of their influence, and the growing season cannot be suspended or relocated. However, a positive point in the interaction of man and nature is that the absence of electricity and the Internet does not affect the growing season in open systems. If favorable conditions are not observed during the growing season and if unsustainable farming methods are used (for a period of 3–9 months), there may be no harvest. Adherence to crop rotation, soil analysis and maintenance of its fertility, temperature and precipitation dynamics after extensive observation, and examination of global food markets and supply chains will make it possible to predict the most appropriate development strategy at various levels in modern information and communication parameters.

Recently, there have been integrated ecological solutions in the fields and sustainable resource-saving crop and livestock farming that combines different types of sensors, Internet of Things technologies, automated and unmanned vehicles, robotic manufacturing systems, and platform technologies for processing big data and machine learning, which correspond to the increasing attention of society to a sustainable and ecologically clean consumption model. Digitization in the agricultural sector has the potential to achieve a number of indirect and social effects, including reducing differences in the quality of life between urban and rural areas, ensuring the economic and social integration of smallholder farmers into food systems and supply chains, and giving rural people the tools to improve digital literacy and increase recruitment competencies.

Sensor systems, remote sensors, equipment, and smartphones do not produce food but are intended to provide food growth and resource efficiency. Forecasts for the development of the concept of "digital agriculture" require coordination and training of users, especially young farmers, who want to understand and use contemporary innovations in farming.

The implementation of precision agriculture and the digital revolution in rural regions can assist Ukraine in meeting or surpassing these projections, thereby reinforcing the nation's status as a global frontrunner in food production and export through enhanced productivity and sustainable utilization of natural resources. Enterprises that have embraced and employed these technologies have demonstrated advantageous outcomes, including enhanced administration, heightened productivity, diminished expenses, reduced environmental footprint, and improved ecological integrity. Digitization in agriculture should be considered from two aspects: who will implement it and adapt it to the needs of a specific agricultural enterprise (in Ukraine, there is currently no systematic training of specialists in the digitization of business processes in the agricultural sector, while the age of most farmers is 50+, that is, it is necessary to create a new generation of young farmers who are interested in the digital segment and like life in the countryside). In our opinion, radical changes cannot be thoroughly considered without the formation of a team and the administration of business processes, where significant attention is paid to the environmental culture of the company's reputation, which meets global social expectations, and the existing procedures must be accompanied by sustainable development coaching. Having a robust and sustainable data-driven strategy forces organizations to pay more attention to developing learning capabilities, which improves the quality of change. Managers must promote environmental strategies of human resources and the importance of a sustainable culture based on the positive dynamics of relevant statistical and reporting data of organizations [24].

Secondly, it is essential to carefully shape the ecological direction of development in accordance with the landscape and climatic features of the area and the sufficiency of resources (water, average annual temperature, acceptable for the vegetation process, climatic conditions, social and political aspects capable of containing risks) in the next 50 years, taking into account regional differences in terms of socioeconomic and structural profile, where larger and more technical facilities show a higher level of use of digital technologies.

If large-scale enterprises and multinational corporations have the personnel and financial resources to digitize and create a complete food chain "from farm to table," this can bolster the country's food security at a national level while promoting the development of an environmentally and socially conscious food system and supply chain. So, small farms need help in optimizing innovative solutions and calculating the economic effect. It is necessary to present the advantages of using remote sensors, satellite systems, drones, and software, especially developed for the requirements of growing ecologically clean and organic products (which can be done qualitatively only in small-sized enterprises), and using smartphones for the feasibility of their implementation in a specific agricultural enterprise.

Today, large enterprises demonstrate a higher level of utilization of electronic devices, yet they produce sustainable products. Unfortunately, Internet coverage in large areas of rural areas will be delayed in Ukraine, as there is a small number of people, mostly elderly people, living there. That is, mobile applications, digital platforms, and quality software are concentrated in cities or the suburbs. All processes of identifying and controlling nutrient deficiencies, diseases, pests, weeds, and water shortages take place without the help of online applications and programs, and measures related to the certification and tracking of ecological agricultural products are also carried out mainly by relevant experts using outdated methods.

Software, digital platforms, and mobile apps are modern technologies with high profitability, especially for improving marketing chains and increasing the share of online sales, without the participation of intermediaries. Digital technologies help to annually accumulate planned and actual data, which improves the quality of management and the search for management solutions regarding risks, and combining technical information with organic, financial, and investment data can help suppliers, producers, and consumers in making choices by planning agricultural activities. For example, the growing season of spring wheat is 90–120 days, the growing season of winter wheat lasts from 190 to 210 days, and the pregnancy of pigs is 3 months, 3 weeks, and 3 days, and these stages are repeated every day every year, so it is worth forming a digital technology map of all operational processes for each type of product. Field sensors for monitoring ecological norms of cultivation and machines and equipment are definitely capable of optimizing the use of agricultural resources, increasing productivity and ensuring higher ecological quality of products produced in rural areas. All farmers are concerned about implementing measures that can lower production expenses and boost yields. Nowadays, this is achievable through the utilization of machinery and equipment that are connected to global satellite positioning systems.

Digital solutions will help reduce climate and environmental risks, which urgently require workers who can manage data through platforms. In the next 10 years, we expect that there may be food shortages where human participation is most needed because it is not prestigious to work in agriculture. The problem of labor shortages in the agricultural sector, artificial intelligence, and the advantages of the younger generation will only increase this trend of food security risks in the future. The agrarian platform must control all resources included in agricultural production, as well as the complete production chain of production, sale, and consumption of ecological products. It is a difficult analytical task to collect information and communication links of various industries and regions, but with the help of modern digital capabilities, it will be realized.

Informational and analytical support for sustainable business development is determined by a set of elements that have undergone significant changes and improvements in recent years due to the emergence of new methodological approaches, standards, and requirements for reflecting the practical aspects of the companies' activities related to the implementation of sustainable development projects and programs. Among such elements, the following should be noted: the general concept and philosophy of the company's development, which defines the strategic priorities and tasks of business development, taking into account the goals of sustainable development; the nature of management reporting, in particular, non-financial content; management reports (which in modern practice, in addition to traditional financial reporting, include an environmental report, a sustainable development report, a social report, audit reports, etc.); the field of corporate social responsibility of business; and professional standards of accounting, financial reporting, and auditing. System digitization, which creates new opportunities for collecting, accumulating, and using analytical data, is of exceptional importance in the organization of such a system of information and analytical support for sustainable agricultural management.

The implementation of sustainable solutions in the agro-food sector requires full and timely information support of the management process [25]. So, this involves increasing the level of activity in the use of digital tools in the accounting and financial reporting of agricultural companies.

5.6 Conclusions

The trend of environmentally safe production is an essential element of the growth of the company's capitalization, and a business that does not consider environmental risks gradually loses the best employees, partners, value, and reputation and is less successful in terms of profitability, growth, and retention of market share. By presenting publicized reporting of business strategy as a global principle of survival, the agrarian business will surely achieve success through the implementation of planning and accounting, public reporting, transparent measurement, and publication of enterprise quality parameters. A critical competitive advantage lies in developing and deploying AI and cloud business strategies that meet enterprise and stakeholder needs while protecting, preserving, and enhancing the human and natural resources that future generations will need.

An increasing number of businesses now adopt ecologically friendly management practices and prepare reports taking into account its key indicators. In Ukrainian companies, such activity is currently voluntary and proactive; in foreign countries, components of environmental and social engagements are regulated by current standards and norms that are constantly updated. Today, there are several problematic issues related to the implementation and adoption of environmentally friendly approaches to accounting and financial reporting of agricultural companies, particularly the following:

1) the integration of sustainable growth programs, as a rule, is of a long-term nature and reduces the size of the company's profits in the short term, which reduces the economic interest of business owners;
2) the difficulty of allocating the costs of the long-term stability measures (in particular, ecology) to pertinent objects;
3) non-systematic activity of companies not contributing to the formation of a complete accounting system;

4) methodological controversy of individual standards regulating the display of accounting objects and results of the healthy development activities in the reporting of companies; and

5) existing issues with the perception of the values of the concept of sustainable business development by society, business, and company personnel.

In this regard, with the vision of sustainable accounting and reporting, becoming crucial elements of the company's capitalization and successful strategy, we see the creation of a new system of accounting and analytical support for sustainable agricultural management, the action of which is aimed at creating new long-term values for business, society, national economies, and the subsequent generations by providing information that is capable of radically changing the perception of principles and form the prerequisites for their execution in practical activities.

Informational and analytical backing for the development of sustainable business practices is determined by a set of elements that have undergone significant changes and improvements in recent years due to the emergence of new methodological approaches, standards, and requirements for reflecting the practical aspects of companies' activities related to the enactment of environmentally friendly practices, projects, and programs. Among such elements, the following should be noted: the general concept and philosophy of the company's development, which defines the strategic priorities and tasks of business development, taking into account the goals of equitable growth; the nature of management reporting, particularly, non-financial content; management reports (which in modern practice, in addition to traditional financial reporting, incorporate an ecological report and a report on sustainable growth, a social report, audit reports, etc.); the field of corporate social responsibility of business; and professional standards of accounting, financial reporting, and auditing. System digitization, which creates new opportunities for collecting, accumulating, and using analytical data, is of exceptional importance in the organization of such a system of information and analytical support for environmentally friendly development of agricultural management. The level of professional competence of the staff; the basic perception of the concept of equitable growth in combination with the comprehension of the ecological component, which should be seen as a competitive advantage of the business owners; and the company's management and its employees are also of exceptional importance. Every Ukrainian will be able to easily capitalize on himself, his knowledge, skills, and abilities, thanks to the use of digital technologies. The digital economy is a type of economy where the key factors and means of production are digital data (binary, informational, etc.) and network transactions, as well as their use as a resource, which makes it possible to significantly increase the efficiency and productivity of activities and value for the resulting products and services.

Digital transformation of the ecological direction is the transformation of existing analog (sometimes electronic) products, processes, and business models of agrarian organizations and farms, which is based on the effective use of digital technologies.

Digital technologies (according to the analytical reports of the Davos Economic Forum) include the Internet of Things, robotics and cyber systems, artificial intelligence, big data, paperless technologies, additive technologies (3D printing), cloud and fog computing, unmanned and mobile technologies, biometric technologies, quantum technologies, identification technologies, and blockchain (the list is not exhaustive and is being supplemented). Recently, we have been observing the introduction of digital technologies into all spheres of life: from interaction between people to industrial and agricultural production and from household items to the service sector. This is the transition of biological and physical systems into cyberbiological and cyberphysical ones (a combination of physical and computing components). In the end, the state should become a customer and the first buyer of innovations and services, which will be a positive example and an impetus for the formation of new markets. In the conditions of the military invasion of the Russian Federation on Ukrainian territory, the processes of transformation of the economy are based on the introduction of innovations, optimization, and transfer of tools to national regulation of business in electronic form, as well as the integration of the Ukrainian innovation ecosystem into the European network. Total digitalization in Ukraine will lead to an additional loss of jobs for citizens in the branches and sectors of the agro-industrial complex, but it is digitalization that will create new directions, which will eventually lead to new demands in a few years (or a few months). Moreover, this demand for "hands and brains," as the experience of industrial revolutions shows, will be much greater than the demand in the past period. Also, the digitalization of all spheres of life will lead to the fact that Ukrainian citizens and businesses will increasingly suffer from the growth of cybercrime. That is why the state should make every effort to make society aware of existing risks, as well as provide consulting and technological support in the implementation and use of protected information and communication systems, infrastructures, and platforms.

The possibilities and technologies of digital optimization were analyzed and recommendations were offered regarding the quality of environmental data analysis in real time. The active implementation of digital platforms will have a positive effect on optimizing the efficient utilization of resources, reducing waste and increasing the effectiveness of risk management, corporate sustainability reporting, and investment attraction. It offers high-quality administration of business processes, in which due attention is paid to the reputation culture based on strategic data and social expectations and the existing procedures should be accompanied by coaching in order to strengthen the trend of sustainable development. Having a reliable and sustainable data-driven strategy forces organizations to pay more attention to the development of learning capabilities, which helps to increase the quality of change. Managers must promote environmental strategies of human resources and the importance of a sustainable culture, based on the positive dynamics of relevant statistical and reporting data of organizations.

Such actions will ensure the attainment of the set strategic plan within the designated time frame and will have a favorable impact on the progress of the nation's image as a producer of high-quality products in compliance with world standards.

References

1. *Law of Ukraine On Basic Principles and Requirements for Organic Production, Circulation and Labeling of Organic Products*, The Official Bulletin of the Verkhovna Rada of Ukraine, Kyiv, 2018, http://zakon2.rada.gov.ua.
2. Market of organic products of Ukraine-2018: Status and challenges, *Legal newspaper*, 44, 490, pp.1-4, 2019. https://agropolit.com.
3. Fedun, A., Orhanika: doliderstva cherez perepony. *Yurydychna hazeta*, 44, 490, 3, 1-4, 2015. https://yurgazeta.com/publications/practice/inshe/organika-do-liderstva-cherez-pereponi.html.
4. Skydan, O., Ramanauskas, Y., Zinovchuk, V., *et al.*, *Orhanichne vyrobnytstvo i prodovolcha bezpeka*, Polissia, Zhytomyr, 2013.

5. Organic in Ukraine, OrganicInfo, *Federation of Organic Movement of Ukraine*, OrganicInfo, Kyiv, 2023, https://organicinfo.ua.
6. *Law of Ukraine "On State Support of Agriculture of Ukraine"*, The Official Bulletin of the Verkhovna Rada of Ukraine, Kyiv, 2004, http://zakon2.rada.gov.ua.
7. *Resolution of Ukraine "On Approval of the National Economic Strategy for the Period Until 2030"*, The Official Bulletin of the Verkhovna Rada of Ukraine, Kyiv, 2021, http://zakon2.rada.gov.ua.
8. Annual report, *The results of the association of participants of the organic sector of Ukraine "Organic Initiative" in 2022*, Organic Initiative, Kyiv, 2022, https://organicinitiative.org.ua.
9. *Statistical Yearbook of Ukraine–2021*, State Statistics Service of Ukraine, Kyiv, 2022.
10. The World of Organic Agriculture, *Statistics and emering trends*, IFOAM, Hachenburg, 2004-2023, https://www.fibl.org/.
11. Trofimtseva, O., Prokopchuk, N., Halashevskyi, S., Organic in Ukraine, article posted on the the Ministry of Agrarian Policy and Food of Ukraine (MAPF), pp. 1-4, 2019. https://organicinfo.ua.
12. Dashboard regarding the export of Ukrainian organic products 2021-2023, Diia Business, Trade with Ukraine, 2023. https://export.gov.ua/740-eksport_ukrainskoi_organichnoi_produktsii.
13. Analysis of the Ukrainian organic sector. 8 months since the beginning of the full-scale war in Ukraine, OrganicInfo, Kyiv, 12, 2022. https://organicinfo.ua.
14. Ukraine increased exports of organic products to the EU and Switzerland last year. UKRINFORM, 2023. https://www.ukrinform.ua/.
15. In 2021, Ukraine exported organic products worth 222 million dollars, Novyny APK, Ukrainian agricultural conference, 2002. http:// agroconf.org/.
16. Levina-Kostiuk, M.O., Perspektyvy rozvytku ekolohichno bezpechnoho vyrobnytstva produktsii ahroprodovolchoi sfery, in: *Zbirnyk materialiv I Mizhnarodnoi naukovo-praktychnoi konferentsii NPP ta molodykh naukovtsiv «Aktualni aspekty rozvytku nauky i osvity»*, pp. 444–446, OSAU, Odesa, 2021.
17. Levina-Kostiuk, M.O. and Nehodenko, V.S., Ekolohichna bezpeka produktiv ahroprodovolchoi sfery. *Naukovi zapysky Instytutu zakonodavstva Verkhovnoi Rady Ukrainy*, 5, 66–74, Kyiv, 2017.
18. *The Green Deel and the Cap: policy implications to adapt farming practices and to preserve the EU`s natural resources*, Agriculture and Rural Development, European Union, 2020, https://www.europarl.europa.eu/.
19. *Strategic plans of the SSP. Problems and forecasts regarding EU agriculture. Briefing of the European Parliament*, Research Service of Members of the European Parliament, European Union, 2021, https://www.europarl.europa.eu/.
20. Kernasiuk, E.V., Hlobalna ahroproduktyvnist: lidery, innovatsii ta maibutnie. *Ahrobiznes sohodni*, Article dated 15.03.2021, http://agro-business.com.ua/agro/ekonomichnyi-hektar/item/20860-hlobalna-ahroproduktyvnist-lidery-innovatsii-ta-maibutnie.html.
21. Use of drones in agriculture, Drone Center, 2023. https://dronecenter.ua/review-of-the-dji-phantom4-pro-quadcopter.
22. MHP: the example of Ukrainian-German eco-innovative partnership, 2021. https://www.epravda. com.ua/publications/2021/01/19/670097/.
23. Chukurna, O. and Zamlynskyi, V. (Eds.), *Modern Trends in Digital Transformation of Marketing & Management, Collective Monograph, Vysoká škola bezpečnostného manažérstva v Košiciach, Košice*, Vysoká škola bezpečnostného manažérstva v Košiciach, Košice, 2023, https://www.researchgate.net/publication/368450165.
24. V. Zamlynskyi *et al.* Corporate sustainability reporting and management of agricultural businesses in Ukraine, *IOP Conf. Ser.: Earth Environ. Sci.*, 1126 012002, 2023, DOI 10.1088/1755-1315/1126/1/012002
25. Kryukova, I., Zamlynskyi, V., Vlasenko, T., Architecture of corporate reporting on the sustainable development of business entities in the agrarian sector as a tool of sustainable agri-management. *Ekonomika APK*, 30, 2, 38–48, 2023, doi: 10.32317/2221-1055.202302038.

Adoption and Impact of Blockchain Technology on the Silk Industry's Supply Chain

G.S. Vijaya[1], Lakshmi Sevukamoorthy[1]* and Divakar Rajamani[2]

*[1]Faculty of Management Studies, CMS B School, Jain (Deemed to be University),
Bengaluru, Karnataka, India*
[2]Center for Intelligent Supply Networks at the University of Texas at Dallas, Dallas, Texas, United States

Abstract

The digital profoundness of technology with its disruptive techniques like machine learning, deep learning, and blockchain technology (BCT) has made many challenging tasks with tangible resources in communication media, money, and land and intangible resources such as patents and copyright intellectual property. Increased efficiency and reduced risk with the parties involved in the blockchain network enable the harnessing of its productiveness in the supply chain networks and especially the silk industry. Silk, the uncrowned queen of the textile sector across Asian countries like India, China, and Japan, has also influenced the West textile creating the silk route dating back to the 15th century. In India, silk has a strong impact on the life and culture of the people whose supply chain is so laborious and spans around 45–55 days of a cycle where care and hygiene have to be perpetuated across all stages from egg, larval, chawki, and pupal rearing to form the cocoons which are then woven for colorful silk garments. Hence, we propose a multiphase model for the adoption of BCT in the supply chain of the silk industry with secured decentralized access to information across each stage for a healthy and robust sericulture. This chapter details an analysis of BCT, its challenges, and its adoption into the silk industry.

Keywords: Blockchain technology (BCT), silk industry, supply chain

6.1 Introduction

Sericulture provides stable work and prevents people from moving from rural to urban areas reducing the population and pollution in urban areas. It does play a significant role in job creation being lucrative and remunerative for the rural population and is a crucial tool for rural development in raising the standard of living for the rural [7] where the revenue generated is approximated at some hundred billion dollars from the products made from silk. Being such a flourishing textile industry over a millennium, the silk strand of the *Bombyx mori* silkworm, whose exceptional biocompatibility and mechanical characteristics do not fluoresce under ultraviolet (UV) light [8, 10], is an industry more of economic

---

*Corresponding author: dr.lakshmis@cms.ac.in

Kuldeep Singh and Prasanna Kolar (eds.) *Digital Agricultural Ecosystem: Revolutionary Advancements in Agriculture,*
(91–122) © 2024 Scrivener Publishing LLC

preference rather than a cultural heritage. India being the world's largest consumer and the fourth largest exporter of natural silk has a steady boom in the country's silk market. But still, the gap between supply and demand for mulberry raw silk is growing and so is the need for transparency across the transactions of this industry. As a result, there is a pressing need to increase Indian silk's productivity, manufacturing, and standard of quality to compete on the global market and provide domestic consumers with benchmark quality and clarity on the processes.

6.2   Mulberry—The Fodder

The proverb "You are what you eat" reflects the quality, luster, and glossy look of silk, which the silkworm produces as it eats mulberry leaves that are highly nutritious containing ash,

Table 6.1 Mulberry varieties.

Variety	Botanical name	Character traits
Mysore local	*Morus indica*	Unequal teeth of the leaves, medium to long, hairy, fruit ovoid, bud is dark brown elongated
Bombay Piabari	*Morus indica*	Unequal teeth of the leaves, medium to long, hairy, fruit ovoid, bud is dark brown elongated
Kanva-2	*Morus indica*	Unequal teeth of the leaves, medium to long, hairy, fruit ovoid, bud is dark brown elongated
Bilidevalaya	*Morus indica*	Unequal teeth of the leaves, medium to long, hairy, fruit ovoid, bud is dark brown elongated
Kajli	*Morus indica*	Unequal teeth of the leaves, size medium to long, hairy, fruit ovoid, bud is dark brown elongated
S1	*Morus alba*	Uniform teeth of the leaves, perianth of female flowers four in number, bud is brown oval
$BC_2 59$	*Morus indica* × *Morus latifolia*	Leaves are spirally arranged, dark green in color, from Berhampur
C776	*M. nigra* × *M. multicaulis*	Victory-1 name is C776 in the 1990s
S-36	*Morus indica*	Unequal teeth of the leaves, medium to long, hairy, fruit ovoid, bud is dark brown elongated
RFS-175	*Morus indica*	Unequal teeth of the leaves, medium to long, hairy, fruit ovoid, bud is dark brown elongated
Victory-1	*M. nigra* × *M. multicaulis* × *Morus indica*	Erect branches, grayish stem color, leaves thick and ovate, smooth and glossy, high rooting ability, and fast growth with high yield

Sources: [38, 39, 92].

201 crude protein, 120 crude fiber, 37 ether extracts, 479 nitrogen-free extracts, 268 neutral detergent fiber, 148 acid detergent fiber, 41 acid detergent lignin, 121 cellulose, and 107 hemicelluloses [41]. Mulberry is the best supplement for the silkworm. The nitrogen solubility of these leaves ranges from 11.6% to 14.9% and protein is 14.4%, where the soluble constituents after protein fractionation are albumin 11.1, globulin 9.7, prolamins 44.1, glutelins 8.5, and the insoluble constituent consisted of 26.6% of the total, which qualifies the mulberry as the best fodder not only for the silkworms but also for cattle [11, 21, 22, 79].

For the effective yield of silk production, the principal aim of the sericulture industry is to adapt and adopt scientific breeding conditions with live information streaming for increased output [2, 3, 6], like proper nutrition, proper maintenance of environmental temperature, appropriate humidity, sufficient light, perfect hygiene, compliance with the best sustainability of the silkworm and also on fodder quality, quantity, and condition. So to manufacture fluorescent silk, it is mandatory to feed the silkworms with non-toxic, biocompatible, environmentally friendly, highly luminous, and affordable best yield [9] as the leaf quality influences the rising outcome of the next generation of the cocoon [31].

The mulberry genus *Morus* has about 68 species that are predominant in Asia, with China having 24 species and Japan with 19 species. The *Morus* species are widespread in North America [38], a few species are found in Africa, Europe, and the Near East, and none are found in Australia. Varieties like *M. multicaulis*, *M. nigra*, *M. sinensis*, and *M. philippinensis* have also been introduced, but the majority of Indian mulberry varieties are *M. indica* [39] and Table 6.1 throws more insights into this.

6.2.1 Plantation Technique

The governing method for this perennial crop for succulent production takes into account the following:

- *Soil type* is loamy, clayey loam (with the acidic condition of the soil 6.2–6.8 pH, but in case of less acidity that is below 5, the corrective measure is to add dolomite or lime for less acidic and gypsum salt for alkalinity).
- *Nursery production* is the birthplace of the mulberry plantation, where the nursery bed has dimensions of 4 × 5 and 1.5–2 m and 30 cm raised from the ground level in a shady place preferably with an equal quantity of red soil, sand, and farm yield manure. The mulberry cuttings are planted at a distance of 15–20 cm, and if necessary, a small amount of fertilizer is applied after 1 month of planting the cutting. For ease of transportation, it is easier if the cuttings are planted across individual plastic bags.
- *Planting type*: A pit system with a paired row system of plantation with a plant spacing of (90 +150) cm × 60 cm is preferable for intercultural operations and transportation of the leaves, which accommodates more plants.
- *Planting season*: The beginning of spring and the fall of autumn are the prime and apt seasons, and the winter and summer seasons are the inappropriate seasons for these plantations. In India, the cultivation season varies among the states: in Karnataka, it is done during the months of July–August with the dawn of the southwest monsoon rains; in West Bengal, it is done during

November, which is the late autumn; in Tamil Nādu, it is again June–July and November–December; and in Andhra Pradesh, it is June–September.

- *Land preparation*: A depth of 2 feet for plains and 15% more for sloping lands are the measures for contour bunding, and bench terracing has to be adopted for the cultivation. The field is deeply plowed for a depth of 30–45 cm with the addition of a basal dose of farmyard manure at a rate of 20 tons per hectare [42].

- *Propagation material*: The propagation can be done through seeds, cuttings, or saplings, but saplings are recommended for fast and excellent inception of the plant with two cuttings/one sampling [40].

- *Climatic conditions*: With South Asia being its habitat, the optimal climate conditions that support the flourishing of mulberry [3, 5, 43] are as follows:

  o The plant requires an atmospheric temperature between 24°C and 28°C in a tropical area as it cannot grow below 13°C and above 38°C; thus, mulberry is reared from May to October.

  o The plant requires 600 mm to 2500 mm of rainfall; hence, if there is irrigation, the plant requires 80–120 mm every week.

  o Daylight is one of the important factors that boost the healthy production of mulberry, and it has to be from 5.00 to 10.20 h a day in the tropics, but the growth is extraordinary with the light of the sunshine ranging between 9.00 and 13.00 h a day.

  o Elevation: Mulberry propagation is best at altitudes ranging from 22 m to 1,735 m above MSL (mean sea level) in Japan and 400 to 2,000 m in the USSR. Mulberry is grown in India at altitudes ranging from 300 to 800 m above sea level. However, MSL up to 700 m is appropriate for mulberry growth.

  o Relative atmospheric humidity is 65%–80%.

- *Irrigation methods* can be either *ridges* and *furrows*, which are efficient, requiring less water, and during the rainy season, the furrows serve the best drainage besides the *flatbed method* where beds of rectangular dimensions are formed, which sometimes wastes the land utility and is costly.

- *Weed management* can be done by traditional methods like the *cultural method*, the *mechanical method* of plowing to remove weeds, and the *chemical method* of spraying a weedicide mixture prepared from Glycel 7.5 ml and 10 g of ammonium sulfate per liter of water (600 L of such proportion per hectare) as a post-emergence application, as well as *mulching* and *intercropping*. The weed flora across the mulberry bed are nut grass (*Cyperus rotundus*), Bermuda grass (*Cynodon dactylon*) of grassy weeds, velvet leaf (*Abutilon indicum*), pigweed (*Amaranthus viridis*), copper leaf (*Acalypha indica*), hogweed (*Boerhevia diffusa*), croton (*Croton sparsiflorus*), carrot grass (*Parthenium hysterophorus*), carpet grass (*Trianthema portulacastrum*), and tridax (*Tridax procumbens*) [77]. The predominant ones are *Cynodon* and *Cyperus* which require cautious and constant care in weeding as they compete with the health of the mulberry in terms of nutrients, water, sunlight, etc. [44, 45].

Hence, deep plowing to remove the weed flora has to be done, and rather than adopting a single method of weeding like manual, cover crop intercropping, herbicide, or mulching, it is best to adopt an integrated method of weed control [47]. In the early stage, spraying herbicide pre- and post-emergence is done, and in the later stage, hand weeding followed by intercropping of leguminous plants had a compelling and categorical influence on the growth and yield of the crop [44].

– *Intercropping* is the process of cultivating two or more crops simultaneously for the effective utilization of the field, for economic and financial benefits, and sometimes for mutual association among the crops. In mulberry cultivation, besides having leguminous plants as intercrops in the weeding process, it is best to have crops like soybean that increase the alkali salt due to the presence of bacterial communities like Acidobacteria and Proteobacteria in the soil [46]. It is also recommended to grow turmeric with proper interspacing where both crops mutually benefit [47]. Financial benefits were consistently higher when mulberry was intercropped with maize and finger millet than when mulberries were only grown alone. Mulberry–maize intercropping increased overall yield by up to 43%, and mulberry–finger millet intercropping increased production by up to 3% [73]. In comparison to other row arrangements, the 1:2 row configurations were shown to have the best plant population for maximum production [48]. In some places in India, an intercropping technique is used that involves growing garlic, onions, carrots, or cowpeas (45, 120.34, 29, 7,955.82) which had no impact on the yield of mulberry leaves [49], resulting in increased soil fertility and higher leaf yield and cocoon yield, which may help generate an additional income [50].

– *Pruning and leaf harvest*: For a better yield of the leaf, a good and robust pruning technique needs to be adopted. The first pruning starts when the sprouted flora is about 10–15 cm above the ground within a week, and bottom pruning is then done to the plants at a height of 25 cm after 6 months leaving three to four branches [51]. Pruning is done across the harvesting of the leaf; in the *leaf-picking* method, the first pruning happens when the shoot length is about 20–25 cm above the ground, and the second pruning is done after three leaf harvests at the height of the shoot 30 cm from the ground. However, in the *leaf-harvest* method, the pruning is done at a height of 60–70 cm once a year during the months of January–February. The duration of this harvest is done at 70 days of the cultivation of the plants, and the second and third pruning is done with an interval of 55 days of the first pick, and the fourth harvest is done after 70 days of the third one. Finally, the fifth and sixth pruning is done again at an interval of 55 days from the previous pruning. In the *shoot-harvest method*, the offshoot is harvested at a height of 25 cm from the ground which itself becomes a pruning which is done within 10–12 weeks of consumption of the plant which roughly goes for five to six harvests in a year. In branch cutting, the entire branch having matured lower leaves is harvested as fodder [43].

– *Manuring and fertilizers*: The garden bed is initially treated with the application of rudimentary organic manure like compost and cattle manure, which supports and gives vigorous growth after which periodic application of bio-fertilizers is done [52]. The applicable manure for the garden bed per hectare per year under the rainfed condition is as follows:

- FYM (farm yard manure) of 10 tons in quantity is to be mixed with the bed before the onset of the monsoon.
- Application of biofertilizers like *Azospirillum* at a rate of 20 kg per hectare in five doses across the leaf pruning, application of *Azotobacter* biofertilizers at 4 kg per hectare given twice a year during the rainy season, and application of phosphobacterium at a rate of 10 kg per hectare in two splits. Care is taken to mix these biofertilizers with FYM [53].
- VAM inoculum through maize rootlets 1,000 kg once in the life span of the plant.
- Suphala, 167 kg, single super phosphate, and muriate of potash during the first crop.
- Urea (55 kg) or cam (100 kg) during the third crop.
- Application of micronutrients is done based on the deficiency syndrome on testing the soil. But the recommended application of micronutrients is as a foliar spray which has a combination of zinc sulfate (5 g), ferrous sulfate (10 g), borax (2.5 g), copper sulfate (2.5 g), manganese (2.5 g), or sodium molybdate 100 mg per of water and sprayed with a high-volume sprayer for a spray fluid of 500 L per hectare.

Table 6.2 Recommended NPK dose for cultivation.

Details	N	P	K
Recommended for row method	300	120	120
Split doses			
First crop	60	60	60
Second crop	60	–	–
Third crop	60	60	60
Fourth crop	60	–	–
Fifth crop	60	–	–
Sixth crop	–	–	–
Rainfed doses			
Recommended	100	50	50
First crop	50	50	50
Second crop	50	–	–

- The recommended NPK dose detail across the first, second, and third up to the sixth crop and the rainfed season are given in Table 6.2.

  But for the pit mode of planting, the recommended NPK is 280, 120, and 120, which is the same as the first crop, but for the second crop and third crop, it is 40, and for the fourth crop, it is 60 across the three fertilizers, and for the fifth and sixth, it is 40 across N.

- *Preferred varieties*: Kanva-2, S-36, S-54, MR-2, and Victoria 1 are the most preferred and recommended varieties of mulberry [88].

6.3   Embryogenesis of the Silkworm

In insect embryogenesis, the insects shed or molt their cuticular covering throughout the process with the lining of interior portions which is ectodermal in nature, but in the case of silkworms, in addition to the pupal stage, there are five of these growth stages, also called "instars" [29]. The majority of silkworm larvae are tetramolters, going through four instars and molting after each one. The larval instar stages of the silkworm are as follows:

- The first instar lasts for 3 to 4 days,
- the second instar for 2 to 3 days,
- the third instar for 3 to 4 days,
- the fourth instar for 5 to 6 days, and
- the fifth instar for 6 to 8 days.

However, the length of the larval stage depends on the type of silkworm and the temperature of the rearing environment. Also, the rearing of silkworms across each of these instars has a name which is *infant rearing*—the stage from the first to third instar where the body development takes place. *Chawki rearing* is the rearing of the worms up to stage two instar where the larvae are called chawki from the day of its hatching to the second molt, i.e., for 7 days with special care and hygiene [43]. Next is *late age rearing* from the third instar where they feed voraciously on the leaves, and careful attention is done on the rearing. The last is the *developed stage* (fourth and fifth instars) *rearing*, where they are gluttonous, allowing the reproductive cells and silk glands to expand and develop. Experiments have shown that the number of eggs produced correlates closely with the nutrients ingested by larvae in their fourth and fifth instars.

6.4   Silk Rearing—An Art by Itself

The primary requirement for a positive growth of the overall silk operations is dependent more on healthy egg production. Hence, the protection of wild silk cocoons raised in an inhospitable environment is very crucial as it hampers the inventory of the silk production supply chain, which elevates us to understand the process of silk rearing from the onset. Except for the egg stage, the pupa and adult stages of the silkworm are also considered feeding stages, so proper raising of the silkworms requires knowledge and wisdom on the feeding habits and the hygiene conditions in all the five larval instars. The entire life cycle lasts 45 to 55 days, consisting of an egg stage of 10 to 12 days, a larval stage of 25 to 30 days, a spinning stage of 1 to 2 days, a pupal stage of 5 to 7 days, and an adult stage of 4 to 5 days [34, 36, 84].

6.4.1 The Procedural Outlay

The tensile of the silk filament is dependent on disease-free quality cocoon harvest with good quantity yield, which in turn is directly and indirectly more pivotal on the egg rearing of the silkworm which can be summarized as follows:

1. *Copulation* (1–2 days): One Chinese proverb says, "With time and patience the mulberry leaf becomes a wonderful silk gown." Patience and care in rearing silkworm starts with copulation which is the pairing and depairing of the silkworm moths. It begins with the birth of the moths from the cocoon which are kept in sterile conditions [2] like a darkroom with the optimum temperature of 25°C plus or minus 1°C and RH of 75% plus or minus 5. After careful observation, the active, healthy moths are paired in a disinfected grainage wire mesh tray for 3.5 to 4 h and sometimes 6 h [32]. The female silkworm moth releases a chemical called bombykol, a sex hormone, in minute quantities in the air, which attracts males from a distance of more than 7 km, and copulation starts. The pairing is done in a grainage wire mesh tray or a perforated cotton cloth where the safety measure is that the mating cloth is washed initially with running water and then disinfected with a 2% formalin solution. After the copulation period, the male and female are depaired without injuring the reproductive organs, where the mated female moths are separated and induced for urination. After this, they are placed in a cellule for Pasteur's method of hatching eggs, where the female lays about 300 eggs that are pebrine-free; if the entire group of moths is infected with pebrine disease, the eggs produced and the cocoon batch have to be destroyed completely [34]. The male moth can be preserved under a temperature of 5–6°C for a second pairing with a resting period of 1–2 h.

2. *Egg preparation and rearing* (9–10 days): The methods of egg preparation can be either *segregated* or *mixed* [34], which are detailed as follows:

   A. *Segregated*: This method can be in either *Pasteur* or *cellular*. In *Pasteur*, the F1 hybrids are used for the production of parental silkworms' strains and grandparents on a big sheet of paper of 32 × 18 cm dimension divided into 22 partitions with sufficient in-spacing and between-spacing to place the cellule—the cone-shaped instrument to place the female moth to lay eggs or *rings* where individual moths are placed to prevent mixing (Figure 6.1). After the egg is laid, the moth is transferred to another sheet of the same dimension after oviposition with labels for further examination in the microscope. The advantages are it is convenient for the examination of the mother moth and the elimination of inferior eggs aside

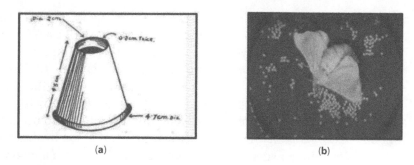

Figure 6.1 (a) The cellule [17]. (b) The ring for the moth to lay eggs [86].

from being less expensive, and the disadvantages are it is laborious and consumes a lot more paper [34, 36, 86].

However, in the *cellular* method invented by Pasteur, a small cellular bag with perforation for the female moth to lay eggs is used, after which the bag is tied. The advantages are more eggs are produced using this method and the examination of the moth is also perfect. For the disadvantages, it is more laborious than the Pasteur method and is also expensive.

B. *Mixed* is otherwise called the *collective moth egg* collection method, which is further divided into *sheet/flat* and *loose-formed* [86]. The *sheet/flat card method* involves a certain number of moths that are allowed to lay in a definite area of 400 cm² (20 × 20 cm), i.e., *sheet*, where the egg-laying area is full and flat with no overlapping of eggs. After oviposition, the moths are examined individually or the moth mother is examined to check for the quality of the eggs and placed on a sheet with a count of 20 moths/sheet to lay eggs, separated by cellule. The advantages are that they are simple and convenient and it is popular for seed crop or commercial rearing, while the disadvantages are that they are prone to washing disinfection, incubation, and brushing of newly hatched larvae.

The second is the *loose-formed method* practiced in China, Japan, Thailand, and Brazil, where industrial eggs are produced as loose eggs, and it is also popular in India for commercial rearing [36, 79, 86]. The process starts by preparing the starched craft sheet of 110 g having a brown color of 90 × 60 cm dimensions for 250 to 300 moths to lay eggs. The starch is prepared by mixing 100 g of Maida with 1 L of water and then adding it to a boiling 3 L of water to make a thin paste to which talcum powder (10 g) is added to the paste for a smoother finish and boric acid (5 g) is also added to prevent mold which is then dried and done with a *roller drum*.

In *oviposition*, the floor of the tray is spread evenly with starch paper and the female and male are allowed to mate for the same duration [23]. After depairing, the female moths are broadcasted uniformly with 40–50 bivoltine and 50–60 multivoltine in a tray. No cellule is used and the moths are spread free on the sheet which is kept in a dark room with optimum hygiene conditions. In *egg collection*, the mother moth is examined for any absurdity and pebrine disease, where the egg sheets are soaked in water for 20–30 min to dissolve the gum, which is then transferred to the egg washing tray from which the eggs are dislodged into a collection bag [34, 36, 86]. In *gum removal*, the female moth lays about 200–300 eggs which are a bit sticky because of the gum which helps the eggs to stick to the surface on which it is laid by not being affected by the wind and the rain [78]. This gum is removed with an optimal solution that contains 0.3%–0.5% bleaching powder solution (obtained by dissolving 3–5 g of bleaching powder which has 30% active chlorine in a nylon bag dissolved in 1 L of water) as the condition beyond this optimality would have an ovicidal effect on the eggs. The washing process starts by washing in this solution for 10–15 min followed by washing with 2% formalin solution for 10 min and finally washing with freshwater. Next, in *shading*, the egg sheets are squeezed for water and placed in the drying unit with the fans on for the drying of the eggs followed by *acid treatment* where the hibernating eggs are washed in hydrochloric acid of 1.076 to 1.1 specific gravity (the density of the acid) with a temperature of 25°C to 48.6°C for a time duration of 5 to 90 min and then washed in running water for 20–30 min to remove acid stains and the sheets are dried in the shade. The eggs after acid treatment have an increase in cell number [33, 86]. Next is the *winnowing of eggs* which is the procedure of removing the lighter eggs, where the egg sheets are fed into the hopper of the winnowing unit with the fans on to blow off the light one, and the good ones are collected [26], followed by *packing of eggs* which is done by weighing 1 g of eggs in a weighing machine where the eggs are counted and divided over 20,000 to get the grams of eggs per box which gives the count of disease-free layings (DFLs) which is then put into the box and sealed with details on race name, quantity, laid-on date, release-on date, and probable day of hatching (as shown in Figure 6.2 & 6.3).

The advantages are as follows: support for the supply of quality eggs, quality cocoon production, and elimination of defective eggs, independent of race and season; and healthy laying with low fecundity is achieved. Eggs are also supplied by standard weight with an equal number of eggs for the same DFLs. The disadvantages of this method are that it cannot be advocated for reproductive egg production, which is laborious, and the calculation of the hatching % is not accurate.

(a)

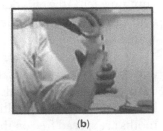
(b)

Figure 6.2 (a) Egg box carrier. (b) The counted eggs are placed inside the egg box [86].

Figure 6.3 The sealed egg packets [86].

C. In the *industrial method*, 50–100 seed cocoons are preserved under hygiene conditions at 30°C and relative humidity of 70%, and the evolved moths are observed under a microscope for pebrine disease and are allowed for pairing. Then, they are depaired and the female moths are allowed to lay eggs in the cards after which they are not subjected to examination. The advantages of this method are it is simple, labor-saving, and less expensive and requires less equipment. This method is feasible only for areas where pebrine is not prevalent [34, 37].

D. In the *biological method* invented by Prof. E. F. Pervakov, once larvae start to emerge from the cocoon as shown in Figure 6.4, they are subjected to a temperature of 33.8°C and RH 55%–65% in a special compartment for 16 h a day, for the moth to emerge. The moths are allowed for pairing, depairing, and egg laying. The advantage of this method is that on the subjection to high temperature, the pupae are activated by phagocytes which reduces the pebrine disease so no examination of the eggs is required. The disadvantages are high mortality and an increased number of defective moths due to exposure to high temperatures [89].

2.1 *Egg-rearing hygiene*: A silkworm seed is said to be of excellent quality if its eggs are completely free of diseases. However, looking at the supply of eggs, only 10% of the total amount of eggs required is produced by the government grainages and 90% of the remaining seeds are generated by farmers for their own needs without using scientific methods, which results in a disease-prone breed [1]. The eggs are always considered as *superior* if the weight

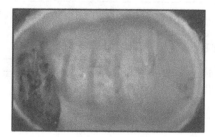

Figure 6.4 Biological method of moth emergence from the cocoon [86].

is 0.0078 g and 2.8 mm in diameter which happens in the summer season and *inferior* if the weight is 0.0069 g and 2.0 mm in diameter which happens in spring. Being a poikilothermic creature, maintaining the ideal temperature, relative humidity (RH), light, and ventilation at each stage of silk rearing is of utmost importance for the successful cultivation of silkworms [28]. For pristine quality cocoons, the following hygiene conditions in egg rearing at the grainages must be observed:

i. *Equipment hygiene*: The grainage equipment like egg laying tray, grainage wire mesh tray, moth examination table and chair, cellule, moth crushing set, mortar and pestle, loose egg container, deflossing machine, cocoon cutting machine, and dry and wet bulb thermometer is disinfected with 5% bleaching powder solution which should have 30% more chlorine content.

ii. *Grainage hall hygiene*: The quality and quantity of rearing is determined by the size of the rearing home where 100 disease-free layings (DFLs) are raised in 400 square feet of space (one DFL is equal to 500 larvae) [24]. On acquisition, the grainage hall is disinfected 3 days ahead of the activity [30]. The hall is sprayed with 2% formaldehyde solution mixed with 0.5% slaked lime mixture and 0.5% detergent solution at 1 L per 2.5 m^2, and the hall is sealed [26]. Alternatively, it can be fumigated with 5% formaldehyde solution for 24 h during high humidity conditions, at least 3–4 days before and also shortly following the grainage activity [76]. Table 6.3 lists the

Table 6.3 Grainages in India [74, 87].

State	Grainage places	Silk variety
Assam	Kamrup, Sonitpur, Darrang, Nagaon, Morigaon, Sivasaga, Golaghat, Lakhimpur, Dhemaji, Dibrugarh, Tinsukia, Cachar, Karimganj, Goalpara	Eri, Muga
Andhra Pradesh	Anantapur, Chittoor, Kurnool, Adilabad, Warangal, Karimnagar, Khammam	Mulberry and Tasar
Karnataka	Bagalakore, Belgaum, Bidar, Chitradurga, Chikkaballapur, Thandavapura, B. R. Hills	Mysore and mulberry
Kashmir	Srinagar, Rajbagh, Anantnag, Budgam, Pulwama, Kathua, Udhampur, Baramulla, Kulgam, Poonch, Batote	Kashmiri
West Bengal, Orissa	Birbhum, Darjeeling, Malda, Murshidabad, Purulia, Bankura, Nadia, Siliguri, Uttar Dinajpur, Cooch Behar	Mulberry, Eri, Tasar
Tamil Nadu	Hosur, Krishnagiri, Sogathur, Pennagram, Coimbatore, Erode, Talavady, Vaniayambadi, Trichy, Dindigul, Courtallam	Mulberry

Sources: [26, 27].

well-established government-supported grainages with their corresponding silk varieties [26, 27].

iii. *Egg hygiene*: The laid eggs are spread on the paraffin paper of the egg-rearing tray. Special care is taken to ensure that the eggs are kept under standard conditions like 25–26°C of temperature and 80% of relative humidity.

iv. *Egg transportation hygiene*: The transportation of the egg from the grainage to the rearing house is done with agile care with no exposure to direct sunlight resulting in irregular hatching and also no exposure to chemicals, fertilizers, and pesticides. It is best to transport the DFLs in disinfected egg boxes to avoid injury to the eggs from any physical shock under a perfect temperature of 25°C and proper ventilation to prevent choking of the embryos. For bulk quantity transfer, transportation through boxes made of muslin cloth or mosquito net with a capacity size of 50 DFLs fitted in a wooden frame is preferable.

3. *Worm evolution*: The eggs received from either of the above processes are brought to the incubation center and are cautiously spread on a paraffin paper placed on the egg-rearing tray. They are covered again with another paraffin paper to avoid infections with sustainable conditions of 25°C to 26°C temperature and 80% relative humidity. Within a day or two, blue-colored pinhead starts appearing from the eggs (Figure 6.5), which are wrapped in tissue paper with a count of 25 to 50 DFLs, and then placed in a black-colored box or black cloth for 1 to 2 days, with exposure to dim sunlight or sunlight diffused shade, where the worms evolve from the eggs as shown in Figure 6.5 the moth emerges from the egg [26].

4. *Brushing in chawki rearing*: These young worms are cautiously transferred to a rearing tray with paraffin-coated paper with the help of a soft brush or a feather without affecting these tiny tender creatures; hence, the process is called *brushing*. The worms are then fed with fresh tender disease-free mulberry leaves pruned from the third and fourth leaves from the apex sliced and diced with a dimension between 0.5 and 1 cm (as shown in Figure 6.6) to emerge as larvae. The feeding timings are 3 to 4 meals per day, and the feeding discipline is 5 kg per 100 DFLs for the first instar, 18 kg per 100 DFLs for the second instar where the diced leaves' dimensions are 2 to 4 cm^2 on a meal of 3 to 4 per day. The optimal conditions in brushing are a temperature of 27°C to 28°C and humidity of 80% to 90%.

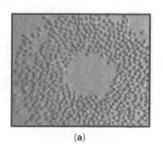
(a)

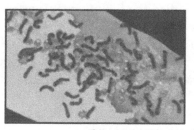
(b)

Figure 6.5 (a) Blue-colored pinhead egg. (b) Moth emergence [85].

Figure 6.6 Worm fed with fresh mulberry in the rearing tray [76].

5. *Bed cleaning* is removing the unused, leftover leaves and stripping the frail and fragile unhealthy ones from the bed and putting in a solution of 2% of bleaching powder and 0.3% slaked lime with 1 L of water [80] before feeding the worm, where during the first and the second molt it is done once in 2 days, and from the third stage, it is almost done daily with the help of a cotton cleaning net with a mesh size of 0.5 cm^2. Care is taken to ensure that the rejects from the bed are not spilled over the floor of the rearing which becomes the breeding place for all infections. Bed cleaning is done using disinfectants like Vijetha, Vijetha green, and Ankush, taken in a white cloth tied and dusted on the body of the silkworm at a dimension of 5 g per square foot across every molt and in a gap of once in 4 days of the final instar with ideal care not to dust the disinfectant under molting conditions or eating conditions.

6. *Larvae* (22–30 days): Larvae hatched are from 4 to 6 mm in length with a rough body, wrinkly, hairless, and yellowish-white or gray in color and 6 and 8 cm in length when fully grown. The larva is extremely sociable and a ferocious eater fed initially with fresh, young virginal mulberry leaves in chopped form but then with whole, mature mulberry leaves in the mature stage. The larvae also called *caterpillars* make movements similar to loops and undergo the four molts discussed in the embryogenesis of silkworms where they grow quickly. The fully grown larva is 8 cm long with a transparent and golden light brown-colored body with a pair of long, sac-like silk glands which are the modification of salivary glands appearing on the lateral side. At this stage, they stop feeding and start to release the transparent, viscous fluid that is produced by their salivary glands through a tiny orifice on their hypopharynx called the spinneret. This viscous substance turns into a firm, fine, long thread of silk when exposed to the atmosphere, and the cocoon is formed which varies in color from white to yellowish which is about the biological phenotypic diversification [20], which leads to mounting.

7. *Mounting* is when the silkworm larvae are mounted on the seventh day of the fifth instar, when they cease eating and start looking for a place for developing cocoons on mountages to produce cocoons of excellent caliber. Silkworms reach adulthood. The larvae are picked carefully with clean hands and mounted onto the mountages or on Chandrika (Figure 6.7) with

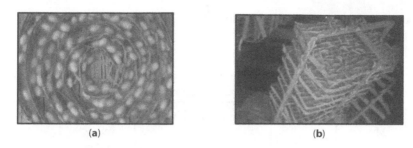

(a)   (b)

Figure 6.7 (a) The mounting instrument Chandrika. (b) Mountages [77].

precautions that the number of larvae on mountages does not exceed each mountage's capacity [81]. The optimal conditions here are 24°C temperature, 60% to 70% relative humidity, and good aeration. It is advised to use rotary mountages to produce cocoons of higher quality and for mounting worms of 100 DFLs, and approximately 35 sets of rotating mountages are needed.

8. *Pupa* (8–10 days) is the stage when the caterpillar larva's body is completely covered by the thread, called the *cocoon* also known as the *pupal case*, which takes about 3 to 4 days to complete this form. This cocoon, an oval thick capsule of white or yellow color, acts as a protective cozy home for the pupa to undergo its metamorphic development of discarding the larval organs like abdominal pro-legs, horn, and mouth and developing pupal organs like antennae, wings, and copulatory organs. This wonderful natural capsule is crafted from one long continuous thread where the outer filaments are uneven and crooked and the inner ones are even and long about 300 m in length obtained from the constant motion of the head from one side to the other at a rate of 65 times/min [82] producing a filament at a rate of 150 mm/min, which is an inconceivable mission. The optimal care here is sufficient spacing (equivalent to the length of the body) for spinning, with a temperature of 22°C and humidity of 65% ± 5%, and mountages are placed in an inclined position at 90° for the urine to drain and prevent staining of the cocoons.

9. *Cocoon harvesting* is done on the fifth day though the cocoon spinning is completed in 2 to 3 days for the worms inside to be matured [77, 84]. The larvae undergo metamorphosis and transform into pupae inside the cocoons which is supposed to be the last stage of sericulture as it is where the extraction of silk is done. The seed cocoon is selected which is pebrine-free, and cocoon hygiene is a must till they are marketed for the best price. Hence, the procedure is as follows: they are stored in moth cages to avoid contamination; the deformed, dead cocoons are removed, burnt, or buried; the hall is disinfected (bleaching powder to lime = 100:900); the cocoon is disinfected (solution containing 2% formalin with 5% bleaching powder); and the hands are sanitized with alkaline soaps. Table 6.4 is a quick revelation of various breeds of these worms.

10. *Silk reeling* is the procedure where the silk threads are separated by decomposing the cocoon. A single cocoon comprises one raw silk thread which is 300 to 900 m (1,000 to 3,000 feet) in length [33]. The fibers are extremely

Table 6.4 Various traits of the silkworm and its characteristics.

Traits breed	Origin/ donor institute	Fecundity no.	Hatching %	Voltinism	Cocoon shape and color	Weight of the cocoon	Denier
PM (pure Mysore)	India/ Mysore	473	96.13	Multivoltine	Greenish yellow and oval	0.942	1.7
C. nichi	India/ Mysore	454	95.34	Multivoltine	White and dumbbell	1.08	1.6
NB_4D_2	India	586	95.34	Bivoltine	White and dumbbell	1.82	2.2
KA	India/Ooty	540	94.9		White and oval	1.62	2.1
CSR_2	India/ Mysore	550	97	Bivoltine	White and round oval	1.8	2.1
BL67	India			Multivoltine	Greenish yellow and oval	1.3–1.4	2.0
DHP5	India	451.6	93.67	Bivoltine	Round	–	2.52
DHR4	India	436	96.49	Bivoltine	Round	–	2.69
SHP2	India	479	97.8	Bivoltine	White and oval	–	2.93
SHR1	India	466	98	Bivoltine	White and oval	–	2.65
MH1	India	502	95.3	Multivoltine	Greenish yellow and elongated oval	1.24	
Nistari	India/ Mysore			Multivoltine	Golden yellow and spindle	0.9–1.0	1.91
S8	India/ Mysore	521	96.8		White and oval	1.69	1.98

Sources: [18, 19, 91].

Figure 6.8 Ramanagara marketplace in Karnataka [83].

thin; hence, a pound of silk requires between 2,000 and 5,000 cocoons, where silkworm cocoons are immersed in boiling water for 15 min to disintegrate the filament from the stickiness, making the silk unravel. Now with a series of guides and pulleys, these filaments are wound into a thread, and to enhance its glossiness, this silk is boiled again.

11. *Marketing* the cocoon for the weavers to buy is done by carrying the disease-free undamaged cocoon to the local marketplace. The marketplace (Sample Ramanagara market place as shown in Figure 6.8) is where the buyers and the sellers of the cocoon transact by an open auction system under the regulation of the government where the process starts when the manufacturers after inspecting the cocoons bid them by a process called e-auction. The prices are fixed under the regulation of the government.

6.4.2 Diseases and Predators of Silkworms

Diseases and predators have a negative impact on the quality and production of the silkworm, where the average loss in this trade accounts for about 15%–47% in India and 10%–15% in other countries [4, 84] due to improper prevention and precautionary measures.

6.4.2.1 Diseases

On account of the proteinaceous matter and the sticky nature of the egg and cocoon, many species of microsporidia infect the silkworms, infecting disease and evolving into a more complicated form causing significant loss to the sericulture [90]. The most prevalent and dreadful diseases in the silkworm are discussed below.

6.4.2.1.1 Grasserie

The source of infection of this viral disease is contaminated by mulberry leaves, occurring throughout the year which is rigorously high in the summer and rainy seasons. The symptoms of this disease in larvae are shining skin before the molt and inner segmental swelling with the body taking a yellowish color, restless movement, and body ruptures oozing out the hemolymph (as shown in Figure 6.9). The remedial measures are disinfecting with 0.3% slaked lime and the best-recommended bed disinfectant, while the disinfected larvae are properly disposed of, either burnt or buried 5 km away from the grainages [25, 34].

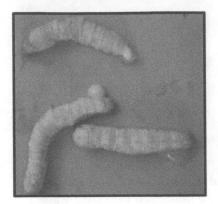

Figure 6.9 Grasserie-infected worm [12].

6.4.2.1.2 Flacherie

This disease, caused by a *virus* or *pathogenic bacteria* (*Bacillus thuringiensis*), infects silkworms when they eat contaminated mulberry leaves, and this disease is more prevalent in the summer and rainy seasons. The disease indications are as follows: the larval body becomes soft and flaccid, impeded growth, vomiting gut juice, sudden death, and paralysis of the larvae turning black in color or red when infected with *Serratia* (as shown in Figure 6.10). The preventive measure is feeding with good succulent, disease-free mulberry, regular bed cleaning, and giving Amruth, an eco-friendly botanical-based, non-toxic, non-polluting, and biodegradable powder formulation [12, 34].

6.4.2.1.3 Muscardine

This *fungal disease* caused by *Beauveria bassiana* is seen during the rainy and winter seasons when the fungal conidia—the asexual non-motile spore of the fungus—comes in contact with the silkworm. The symptoms are larvae losing their appetite, vomiting, and turning flaccid with the presence of moist specks on the skin (as shown in Figure 6.11), and the control measures are disinfecting the rearing house and burning the diseased ones. The preventive measures are adhering to the optimal condition in the rearing house, regulating the

Figure 6.10 Flacherie-infected worm [12].

Figure 6.11 Muscardine-infected worms [12].

breeding bed by dusting slaked lime powder, and applying any recommended disinfectants like Vijetha, Vijetha green, and Ankush [12, 34].

6.4.2.1.4   Pebrine

This *parasitic infection* occurs at the egg stage or by eating contaminated mulberry leaves and also through infected appliances in rearing houses. The symptoms are irregular hatching of the eggs, laying clumped non-sticky eggs, black pepper-like spots on the body, and the infected larva ceasing to eat or showing less food intake and becoming inactive (as shown in Figure 6.12). As it spreads through fecal matter and contaminated leaves, the application of the bed disinfectant Vijetha/Ankush is recommended, and proper disposal of the infected ones is the remedy [12, 34].

6.4.2.1.5   Kenchu

This *viral disease* prevails during high temperature and humidity between May and September and during chawki rearing which enters through the mouth of the silkworm. The pathogen is discharged through the litter and so it remains in the rearing for more than 6 months. The symptoms of the disease are as follows: the infected ones have bodies that become flaccid, swollen head regions, and the larvae appear translucent with a reddish body tinge, for which they are called red flacherie (as shown in Figure 6.13) [12, 34].

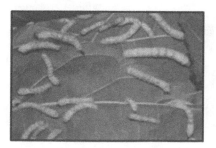

Figure 6.12 Pebrine-infected worms [12].

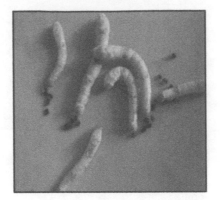

Figure 6.13 Kenchu-infected worms [12].

6.4.2.2   Predators

Insects and small animals can be the worst enemies of the silkworm and wreak havoc in silkworm production. Although there are nine predators of silkworms which include *Canthecona furcellata*, *Hierodula bipapilla* (Asian mantis), *Vespa orientalis* (the Oriental hornet), *Ocecophylla smaragdina* (weaver ant), and *Myrmicaria brunnea* (the winged ant) contributing to crop reduction by 4% to 5% [72], the major damage is caused by two predators, the Uzi fly and Dermestid beetle, in India.

6.4.2.2.1   Uzi Flies

Uzi fly attack is the worst predator in silkworm rearing, and their attacks are characterized by the presence of eggs or black scars on the body of the silkworm, with maggot emergence at the tip of the cocoon (as shown in Figure 6.14(a)). The fly lays eggs on the silkworm larva, the egg hatches after 2–3 days and feeds on the internal content of the silkworm rupturing the larva, and if the fly infects the pupal stage, the Uzi maggot emerges out whence the cocoon is formed by making a circular hole. These predators can be prevented by having wire mesh/nylon nets across the windows and doors that can be automated on closing, providing a small anteroom at the front of the rearing house, and covering the rearing tray with a nylon net. Besides the *physical way* to control the Uzi fly, another method is to use Uzi trap powder (as shown in Figure 6.14 (b)), an exclusive product of Mysore Sericulture, which is dissolved in 1 L of water, and this solution can be poured into white trays which are placed inside and outside of the rearing house. Biologically [35], biocontrol parasite insects

(a)   (b)

Figure 6.14 (a) An Uzi fly-infected worm. (b) Uzi trap from the Sericulture Department of Karnataka [75].

Figure 6.15 Dermestid beetles.

like *Nesolynx thymus* and *Exoristobia philipinensis* have been identified to control Uzi fly infestation, and these insects should be dispersed in pouches in the fourth and fifth stages of silkworm rearing and 1–2 days before cocoon harvesting especially in the Chandrika. The parasite worms feed on the pupae and emerge as mature insects, and the Uzi pupae die as a result of this.

6.4.2.2.2   Dermestid Beetles

The next beastliest predator is the Dermestid beetle (as shown in Figure 6.15) that attacks cocoons, where the female beetles lay 150–250 eggs in the floss of the cocoons as they migrate from the cocoon storage room to the grainage, attaching themselves with the moths with an estimated damage of about 16.62% on the cocoons and 3.57% on the moths. These beetles can be prevented by providing wire mesh to the door and windows of the storage rooms and dipping the storage equipment in 0.2% malathion solution for 2–3 min [84]. The *mechanical control measure* is to use a vacuum cleaner to sweep the grubs, and the *chemical control* includes storing the cocoons in deltamethrin-treated bags, spraying deltamethrin solution on the walls once in 3 months, and sprinkling bleaching powder all around the inner wall to curb the crawling of the grubs into the storage room.

6.5   Blockchain Technology

History dates back to 1991 when two researchers Stuart Haber and W. Scott Stornetta wished to have a technique that would not tamper the document time stamps. Later, the blockchain concept appeared ambiguously in the publication of the white paper on Bitcoin in 2008 by Satoshi Nakamoto. The current prominence of this technology is attributed to the huge set of users of cryptocurrencies which started from Bitcoin, and thence, it started having diversification when the users started to apply it across decentralized transactions and tasks till 2017 [59]; after 2018, the strict regulation consensus started.

Data distributed over the network are vulnerable to being stolen and replicated by cyber-criminals who are equally dominating the cyberworld and whose identities are difficult to track. This issue in question has been entirely resolved thanks to blockchain technology. Blockchain technology is characterized as a written document or a distributed database that contains information about events and the transactions that happened or communicated among parties of common interest [62] and provides decentralization, enhanced transparency, security, and immutability. It is an innovative technology that can replace any existing system and enhance the performance of a network [56]. The information and the transactions entered cannot be deleted as the information and the transactions made are approved, verified, and documented. It is more interesting that both financial and non-financial sectors have also made room for the application of blockchain technology. Blockchains are open ledgers that compile all of the transactions into a series of blocks, and when multiple transactions are happening, multiple blocks continue to add, creating a chain-like structure of the event, hence the name blockchain technology [54].

6.5.1   Blockchain Categories

Based on the category of network and functionality, blockchains are categorized into three types as follows [65]:

- *Public blockchain*: where everyone has permission to read, write, and edit and the consensus mechanisms are proof of work (POW) and proof of stake (POS). Ethereum and Bitcoin are some examples of these kinds of blockchains.
- *Private blockchain*: where the access permissions are limited, which means the read–write operations are vested across a few authorized personnel and it is used across organizations and individuals. This is more of a centralized system, and bank blockchain is a good example of this kind.
- *Consortium or federal blockchains*: where the access permission or the decision-making can be vested across some reliable group of people, and R3 and Energy Web Foundation (EWF) are examples of this blockchain.

In the workflow of this technology, the user of the network would first request a transaction which initiates the creation of a *block* that represents the transaction and is broadcast to all other nodes in the system. The nodes are people or objects that a network user can access to log into the system. If the data are accurate, the block is confirmed and added to the *ledger* with proper validation; otherwise, it is rejected [57].

6.5.2   Blockchain Framework

A typical representation of the blockchain framework in the network tier of operations is given in the below diagram (Figure 6.16) [55].

From a data structure perspective, blockchain is a burgeoning linked list of data records or blocks where the primary input is the lightweight transactions called data records that involve the transfer of funds.

6.5.3   Blockchain Concept

The functioning of the BCT is well explicable in the below diagram (Figure 6.17) [60], and the consensus can be either of the following: proof-of-work, proof-of-stake (delegated or leased), proof-of-elapsed time, practical Byzantine fault tolerance (simplified or practical or delegated or federated), proof-of-activity, proof-of-authority, proof-of-reputation, proof-of-history, proof-of-time, proof-of-capacity, proof-of-weight, etc. [63].

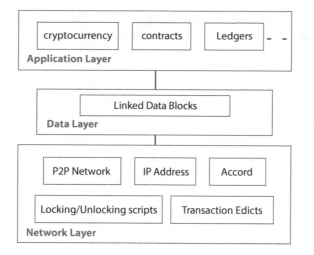

Figure 6.16 The blockchain framework.

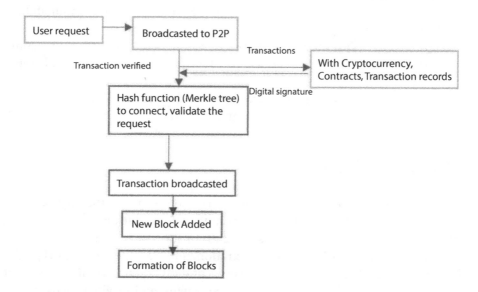

Figure 6.17 User process of information of BCT [64].

6.5.4 Blockchain Technology Features

Bitcoin is the most extensively used blockchain technology for electronic transfer. The benefits reaped by this technology according to its creator [58] are as follows:

- *Decentralization*: The information and the process are decentralized, which makes the service easy and fast while approaching deadlines, facilitating transparent operations.
- *Autonomy*: As blockchain uses cryptography, it verifies the identity of the sender for a reliable transaction. Moreover, the autonomy of all transactions is preserved by the distributed consensus algorithm of the technology.

- *Immutability*: Alteration or tampering with the record and transactions are not possible as the data blocks are encrypted with the hash algorithm and time-stamped which prevents any changes, deletion, or alteration, though there are many views.
- *Traceability*: As it involves time stamping of the transaction, the data traceability is easily preserved along with these features and the hash value is stored in the block.
- *Pseudonymity*: This means the person who initiates any transaction is not required for any identity; instead, the protocol analyzes the previous transaction, checks for credibility and authorization if any, and then starts the transaction.
- *Transparency*: The height of transparency is so unique that any details with the history of any transaction/ledgers can be seen by anyone.
- *Security*: The security of the technology with the hash and the consensus mechanism ensures all information with integrity, confidentiality, and authorization features.
- *Integrity*: Integrity is ensured because of the centralized and immutability feature of the technique.
- *Fault tolerance*: With the feature of the P2P framework and Byzantine consensus, the recovery of any handicapped/failed node or from any malicious attack is so fast.
- *Automatic*: All the transactions across the nodes are maintained and validated automatically with no manual intervention.

6.6   BCT and the Supply Chain

The basis and underpinning of almost every industry and business is the huge supply chain management sector [66]. Traditional SC systems are not adaptable and transparent enough to meet the increasing needs and requests and calls of the future, leading to considerable costs for mistake handling, penalties, administration, and fraud regulation [61]. With the use of blockchain technology, several key processes of the supply chain like SC reengineering, security, resilience, provenance, process management, and product management can be revamped. Moreover, blockchain helps incredibly with sustainable supply chain operations as it benefits the ecosystem and the rational of the business environment, providing end-to-end visibility, traceability, decentralization, improved data sharing, storage, and security [67]. Furthermore, the technology has a profound application in the supply chain operations of sectors of finance, healthcare, manufacturing, IoT, social service, shipping, agriculture, food, and education in terms of scalability, privacy, interoperability, auditing, product provenance, latency, visibility, and disintermediation [68]. Z. Wang *et al.* [69] proposed a blockchain-enabled data sharing model in the supply chain that is equipped with data valuation and pricing mechanisms for fair data sharing in the supply chain, which helped them overcome the challenges of information leak, distribution of values from the shared data to the data provider, and the lack of trust and consensus on the quality of data shared among the data-sharing parties.

Despite numerous benefits and security, there are very few successful implementations of this technology across the supply chain. The research question on why supply chains find it difficult to adopt BCT despite the encouraging advantages stated by other studies was addressed in one such work using the IOS adoption theory [76]. According to the investigation, it was found that there are several unresolvable trade-offs between advantageous and disadvantageous IOS characteristics in adopting BCT with the supply chain in terms of management of distributed ledgers, blockchain role in multi-actor scenarios, and data governance [70]. In one attempt of integrating blockchain with the sustainable food supply chain, a complex industry involving vulnerable perishable processes with reverse logistics in terms of the risk of adaptation [71] found that the data security risks and the data management risk had the highest value among other risks identified as 14.

6.7 The Proposed Model: VL-SS-23

The sericulture industry accounts for 60% of the total world production of silk across India and China alone. The supply chain management across any business is complex and more complicated in interconnectedness and interdependencies of all the elements in this network, and to the extent of transparency, they hold on to any external users. Hence, a decentralized trustworthy, transparent system that holds all the details in a shared but immutable mode is the pressing priority of these two industries. The principal owners of the details or the information about the silk industry are the Sericulture Department of the States and the government officials who are in that department. The rearing of the feeble and precious silkworm whose metamorphic outcome is the lavish lustrous silk filament is a hectic, cautious, orderly, meticulous, and methodical task lasting for a month. So, a clear notion of the processes and the rudimentary details of the live condition of the breeding activity, a conscious understanding of the sequence and the pace of the chronological ordering, and the support and assistance facility for any backing or comprehension of the operation on the silkworm rearing are an absolute necessity. Hence, we have proposed the model *VL-SS-23*, integrating the affairs of both sericulture and the supply chain to overcome the challenges and demands of any external actor who does not belong to this framework (Figure 6.18).

Here, the data about the plan of action, strategies, operation procedures, livable conditions for good rearing, precautionary measures, and the details of the grainages related to the silk work are collated across agriculture universities, state government sericulture departments, grainage rearers across the countries, and any third party/private NGOs, which are validated by some recognized members of the government/sericulture professors with encryption. These data get straight into the blockchain as bulletin ledgers in the form of documents, which can then be broadcasted with any further transaction information with the consensus on the SHA-256 algorithm and the Merkle tree. The inclusions in this process are added to the bulletin ledgers to become a block. The access right for anonymous or any third party/NGO-involved users is a bit stringent with user verification with blind signature, group signature, and ring signature for data integrity and security.

SHA-256 is a secure hashing algorithm, known for its unkeyed cryptographic hashing functions which take any input variable and produce a 256-bit hash as output. In a blockchain, SHA-256 is employed in many stages, most preferably in the following:

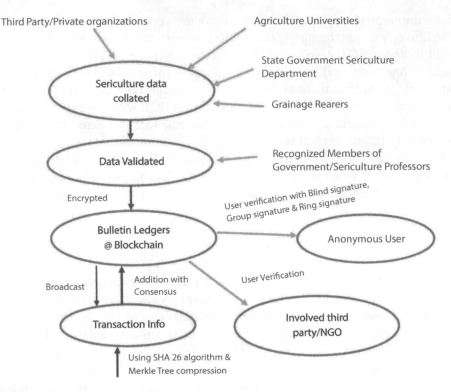

Figure 6.18 The proposed VL-SS-23 model.

Consensus mechanism: Where SHA-256 is used to determine the hash of new blocks that will be generated. The block can then be approved for entry into the ledger.

Blockchains: Each block in the ledger has an SHA-256 digest referring to the block preceding it in the chain.

Digital signatures: To ensure the integrity of a transaction, the data used in the transaction are hashed using the SHA-256 algorithm.

The Merkle tree otherwise called a binary hash tree is a cryptographic security technique, and in blockchain technology, the purpose of the Merkle tree is to preserve the integrity of the block and the transactions, where each leaf node representing the block is labeled with the cryptographic hash, while the non-leaf node has the hash of the prior hash which uses the popular hash algorithm SHA-256. Hence, the Merkle tree is the digital fingerprint of the entire activities that involve all kinds of transactions, document sharing, etc. in the block that enables the user to vouch for the credibility and integrity of the data in the block.

6.8   Conclusion

In this competitive world, the adoption of blockchain technology in the silk industry supply chain area is the need of the hour. An attempt has been made to understand the classical history of sericulture research and its development. India has four silk varieties, namely, mulberry silk, eri silk, wild tussar silk, and wild golden Muga silk. Silkworm classification is done based on biological, geographical, and taxonomical hierarchy. Insights into fodder details, plantation technique, and embryogenesis of the silkworm have to be clearly understood. Silk-rearing methods have to be understood clearly. However, there is a threat of various types of diseases to the silkworm. The authors have suggested the VL-SS-23 model, which focuses on sericulture and supply chain data integration. These integrated data will be stored in the blockchain as bulletin ledgers in the form of documents. This system is secured and integrated as it has three levels of signatures, namely, blind, group, and ring. With the proper adoption of blockchain technology, the producers of silk yarn will get accurate data which helps in making the right decisions at the right time and selecting the correct ways of producing yarn and marketing the same with a good profit margin.

References

1. Pereira, R.F.P., Silva, M.M., de Zea Bermudez, V., *Bombyx mori* silk fibers: An outstanding family of materials. *Macromol. Mater. Eng.*, 300, 12, December 2014.
2. Bajwa, G.A., Nawab, Y., Umair, M., Rizwan, Z., Techno-mechanical properties of the cocoon, raw silk and filament of two mulberry silkworms (Bombyx mori L.) strains. *Meterialwiss. Werkstofftech.*, 50, 10, 1287-1294, October 2019.
3. Pandiarajan, J., Cathrin, B.P., Pratheep, T., Krishnan, M., Defense role of the cocoon in the silk work *Bombyx mori* L. *Rapid Commun. Mass Spectrom.*, 25, 21, October 2011.
4. Shrikanti, M., *Silkworm: Species and Diseases Zoology, Zoology Notes*, Wiley. https://www.notcsonzoology.com/silkworm/silkworm-species-and-diseases-zoology/13207
5. Agustarini, R. *et al.*, Conservation and breeding of natural silkworm (Bombyx mori L.) in Indonesia. *IOP Conf. Ser.-Earth Environ. Sci.*, 533, 012004, 20202020.
6. Hemmatabadi, R.N., Seidavi, A., Gharahveysi, S., A review on correlation, heritability and selection in silkworm breeding. *J. Appl. Anim. Res.*, 44, 1, 9–23, 2014.
7. Trivedi, S. and Sarkar, K., Comparative study on income generation through agriculture crop and sericulture at farmers' level in Murshidabad district. *J. Entomol. Zool. Stud.*, 3, 1, 242–45, 2015.
8. Liu, J., Kong, T., Xiong, H.-M., Mulberry leaves derived red emissive carbon dots for feeding silkworms to product brightly fluorescent silk. *Adv. Mater.*, 34, 16, 2022.
9. Jin, Y.X., Chen, Y.Y., Jiang, Y.H., Xu, M.K., Proteome analysis of the silkworm (Bombyx mori. L) colleterial gland during different development stages. *Arch. Insect Biochem. Physiol.*, 61, 42–50, 2006.
10. Sen, K. and Babu, K.M., Studies on Indian silk I. Macrocharcterization and analysis of amino acid composition. *J. Appl. Sci.*, 92, 1080–1097, 2004.
11. Nakamura, S., Saegusa, Y., Yamaguchi, Y., Magoshi, J., Kamiyama, S., Physical properties and structure of silk. XI. Glass transition temperature of wild silk fibroins. *J. Appl. Polym. Sci.*, 31, 955–56, 1986.
12. https://silks.csb.gov.in/bastor/diseases-and-pests-of-silkworms/
13. Konwarh, R., Bhunia, B.K., Mandal, B., Opportunities and challenges in exploring Indian non-mulberry silk for biomedical applications. *Proc. Indian Natl. Sci. Acad.*, 83, 85–101, 2017.
14. Xu, P.-Z., Zhang, M.-R., Wang, X.-Y., Wu, Y.-C., Precocious Metamorphosis of silkworm larvae infected by BmNPV in the latter half of the Fifth Instar. *Front. Physiol., Invertebrate Physiol.*, 12, 50, 10, 2021.

15. Reddy, N.S., Kumar, T.P., Babu, K.S., Moulting patterns in the silkworm, Bombyx mori L. (PM x NB4D2) under different photoperiodic conditions. *Indian Acad. Sci.*, 99, 467–75, 1990.

16. Usui, K., Nishida, S., Sugita, T., Ueki, T., Matsumoto, Y., Okumura, H., Sekimizu, K., Acute oral toxicity test of chemical compounds in silkworms. *Drug Discov. Ther.*, 10, 1, 57–61, 2016.

17. Kasmaei, F.G. and Mahesha, H.B., Studies on the esterase and its relationship with commercial characters of silkworm Bombyx mori L. *Ann. Biol. Res.*, 3, 11, 52735292, 2012.

18. Singh, R., Rao, D.R., Premalatha, V., Mondal, S., Kariappa, B.K., Jayaswal, K.P., Datta, R.K., Manifestation of hybrid vigour and cocoon shape variability in f1 hybrids of the mulberry silkworm, Bombyx mori L. *Int. J. Ind. Entomol.*, 2, 2, 133–139, 2001.

19. Maske, S.K., Latpate, C.B., Matre, Y.B., Studies of the biology and economic traits of mulberry (Bombyx mori L) single CSR hybrids on V-1 mulberry variety. *Int. J. Curr. Microbiol. Appl. Sci.*, 12, 1, 2476–2482, 2020.

20. Lu, Y. *et al.*, Deciphering the genetic basis of Silkworm cocoon colours provides new insights into biological colouration and phenotypic diversification. *Mol. Biol. Evol.*, 40, 2, 2023.

21. Zurovec, M., Yonemura, N., Kludkiewicz, B. *et al.*, Sericin composition in the silk of Antheraea Yamamai. *Biomacromolecules, Am. Chem. Soc. (ACS)*, 17, 5, 1776–1787, 2016.

22. Kweon, H.Y., Um, I.C., Park, Y.H., Structural and thermal characteristics of Antheraea pernyi silk fibroin/chitosan blend film. *Polym.* Elsevier, 42, 15, 6651–56, 2001.

23. Abdelmegeed, S.M., Effect of mating duration and the number of female/male moth of *Bombyx mori L* on eggs fertility. *Ann. Agric. Sci.,* Elsevier, 60, 2, 341–343, 2015.

24. https://sericulture.assam.gov.in/information-services/detail/eri-seed-grainage

25. https://silks.csb.gov.in/westgodavari/seed-distribution-centres/

26. https://tnsericulture.tn.gov.in/deptunits

27. http://www.seriwbgov.org/tech_service_centres.aspx

28. Games, A.M. and Leon, S.P., The role of learning in the oviposition behaviour of the silkworm moth (Bombyx mori). *Behav. Processes*, 157, 286–290, 2018.

29. Wachter, S., The Moulting of the Silkworm and a Histological study of the moulting gland. *Ann. Entomol. Soc. Am.*, 23, 2, 381-389, Stanford University, 1930.

30. Prasobhkumar, P., Venukumar, A., Francis, C.R., Gorthi, S.S., Pebrine diagnosis using quantitative phase imaging and machine learning. *J. Biophotonics*, 14(3):e202100044. 2021.

31. Chen, F., Lu, J., Zhang, M., Wan, K., Liu, D., Mulberry nutrient management for silk production in Hubei Province of China. *J. Plant Nutr. Soil Sci.*, 172, 2, 245–253, 2009.

32. Ando, T., Kasuga, K., Yajima, Y., Kataoka, H., Suzuki, A., Termination of sex pheromone production in mated females of the silkworm moth. *Arch. Insect Biochem. Physiol.*, 31, 2, 207-218, 1996.

33. Wyatt, S.S., Culture *in vitro* of tissue from the silkworm, Bombyx Mori L. *J. Gen. Physiol.*, 39, 6, 841–852, 1956.

34. Naraaimhanna, M.N., *Manual on Silkworm Egg Production*, Central Silk Board, 1988.

35. Aruna, A.S. and Manjunath, D., Reproductive performance of Nesolynx thymus (Hymenoptera: Eulophidae), in relation to the age of Musca domestica (Diptera: Muscidae). *Biocontrol Sci. Technol.* 10, 2, Taylor & Francis, 2009. https://doi.org/ 10.1080/09583150802624303.

36. San-ming, W., Ping-yi, L., Run-shi, P., Bing-sen, O., *Silkworm Egg Production, Vol. III, 73/3*, Food and Agriculture Organization of the United Nations, 1989.

37. Murugesh Babu, K., *Silk–Processing, Properties and Application*, Woodhead Publishing Limited, Elsevier Science, 2013.

38. Sastry, C.R., Mulberry varieties, exploitation and pathology. *Sericologia*, 24, 3, 333–350, 1984.

39. Vijayan, K., Awasthi, A.K., Srivastava, P.P., Saratchandra, B., Genetic analysis of Indian mulberry varieties through molecular markers. *Hereditas*, 141, 8–14, 2004.

40. Pawan, S., Rohela, G.K., Kumar, J.S., Shabnam, A.A., Kumar, A., Cultivation, utilization and economic benefits of Mulberry, in: *The Mulberry Genome*, pp. 13–56, 2023.

41. Kandylis, K., Hdjigeorgiou, I., Harizanis, P., The nutritive value of mulberry leaves (Morus alba) as a feed supplement for sheep. *Trop. Anim. Health Prod.*, 41, 17–24, 2009.

42. Shabnam, A.A., Chauhan, S.S., Khan, G., Mulberry breeding strategies for North and North West India. *Int. J. Adv. Res. Sci. Eng.*, 07, 04, 2018.

43. Datta, R.K., Chapter 2 Mulberry cultivation and utilization in India, in: *Mulberry for Animal Production*, 2002.

44. Shanmugam, R., Krishnan, R., Chinnuswamy, C., Muthuswami, M., Post-emergence management of Cynodon dactylon(L) Pers in Mulberry plantation. *Indian J. Weed Sci.*, 41, 3 & 4, 207–210, 2009.

45. Khare, T.R., Sobhana, V., Kalpana, G.V., Weed management in Mulberry (Morus alba): A review. *Agric. Rev.*, 44, 1, 60.65, 2023.

46. Li, X., Sun, M., Zhang, H., Xu, N., Sun, G., Use of mulberry-soybean intercropping in salt-alkali soil impacts the diversity of the soil bacterial community. *Microb. Biotechnol.*, 9, 3, 293-304, 2016. https://doi.org/10.1111/1751-7915.12342.

47. Khan, S.A., Hussain, M., Noureen, N., Fatima, S., N. ul Ane, Z., Abbas, Yield performance of turmeric varieties intercropped with the mulberry plantation. *Am.-Eurasian J. Agric. Environ. Sci.*, 15, 10, 2076–2079, 2015.

48. Yadav, B.R.D. and Nagendra Kumar, T.D., Effect of row arrangements on yield and monetary benefits in mulberry (Morus Indica) Maize (Zea Mays) and Mulberry-finger millet (Eleusine Coracana) intercropping. *Sericologia*, 44, 3, 351-360, 2004.

49. Singhvi, N.R. and Katiyar, R.L., Intercropping of mulberry with garlic, onion, and carrot in Maharashtra. *Plant Arch.*, 9, 1, 265–266, 2009.

50. Rajegowda Vinuth, B.S., Vinitha, C., Sanathkumar, V.B., Effect of intercrops on growth and yield of tree mulberry in turn its influence on and cocoon yield. *Int. J. Curr. Microbiol. Appl. Sci.*, 9, 5, 3134–3139, 2020.

51. Suzuki, T. and Kohno, K., Effects of pruning on the branching habit of Morus alba and the abscission of the apices of the short shoots. *New Phytol.*, 106, 4, 753–758, 1987.

52. Chen, F., Lu, J., Zhang, M., Wan, K., Liu, D., Mulberry nutrient management for silk production in Hubei Province of China. *J. Plant Nutr. Soil Sci.*, 172, 2, 245–253, 2009.

53. Sudhakar, P., Chattopadhyay, G.N., Gangwar, K., Ghosh, J.K., Effect of foliar application of Azotobacter, Azospirillum, and Beijerinckia on leaf yield and quality of mulberry (Morus alba). *J. Agric. Sci.*, Cambridge Univ. Press, 134, 227–234, 2000.

54. Priyadarshini, I., Chapter 6: Introduction to blockchain technology, in: *Cybersecurity in Parallel and Distributed Computing- Concepts Techniques Applications and Case Studies*, Wiley Publications, 2020.

55. Gao, W., Hatcher, W.G., Yu, W., *A survey on Blockchain Technology: Techniques, Applications, and Challenges*, IEEE Xplore, 2018.

56. Akram, S.V., Malik, P.K., Singh, R., Anita, G., Adoption of blockchain technology in various realms: Opportunities and challenges. *Secur. Privacy*, 3, 5, 2019. DOI: 10.1002/9781119488330.

57. Latif, S., Idees, Z., e Huma, Z., Ahmad, J., Blockchain technology for the industrial Internet of Things: A comprehensive survey on security challenges, architectures, applications, and future research directions. *Trans. Emerg. Telecommun. Technol.* 32, 11, Wiley, 2021. https://doi.org/10.1002/ett.4337.

58. Nakamoto, S., *Bitcoin: A Peer-To-Peer Electronic Cash System*, http://bitcoin.org/bitcoin.pdf.

59. Williams-Grut, O., Here are all the theories explaining the crypto market crash, Jan 2018. http://www.businessinsider.com/bitcoin-cryptocurrency-market-crash-explained-causes-2018-1. Accessed: 2018-04-02.

60. Gamage, H.T.M., Weerasinghe, H.D., Dias, N.G.J., A Survey on Blockchain Technology concepts, applications, and issues. *SN Comput. Sci.*, 1, 114, Springer, 2020.

61. Wang, Y., Singgih, M., Wang, J., Rit, M., Making sense of blockchain technology: How will it transform supply chains. *Int. J. Prod. Econ.*, 211, 221–236, 2019.

62. Zheng, Z., Xie, S., Dai, H.-N., Chen, X., Wang, H., Blockchain challenges and opportunities: A survey. *Int. J. Web Grid Serv.* Inderscience, 14, 4, 352-375, 2018.

63. Altaf, A., Iqbal, F. *et al.*, A survey of blockchain technology: Architecture, applied domains, platforms, and security threats. *Soc Sci. Comput. Rev.* 41, 5, SAGE, 2022. https://doi.org/10.1177/08944393221110148.

64. Saurabh, S. and Dey, K., Blockchain technology adoption, architecture and sustainable agri-food supply chains. *J. Clean. Prod.*, 284, 2021. https://doi.org/10.1016/j.jclepro.2020.124731.

65. Seebacher, S. and Schuritz, R., Blockchain technology as an enabler of service systems: A structured literature review. *8th International Conference*, IESS, Springer, 2017.

66. Hughes, A., Park, A., Kietzmann, J., Archer-Brown, C., Beyond Bitcoin: What blockchain and distributed ledger technologies mean for firms. *Bus. Horiz.*, 62, 3, 273–281, 2019.

67. Feng, Q., He, D., Zeadally, S., Khan, M.K., Kumar N. A survey on privacy protection in the blockchain system. *J. Network Comput. Appl.*, 126, 45–58, 2019.

68. Dutta, P., Choi, T.M., Somani, S., Butala, R., Blockchain technology in supply chain operations applications, challenges and research opportunities. *Transp. Res. E Logist. Transp. Rev.*, 142:102067, 2020.

69. Wang, Z., Zheng, Z., Jiang, W., Tang, S., Blockchain-enabled data sharing in supply chains: Model, operationalization and tutorial. *Prod. Oper. Manage. Soc.*, 30, 7, 1965-1985, 2021.

70. Sternberg, H.S., Hofmann, E., Roeck, D., The struggle is real: Insights from a supply chain blockchain case. *J. Bus. Logist.*, 42, 1, 71–87, 2021.

71. Kazancoglu, Y., Pala, M.O., Sezer, M.D., Luthra, S., Kumar, A., Resilient reverse logistics with blockchain technology in sustainable food supply chain management during COVID-19. *Bus. Strategy Environ.*, 32, 4, 2327–2340, 2022.

72. Gathlkar, G.B. and Barsagade, D.D., Parasites-predators- their occurrence and invasive impact on the tropical Tasar silkworm in the zone of Central India. *Curr. Sci.*, 111, 10, 1649–1657, 2016.

73. Tikader, A. and Kamble, C.K., Mulberry wild species in India and their use in crop improvement-a review. *Aust. J. Crop Sci.*, 2, 2, 64–72, 2008.

74. https://silks.csb.gov.in/malda/wp-content/themes/Common_District/malda/dpm-frame2.html

75. Iacovou, *et al.*, Electronic data interchange and small organization: Adoption and impact of technology. *MIS Q.*, 19, 465–485, 1995. https://doi.org/10.2307/249629.

76. https://silks.csb.gov.in/bagalkote/rearing-of-mulberry-silkworm/

77. http://www.agritech.tnau.ac.in/sericulture/seri_mulberry%20cultivation.html

78. TNAU AGRITECHPORTAL; Sericulture, *Sericulture Technology: Mulberry Cultivation, 2014.* http://www.agritech.tnau.ac.in/sericulture/seri_mulberry%20cultivation.html

79. Rahmathulla, V.K. and Srinivasa, G., Quality silkworm seed production–a boom for Indian silk industry. *Man-Made Text. India*, 41, 2, 57-61, 2013.

80. Tilahun, A., Shifa, K., Ibrahim, A., Terefe, M., Study on silkworm bed cleaning frequency during larval growth period. *Sci. Technol. Arts Res. J.*, 4, 2, 39-47, 2015. http://dx.doi.org/10.4314/star.v4i2.5.

81. Ueda, S., Effects of silkworm rearing and mounting condition on cocoon reelability. *Jpn. Agric. Res. Q.*, 19, 2, 1985.

82. Zhao, M. *et al.*, Global expression profile of silkworm genes from larval to pupal stages: Toward a comprehensive understanding of sexual differences. *Insect Sci.*, 18, 6, 607-618, 2011.

83. https://ramanagara.nic.in/en/district-produce/cocoon-market/

84. Chauhan, T.P.S. and Tayal, M.K., Mulberry sericulture, in: *Industrial Entomology*, Springer, 2017.

85. http://www.wormspit.com/bombyxsilkworms.htm

86. Mysore University (2020, June 10) Sericulture Department | Lecture 2, 3 [Video]. Youtube. https://www.youtube.com/watch?v=SQ GQdI4QQn8.

87. https://kssrdi.karnataka.gov.in/page/Contributions/Silkworm+Breeding+and+Genetics/en

88. http://www.agritech.tnau.ac.in/sericulture/seri_mulberry%20cultivation.html#:~:text=Slightly%20acidic%20soils%20(6.2%20to,good%20growth%20of%20mulberry%20plant.)

89. Zhou, W., Gong, C., Xue, R., Cao, G., Cao, J., Ye, A., Weng, H., Wang, Y., Germline transformation of the Silkworm Bombyx mori L by sperm-mediated gene transfer. *Biol. Reprod.*, 87, 6, 144, 1-5. 2012.

90. Chopade, P., Raghavendra, C.G., Mohana Kumar, S., Bhaskar, R.N., Assessment of diseases in Bombyx mori silkworm-a survey. *Glob. Transit. Proc.*, 2, 1, 133-136, 2021.

91. Ahmad, M.N., Shivkumar, B.K., Ghosh, M.K., Evaluation of selected genotypes of Bivoltine silkworm Bombyx mori L during different seasons of Kashmir. *J. Entomol. Zool. Stud.*, 7, 1, 1030-1035, 2019.

92. Sharma, A., Krishna, V., Kaur, P., Rayal, R., Characterization and Screening of Various Mulberry varieties through morpho-biochemical characteristics. *J. Global Biosci.*, 4, 1, 1186-1192, 2015.

Transforming Indian Agriculture: Unleashing the Potential of Digital Agriculture Using Efficiency Analysis

Neetu Mishra*, Anil Vashisht and Sandeep Raghuwanshi

Amity University Gwalior, Madhya Pradesh, India

Abstract

This paper explores the vital role played by ethnic groups in preserving biodiversity within their natural habitats, focusing on agriculture as the oldest occupation and foundation of all other industries. With market liberalization and globalization, there is a growing need for quick access to reliable information on crop options, technology, inputs, production techniques, services, and the market. Indian farmers have successfully adopted information and communication technology (ICT) models, programs, and projects, enhancing their agricultural practices and global market presence. To demonstrate this, the study employs data envelopment analysis (DEA) methodology to analyze the efficiency of the top 17 states in India. This research aims to harness the country's potential and formulate growth plans by providing policymakers and decision-makers with valuable guidance. The research presents evidence from secondary data, highlighting the integration of tribal and rural communities into the digital age within a changing society.

Keywords: Information communication technology (ICT), data envelopment analysis (DEA), digital marketing, social media

7.1 Introduction—The Role of Agriculture as the Foundation of All Industries

The first occupation of mankind was agriculture, which encompasses the entire globe and is the foundation of all industries. Through their traditional knowledge and practices, farmers ensure the availability of genetic resources for future agricultural endeavors, preserving various plant species, handlooms, handicrafts, plant products, etc. In today's globalized and liberalized market, farmers face the challenge of adapting their production methods to meet changing trends in food consumerism. As we all know, farming is the oldest and most demanding task, and information communication technology (ICT) is utilized to make

---

Corresponding author: onemishraneetu@gmail.com; ORCID: https://orcid.org/0000-0002-5871-6541

Kuldeep Singh and Prasanna Kolar (eds.) Digital Agricultural Ecosystem: Revolutionary Advancements in Agriculture, (123–144) © 2024 Scrivener Publishing LLC

difficult tasks easier while also allowing farmers to demonstrate their worth in the globalized world.

The goal is to create a society that meets human needs without harming the natural system's dignity and stability [1]. Among the technological advances encompassed by digital agriculture are indoor home vertical farming, robots and automation, livestock technology, sophisticated greenhouse techniques, precision farming, blockchain technology, and artificial intelligence (AI) [2]. Software systems assist farmers in seed selection and precise application of pesticides and fertilizers [3]. By utilizing mobile technology, farmers can remain connected, access information, and make informed decisions, increasing agricultural productivity and efficiency. New and improved technologies have enabled farmers to enhance their productivity and livelihood by utilizing new and improved technologies.

According to the Ministry of Finance's most recent economic survey, it was a pitiful 16.5% in 2019–2020 (down from 18.2% in 2014–2015). It is also true, however, that more than 70% of rural households still rely on agriculture for a living (The Economic Survey of India, 2019–2020). The globe has grown more complex in recent years as a result of a variety of causes, such as our population's expansion and the resulting increase in the need for increasing pressures on natural resources, a lack of fertile land for increased food production, and a lack of food, water, and energy. Climate change, which will result in many changes, further complicates these issues, and it is necessary to draw inferences about the whole system from the research of individual components [4]. We prefer the DAE method through which we learn about comparing the 17 states with the analysis of the import and export of agricultural products with others. First, we can get information about agriculture; hence, the history of agriculture will help us know about the deep knowledge of agriculture changes.

The remainder of the paper contains the below details. Section 7.2 discusses the agriculture sector in India and its implications on the country's overall development. The section elaborates on biodiversity and agriculture practices, the impact of globalization, the importance of data envelopment analysis, and the importance of technology in rural tribal communities. Section 7.3 talks about the methodology of the paper, the variables included in data collection, and the result of data envelopment analysis. Section 7.4 analyzes the results received and discusses the importance of data envelopment analysis used in different states (provinces) of India. Section 7.5 talks about the implication of the study, where managerial as well as theoretical implications are elaborated. Section 7.6 talks about limitations and future directions, while Section 7.7 concludes the paper.

7.2   Analysis of the Agriculture Sector in India

7.2.1   Brief Background

The Indian subcontinent witnessed the domestication of wheat, barley, and jujube around 9000 BCE, followed by the taming of sheep and goats. Agriculture of wheat and barley and domestication of cattle, mainly sheep and goats, were evident in Mehrgarh by 8000–6000 BCE. Cotton cultivation began between the fifth and fourth millennia BCE, establishing a well-established industry in the Indus Valley. Rice, sugarcane, millet, black pepper, cereals, coconuts, and other crops were cultivated during the Early Common Era (200–1200 CE), alongside the development of water storage techniques and hydrological knowledge [1]. The Colonial British Era (1757–1947 CE) saw the export of rice, cotton, indigo, and opium. After India's independence in 1947, agricultural growth became a key focus, leading to several production revolutions, such as the Green Revolution and Operation Flood, and significant expansion in the agricultural industry due to economic changes and advancements in biotechnology and agro-processing.

7.2.2 Preserving Biodiversity and Agricultural Practices

Ethnic communities have a profound knowledge of the value of protecting biodiversity and their particular ecosystems. They have created conventional farming methods that support conservation and sustainable land management. Crop rotation, agroforestry, and using conventional seed varieties are common elements of these practices [5]. Farmers now more easily access resources, training, and financial support with modern technologies, such as ICT. By recognizing and supporting the vital role of ethnic groups in preserving biodiversity and agricultural practices, we can imagine a significantly more robust and inclusive future for farming and the environment.

The Internet of Things (IoT) plays a critical role in modern agriculture by monitoring and managing the variables that impact plant growth [6]. This cutting-edge technology service takes as inputs data on soil fertility, temperature, and moisture and produces outputs on the availability of crops. Machine learning keeps tabs on and forecasts crop availability by predicting the infiltration of weeds, water, arthropods, and animals and grain diversification [7]. Agroforestry has the potential to achieve agricultural sustainability by maximizing productivity while reducing the effects of climate change [8].

7.2.3 Traditional Agricultural Practices and Challenges

Traditional agricultural practices (TAPs) are a group of procedures used in traditional agriculture. Seventy percent of India's population, the second-most populated nation in the world, following China, depends on agriculture for food and a living. TAPs are widely spread across India, particularly where the Himalayas are, and locals rely on a nearby supply [9]. Sustainably, traditional agricultural methods like mixed cropping can reduce the danger of insect infestation and monocrop failure [10]. The tribal people of Northeast India, Orissa, and Maharashtra mostly engage in ecologically nutrient-conserving practices, including agroforestry and shifting cropping [10, 11]. India's northeastern province has a wealth of natural, cultural, and biological diversity, all protected because of the environmentally responsible indigenous wisdom of more than 120 scheduled tribes [9, 12].

Creating food and maintaining a sustainable environment rank among today's most pressing challenges. Two of the biggest issues facing the Indian agricultural sector are providing for the expanding population and maintaining the environment's quality. Since ancient times, traditional agricultural methods have been a crucial component of India's food supply. There is pressure to adopt modern agriculture as a result of the growing population and a sharp rise in per capita food resource consumption, which puts more strain on natural resources [13–15]. By 2050, the production capacity must expand by 60% to feed this increasing population, which raises serious worries about TAPs considering habitat loss, harm by nuisance species, an increase in modernized farming practices, and a change in people's lifestyles [18]. In light of the aforementioned study, it is uncommon for TAP studies to concentrate primarily on the sustainability and production effectiveness of conventional farming techniques [16, 17]. However, comprehensive data covering all three facts of traditional agriculture, such as cultivating land, controlling pests, and protecting crops, are unavailable. To reach the goal of sustainability, it is important to review and reimplement TAPs. This review's main objective is to analyze India's diverse indigenous agricultural practices for food security. This paper's objective is to provide information on some of the native approaches used by traditional farmers in northeastern India and elsewhere to manage pests that affect several popular crops grown there [18]. Figure 7.1 indicates the conventional techniques applied to agriculture.

Competitiveness is more probable to influence concurrent agroforestry systems than sequential ones [19]. Contesting, convolution, expediency, and sustainability should be the four cornerstones for the establishment of agroforestry as a scientific discipline [20]. Resource-conserving practices like agroforestry are heavily influenced by expectations of improved productivity, risk reduction, and economic viability [21, 22].

Intercropping is an essential element of the conventional farming method [23]. Intercropping is still widely practiced, and mounting data suggest that, in many cases, it may represent a more effective use of natural resources, despite the focus of research and development on the intensification of monocrop systems [5]. Traditional knowledge heavily relies on shifting cultivation, a tried-and-true agriculture method. Many socioeconomic conditions used to make it a good land use practice. However, shifting cultivation is now considered by scientists to be an inefficient kind of land use with very low productivity. The increasing population and rising food demand were the main reasons why shifting cultivation could no longer be sustained [24].

Rotation diversity and perennially are common characteristics of ruminant farming systems, as are nutrient recycling and energy efficiency. A type of mixed production known as an "integrated crop–livestock system" makes use of crops and livestock in a way that allows for their spatial and temporal complementarity.

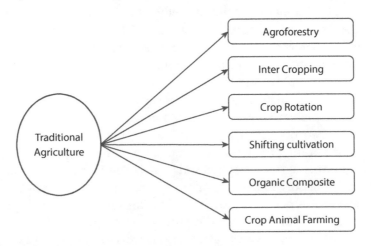

Figure 7.1 Conventional techniques applied to Indian agriculture.

7.2.4   Impact of Globalization on Indian Agriculture

Globalization is the process of cross-cultural interaction that results in the fusion of ideas, products, and other aspects of culture. Every country's necessities are met by agriculture, which also contributes to economic strength, stability, and sustainability. The nation produced 3.5% of its food grains during the pre-globalization era but just 1.7% during the post-globalization era [3]. Reduction in farmer subsidies, which led to increased market prices for food grains, is one reason for this autumn. In a globalized India, the average national income decreased from 193 points to 122 points, while the wholesale food grain index spiked from 179 points to 410 points. According to the most recent FAO data, agriculture and forestry use 2% of the total energy consumed globally [11]. Agriculture gives the gift of goods for industries like manufacturing, exports, and healthier consumption. Market intelligence helps to improve pricing formation and boosts the effectiveness of the marketing system. Marketing needs to focus on the needs of the consumer and benefit farmers, transporters, traders, and processors [25].

Today's farmers stay current with emerging technologies and knowledge. The youth are affected by knowledge and information, whereas socioeconomic factors still influence women [26]. Except for a few lifestyle-based products that primarily rely on urban India, leadership in any product or service is correlated with leadership in rural India. The following factors significantly impact India's rural and agricultural marketing potential: rising income and purchasing power, market accessibility, shifting consumer behavior, competition in urban markets, new job opportunities, green revolution, and improved credit facilities [27].

7.2.5   Data Envelopment Analysis (DEA)

The DEA compares the effectiveness and productivity of decision-making units (DMUs) across different industries. It is especially helpful when numerous inputs and outputs are involved in production. The goal of the DEA is to pinpoint the DMUs that perform the best and offer suggestions for boosting the effectiveness of less effective units.

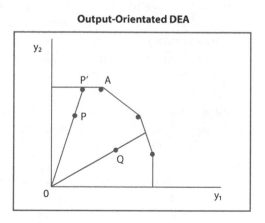

Figure 7.2 The output-oriented DEA model.

A "data-oriented" method known as DEA is used to assess the effectiveness of a group of peer entities (DMU), in our case, the province (states) in India, which transforms numerous inputs into multiple outputs (Figure 7.2) [28]. A nonparametric linear programming technique is used to evaluate the effectiveness and productivity of DMUs. Since DEA was first launched as a managerial and performance-measuring tool in the late 1970s, its application fields have expanded [29].

The output-oriented model is pertinent to the topic at hand because it enables us to compare the agricultural output of various Indian states while considering their various inputs. The model accounts for the production of agricultural products (output) and elements like land acreage and government spending (input). Output-oriented measures can include cases where a production involves two outputs (Yl and Y2) and multiple inputs (I). Using a two-dimensional space, a unit production possibility curve represents the technology. The position of an inefficient unit is at P, and the scope of improvement t is the gap till P′, and point A represents an efficient firm. We determine the states that are utilizing their inputs effectively to produce increased agricultural production by evaluating the efficiency scores of each state. Policymakers may use this information to identify the states performing well and possibly use them as models for other states to increase their efficiency. Due to its ability to concurrently consider various inputs and outputs, DEA is an ideal tool for comparing agricultural production in India. It thoroughly evaluates each state's performance by considering how much agricultural production they produce with the resources they use. Instead of concentrating exclusively on production volume, DEA enables us to assess the effectiveness and productivity of states in producing outputs given the resources at their disposal. In agriculture, efficient resource use is crucial to productivity and sustainability.

7.2.6   Implementation of ICT (Information and Communication Technology) in Rural Tribal Farming Communities

This case study focuses on providing agricultural extension services to rural tribal farming communities through ICT, which helps save farmers time and money. Digital technologies, such as indoor home vertical farming, livestock technology, advanced greenhouse methods, precision agriculture, and blockchain, have revolutionized the agricultural sector [2]. Adopting ICT for political, economic, and social development, focusing on aiding the underprivileged and organizations, has become increasingly dependent on technology over the past 50 years to facilitate communication and information processing across all facets of their business. Academics in the marketing field have likewise struggled to create the proper explanatory and prescriptive frameworks to permit a thorough analysis of this evolution [30]. This is supported by the contribution of ICT to decision quality, information exchange, and interorganizational connections [31]. There are many indications that the use of ICT has significantly influenced how marketing practices have evolved, and many people believe that technical difficulties will continue to play a major role in how marketing develops in the future [30, 32].

The country's economic and social development depends heavily on agro-informatics. Traditionally, the two most important agricultural improvement variables were infrastructure and human resources. ICT, consisting of the three major technologies listed below, can play a significant role in keeping feasible information. According to the task group on

"India as knowledge superpower," ICT must be connected for society to change. India and other developing nations with strong agricultural sectors cannot ignore agriculture in this shift. The progress of agriculture has historically been aided by rising ICT. ICT can be integrated into agriculture to benefit rural and agricultural development [33].

7.2.7   Data Management

In recent years, agriculture has been working on data management, and the agricultural database management system aids farmers in various ways, including crop planning advice, farm machinery, timely delivery of soil test results, and much more. Changing weather patterns, rainfall, fertilizer use, rainfall, and other elements that affect crop output are all tracked by farmers using big data. All of this knowledge aids farmers in making reliable judgments that maximize the output of their land cultivation. Data management has been a topic of discussion in the agricultural sector, as smart farming technology and increased data creation and use have increased [34]. Analysis of the 2013 Office of Science and Technology Policy Memo replies from 19 government agencies (*Office of Science and Technology Policy OSTP 2013*) [35]. Improving best data handling practices is imperative to expand access to research findings [36]. "The Data Management Plans as a Research Tool (DART)" project strives to increase efficiency and openness [37]. In data management, the following technologies have helped promote the introduction of farming, as illustrated in Figure 7.3.

7.2.7.1   Variable Rate Treatment (VRT)

The VRT is known as the variable rate treatment here; examples of VRT implementation include managing weeds with flow rate-controlled sprayers to match previously gathered weed incidence maps and using different flow rate fertilizer spreaders that change application across the field to match local requirements. The creation of VRT herbicide applicators [38] and sprayer design was looked at by Schueller and Wang [39].

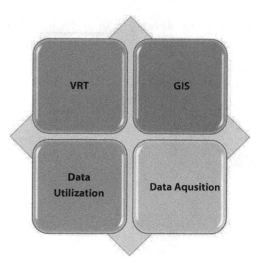

Figure 7.3 Data management tools.

7.2.7.2 Geographic Information System (GIS)

All types of data are gathered, arranged, processed, and mapped by a system known as a geographic information system (GIS). A GIS connects data to a map by fusing descriptive (the qualities of a place) and location (the places where things are). The benefits include improved management, decision-making, communication, and productivity. GIS has long been applied to agricultural management [40]. Using GIS techniques, most agricultural management techniques have been applied to develop yield surface maps and analyze data quality using GIS and GPS [41, 42].

7.2.8 Data Utilization

Due to its assistance or effort in data collection via technology, radio frequency identification (RFID) and other means serve as the foundation of modern agriculture [43]. However, with the usage of IoT, agricultural harvesting might be done using robotic arms, drones, and a few sensors. With the aid of RFID technology, it would be simple for us to periodically gather product-related data. Sensors that identify ripe crops could be employed during packing and grading. IoT is crucial in the process of getting the product to its destination. While employing GPS, the products may be easily traced. Following are the technologies that farmers use. Figure 7.4 indicates the technologies used by farmers and the interconnected network of technologies.

7.2.8.1 Internet of Things (IoT)

IoT devices use embedded technology to communicate, detect, and act on their internal and external states [44]. A lot of work has been put into using IoT technologies in the agriculture sector to build smart farming solutions [45]. Therefore, IoT is essential to agriculture and helps farmers adopt the technology.

7.2.8.2 Robotics

New robotics systems are also being developed in agriculture, allowing for the fusion of several technologies while offering modularity, flexibility, and adaptation. Fleets of robots

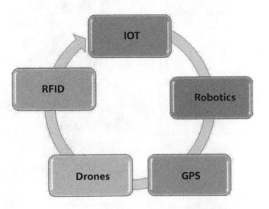

Figure 7.4 Technologies used by farmers.

can offer various benefits. Intelligent machines may replace time-consuming, expensive, and repetitive labor in high-value crops with complex, expensive systems [46].

7.2.8.3   Global Positioning System (GPS) and Geographic Information System (GIS)

Mobile computing, advanced information processing, and telecommunications are just a few of the technologies that have been developed and converged to support this new methodology [47]. Using GPS receivers attached to yield monitors, yield maps will be generated to identify fields that need treatment [48].

7.2.8.4   Drones

Drones are most frequently employed in agriculture as a platform for remote sensing to assess and monitor crops, but they can also be used for remote sampling, targeted pesticide and biological control agent administration, and livestock health monitoring. According to a thorough study, integrating drones into traditional farming practices results in smart farming [49].

7.2.8.5   Radio Frequency Identification (RFID)

In the past 20 years, RFID technology has been extensively studied as an IoT pillar. RFID-based sensing technology has recently been researched for use in industries and educational institutions, including agriculture [50], monitoring the quality of food products as they are being moved and stored [51]; medical care and health [52]; and structural monitoring of health [53]. Different RFID sensors may be created to meet certain requirements for smart agriculture and provide distinctive advantages because of their design flexibility. RFID can also track soil conditions.

7.2.9   Data Acquisition

We measure mass, volume, temperature, relative humidity, gas flow, and more in horticulture and agriculture. All can operate dependably and accurately enough for most purposes in an agricultural setting [54]. There are four different types of sensors, as indicated in Figure 7.5.

7.2.9.1   Remote Sensing

It was during the 1960s that aircraft and satellite platforms were developed for remote sensing of land surface features. Large forests are particularly important for remote sensing surveys because they are considered crucial components of a healthy, sustainable global ecosystem and could be damaged by fires that were not detected initially.

7.2.9.2   Close-Range Sensing

GPR equipment operating at 500 MHz to 5 GHz has been useful in gauging water table levels in some soils [54]. CCD cameras have been used for crop harvesting and grading for

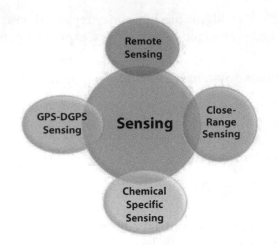

Figure 7.5 Data acquisition sensing.

the last few decades [55]. Typically, they are built around a sensor in close contact with the relevant solid, liquid, or gas [56, 57]. Finally, a reference to the transponders that many agricultural creatures maintain throughout their career is necessary for a section on sensing.

7.2.9.3 Chemical-Specific Sensors

Chemical data are converted into a useful output signal by a chemical sensor. Typically, it transforms chemical interactions or physicochemical qualities. Horticultural and agricultural sensors can detect the presence and quantity of certain chemicals. Individual liquid nutrients have been monitored for and controlled using solid-state, ion-selective electrodes (ISFETS) [54].

7.2.9.4 Global Positioning System and Differential Global Positioning (GPS-DGPS)

GPS and DGPS are satellite navigation systems. When employed in high-precision differential mode, GPS can steer a tractor and an implement with 1–2-cm level relative accuracy along a predetermined course. High-precision GPS is used to identify the actual machine position [42]. The following section analyzes the data obtained from the official Indian government website. Our objective is to assess the agricultural performance of the top 17 states and determine their efficiency[1].

7.2.10 Analysis of Imports and Exports

Agriculture imports and exports play a critical part in the rise in agricultural productivity; the larger a country's exports, the greater the demand for its products, which may lead to increased agricultural production. The import of agricultural products is dependent on the inflation rate; therefore, if there is a difference in the inflation rates of two nations,

---

[1]https://iasri.iar.gov.in/

the nation with a lower inflation rate will experience an increase in domestic demand for its products, which may result in product imports that increase agricultural productivity. Because of the difference in inflation rates, the demand for domestic goods will decline if cheaper agricultural inputs are imported. As a result, imports of agricultural products may increase agricultural productivity [58]. Table 7.1 indicates the trends of imports and exports in India pre-COVID time.

Table 7.1 Imports and exports of agricultural commodities.

India's imports and exports of agricultural commodities (Rs. Cr.) year* (Considering pre-COVID data for analyzing the pre-disruption demographic situations)	Imports (Rs. Cr.)	Exports (Rs. Cr.)
1999–2000	1,205.86	6,012.76
2000–2001	12,086.23	28,657.37
2010–2011	51,073.97	113,046.58
2011–2012	70,164.51	182,801.00
2012–2013	95,718.89	227,192.61
2013–2014	85,727.30	262,778.54
2014–2015	121,319.02	239,681.04
2015–2016	140,289.22	215,396.55
2016–2017	164,726.83	226,651.94

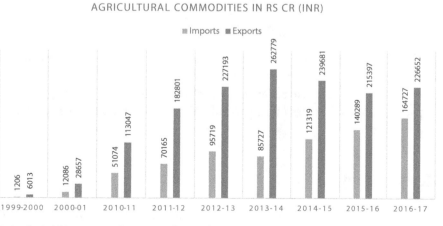

Figure 7.6 Analysis of imports and exports of agriculture.

The dynamics of India's agricultural commerce demonstrate rising demand for agricultural products, substantial reliance on substantial imports, and the possibility for increased exports [58]. Policymakers and other stakeholders can use these findings to design plans to strengthen India's agriculture industry and balance trade in the future. We can infer the following inferences from Figure 7.6.

7.2.10.1   Increasing Trend

Agricultural commodity imports and exports have generally tended upward over time. From 1999–2000 to 2016–2017, import and export numbers grew considerably. This shows a rising domestic and global demand for agricultural products.

7.2.10.2   Import–Export Gap

India has exported more agricultural products than it has imported. The fact that import numbers are routinely greater than export numbers each year proves this. Over time, the widening disparity between imports and exports shows a significant reliance on imported agricultural commodities.

7.2.10.3   Trade Balance

Agricultural commodities have had a negative trade balance throughout the period. India has therefore become a net importer of agricultural products. Increased demand for particular commodities that are not being sufficiently fulfilled by domestic production is indicated by rising imports.

7.2.10.4   Steady Export Growth

Exports have likewise demonstrated a consistent growth tendency, while imports have increased dramatically. This shows that agricultural products from India are becoming more competitive in the international market. Nonetheless, it is noticeable that recent years seem to have seen a slowdown in the export growth rate.

7.2.10.5   Potential for Export Expansion

Agricultural exports have increased positively, but there is still room for growth. The difference between imports and exports emphasizes India's ability to enhance agricultural commodity exports and decrease reliance on imports. This can be accomplished by taking several steps, like enhancing the quality, productivity, and market accessibility of Indian agricultural products.

7.3   Methodology

Initially, we collected the data from the ICAR-Indian Agricultural Statistics Research Institute (IASRI), the official body of the Government of India responsible for collecting data and research-related information about agriculture in the country. Below, Table 7.2 indicates the top 17 states based on the area in hectares. We may make some inferences based on the facts given that illustrate some inputs and outputs of the states.

7.3.1   Production

Following Punjab and Madhya Pradesh in terms of agricultural product production is Uttar Pradesh. This shows that these states contribute significantly to the agricultural output of India.

Table 7.2 Ranking of the top 17 states based on available agricultural land.

State name	Agri production— million tons	Area (million hectares)	Population % under the poverty line	Government expenditure (Rs. in crore at current prices)
Uttar Pradesh	49.14	19.92	37.7	14,164.8
Madhya Pradesh	32.98	17.03	36.7	6,057.09
Punjab	27.99	6.42	15.9	1,410.77
Rajasthan	19.28	14.11	24.8	5,990.67
Haryana	17.16	4.59	20.1	2,733.02
West Bengal	17.06	5.98	26.7	3,339.26
Maharashtra	15.79	12.16	249	10,636.4
Bihar	15.58	6.61	539	4,805.33
Andhra Pradesh	10.37	3.97	21.1	9,510.46
Karnataka	9.64	7.29	23.6	10,484.4
Chhattisgarh	9.23	5.05	48.7	5,637
Odisha	9.06	4.8	37	725.08
Gujarat	7.42	3.8	23	8,879.8
Tamil Nadu	6.22	2.99	17.1	8,170.01
Assam	5.47	2.67	37.0	2,335.56
Jharkhand	5.37	2.89	39.1	2,319.85
Uttarakhand	1.87	0.88	18	2,079.25

7.3.2 Area

Most land is used for agriculture in Uttar Pradesh, followed by Madhya Pradesh and Maharashtra. This implies that these states have a wealth of agricultural land resources, which may help explain their high productivity levels.

7.3.3 Poverty Levels

Following Bihar and Chhattisgarh in terms of population percentage of those living in poverty are Jharkhand and Chhattisgarh. This demonstrates the states' economic difficulties and the requirement for programs to reduce poverty.

7.3.4 Government Expenditure

The biggest government spending is in Karnataka, followed by Maharashtra and Uttar Pradesh. These jurisdictions prioritize agricultural support and development through investments and financial allocations.

7.3.5 Regional Disparities

The states differ significantly in output, area, poverty rates, and government spending. While states like Bihar and Chhattisgarh struggle with poverty levels and Jharkhand has a high percentage of poverty, states like Uttar Pradesh, Punjab, and Madhya Pradesh have great output and big land areas. These variations emphasize the necessity for specialized treatments and strategies to address particular problems in each state.

7.3.6 Data for 2018–2019 of the Top 17 States Based on Agricultural Land

Among the states in India, Uttar Pradesh takes the lead in agricultural production with 49.14 million tons, utilizing 19.92 million hectares of land. Madhya Pradesh follows closely with 32.98 million tons produced on 17.03 million hectares. Punjab stands out due to its smaller size of 6.42 million hectares but strong agricultural output of 27.99 million tons annually. Rajasthan boasts a substantial agricultural area of 14.11 million hectares and produces 19.28 million tons. Despite its relatively modest 4.59-million-hectare agricultural area, Haryana demonstrates great productivity by producing 17.16 million tons. West Bengal utilizes 5.98 million hectares of agricultural land, yielding 17.06 million tons. Maharashtra generates 15.79 million tons on a significant agricultural area of 12.16 million hectares. Bihar utilizes a 6.61-million-acre agricultural area to produce 15.58 million tons.

Andhra Pradesh, with a smaller 3.97-million-acre agricultural area, still produces 10.37 million tons. Karnataka yields 9.64 million tons of agricultural output from a substantial agricultural area of 7.29 million hectares. Chhattisgarh utilizes 5.05 million hectares for agriculture, generating 9.23 million tons. Odisha produces 9.06 million tons from a moderate 4.8-million-hectare agricultural area. Gujarat generates 7.42 million tons on a smaller 3.8-million-hectare agricultural land. Tamil Nadu generates 6.22 million tons from a comparatively modest area of 2.99 million hectares. Assam, with a 2.67-million-acre agricultural area, produces 5.47 million tons. Jharkhand generates 5.37 million tons on a smaller area of 2.89 million hectares. Finally, Uttarakhand has the smallest agricultural area of 0.88 million hectares but manages to produce 1.87 million tons. To assess the effectiveness of the

Table 7.3 Results and ranking.

Efficiency ranking	Name of the province (state) in India	Constant return to scale	Variable return to scale	Scale efficiency	Orientation (input or output)
1	Punjab	1	1	1	–
2	Haryana	0.855	0.897	0.953	IRS
3	West Bengal	0.651	0.684	0.953	IRS
4	Maharashtra	0.296	0.314	0.943	IRS
5	Bihar	0.54	0.574	0.942	IRS
6	Chhattisgarh	0.412	0.478	0.862	IRS
7	Uttar Pradesh	0.74	1	0.74	**DRS**
8	Andhra Pradesh	0.594	0.809	0.735	IRS
9	Madhya Pradesh	0.511	0.731	0.698	**DRS**
10	Rajasthan	0.442	0.641	0.689	IRS
11	Odisha	0.628	1	0.628	IRS
12	Gujarat	0.445	0.748	0.595	IRS
13	Jharkhand	0.426	0.747	0.57	IRS
14	Uttarakhand	0.483	1	0.483	IRS
15	Tamil Nadu	0.472	1	0.472	IRS
16	Karnataka	0.301	0.694	0.433	IRS
17	Assam	0.118	0.312	0.379	IRS

aforementioned states, we conducted a data envelopment analysis (DEA) on the provided data set. In the following section, we will outline the procedure of DEA and explain its significance in relation to the study.

Following the implementation of the DEA, the analysis of exports and imports is as follows. Table 7.3 indicates the results of DEA in constant return to scale and variable return to scale with scale ranking and also indicates the orientation of the results.

7.4   Discussion

7.4.1   Analysis of DEA Results

The DEA results emphasize the states that exhibit high agricultural production efficiency and offer recommendations for optimizing resource use to raise agricultural output in India. The following conclusions were drawn:

1) Punjab emerges as the state with the highest efficiency ranking in terms of agricultural production. This shows how effectively Punjab uses its resources to achieve its agricultural goals.

2) Haryana and West Bengal, which both scored well in all three categories, are closely behind Punjab in terms of efficiency. These states perform exceptionally well in terms of resource use and agricultural productivity.

3) Although Maharashtra, Bihar, and Chhattisgarh produce agricultural goods with a respectable amount of efficiency, these states may further optimize their resource utilization to enhance agricultural output.

4) Uttar Pradesh and Madhya Pradesh have different DEA model types (DRS) among the top rankings. This shows that Uttar Pradesh and Madhya Pradesh should increase output, keeping the input constant.

5) The agricultural output efficiency varies among the states of Rajasthan, Gujarat, Jharkhand, Uttarakhand, Tamil Nadu, Karnataka, and Assam. These states could allocate better and manage their resources to increase their agricultural output.

7.5   Implications

7.5.1   Managerial Implications of the Study

The findings provide managers and policymakers with useful information to help them decide how best to allocate resources, formulate policies, share expertise, reduce poverty, and provide government funds to the agricultural sector. These consequences may help raise agricultural output's general effectiveness and productivity across different Indian states.

7.5.1.1   *Performance Benchmarking*

Managers may compare the efficiency of agricultural production in various states using the DEA data. Managers can discover the states that are operating well and use them as benchmarks for improving the performance of less efficient states by comparing the efficiency rankings and ratings.

7.5.1.2   *Resource Allocation*

The states with the highest efficiency scores produce the most agricultural products with their available resources. Managers can use these data to strategically allocate resources, concentrating on states with lower efficiency scores to increase resource utilization and productivity.

7.5.1.3   *Best Practice Sharing*

High-efficiency states like Punjab may serve as role models for others. Policymakers may promote knowledge exchange and cooperation between governments to spread best practices and tactics that boost agricultural production efficiency.

7.5.1.4   Policy Formulation

The DEA results provide light on the elements influencing agricultural production efficiency. Policymakers may create policies and interventions that support resource optimization, technology adoption, and skill development in the agriculture sector by analyzing the traits and practices of the top-performing states.

7.5.1.5   Poverty Alleviation

The result can help targeted initiatives that increase agricultural productivity, and income creation may reduce poverty in states with high rates of poverty but low-efficiency ratings.

7.5.1.6   Government Expenditure Analysis

Managers can gain insight into the effectiveness of government investments from statistics on government spending concerning agriculture productivity. Managers can assess the effect of public spending on agricultural productivity and pinpoint areas where investments might be optimized for better results by comparing efficiency ratings with government spending.

7.5.2   Theoretical Implications

For policymakers and stakeholders, the theoretical ramifications of the study based on the DEA methodology and the supplied data set give insightful information. These implications cover resource use, input and output orientations, policy formulation, poverty alleviation, and sustainable agricultural development. They serve as a basis for interventions and decision-making in the agricultural sector.

7.5.2.1   Efficiency Rankings

The states are ranked in the DEA analysis based on their efficiency rankings. Identifying the best-performing states in terms of agricultural production efficiency (Punjab being the most effective in this case) is one of the theoretical implications of these rankings. With these rankings, policymakers can better grasp the elements that contribute to a state's effectiveness and note its best practices.

7.5.2.2   Resource Utilization

The DEA data provided insight into how well resources were used in various states. States with better efficiency scores, including Punjab, Haryana, and West Bengal, effectively use inputs, including land, government spending, and demographic characteristics. Theoretical conclusions imply that states with effective resource allocation and utilization can increase agricultural output without incurring significant resource waste.

7.5.2.3   Input and Output Orientations

Input- and output-based DEA models have theoretical ramifications on where to concentrate efficiency improvement efforts. States with higher input-oriented efficiency scores (IRS) may profit from tactics designed to cut back on inputs while keeping output levels constant. In contrast, states with lower output-oriented efficiency (DRS) ratings might need to concentrate on increasing outputs while maintaining constant inputs to increase efficiency.

7.5.2.4   Policy and Decision-Making

The study emphasizes the variability in efficacy among various states. Theoretical ramifications imply that decision-makers can use the DEA data to identify states with lower efficiency ratings and create targeted policies and actions to raise their agricultural production efficiency. This can entail improving infrastructure, improving access to resources, encouraging agricultural research and development, and putting efficient poverty alleviation programs in place.

7.5.2.5   Poverty Alleviation and Sustainable Agriculture

An essential aspect of agricultural development to consider is the proportion of the population below the poverty line. According to theoretical repercussions, states with greater efficiency ratings are better positioned to bring their inhabitants out of poverty through increased agricultural production. Therefore, authorities might prioritize initiatives to improve efficiency in states with high poverty rates to alleviate poverty and promote sustainable agricultural growth.

7.6   Limitations and Future Directions

The limitation of the study relies on secondary data and DEA analysis, which may be subject to data limitations and assumptions. Future research could address this limitation by collecting primary data and incorporating additional variables that may influence agricultural efficiencies. Furthermore, the study mainly focuses on resource allocation and efficiency rankings, but exploring the impact of specific interventions or policies on agricultural productivity would be beneficial. Future research could also investigate the long-term sustainability of agricultural practices and their implications for poverty alleviation. Additionally, considering the growing importance of international markets, future studies could examine the relationship between agricultural efficiency and India's competitiveness in global trade, analyzing the role of import–export dynamics and their impact on the overall economy.

7.7   Conclusion

The study sheds light on the significant contribution of agriculture and innovative individuals to India's economy, highlighting the role of ICT in enhancing agricultural productivity.

By utilizing the DEA method, the study identifies states with high agrarian production efficiency, such as Punjab, Haryana, and West Bengal, which can serve as benchmarks for less efficient states. The findings provide valuable insights for managers and policymakers to strategically allocate resources, formulate policies, promote knowledge exchange, and address poverty alleviation. The study encompasses efficiency rankings, resource utilization, input and output orientations, policy formulation, and the potential for poverty reduction and sustainable agricultural development. Future research should focus on primary data collection, considering technological advancements, environmental factors, and the impact of international trade dynamics on India's agricultural sector.

References

1. Alam, A., Rizvi, A.H., Verma, K., Gautam, C., The changing scenario in Indian agriculture: A review. *Int. J. Sci. Res. Agric. Sci.*, 1, 7, 118–127, 2014.
2. Mishra, N.K., Raj, A., Jeyaraj, A., Gupta, R., Antecedents and outcomes of blockchain technology adoption: Meta-analysis. *J. Comput. Inf. Syst.*, 1, 1–18, 2023.
3. Mittal, S., Gandhi, S., Tripathi, G., Socioeconomic impact of mobile phones on Indian agriculture. Working paper, Q16 - 18, 2010.
4. Hieronymi, A., Understanding systems science: A visual and integrative approach. *Syst. Res. Behav. Sci.*, 30, 5, 580–595, 2013, doi: 10.1002/sres.2215.
5. Fordham, R., Intercropping—what are the advantages? *Outlook Agric.*, 12, 3, 142–146, 1983.
6. Alqahtani, A.S., Mubarakali, A., Parthasarathy, P., Mahendran, G., Kumar, U.A., Solar PV fed brushless drive with optical encoder for agriculture applications using IoT and FPGA. *Opt. Quantum Electron.*, 54, 11, 715, 2022.
7. Anitha, R. and Rai, D., Internet of things with artificial intelligence detection and blockchains of crop availability for supply chain management. *Int. J. Knowl.-Based Dev.*, 12, 3–4, 444–459, 2022.
8. Ahmad, F., Goparaju, L., Qayum, A., FAO guidelines and geospatial application for agroforestry suitability mapping: Case study of Ranchi, Jharkhand state of India. *Agrofor. Syst.*, 93, 2, 531–544, 2019.
9. Jeeva, S.R.D.N., Laloo, R.C., Mishra, B.P., Traditional agricultural practices in Meghalaya, North East India. *IJTK*, 5, 1, 7-18, 2006.
10. Singh, R. and Singh, G.S., Traditional agriculture: A climate-smart approach for sustainable food production. *Energy Ecol. Environ.*, 2, 296–316, 2017.
11. Murthy, I.K. *et al.*, Carbon sequestration potential of agroforestry systems in India. *J. Earth Sci. Clim. Change*, 4, 1, 1–7, 2013.
12. Chhetry, G.K.N. and Belbahri, L., Indigenous pest and disease management practices in traditional farming systems in North East India. A review. *J. Plant Breed. Crop Sci.*, 1, 3, 28–38, 2009.
13. Rands, M.R. *et al.*, Biodiversity conservation: Challenges beyond 2010. *Science*, 329, 5997, 1298–1303, 2010.
14. Patel, S.K., Singh, A., Singh, G.S., Food production through traditional agriculture: An urgent need to improve soil health by sustaining soil microbial diversity. *Int. J. Curr. Microbiol. Appl. Sci.*, 8, 1, 183–196, 2019.
15. Varma, V. *et al.*, Perceptions of priority issues in the conservation of biodiversity and ecosystems in India. *Biol. Conserv.*, 187, 201–211, 2015.
16. Joshi, C.P. and Singh, B.B., Indigenous agricultural knowledge in Kumaon hills of Uttaranchal. *IJTK*, 5, 1, 19-24, 2006.

17. Pradhan, A., Idol, T., Roul, P.K., Conservation agriculture practices in rainfed uplands of India improve maize-based system productivity and profitability. *Front. Plant Sci.*, 7, 1008, 2016.
18. Chhetry, G.K.N. and Belbahri, L., Indigenous pest and disease management practices in traditional farming systems in North East India. A review. *J. Plant Breed. Crop Sci.*, 1, 3, 28–38, 2009.
19. Sanchez, P.A., Science in agroforestry. *Agrofor. Syst.*, 30, 5–55, 1995.
20. Sain, G.E. and Barreto, H.J., The adoption of soil conservation technology in El Salvador: Linking productivity and conservation. *J. Soil Water Conserv.*, 51, 4, 313–321, 1996.
21. Salam, M.A., Noguchi, T., Koike, M., Understanding why farmers plant trees in the homestead agroforestry in Bangladesh. *Agrofor. Syst.*, 50, 77–93, 2000.
22. Scherr, S.J., On-farm research: the challenges of agroforestry. *Agrofor. Syst.*, 15, 95–110, 1991.
23. Jodha, N.S., Intercropping in traditional farming systems. *J. Dev. Stud.*, 16, 4, 427–442, 1980.
24. Tripathi, R.S. and Barik, S.K., Shifting cultivation in North East India. *Proc Approaches Increasing Agric. Product. Hill Mt. Eco Syst. ICAR Res. Complex NEH Reg*, Umiam Meghalaya, pp. 317–322, 2003.
25. Mahadevan, R. (2003). Productivity growth in Indian agriculture: The role of globalization and economic reform. *Asia Pacific Development Journal*, 10, 2, 57-72.
26. Antov, P., Savov, V., Neykov, N., Utilization of agricultural waste and wood industry residues in the production of natural fiber-reinforced composite materials. *Int. J.–Wood Des. Technol.*, 6, 64–71, 2017.
27. Das, M. and Gogoi, B., Agricultural intensification, diversification and migration as livelihood strategies among rural scheduled tribe population of Palasbari Revenue circle: A case of India. *Asian J. Agric. Rural Dev.*, 10, 2, 598–611, Aug. 2020, doi: 10.18488/journal.ajard.2020.102.598.611.
28. Banker, R.D., Cooper, W.W., Seiford, L.M., & Zhu, J., Returns to scale in DEA. *Handbook on Data Envelopment Analysis*, 41-70, 2011.
29. Ji, Y. and Lee, C., Data envelopment analysis. *Stata J.*, 10, 2, 267–280, 2010.
30. Brady, M., Fellenz, M.R., Brookes, R., Researching the role of information and communications technology (ICT) in contemporary marketing practices. *J. Bus. Ind. Mark.*, 23, 2, 108–114, 2008.
31. Mohamed, M., Murray, A., Mohamed, M., The role of information and communication technology (ICT) in mobilization of sustainable development knowledge: A quantitative evaluation. *J. Knowl. Manage.*, 14, 5, 744–758, 2010.
32. Mintzberg, H., Quinn, J., Ghoshal, S., *The Strategy Process–European Revised Edition*, Prentice Hall Hertfordshire, UK, 1998.
33. Singh, V., Sankhwar, S., Pandey, D., The role of information communication technology (ICT) in agriculture. *Glob. J. Multidiscip. Stud.*, 3, 4, 2–10, 2015.
34. Kunisch, M., Big data in agriculture–perspectives for a service organization. *Landtechnik*, 71, 1, 1–3, 2016.
35. Office of Science and Technology Policy (OSTP), Increasing access to the results of Federally-funded scientific research. *Socio-Econ. Plan. Sci.*, 89, 7, 1–5, 2013.
36. Kriesberg, A., Huller, K., Punzalan, R., & Parr, C., An analysis of federal policy on public access to scientific research data. *Data Sci. J.*, 16, 27-27, 2017.
37. Whitmire, A., Carlson, J., Westra, B., Hswe, P., Parham, S.W., The DART Project: Using data management plans as a research tool. 2016.
38. Shearer, S.A. and Jones, P.T., Selective application of post-emergence herbicides using photoelectrics. *Trans. ASAE*, 34, 4, 1661–1666, 1991.
39. Schueller, J.K. and Wang, M.-W., Spatially-variable fertilizer and pesticide application with GPS and DGPS. *Comput. Electron. Agric.*, 11, 1, 69–83, 1994.

40. Wylie, B.K., Shaffer, M.J., Brodahl, M.K., Dubois, D., Wagner, D.G., Predicting spatial distributions of nitrate leaching in northeastern Colorado. *J. Soil Water Conserv.*, 49, 3, 288–293, 1994.

41. Everitt, J.H., Escobar, D.E., Summy, K.R., Davis, M.R., Using airborne video, global positioning system, and geographical information system technologies for detecting and mapping citrus blackfly infestations. *Southwest. Entomol.*, 19, 2, 129–138, 1994.

42. Larsen, W.E., Nielsen, G.A., Tyler, D.A., Precision navigation with GPS. *Comput. Electron. Agric.*, 11, 1, 85–95, Oct. 1994, doi: 10.1016/0168-1699(94)90054-X.

43. Mani Sai Jyothi, P. and Nandan, D., Utilization of the Internet of Things in agriculture: Possibilities and challenges, in: *Soft Computing: Theories and Applications, Advances in Intelligent Systems and Computing*, M. Pant, T. Kumar Sharma, R. Arya, B.C. Sahana, H. Zolfagharinia (Eds.), pp. 837–848, Springer, Singapore, 2020, doi: 10.1007/978-981-15-4032-5_75.

44. Lee, I. and Lee, K., The Internet of Things (IoT): Applications, investments, and challenges for enterprises. *Bus. Horiz.*, 58, 4, 431–440, 2015.

45. Stočes, M., Vaněk, J., Masner, J., Pavlík, J., Internet of things (IoT) in agriculture-selected aspects. *Agris-Line Pap. Econ. Inform.*, 8, 665-2016–45107, 83–88, 2016.

46. Bochtis, D.D., Sørensen, C.G., Vougioukas, S.G., Path planning for in-field navigation-aiding of service units. *Comput. Electron. Agric.*, 74, 1, 80–90, 2010.

47. Mishra, N. K., Pande Sharma, P., & Chaudhary, S. K. (2024). Redefining agile supply chain practices in the disruptive era: A case study identifying vital dimensions and factors. *J. Glob. Oper. Strateg.*

48. Smith, K.R., Research & technology-does off-farm work hinder "smart" farming? *Agric. Outlook*, 294, 294, 28–30, 2002.

49. Ram Kumar, R.P., Sanjeeva, P., Vijay Kumar, B., Transforming the traditional farming into smart farming using drones, in: *Proceedings of the Second International Conference on Computational Intelligence and Informatics: ICCII 2017*, Springer, pp. 589–598, 2018.

50. Deng, F., Zuo, P., Wen, K., Wu, X., Novel soil environment monitoring system based on RFID sensor and LoRa. *Comput. Electron. Agric.*, 169, 105169, 2020.

51. Fathi, P., Karmakar, N.C., Bhattacharya, M., Bhattacharya, S., Potential chipless RFID sensors for food packaging applications: A review. *IEEE Sens. J.*, 20, 17, 9618–9636, 2020.

52. Abugabah, A., Nizamuddin, N., Abuqabbeh, A., A review of challenges and barriers implementing RFID technology in the Healthcare sector. *Proc. Comput. Sci.*, 170, 1003–1010, 2020.

53. Wang, C., Wang, C., Wan, G.C., Tong, M.S., Guan, S., Xie, L.Y., RFID antenna sensor for quantitatively monitoring surface crack growth, in: *2019 IEEE International Conference on Computational Electromagnetics (ICCEM)*, IEEE, pp. 1–3, 2019.

54. Cox, S.W.R., *Measurement and Control in Agriculture*, Carlton, Vic: Blackwell Science, Oxford, England, 1997.

55. Mason, R.J., Buist, A.S., Fisher, E.B., Merchant, J.A., Samet, J.M., & Welsh, C.H., Cigarette Smoking and Health: This Official ATS Statement was Adopted by the ATS Board of Directors, November 1984. *Am. Rev. Respir. Dis.*, 132, 5, 1133-1136, 1985.

56. Frost, A.R., Special issue: Livestock monitoring. *Comput. Electron. Agric.*, 17, 139–261, 1997.

57. Jahns, G., Navigating agricultural field machinery. *Comput. Electron. Agric.*, Elsevier Science, Amsterdam, Netherlands, 25, 1–2, 1–2, 2000.

58. Gilani, S.W., The impact of agricultural imports and exports on agricultural productivity. *J. Econ. Sustain. Dev.*, 6, 11, 1–6, 2015.

8

Digital Agriculture: Transforming Farming Practices and Food Systems for a Sustainable Future

D. Pushpa Gowri[1]* and Anitha Ramachander[2]

[1]Manipal University Jaipur, Jaipur, Rajasthan, India
[2]Indus Business Academy, Bangalore, Karnataka, India

Abstract

Digital agriculture refers to the use of technology in agriculture to improve farm efficiency, productivity, and profitability. It has the potential to revolutionize farming practices, improve food security, and promote sustainability. Feeding a growing population, climate change, better decision-making, cost savings, access to markets, economic benefits, optimum resource management, and job creation are some of the important objectives of digital agriculture. The digital technologies used create a value chain of food systems by enhanced traceability, supply chain optimization, consumer engagement, enhanced food safety and quality, promotion of sustainable practices, and innovative business models. Innovation in digital agriculture has the potential to transform the way food is produced and distributed. It includes precision agriculture, artificial intelligence, farm management software, big data analytics, the Internet of Things, robotics and automation, and blockchain technology to promote sustainable and environmentally responsible practices. It has its limitations of cost, infrastructure, security concerns, connectivity, knowledge, and skill gaps. Agriculture is the backbone of India, and the government has taken initiatives to promote digital agriculture and has launched various mobile applications to reconstitute the sector. The future of digital agriculture is promising as it revamps the potential for the production and consumption of food from farm to fork.

Keywords: Digital agriculture, farmer, producer, economy, value chain, food security, sustainability, innovation

8.1 Introduction

Most of the world's food and fabrics are produced by agriculture. Digital agriculture has evolved as a technical platform for improving agricultural profitability and sustainability. It intends to revolutionize the agricultural sector by harnessing computer and communication technology [1]. This topic includes the use of intelligent technologies such as the Internet of Things (IoT), artificial intelligence (AI), robotics, big data, and biotechnology to improve agricultural practices as well as to secure long-term food production.

**Corresponding author*: pushpagowri31@gmail.com

Kuldeep Singh and Prasanna Kolar (eds.) Digital Agricultural Ecosystem: Revolutionary Advancements in Agriculture, (145–160) © 2024 Scrivener Publishing LLC

The concept of digital agriculture is an extension of the "digital earth" concept proposed in the 1990s [4]. It aims to use sophisticated technology to address many agricultural industry concerns, such as increasing production, optimizing resource utilization, minimizing environmental consequences, and improving food security.

Digital agriculture is a multidisciplinary field that links aspects of engineering, computer science, mathematics, and agriculture. It promotes teamwork and knowledge sharing among specialists with various backgrounds in order to create original solutions for the agricultural industry [35]. Agriculture plays a vital role in many developing countries, driving economic growth and raising national wealth. Initiatives like the 2013 National Food Security Act (NFSA), which promotes better farming methods, higher crop yields, and easier market access, also boost the agricultural sector [3]. By offering technical innovations that can empower farmers and increase the general effectiveness and productivity of the agricultural value chain, digital agriculture is in line with these objectives [20].

The ultimate objective of digital agriculture is to ensure that everyone has access to adequate nutritious food that suits their dietary needs and tastes. Digital agriculture can transform farming practices, improve resource management, and build a more resilient and sustainable food system in the future by utilizing intelligent technologies.

8.2 Need for Digital Agriculture and Food Security

To achieve the Sustainable Development Goals, agriculture and food play a crucial role, and the global population has been anticipated to increase by 34% by 2050. Increasing productivity is essential for tackling global food shortages, malnutrition, and the need to feed a growing population in areas with limited land resources, as stated by the Food and Agriculture Organization of the United Nations (2010) [7, 34].

To boost agricultural productivity, effective management of agricultural inputs, crop yield, soil quality, and climate-related risks is required. Farmers can make more informed decisions about resource allocation with the help of digital technology, which boosts productivity [22]. Digital technologies play an important role in promoting equal consumption and

Figure 8.1 Farmer with his crop (www.freepik.com).

distribution of food items across the country in the field of food supply chains. Transparency and traceability afforded by digitization ensure adequate food availability during crises and increase resilience against global shocks like pandemics, wars, or natural disasters [44]. Digital platforms help farmers by simplifying access to local, regional, and global markets and enabling customization to satisfy consumer demands everywhere. The efficacy and efficiency of agricultural goods have significantly increased, thanks to the integration of digital technologies into food and agriculture supply chains which has benefited farmers, consumers, and the entire nation [42].

8.3 Role of Digital Agriculture in Economic Transformation

Agriculture is one of the most promising areas for adopting digital technology, with the potential to develop a worldwide digital economy. Digital agriculture can help drive economic transformation, especially in developing nations where agriculture is economically important and employs a large part of the workforce. It promotes economic growth, stability, and national food security by encouraging improvement in production, distribution methods, and holistic agricultural development.

Big data and analytics are driving a rise in investments in Agricultural Revolutions 4.0 and 5.0, opening new prospects for all economic actors involved. Digital agriculture improves sustainability and profitability by utilizing computer communication technology. Farmers gain knowledge, empowerment, and improved revenue by developing, managing, and applying digital solutions. Smart farming, which blends physical and digital elements, enables a deeper understanding of the environmental impact. Small and marginalized farmers specifically benefit from the convergence of physical and digital infrastructures, which spurs revenue development [41].

A digital agricultural system encompasses a comprehensive database that includes various types of agricultural data, ranging from soil conditions to market analysis. Using digital networks, farmers may connect with the proper markets and sell their produce at the right

Figure 8.2 Transport of food grains (www.freepik.com).

time and price, improving yields, reducing food loss and waste, and ensuring fair recompense for their produce. Modern national food systems must consider important factors such as the pace of economic growth, agricultural productivity, and active engagement in the global food market. Enhancing food safety and nutritional value through improved product traceability from farm to consumer eventually benefits consumers. In order to meet the world's need for food, developed nations like the United States and Germany, as well as growing economies like China, India, and Brazil, contribute to national food security [2, 8].

8.4   Digital Value Chain and Food Systems

Global agriculture is changing due to digitization, and it has strengthened food systems, value chains, and supply chains. Value-based food supply chains focus on large quantities of distinctive and high-quality food products while ensuring equitable benefit distribution along the entire chain. They are collaborative partnerships between farms and other supply chain players. These chains cover every step of a product or process life cycle, from resource sourcing to manufacturing, consumption, disposal, and recycling. A digital food value chain emerges in the context of the digital era as a business model where sellers and buyers of agricultural products develop deliberated alliances with other supply chain members, such as aggregators, processors, distributors, retailers, and consumers. The aim is to enhance financial returns through product differentiation that upholds social values and caters to the specific preferences of consumer groups [5, 26].

An effective and efficient food value chain clearly articulates its principles, incorporates them across the chain, enhances the product at each level, and cultivates client loyalty by assuring transparency and meeting client expectations. Partners in the chain understand that

Digital Food Value Chain

Figure 8.3 Digital food value chain (authors' own).

Figure 8.4 ITC's e-Choupal (www.freepik.com).

maximizing the value of their products requires collaboration, interdependence, and mutual assistance. A digital food value network functions as a strategic engine, addressing customer needs for food safety, quality assurance, sustainability, and other factors through an ecosystem-based business model. Technology is enabling new kinds of collaboration in the current dynamic environment that prioritizes sustainability in potential investment decisions [9, 10].

An exemplary instance of a digital food chain is ITC's e-Choupal ecosystem, which empowers four million farmers across 10 states [50].

8.5   Innovation in Agriculture

The lifestyle of the people is changing as a result of digital innovation. A consolidated and automated system that integrates technological, modeling, and data features into a unified body of digital information for efficient management across many domains is referred to as a "digital platform" [17]. By 2050, global agriculture might enhance production by 70% by digitalizing critical agricultural systems like technology, logistics, management, marketing, and finance. Information, infrastructure, and dependable delivery systems will serve as the three main pillars of the modern agricultural environment, which replaces manual labor-intensive farming methods with data-driven management strategies. By bridging the physical and digital worlds, this change ushers in the era of cyber-physical systems, which rely on innovative techniques like machine learning and data mining for intelligent analysis [6, 25, 40].

Precision farming and smart farming are other terms for digital agriculture. Precision agriculture in modern agriculture refers to monitoring, measurement, and response to diverse intra- and interfield variable inputs. It is a method of managing agriculture that maintains track of metrics and assesses the demands of various locations and crops. Precision farming aims to maximize efficiency and productivity while decreasing input costs and improving

Figure 8.5 Smart farming (www.freepik.com).

environmental sustainability. The application of robotics and artificial intelligence in modern agriculture is centered on the creation of autonomous decision-making systems and the ability to execute tasks without the assistance of humans [13, 48].

8.5.1   Innovative Techniques in Agriculture

Agriculture has seen massive breakthroughs in numerous technologies and tools aimed at increasing output, sustainability, and efficiency in recent years. The IoT is a crucial technology in the agricultural sector, which is a network of networked computers, sensors, and devices, each with its own unique identity that enables remote sensing and monitoring, where remote sensing enables farmers to monitor natural resources in real-time and with pinpoint accuracy, allowing them to make informed decisions. Big data analysis in agriculture enables farmers to identify new market trends and client preferences, resulting in better customer service and decision-making. Farmer's workload can be reduced by incorporating multiple strategies like system integration and cloud computing. Satellite imaging and field mapping are applied to map and monitor fields and crops more efficiently, resulting in higher agricultural productivity [11, 12].

Autonomous robotic systems, including ground vehicles and aerial vehicles (drones), are being employed to reduce the need for human intervention in outdoor applications such as planting, spraying, and manuring. Farmers use computer model systems such as artificial intelligence, deep learning, and digital twins to solve complicated tasks such as market forecasting, demand analysis, and risk assessment. Augmented reality is applied to envisage data from soil analysis, pest and weed identification, crop monitoring, and disease detection, providing significant insights into crop health.

In contrast to previous methodologies, today's agriculture relies on data-driven, model-driven, communication-driven, document-driven, and knowledge-driven decision support systems. Furthermore, genetically altered technology, such as bioengineering, helps to improve crop quality. This holistic approach to farming is frequently practiced through regenerative agriculture, which highlights the necessity of ecosystem restoration and revitalization, soil health, and general sustainability in agricultural practices [13, 14, 16].

Figure 8.6 Innovation in agriculture (www.freepik.com).

8.5.2   Transition to Agriculture 5.0

Agriculture 5.0 is the next stage of agricultural growth, building on the advances of Agriculture 4.0. To further optimize and improve systems, it includes techniques such as IoT, AI, wireless sensor networks (WSNs), and robotics.

Agriculture 5.0 expands on Agriculture 4.0 to produce healthy, inexpensive food while minimizing the harm to the ecosystems that sustain life. Assigning arduous, repetitive work to robots and critical-thinking activities to humans can improve crop quality and production efficiency in Agricultural 5.0 settings [21].

8.6   Benefits and Limitations of Digital Agriculture

Digital agriculture refers to a range of technological innovations that has the potential to increase farming productivity while improving environmental sustainability and farmer living standards. Technology has the potential to improve agricultural output, consistency, optimum utilization of resources, and time management. It provides considerable benefits to farmers as well as worldwide social rewards. Agricultural enterprises can share information across industry lines to create new and disruptive opportunities.

8.6.1   Benefits

The agricultural sector's digital transformation has various advantages. Farmers acquire knowledge, power, and revenue by utilizing digital technologies that allow them to comprehend the environmental impact of their practices. Data-driven decision support systems and digitized platforms boost productivity, minimize food loss and waste, and improve access to national and international markets. Furthermore, digital agriculture enhances food product transparency, traceability, and customization, benefiting both farmers and customers. Digital agriculture improves individual health and production while also affecting numerous areas of the environment by boosting food safety and nutritional value [18, 34].

Digital technology guides farmers to estimate food supply and demand to connect with producers and the market with the help of high-resolution data. Promoting a shared value between commercial success and social good, environmental and digital ecosystems are connected in agriculture [41]. Through the digital green, producers communicate the best management practices with other farmers to adopt intelligent irrigation systems for rain gardens and trees for green infrastructure via interactive films [33].

The Agricultural Bank is developing a method for electronic farmer identification through the application of a single biometric system for authentication and identification. It will enable the provision of package solutions for agricultural enterprises (subsidies, finance, insurance) as well as the identification of the best prospects to sell products directly on the global market [15]. Environmentally friendly digital solutions promote strategic alliances between farmers, sellers, buyers, and other supply chain actors to reduce world hunger and malnutrition and improve food security. Through blockchain technology, the entire food chain is now transparent and visible, offering the product a digital identity and connecting the user to the product's entire journey through a pleasant experience by promoting ecosystem trust and ensuring safe and healthy products for the customer through supply chain optimization.

8.6.2   Limitations

While digital agriculture has the potential to improve food production globally, it confronts several problems that are impeding its wider implementation. High prices, lack of information on long-term advantages, and numerous hurdles are connected with modern farming methods [6, 20]. Digital technology frequently comes at a high cost, prohibitively expensive for farmers in impoverished countries. Furthermore, an overreliance on technology might be a hindrance because it necessitates dependable infrastructure, access to electricity, and Internet connectivity.

Pesticides and genetically engineered crops can generate questions about food safety and long-term health consequences. The application of such technologies must be regulated and monitored to ensure that they fulfill safety requirements and do not pose substantial dangers to human health and the environment. Agricultural systems are becoming increasingly vulnerable to cyberattacks as they are digitized. Farmers and farm workers may be undervalued or displaced because of digital technologies. It can lead to structural unemployment, especially for people who lack digital literacy or are not tech-savvy. Governments and commercial organizations should invest in research and development to enable the transition of digital-driving industries [19].

8.7   Digital Agriculture in India

The agricultural sector in India is vital to the country's economy and the worldwide agriculture business. With more than half of the population employed in agriculture and a sizable section of the population reliant on it for a living, the sector is vital to India [23, 38]. While India is still creating a valuable information and communication technology (ICT) infrastructure, there is considerable potential for using technology in agriculture. Digital agriculture can help farmers overcome challenges, such as increasing productivity, optimizing resource utilization, improving market access, and managing risks. Digitization in agriculture has enhanced the speed with which complaints are resolved, as well as the effectiveness of government support and facilitation of access and operation. A robust cold chain infrastructure is essential for the preservation of perishable items, which increases product shelf life, and regulatory requirements protect food product's safety and quality throughout the supply chain.

To empower Indian farmers, solid research and development are required to address local challenges like establishing market ties, overcoming production stagnation, and improving farm management. Because India is one among the world's top food producers, digitization has implications for the sustainability and security of global food markets. By eliminating intermediaries, digitization enables personalized distribution and connects every farmer in the country to any location [24, 27, 32, 36].

Mr. Narendra Singh Tomar, Union Minister for Agriculture and Farmers Welfare, announced the launch of the Digital Agriculture Mission 2021–2025 in September 2021. Five Memorandums of Understanding (MoUs) were signed to strengthen digital agriculture

Figure 8.7 Indian food chain: creating value for marketing success (www.freepik.com).

with the National Commodity and Derivatives Exchange (NCDEX), National e-markets Limited (NeML), ITC Limited, Jio Platforms Limited, Ninjacart, and Cisco. The Digital Agriculture Mission of 2021–2025 intends to support and develop this field by utilizing cutting-edge technology such as AI, blockchain technology, remote sensing, robotics, and drones [33].

8.7.1 Measures Taken by the Government of India to Improve Digital Agriculture

> The National Mission of Agricultural Extension and Technology—The objective of the mission is to strengthen the farmers to get appropriate technology and agronomic practices. It is accomplished by interactive information transmission techniques, ICT applications, the popularization of modern technology, capacity building, and so on.

> BharatNet—BharatNet, also known as Bharat Broadband Network Limited, was founded by the Department of Telecommunications to develop, manage, and operate the National Optical Fibre Network. To amend communication in India and join the Digital India campaign, it plans to connect all 250,000 Gramme Panchayats in the country.

> Agri Market—It is a software developed to inform farmers about crop prices and deter them from holding distress sales. Farmers can access this app on their own devices to learn about crop pricing in markets within 50 km.

> e-Governance initiatives—The government has launched three portals, the mKisan portal, the farmer portal, and the Kisan call center to support farmers in taking learned decisions for profitable agriculture under various agroenvironmental conditions. Soil health card software and web-based software offer integrated nutrient management advice under this initiative [33].

➤ Jio Krishi—To help farmers, the Jio Agri platform was introduced in 2020, which digitized the ecosystem of agriculture in the whole food value chain.

➤ Unified Farmer Services Interface—This program was implemented by Microsoft and the Indian government with the help of India's small farmers. This alliance aids in raising farmers' earnings through improved pricing management and increased agricultural productivity using AI sensors. The partnership quickens the uptake of AI in agriculture.

➤ Pradhan Mantri Kisan Samman Nidhi—The government is helping the farmers through this plan by providing agricultural loans to enhance natural farming practices, significantly upgrade agriculture, and emphasize agri-waste management. Through this Nidhi, 11 crore farmers have received $26.4 billion.

➤ The India Digital Ecosystem of Agriculture (IDEA)—IDEA is a federated database of farmers built using publicly accessible data that provides a foundation for innovative, agri-focused solutions for utilizing emerging technologies. Its goal is to significantly improve India's agricultural ecosystem and increase the productivity and income of farmers in this sector.

➤ The Food Safety and Standards Authority of India (FSSAI)—FSSAI provides food testing across the country by establishing 52 testing facilities and adding 62 mobile labs.

➤ Kisan Sampada Yojana—Under this scheme, farmers are motivated to construct food processing facilities close to agricultural areas. The creation and configuration of warehouses, as well as packaging, storage, and shipping, are all facilitated by Internet technology.

➤ Sensagri—The Sensor-Based Smart Agriculture program, with the collaboration of six institutions, has developed drone technology. Drones are used to survey land areas, gather data, and immediately relay the findings to farmers.

➤ Krishi Yantra App—The Indian Council of Agricultural Research (ICAR-CIAE) has built a web portal on its website to make sure that businesses choose mechanization technology. It helps farmers to select suitable equipment and financing options easily [37].

➤ Climate-smart farming methods—Using these methods will alter the ecosystem of the country and cut down on greenhouse gas emissions caused by agricultural activity. In the Gujarati village of Dhundi, farmers are now using this solar energy and other renewable energy sources to irrigate their fields.

➤ Water balance simulation model—This model helps in installing a roof-mounted water collecting system that results in water savings and security.

➤ Krishi Vani—It is an agro-advisory service using voice messages in the local language by using unique sim cards in mobiles, which educate farmers about the weather, market, agricultural information, government initiatives, nutrition, health, and livestock. The telecom firm Airtel and the IFFCO Kisan Sanchar Limited (IKSL) are jointly working in Andhra Pradesh, Telangana, and Karnataka.

➤ Krishi Gyan Sagar (KGS)—It is an extension model with ICT skills which is a web-based and mobile application that permits the assortment and allocation of data, the uploading of files, and communication in their native language with small farmers while providing them with personalized suggestions. It is a data collection tool that collects data and provides tailored information regarding soil tests in the local language.

➤ YouTube for agriculture—It is a farmer-centric peer-to-peer model that disseminates brief videos on farmers' experiences with technology in the local language.

➤ Kisan Suvidha—It is a website designed to provide information to farmers regarding soil nutrition cards, cold storage and godowns, soil testing laboratories, veterinary centers, diagnostic labs, and government programs.

➤ The National Mission on Horticulture—This organization works to advance horticulture as a whole, including the development of bamboo and coconut trees. Its name is HORTNET and is a web-based workflow system that offers MIDH financial help.

➤ Agriculture Infrastructure Fund (AIF)—Through this fund, financial support is given digitally in the form of interest subsidies and credit guarantees to beneficiaries like farmers, Primary Agricultural Credit Society (PACS), farmer producer organizations (FPOs), self-help groups (SHG), and state agencies/APMCs for the establishment of post-harvest management infrastructure.

➤ MARKET—This is a platform connecting various stakeholders, including farmers, the industry, policymakers, and academic institutions, to access information about agricultural marketing through a single window. The daily arrivals and pricing of goods at various agricultural marketplaces around the country are easier to access via web-based information flow through this G2C e-governance platform [39].

➤ The National e-Government Plan in Agriculture (NeGP-A)—This is a plan where the Federal Government grants funds to the states for initiatives including the application of cutting-edge technology, such as blockchain, robots, drones, data analytics, and artificial intelligence [43].

8.8   Future of Digital Agriculture

Agriculture has a rich history as one of the oldest industries in the world, experiencing a technological transformation. Digitization has brought about a paradigm shift in agricultural production systems, value chains, and food systems. The advent of digital technology has revolutionized the way farmers manage their operations, transitioning from traditional, hands-on approaches to data-driven decision-making. It has facilitated connectivity and interaction across the agricultural value chain. Farmers can access market information, connect with buyers, and streamline the supply chain through digital platforms. It enables them to make enhanced business decisions, improve market access, and increase profitability [28, 29].

More emphasis is placed on digital education and literacy, addressing climate change, greater adoption of technology, integrated nutrient management, integrated water management, crop diversity, and other factors to increase the productivity of food and ensure long-term food security for a growing population [45, 46, 49]. It is about to bring various disruptive opportunities that will tremendously benefit farmers and people all over the world by increasing agricultural output, consistency, resource, and time efficiency. The G20

Figure 8.8 Digital techniques in India (authors' own).

countries want to use technological advances to boost agricultural output, minimize waste, improve food distribution networks, and eventually, assure sustainable and equitable food access. The digital revolution aims to build an efficient food system and a sustainable environment that connects 570 million farmers to 8 billion people. It aims to increase the efficiency of agricultural policy development and implementation, quality control, traceability, and farmers' access to financial markets [30, 31].

Conclusion

The G20 nations collaborated in establishing a framework for global food security and nutrition. It indicates a recognition of the need for a comprehensive and diverse approach to tackle the food crisis. By working together, the G20 nations aim to bring about positive changes in their respective countries and contribute to addressing global food challenges. The G20 nations seek to leverage technological advancements to enhance agricultural productivity, reduce waste, improve food distribution systems, and ensure sustainable and equitable access to food [47]. Therefore, it aligns with the broader goals of achieving food security, promoting nutrition, and addressing the environmental impact of food production. Through continued investment and collaboration, digitization is paving the way for a better future for farmers, consumers, and the planet.

References

1. Vorotnikov, I.L., Ukolova, N.V., Monakhov, S.V., Shikhanova, J.A., Neyfeld, V.V., Economic aspects of the development of the "digital agriculture" system. *Sci. Papers Ser. Management, Economic Eng. Agric. Rural Dev.*, 20, 1, 1–6, 2020. https://managementjournal. usamv.ro/pdf/vol.20_1/Art78.pdf.

2. Ozdogan, B., Gacar, A., Aktas, H., Digital agriculture practices in the context of agriculture 4.0. *JEFA*, 42, 184–191, 2017. https://dergipark.org.tr/en/download/article-file/370149.

3. Sadiku, M.N.O., Ashaolu, T.J., Musa, S.M., Big data in agriculture. *Int. J. Sci. Adv.*, 1, 1, 1–9, 2020. https://www.researchgate.net/publication/348645848_Big_ Data_in_Agriculture.

4. Shen, S., Basist, A., Howard, A., Structure of a digital agriculture system and agricultural risks due to climate changes. *Agric. Agric. Sci. Proc.*, 1, 10, 42–51, 2010.
International Conference on Agricultural Risk and Food Security, Elsevier, https://doi. org/10.1016/j.aaspro.2010.09.006.

5. wbcsd, Collaboration, innovation, transformation, Ideas and inspiration to accelerate sustainable growth-a value chain approach. *WBCSD Consumption and Value Chain*, 1(11), 1-7, 2011. https://www.wbcsd.org/Archive/SustainableLifestyles/Resources/Collaboration-Innovation-Transformation-Ideas-.

6. Klerkxa, L., Jakkub, E., Labarthe, P., A review of social science on digital agriculture, smart farming and agriculture 4.0: New contributions and a future research agenda. *NJAS-Wagening. J. Life Sci.* Elsevier, 1, 19, 90–91, 2019. https://research.wur.nl/en/ publications/a-review-of-social-science-on-digital-agriculture-smart-farming-a.

7. Baryshnikova, N., Sukhorukova, A., Naidenov, N., Digitalization of agriculture: Strategic opportunities and risks for Russia. *International Scientific and Practical Conference "Digital agriculture-development strategy" (ISPC), Advances in Intelligent Systems Research*, Atlantis Press, p. 167, 2019, https://www.researchgate.net/publication/333721490_Digitalization_of_agriculture_strategic_opportunities_and_risks_for_Russia.

8. Runck, B.C., Joglekar, A., T. Silverstein, K.A., Chan-Kang, C., Pardey, P.G., Wilgenbusch, J.C., Digital agriculture platforms: Driving data-enabled agricultural innovation in a world fraught with privacy and security concerns. *Agron. J.*, 114, 5, 2635–2643, 2022. https://doi. org/10.1002/agj2.20873.

9. Diamond, A., Tropp, D., Barham, J., Muldoon, M.F., Kiraly, S., Cantrell, P., *Food Value Chains: Creating Shared Value to Enhance Marketing Success*, United States, Dept. of Agriculture, Agricultural Marketing Service, 2014, https://www.ams.usda. gov/sites/default/files/media/Food%20Value%20Chains%20Creating%20Shared%20Value.

10. Rushchitskaya, O.A., Kulikova, E., Kruzhkova, T., Rushchitskaya, O.E., Digitalization of agriculture as an element of food security provision at present stage. *International Scientific and Practical Conference "Digital agriculture-development strategy" (ISPC), Advances in Intelligent*

Systems Research, Atlantis Press, p. 167, 2019, https://www.atlantis- press.com/proceedings/ispc-19/125909494.

11. Kundius, V. and Pecuh, N., Digital economy in the agribusiness management and rural areas development. *International Scientific and Practical Conference "Digital agriculture-development strategy" (ISPC), Advances in Intelligent Systems Research*, Atlantis Press, p. 167, 2019, https://www.atlantis-press.com/proceedings/ispc-19/125909494.

12. Kuznetsova, N., Ilyina, A., Pukach, A., Opportunities and problems of digital transformation of small and medium-sized businesses in agricultural production. *International Scientific and Practical Conference "Digital agriculture - development strategy" (ISPC), Advances in Intelligent Systems Research*, Atlantis Press, p. 167, 2019, https://www.atlantis-press.com/proceedings/ispc-19/125909496.

13. Dukeyeva, A., Zhamalova, D., Yesmurzina, A., Yesseyeva, G., Digitization of the agro-industrial complex–a power tool of development. *International Scientific and Practical Conference "Digital agriculture-development strategy" (ISPC), Advances in Intelligent Systems Research*, Atlantis Press, p. 167, 2019, https://www.atlantis-press.com/proceedings/ispc-19/125909500.

14. Dongoski, R., Value networks: Next strategy driver in the food value chain, *E&Y*, 6, 22, 1–4, 2021. https://www.ey.com/en_us/food-system-reimagined/value-networks-next-strategy-driver-in-the-food- value-chain.

15. Benfica, R., Chambers, J., Koo, J., Nin-Pratt, A., Falck-Zepeda, J., Stads, G.J., Arndt, C., *Food System Innovations and Digital Technologies to Foster Productivity Growth and Rural Transformation*, International Food Policy Food Research Institute United Nations Food Systems Summit, Washington, D.C., USA, 2021, https://sc-fss2021.org/.

16. Voronin, B., Chupina, I., Voronin, Y., Digital agriculture as part of an innovative economy. *International Scientific and Practical Conference "Digital agriculture - development strategy" (ISPC), Advances in Intelligent Systems Research*, Atlantis Press, p. 167, 2019, https://www.atlantis-press.com/proceedings/ispc-19/125909529.

17. Rotz, S., Duncan, E., Small, M., Botschner, J., Dara, R., Mosby, I., Reed, M., Fraser, D.G., The politics of digital agricultural technologies: A preliminary review. *Sociol. Ruralis*, 59, 2, 203–229, 2019. https://doi.org/10.1111/soru.12233.

18. Tantalaki, N., Souravlas, S., Roumeliotis, M., Data-driven decision making in precision agriculture: The rise of big data in agricultural systems. *J. Agric. Food Inf.*, 20, 4, 344–380, 2019. https://doi.org/10.1080/10496505.2019.1638264.

19. Soma, T. and Nuckchady, B., Communicating the benefits and risks of digital agriculture technologies: Perspectives on the future of digital agricultural education and training. *Front. Commun.*, 6, 21, 1-4, 2021. https://doi.org/10.3389/fcomm.2021.762201.

20. Pyun, J. and Rha, J.S., Review of research on digital supply chain management using network text analysis. *Sustainability* MDPI, 13, 9929, 2021. https://doi.org/10.3390/su13179929.

21. Vanes, H. and Woodard, J., Innovation in agriculture and food systems in the digital age, in: *The Global Innovation Index 2017 Innovation Feeding the World*, Tenth edition, pp. 97–104, 2017, https://www.wipo.int/edocs/pubdocs/en/wipo_pub_gii_2017-chapter4.pdf.

22. Shamshiri, R.R., Weltzien, C., Hameed, I.A., Yule, I.J., Grift, T.E., Balasundram, S.K., Pitonakova, L., Ahmad, D., Chowdhary, G., Research and development in agricultural robotics: A perspective of digital farming. *Int. J. Agric. Biol. Eng.*, 11, 4, 1–14, 2018. https://www.researchgate.net/publication/326929441_Research_and_development_in_agricultural_robotics_A_p.

23. Bolfe, É. L., Precision and digital agriculture: Adoption of technologies and perception of Brazilian farmers. *Agriculture*, MDPI, Basel, Switzerland, 10, 12, 653, 2020. https://doi.org/10.3390/ agriculture10120653.

24. Seth, A. and Ganguly, K., Digital technologies transforming Indian agriculture, in: *The Global Innovation Index, Innovation Feeding the World*, 10th edition, pp. 105–112, 2017, https://tind. wipo.int/record/28330.

25. Wegner, L. and Zwar, G., Who will feed the world? The production challenge. *Food Chain*, 1, 2, 1–7, 2011. https://www.oxfamnovib.nl/Redactie/Downloads/Rapporten/who-will-feed-the-worldrr-260411-en.pdf.

26. Tavana, M., Shaabani, A., Vanani, I.R., Gangadhari, R.K., A review of digital transformation on supply chain process management using text mining. *Processes*, 10, 842, 2022. https://doi. org/10.3390/pr10050842.

27. Rose, D.C. and Chilvers, J., Agriculture 4.0: Broadening responsible innovation in an era of smart farming. *Front. Sustain. Food Syst.*, 2, 87, 2018. https://doi.org/10.3389/ fsufs.2018.00087.

28. Panday, D., *Digital Farming: Fostering Young People in Agricultural Landscape Technical Report*, WFO F@rmletter, Italy, 2017, https://www.researchgate.net/publication/320188634.

29. McFadden, J., Casalini, F., Griffin, T., Antón, J., *The Digitalisation of Agriculture: A Literature Review and Emerging Policy Issues. Oecd Food, Agriculture and Fisheries paper N°175 © OECD*, OECD, Paris France, 2022, https://ideas.repec.org/p/oec/agraaa/176-en.html.

30. McFadden, J., Casalini, F., Antón, J., *Policies to Bolster Trust in Agricultural Digitalisation: Issues Note. Oecd Food, Agriculture and Fisheries paper N°176 © OECD*, OECD, 1-12, Paris, Italy, 2022, https://ideas.repec.org/p/oec/agraaa/175-en.html.

31. Gómez, M., II, Ricketts, K.D., Dyson, C.H., Innovations in food distribution: Food value chain transformations in developing countries and their implications for nutrition, in: *The Global Innovation Index, Innovation Feeding the World*, 10th edition, pp. 113–120, 2017, https://www. wipo.int/edocs/pubdocs/en/wipo_pub_gii_2017-chapter6.pdf.

32. Agri Farming, Digital agriculture in India–Challenges and Opportunities, *Agri Farming*, 2, 11, 1-11 2023. https://www.agrifarming.in/digital-agriculture-in-india-challenges-and-opportunities.

33. Jain, B. and Dhar, I., Digitalisation of agriculture in India. *Team India Blogs*, 8, 22, 1-12, 2022. https:// www.investindia.gov.in/team-india-blogs/digitalisation-agriculture-india.

34. Bordoloi, P., India's Digital Agriculture Mission is about people, not projects, *AI Origins & Evolution*, 10, 22, 1-7, 2022. https:// analyticsindiamag.com/indias-digital-agriculture-mission-is-about-people-not-projects/.

35. Digital agriculture-the future of Indian agriculture. *IBEF Blog*, 1, 21, 1-11, 2021. https://www. ibef.org/blogs/ digital-agriculture-the-future-of-indian-agriculture.

36. Oyinbo, O., Chamberlin, J., Maertens, M., Design of Digital Agricultural extension tools: Perspectives from extension agents in Nigeria. *J. Agric. Econ.*, 71, 3, 798815, 2020. https://doi. org/10.1111/1477-9552.12371.

37. Nabard, Overview of agri clinic and agri-business centres scheme (acabc), *NABARD*, 2, 22, 1-7, 2022. https://www.nabard. org/content1.aspx?id=595&catid=23&mid=530.

38. Jakku, E., Fielke, S., Fleming, A., Stitzlein, C., Reflecting on opportunities and challenges regarding implementation of responsible digital agri-technology innovation. *Sociol. Ruralis*, 62, 2, 363–388, 2022. https://doi.org/10.1111/soru.12366.

39. Enam–India's nationwide electronic trading portal. *IBEF Blog*, 1, 22, 1-11, 2022. https://www. ibef.org/blogs/ enam-india-s-nationwide-electronic-trading-portal.

40. Pushpa Gowri, D., Ramachander, A., Manohar, C., Brand promise a strategic foundation to develop unique customer value and enter new markets. *IJSMM*, 10, 1, 1–7, 2021. https://archive.org/ details/2.-foc-jun-2021-ijsmmbrand-promise-a-strategic-foundation-to-develop-unique-cus.

41. Mass Challenge, Agriculture Innovation: 10 Tech Trends to Watch in 2023. *Agriculture Innovation*, 1, 23, 1-11, 2023. https://masschallenge.org/articles/agriculture-innovation/.

42. European Commission, Sharing Europe's digital future, Farm to Fork strategy for a fair, healthy and environmentally friendly food system. *European Commission*, 1, 23, 1–8, 2023. https://food.ec.europa.eu/horizontal-topics/ farm-fork-strategy_en.

43. Ministry of Agriculture & Farmers Welfare, Digital Technology in Agriculture. *Ministry of Agriculture & Farmers Welfare*, 1, 22, 1–8, 2022. https://pib.gov.in/PressReleaseIframePage.aspx?PRID=1847506.

44. Joy, S., India paving way for global food security; food production, distribution, schemes framework exemplary. *Financ. Express App*, 1, 21, 1-11, 2021. https://www.financialexpress.com/economy/ india-key-in-paving-way-for-global-food security-food-production-distr.

45. McCampbell, M., Schumann, C., Klerkx, L., Good intentions in complex realities: Challenges for designing responsibly in digital agriculture in low-income countries. *Sociol. Ruralis*, 62, 2, 279–304, 2022. https://doi.org/10.1111/soru.12359igital.

46. Ipe, B.T., Shubham, S., Satyasai, K.J.S., *Food and Nutritional Security in India. Charting the way to a robust agri-food system*, Department of Economic Analysis and Research, National Bank for Agriculture and Rural Development, 2022, https://www.nabard.org/ auth/writereaddata/tender/2501230131nrs-35-food-and-nutritional-security-in-india.pdf.

47. Gautam, R.S., Bhimavarapu, V.M., Rastogi, S., Impact of digitalization on the farmers in India: Evidence using panel data analysis. *IJMH*, 6, 1, 2021. https://sibm.edu/impact_of_digitalization_on_ the_ farmers_in_india.

48. Ahmad, L. and Nabi, F., *Agriculture 5.0 Artificial Intelligence, IoT and Machine Learning*, CRC Press, Location USA, 2021, https://www.routledge.com/Agriculture-50-Artificial-Intelligence-IoT-and-MachineLearning/Ahmad-Nabi/p/book/.

49. Sehgal Foundation, Role of modern technology in agriculture. *Report accessed from Sehgal Foundation*, 1, 23, 1-8, 2023. https://www.smsfoundation.org/role-of-modern-technology-in-agriculture/.

50. What is the food supply chain? *Harvard Report*, 1, 22, 1–8, 2022. https://hwpi.harvard.edu/files/chge/files/lesson_4_1.pdf.

9

Exploring the Impact of Artificial Intelligence on Agriculture - A Study on Farmers' Level of Awareness

Shrinivas Patil[1], Premalatha K. P.[1*] and Iqbal Thonse Hawaldar[2]

[1]CMS Business School, Jain (Deemed-to-be University), Bangalore, India
[2]College of Business Administration, Kingdom University, Riffa, Bahrain

Abstract

Agriculture plays a crucial role in eradicating poverty, promoting prosperity, and supporting a healthy and sustainable economy. This sector is expected to feed 9.7 billion people by 2050 and can effectively raise income and contribute largely to the country's GDP. It is evident that the application of artificial intelligence in the agricultural sector in the form of smart irrigation, harvesting robots, weather forecasting, autodriver tractors, drone-based fertilizers, smart farming, water management, networking, crop quality, adulteration detection, etc. is significant. However, the challenge is the reachability of the technological upgradation to the base level of agriculture, i.e., the usage of innovative AI-based agricultural tools and techniques by farmers all over India. The research considered farmers across 31 districts of Karnataka state and collected data using structured questionnaires in the regional language from 161 respondents. Even though most of the farmers were aware of a few techniques and tools of artificial intelligence, very few farmers have adopted those techniques in their farmland, which shows that the far-reaching implementation of innovative technology is still a challenge. The usage of social media platforms and mobile applications by farmers can spread AI awareness to a larger extent. The successful adoption of AI in agriculture fastens and improves agricultural activities, which in turn contributes to the economic growth of the nation.

Keywords: Artificial intelligence, technology, crop quality, awareness, agriculture

9.1 Introduction

Agriculture has become the main occupation in many countries in the recent past. The UN projected an increase in agricultural occupation from 7.5 billion to 9.7 billion by 2050. With the rising population, food production should increase by 60% more to feed the people [1].

However, crop health monitoring, plant disease diagnosis, harvest management, weed protection, weather forecasting, and plant management are still a challenge. The new technology helps farmers in understanding soil and crop health using technologies [2].

Corresponding author: dr.premalatha_kp@cms.ac.in

Kuldeep Singh and Prasanna Kolar (eds.) Digital Agricultural Ecosystem: Revolutionary Advancements in Agriculture, (161–174) © 2024 Scrivener Publishing LLC

Technologies like artificial intelligence help in identifying crop diseases, soil health, and plant health and also increase soil fertility and productivity as shown in Figure 9.1. This paper aims to study the farmer's knowledge concerning the adoption of artificial intelligence technology in varied activities of agriculture.

The adoption of artificial intelligence technologies like usage of sensors, mobile phones, GPS, automotive, machines, robotics, drones, and much more in the agricultural sector has contributed to improvement in crop management, water management, harvesting, soil testing, yield detection, pest control, weather forecasting, weed detection, fertilizer spraying, disease diagnosis, food safety, etc. These advancements support the economy's growth, food safety, climate change, employment, and production issues [3].

AI helps in early sensing, identifying, and diagnosing plant diseases using image processing techniques [4]. Artificial intelligence is also adopted to monitor food processing and assess product quality [5]. AI tools like e-nose and e-tongue are two important measurement techniques used to understand the quality of food grains for further grading and pricing. Artificial intelligence and blockchain-based farming help farmers in ways such as a) testing the soil health to know which crop to grow and when to seed; b) predicting the expected decrease in the crop yield to recommend the use of fertilizers; c) identifying crop diseases and applying the appropriate pesticides; d) predicting the over- and underuse of pesticides in the plants; e) forecasting weather conditions such as temperature, rainfall, cloud cover, sunlight hours, etc., to facilitate the smooth operation of agricultural activities; and f) maintenance of data security and safety using blockchain technology. Hence, technology is taking the shape of redefining farming in the present era, and this reduces the burden of labor costs leading to better farming practices [6].

Additionally, farmers can access chatbots to have automated interactions to support farming activities. There are robots, autoirrigation systems, autoelectric methods, and

Soil management: Testing and monitoring the soil for proper seeding.

Plant management: Diagnose the health of the soil and crop along with pest management, fertilisation and harvesting.

Diagnosis Process Management: Intelligent spraying/diagnosing of crop diseases.

Weather Management: Forecasting weather for the right time for sowing, spraying, harvesting, transporting, selling, etc.

Harvest Management: Auto farming (use of robots) reduces the labour cost and improves efficiency.

Crop Yield Management: Identify the expected yield and monitoring of crop growth.

Yield Grading: Grading of yield helps to get better price

Marketing: Forecasts the market price and supports with better market connect.

Figure 9.1 Application of AI technology in agricultural activities (source: designed by the authors).

many such things that facilitate farmers to increase yield productivity [7]. Precision agriculture and smart farming utilize the advanced form of information in agricultural processes and equipment to analyze the data for better decision-making. Machine language and deep learning are the two key focus areas of research, and even though AI and automation have reduced human efforts by improving productivity, there are many challenges still unaddressed for ensuring sustainability. Solutions to the technical issues have to be focused on by the researchers for harnessing the benefits at a larger scale [8]. Additionally, social media has impacted the rural youth as the usage of smartphones among the rural community specifically farmers has increased tremendously. Applications such as WhatsApp, Facebook, and YouTube are utilized as a source of agricultural information and for other learning [9]. According to a survey that covered almost 11,000 farmers across India, significant financial illiteracy is found among Indian farmers, i.e., the financial literacy score was just 33%. Inadequate knowledge about borrowings, savings, insurance, crop management, and innovative techniques has adverse impacts on the farmers as well as on the economy [10]. AI research with respect to the agricultural processing and consumer sector was found very low when compared with the input, production, and quality testing activities [11]. This paper analyzes the perception of farmers with respect to the implementation of AI technologies in the farmland and farmer's usage of mobile and social media applications.

According to the state government survey 2022, all the agricultural lands are computerized along with the village maps and geo-tagged survey numbers. The state government has implemented developmental schemes and programs like K-KISAN, FRUITS, Samrakshane, Krishi Bhagya, National Mission for Sustainable Agriculture, Raitha Siri, Krishi Yantra Dhare, Kirshi Abhiyana, and many more, but their reachability is still in question. It is evident from the literature survey that the awareness with respect to the usage of technology and adoption of artificial intelligence in agricultural activities was inadequate or very minimal.

9.2   Review of Literature

Artificial intelligence is a part of computing science that generates expert systems, algorithms, and programs [12, 13]. The main purpose of AI is to support decision-making by imitating the human brain in performing various situations and conditions [14, 15]. It is the ability of a machine or an equipment to think, learn, and act as human beings. The concept of artificial intelligence was introduced in 1956 but gained momentum in recent times [16, 17]. Artificial intelligence is majorly known for its computing capabilities and power and data and genetic algorithms [18–21]. AI is the process of manufacturing enabled by machines that can imitate human activities as original [22–24].

Artificial Intelligence in Agriculture: AI has applications in finance, manufacturing, medical science, security, education, agriculture, industry, and other sectors. The implementation of AI involves the learning process of machines. Young farmers are much more interested in investing their time in automation when compared with older farmers. AI has to be adopted slowly in all areas as it is still a new concept for many. Agriculture is gradually moving toward precision farming and growing at a rapid scale. AI has its applications in the early detection of plant diseases and unwanted weeds in the farmland, water management, usage of robots in seeding and planting activities, automatic fertilizer spray, harvesting, and many more. With the support of AI, database information can be gathered and utilized to communicate at the right time to the right farmer. As a whole, AI improves overall growth and increases the benefits for the farmers as well as for the economy [25].

Social Media Networks: Agricultural information is transferred through social interactions, and the agriculturist's network structures among farmers' neighborhoods determine their information-gathering capabilities [26]. Social networks function as a medium for the exchange of information between individuals who have common social and informational resources to share [27]. Social media platforms can have both positive and negative implications on the users.

H1: Usage of social media platforms has an impact on the level of farmer's awareness about AI.

Mobile Applications: The usage of mobile applications in agriculture essentially helps farmers to access agriculture-related information and avail financial services, get connected to markets, and increase visibility for an efficient supply chain. Unluckily, due to a lack of uptake of these mobile applications, most of the farmers have not realized the actual benefits of innovative technology [1].

H2: Usage of mobile applications has an impact on the level of farmer's awareness about AI. AI-based agricultural applications like weed detection system, precision spraying methods, crop health monitoring systems, and sowing quality testing can significantly decrease the agrochemical requirements to a certain extent, especially when compared with traditional systems. This results in the reduction of wastage of resources to unwanted fields that do not require treatment. AI adoption in a large number of acres reduces the cost, crop damage, and wastage of chemicals and also fastens crop production [28].

H3: The number of acres used for AI adoption has an impact on the increase in agricultural income.

9.3 Research Design

The research design for this study is descriptive in nature and follows a survey research method. The study considers both primary data and secondary data where the primary data are collected from farmers with the use of structured questionnaires. The questionnaire has been translated into a regional language of Karnataka and circulated among respondents in various districts of Karnataka having 31 districts with a rich cultivable land of 118.05 lakh hectares with a cropping intensity of 122%. Karnataka state is famous for the cultivation of crops such as rice, jowar, ragi, maize, tur, Bengal gram, ground nut, sunflower, soybean, cotton, and sugarcane on a larger scale along with exotic varieties of fruits and flowers.

Inclusion Criteria: The respondents were selected for the study based on two main criteria: the farmers should have been involved in agricultural activities for a minimum of 1 year and should be a user of a mobile phone.

The questionnaire was sent both through offline and online modes to farmers across Karnataka with the intention of collecting the data from all the districts; however, we received completed questionnaires only from 16 districts, the samples from other districts were not complete, and some errors were found so those samples were not considered for the study. The questionnaire consists of two divisions: the first for demographic data and the second for awareness of AI in agriculture. The details are as follows:

- Name, gender, age, income
- Educational qualification
- Ownership of land (in acres)
- Usage of mobile applications
- Usage of social media/search engine sites
- Awareness of AI in agriculture
- Reasons for not using AI completely
- Number of acres used for AI adoption
- Awareness of AI applications like GPS, sensors, drones, automatic tractors, and robots
- Usage of AI in activities like crop monitoring, automatic weeding, spraying, water management, and weather forecasting
- Annual savings due to the adoption of AI
- Level of satisfaction from the usage of AI

The researchers used 161 questionnaires which were completely filled and submitted by the farmers. The collected data were analyzed through ANOVA, percentage analysis, and regression analysis, and the representations were designed with the use of Tableau software and MS Excel.

9.4 Analysis

The analysis part consists of two divisions: descriptive and inferential analysis. The descriptive analysis is provided below.

9.4.1 Descriptive Statistics—Farmers' Demographic Profile

Table 9.1 shows that out of the collected samples (161), the majority are male farmers (100) and female farmers account for 61. Generally, in the agricultural sector, women act as a supporting factor, but there are certain instances where women have ownership of lands and are actively involved in agricultural activities. The majority of the respondents (50%) are young who are in the age group of 18–25 years; this shows that the young generation is more futuristic and aspirant toward the agricultural sector. The respondents who were considered in the survey belong to different agricultural income groups, where most of them belong to the Rs. 100,000–250,000 income bracket followed by 45 in the Rs. 50,000–100,000 group (28). Very few farmers were in the group of more than Rs. 250,000.

Most of the farmers surveyed in the research are in the age bracket of 18–25 years, in which many have completed their pre-university education (62) and some of them hold undergraduate degrees (19). It is identified that no farmer considered in the study holds a post-graduate degree. The majority of the farmers considered in the study (132) own land

Table 9.1 Respondents' demographic profile.

Sl. no.	Respondents' profile				
1	Gender	Male	100		
		Female	61		
2	Age (in years)	18–25 years	26–35 years	35–45 years	46 years and above
		8	38	24	12
3	Annual income	Less than Rs. 25,000	Rs. 25,000–50,000	Rs. 50,000 to 100,000	Rs. 100,000–250,000	Rs. 250,000 and above
		0	0	45	88	28
4	Educational qualification	Less than SSLC	SSLC	PUC	UG	PG and above
		28	52	62	19	0
5	Ownership of land	Yes	132		
		No	29		

Source: compiled by the authors.

in their districts, and very few are landless (29). Farmers with their own land have a better opportunity to utilize AI technologies for their farmland as they save land costs.

9.4.2   Awareness of Artificial Technology

   i)   Farmers' Awareness of AI Technology

A dichotomous question was asked to the farmers to understand whether they know about artificial intelligence adoption in agricultural activities. The majority of the respondents are aware of AI, and the percentage is high in the north Karnataka region when compared with other districts. Out of 161 respondents, 96 of them are aware of artificial technology adoption in agricultural activities (60%), and 65 are not informed/aware of the usage of AI (40%).

   ii)   Usage of Mobile Applications

Mobile applications such as GPS, document scanners, banking applications, Google Maps, geotag cameras, and agriculture-related applications were used by farmers, but the percentage is very minimal. Banking applications and agriculture-related apps were the most widely used.

iii) Usage of Social Media/Search Engine Sites
For choices like Google, YouTube, Facebook, Twitter, WhatsApp, and Instagram, the majority (153) selected Google and YouTube as the most used social media websites. Very few are aware of Twitter and Instagram sites.

iv) Adoption of AI Technology—Number of Acres Used
More than 70% of the respondents have used less than 2 acres of agricultural land with the adoption of artificial intelligence. Around 10% have used 2–5 acres of their land, and very few have used 5–10 acres for AI adoption.

v) Awareness of Different AI Technologies
It is highlighted in Figure 9.2 that the majority of the farmers are not aware of different artificial technologies like robots, automatic tractors, drones, aerial remote sensors, and GPS/GNSS. Around 80% of the respondents are aware of the usage of GPS/GNSS and automatic tractors in agricultural activities.

vi) Reasons for not Using AI in Agriculture
The lack of awareness about the technology is the main reason for not adopting artificial intelligence in agricultural activities. Some farmers think that AI is very expensive and there are risks involved in maintenance.

vii) Increase in Income after the Adoption of AI
Even though a very small number of farmers have adopted AI in different activities like water management, soil testing, and crop health monitoring, there was not much increase found in their income.

viii) Usage of AI Technologies in Various Agricultural Activities
The survey result shows that some (30%) of the farmers are using artificial intelligence technologies in agricultural activities like sowing quality testing, soil testing, crop health monitoring, automatic weeding, accessing market connect, accessing suppliers connect, weather forecasting, water management, crop insurance, and digital finance. Even though the percentage is less, there is an opportunity for the government and other private

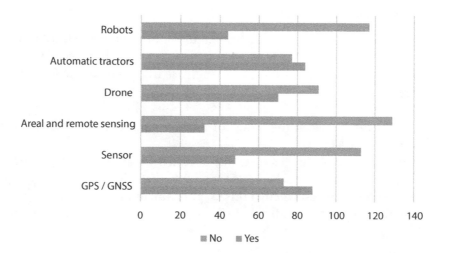

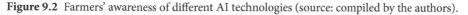

Figure 9.2 Farmers' awareness of different AI technologies (source: compiled by the authors).

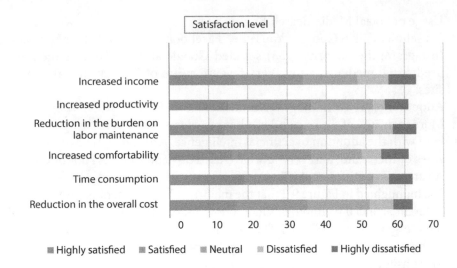

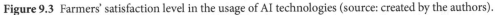

Figure 9.3 Farmers' satisfaction level in the usage of AI technologies (source: created by the authors).

organizations to create awareness among farmers with respect to the usage of different technological applications.

ix) Farmers' Level of Satisfaction

The five-point Likert scale was used to understand the farmers' level of satisfaction concerning the usage of AI. According to the survey, few farmers are using artificial intelligence for the purpose of soil testing, water management, insurance, crop monitoring, and others. From the Figure 9.3, it is clear that the farmers are highly satisfied with the adoption of artificial intelligence technology as it has resulted in increased income, increased productivity, reduction in burden, increased comfortability, and reduction in time and cost. Only a few have shown dissatisfaction toward the adoption of innovative AI-based technology.

9.4.3   Inferential Analysis

Regression analysis is used to check whether the usage of mobile applications and social media platforms influences the level of awareness about artificial intelligence among farmers and also to understand whether there is an increase in income of the farmers with the numbers of acres used for AI.

i) **Relationship Between the Usage of Mobile Applications and Farmers' Awareness of AI**

Farmers use mobile applications like document scanners, geotag cameras, agricultural-related apps, banking apps, and others. Regression analysis has been conducted to test whether this usage has an influence on the awareness about the adoption of artificial intelligence. The test results are as follows:

According to Tables 9.2 and 9.3 on regression analysis, it can be inferred that as the P-value (significance F) is less than 0.05, the alternate hypothesis (H1) is accepted. There is an influence of the usage of mobile applications by farmers on their awareness of artificial intelligence. There is an opportunity for institutions to use mobile applications to spread awareness about the importance and implementation of AI in various agricultural activities.

Table 9.2 Regression statistics for usage of mobile applications and farmer's awareness of AI.

Regression statistics	
Multiple R	0.1810
R^2	0.0328
Adjusted R^2	0.0267
Standard error	0.4867
Observations	161.0000

Source: compiled by the authors.

Table 9.3 ANOVA test for the usage of mobile applications and farmers' awareness of AI.

ANOVA					
	df	SS	MS	F	Significance F
Regression	1	1.275987924	1.275987924	5.386043315	0.02156873
Residual	159	37.66811146	0.236906361		
Total	160	38.94409938			

Source: compiled by the authors.

Table 9.4 Regression statistics for the usage of social media platforms and farmers' awareness about AI.

Regression statistics	
Multiple R	0.167315
R^2	0.027994
Adjusted R^2	0.021881
Standard error	0.487929
Observations	161

Source: compiled by the authors.

Table 9.5 ANOVA test for the usage of social media platforms and farmers' awareness of AI.

ANOVA					
	Df	SS	MS	*F*	Significance *F*
Regression	1	1.090218	1.090218	4.579311	0.033886
Residual	159	37.85388	0.238075		
Total	160	38.9441			

Source: compiled by the authors.

ii) **Relationship between Usage of Social Media Platforms and Farmers' Awareness about AI**

Social media is an information exchange platform where people across boundaries can access large amounts of data. Applications like YouTube, Facebook, and WhatsApp are used by farmers mainly to watch videos and chat with peers. The above table analysis of Tables 9.4 and 9.5 shows that the usage of social media platforms influences the level of farmers' awareness about the adoption of AI technologies in agricultural activities as the P-value (0.033) is less than 0.005, which results in accepting the alternate hypothesis (H2).

iii) **Relationship between the Number of Acres Used for AI Adoption and the Increase in Agricultural Income**

As the *P*-value (0.013) is less than 0.05, the alternate hypothesis (H3) is accepted, and there is a relationship between the number of acres used for adopting artificial intelligence technologies through different forms and an increase in agricultural income.

The regression analysis in the Table 9.6 reveals a weak positive correlation (Multiple R = 0.195334) between mobile app usage and farmers' awareness of AI, with the model explaining approximately 3.82% of the variability (R2 = 0.038155). The adjusted R2 of 0.032106

Table 9.6 Regression statistics for the number of acres used for AI adoption and the increase in agricultural income.

Regression statistics	
Multiple *R*	0.195334
R^2	0.038155
Adjusted R^2	0.032106
Standard error	1.343767
Observations	161

Source: compiled by the authors.

Table 9.7 ANOVA test for the number of acres used for AI adoption and the increase in agricultural income.

ANOVA					
	df	SS	MS	F	Significance F
Regression	1	11.38922	11.38922	6.307344	0.013022
Residual	159	287.1077	1.805709		
Total	160	298.4969			

Source: compiled by the authors.

suggests limited improvement with additional variables, and the standard error of 1.343767 indicates moderate variability in predictions, based on 161 observations.

The regression analysis in Table 9.7 shows a weak positive correlation (R = 0.1810) between mobile app usage and farmers' awareness of AI. The low R-squared value (0.0328) indicates that only about 3.28% of the variation in awareness can be explained by mobile app usage. The adjusted R-squared (0.0267) suggests minimal improvement with additional variables. The standard error (0.4867) indicates a moderate level of variability in predictions. With 161 observations, the model has a reasonable sample size for making predictions.

9.5 Discussion

The adoption of artificial intelligence has remarkable importance in the agricultural sector, but still, it has not been completely implemented across all the villages of the states. The majority of the farmers are not aware of how AI technologies can improve and fasten their agricultural activities [29].

The descriptive statistics with respect to demographic profile highlight that the majority of the farmers are aware of AI technology but most of them are not ready to implement it in farmlands due to lack of knowledge about the usage and benefits of AI. GPS, banking apps, agri-related apps, and document scanners are the most used mobile applications by farmers. Social media platforms like YouTube, WhatsApp, and Facebook are used by a larger number of farmers to watch videos and chat with peers. Few of the farmers have adopted technological changes in areas like sowing quality testing, crop health monitoring, weather forecasting, water management, and crop insurance. A high level of satisfaction is found among farmers who have implemented innovative AI technologies in their activities.

Regression analysis results show that all three alternate hypotheses were accepted leading to rejection of the null hypotheses as the *P*-values of all three analyses are less than 0.05. The test results of the hypotheses are as follows:

H1: Usage of social media platforms has an impact on the level of farmer's awareness about AI. Result—It is proven that there is a relationship between the usage of social media platforms on the farmer's level of awareness of AI.
H2: Usage of mobile applications has an impact on the level of farmer's awareness about AI. Result—The usage of mobile applications influences the level of farmer's awareness about AI.

H3: The number of acres used for AI adoption has an impact on the increase in agricultural income. Result—The number of acres utilized for AI adoption has a significant impact on agricultural income.

9.6   Implications

Academic Implications: There is a huge scope for academicians and researchers to conduct a survey to understand the implementation challenges faced by farmers and the level of awareness about innovative technologies and to support the regulatory bodies and institutions to conduct awareness workshops/trainings to reach the farmers.

Practical Implications: Agriculturists can fasten their process by adopting innovative technologies in their farmland and can reduce the overall cost and time involved not only in farm activities but also in activities like connecting to the market, digital finance, insurance, and other support systems.

Social Implications: As the nation's population is growing, food requirements and its safety and security aspects are also mounting day by day, so it is crucial to take up these aspects of understanding and creating AI awareness among farmers and institutions so that it increases crop production, reduces wastages, increases food safety, and serves the nation's requirement.

9.7   Limitations and Scope for Future Research

The study analyzed the awareness of artificial intelligence technology among farmers of Karnataka and concentrated only on a few applications of artificial intelligence. There is a large scope in understanding the complexities in the implementation of innovative technological aspects in the area of agriculture.

9.8   Conclusion

The implementation aspects and benefits of adopting artificial intelligence technology in agriculture have not reached the farmer's community on a larger scale. Through inferential statistics, it has been proven that there is a relationship between the usage of mobile applications and social media platforms and the level of farmer's awareness about AI. It is also evident that farmers can increase their agricultural income by utilizing more acres of land for crop production with the use of artificial intelligence. Technification in agriculture focuses on multiple areas like production, quality, cost, food security, climate change, and other agri-related issues. Institutions both at the government and private levels can reach farmers in large numbers through digital platforms and support them in the implementation of AI technology in various activities like crop health monitoring, water management, soil testing, automatic weeding, fertilizer spray, sowing quality testing, and weather forecasting. The study concludes that farmers with sufficient technological knowledge and institutional support can revolutionize the agricultural sector and contribute to the growth of the economy as well. Our research results can serve as a yardstick for future research in incorporating recent technologies in agriculture.

References

1. Giovannucci, D., *Sustainable Development in the 21st century (SD21), Food and Agriculture: The future of sustainability*, United Nations Department of Economic and Social Affairs Division for Sustainable Development, New York, NY, 10017, 2012.
2. Jadav, N.K., Rathod, T., Gupta, R., Tanwar, S., Kumar, N., Blockchain and artificial intelligence-empowered smart agriculture framework for maximizing human life expectancy. *Comput. Electr. Eng.*, 105, 108486, 2023.
3. Smith, M.J., Getting value from artificial intelligence in agriculture. *Anim. Prod. Sci.*, 60, 46–54, 2020.
4. Kuma, S.P., Tewari, V.K., Chandel, A.K., Mehta, C.R., Nare, B., Chethan, C.R., Mundhada, K., Shrivastava, P., Gupta, C., Hota, S., A fuzzy logic algorithm derived mechatronic concept prototype for crop damage avoidance during ecofriendly eradication of intra-row weeds. *Artif. Intell. Agric. Chin.*, Roots Global Impact, 4, 116–126, 2020.
5. Singh, V., Sharma, N., Singh, S., A review of imaging techniques for plant disease detection. *Artif. Intell. Agric. Chin.*, Roots Global Impact, 4, 229–242, 2020.
6. Tan, J. and Xu, J., Applications of electronic nose (e-nose) and electronic tongue (e-tongue) in food quality-related properties determination: A review. *Artif. Intell. Agric.*, 4, 104–115, 2020.
7. Talaviya, T., Shah, D., Patel, N., Yagnik, H., Shah, M., Implementation of artificial intelligence in agriculture for optimisation of irrigation and application of pesticides and herbicides. *Artif. Intell. Agric.*, 4, 58–73, 2020.
8. Sood, A., Sharma, R.K. and Bhardwaj, A.K., "Artificial intelligence research in agriculture: A review". *Online Inf. Rev.*, 46, 6, 1054–1075, 2022, https://doi.org/10.1108/OIR-10-2020-0448
9. Singh, G., Singh, P., Tiwari, D., Singh, K., Role of social media in Enhancing Agricultural Growth. *Indian J. Ext. Educ.*, 57, 2, 69–72, April-June 2021. ISSN 0537-1996 (Print) ISSN 2454-552X (Online.
10. Maji, S.K. and Laha, A., Financial literacy and its antecedents amongst the farmers: Evidence from India. *Agric. Finance Rev.*, Emerald Publishing Limited, 83, 1, 124–143, 2023.
11. Ganeshkumar, C., Sanjay Kumar Jena, A., Sivakumar, T., Nambirajan, Artificial intelligence in the agricultural value chain: Review and future directions. *J. Agribus. Dev. Emerg. Econ.*, Emerald Publishing, pp. 379–398, 2023.
12. Aldasoro, U., Merino, M., Perez, G., Time consistent expected mean-variance in multistage stochastic quadratic optimization: A model and a matheuristic. *Ann. Oper. Res.*, 280, 1–2, 151–187, 2019.
13. Colicchia, C., Creazza, A., Menachof, D.A., Managing cyber and information risks in supply chains: Insights from an exploratory analysis. *Supply Chain Manage. Int. J.*, 24, 2, 215–240, 2019.
14. De Sousa Jabbour, A.B.L., Jabbour, C.J.C., Godinho Filho, M., Roubaud, D., Industry 4.0 and the circular economy: A proposed research agenda and original roadmap for sustainable operations. *Ann. Oper. Res.*, 270, 1, 273–286, 2018.
15. Deshpande, P., Sharma, S.C., Peddoju, S.K., Abraham, A., Security and service assurance issues in cloud environment. *Int. J. Syst. Assur. Eng. Manage.*, 9, 1, 194–207, 2018.
16. Dolgui, A., Ivanov, D., Sokolov, B., Ripple effect in the supply chain: An analysis and recent literature. *Int. J. Prod. Res.*, 56, 1–2, 414–430, 2018.

17. Felfel, H., Yahia, W.B., Ayadi, O., Masmoudi, F., Stochastic multi-site supply chain planning in textile and apparel industry under demand and price uncertainties with risk aversion. *Ann. Oper. Res.*, 271, 2, 551–574, 2018.

18. Dubey, R., Altay, N., Gunasekaran, A., Blome, C., Papadopoulos, T., Childe, S.J., Supply chain agility, adaptability and alignment: Empirical evidence from the Indian auto components industry. *Int. J. Oper. Prod. Manage.*, 38129-148, 1, 3-12, 2018a.

19. Dubey, R., Gunasekaran, A., Childe, S.J., Luo, Z., Wamba, S.F., Roubaud, D., Foropon, C., Examining the role of big data and predictive analytics on collaborative performance in context to sustainable consumption and production behavior. *J. Clean. Prod.*, 196, 1508–1521, 2018c.

20. Dubey, R., Luo, Z., Gunasekaran, A., Akter, S., Hazen, B.T., Douglas, M.A., Big data and predictive analytics in humanitarian supply chains: Enabling visibility and coordination in the presence of swift trust. *Int. J. Logist. Manage.*, 29485-512, 2, 2–5, 2018d.

21. Dubey, R., Gunasekaran, A., Childe, S.J., Fosso Wamba, S., Roubaud, D., Foropon, C., Empirical investigation of data analytics capability and organizational flexibility as complements to supply chain resilience. *Int. J. Prod. Res.*, 1, 19, 1–19, 2019a.

22. Coleman, S.Y., Statistical thinking in the quality movement ± 25 years. *TQM J.*, 25, 6, 597–605, 2013.

23. Nguyen, T., Li, Z.H.O.U., Spiegler, V., Ieromonachou, P., Lin, Y., Big data analytics in supply chain management: A state-of-the-art literature review. *Comput. Oper. Res.*, 98, 254–264, 2018.

24. Nie, D., Qu, T., Liu, Y., Li, C., Huang, G.Q., Improved augmented lagrangian coordination for optimizing supply chain configuration with multiple sharing elements in industrial cluster. *Ind. Manage. Data Syst.*, 119, 4, 743–773, 2019.

25. Jha, K., Doshi, A., Patel, P., Shah, M., A comprehensive review on automation in agriculture using artificial intelligence. *Artif. Intell. Agric.*, 2, 1, 1–12, 2019.

26. Pratiwi, A., A. Suzuki Effects of farmers' social networks on knowledge acquisition: Lessons from agricultural training in rural Indonesia. *J. Econ. Struct.*, 6, 8, 2017.

27. Carlsson, B. and Stankiewicz, R., On the nature, function and composition of technological systems. *J. Evol. Econ.*, 1, 93–118, 1991.

28. Okoroji, V., Lees, N.J., Lucock, X., Factors affecting the adoption of mobile applications by farmers: An empirical investigation. *Afr. J. Agric. Res.*, 17, 1, 19–29, 2021, doi: DOI:10.5897/AJAR2020.14909 Article Number: 7CAAE6765726 ISSN: 1991-637X.

29. Eli-Chukwu, N.C., Applications of artificial intelligence in agriculture: A review. *Eng. Technol. Appl. Sci. Res.*, 9, 4, 4377–4383, 2019.

Precision Technologies and Digital Solutions: Catalyzing Agricultural Transformation in Soil Health Management

Anandkumar Naorem[1]*, Abhishek Patel[2], Sujan Adak[3], Puja Singh[4] and Shiva Kumar Udayana[5]

[1]ICAR-Central Arid Zone Research Institute, Jodhpur, Rajasthan, India
[2]ICAR-Central Arid Zone Research Institute, RRS-Bhuj, Gujarat, India
[3]Division of Agricultural Physics, Indian Agricultural Research Institute, New Delhi, India
[4]Department of Soil Science, Horticulture College, Chaibasa, BAU, Ranchi, India
[5]Dr. Y.S.R. Horticultural University, Tadepalligudem, Andhra Pradesh, India

Abstract

The advancement of digital technologies and innovative tools has revolutionized soil health management and transformed agriculture through precision techniques. This abstract explores the key components of soil health monitoring and assessment, including soil sensors, Internet of Things (IoT) devices, remote sensing and imaging techniques, data analytics and modeling, AI-based models, and precision irrigation management. By integrating AI-based models and data analytics, farmers and researchers can accurately evaluate soil conditions, detect anomalies, and make informed decisions for efficient resource allocation. Remote sensing and imaging techniques provide valuable insights into soil properties and spatial variability, aiding in precision agriculture practices. Furthermore, IoT devices and soil sensors facilitate continuous monitoring, enabling timely interventions and precise irrigation management.

Keywords: AI-based models, data analytics, imaging techniques, Internet of Things (IoT) devices, irrigation scheduling, precision irrigation management, remote sensing, soil sensors

10.1 Introduction

Digitalization in any sector offers high flexibility and integration of technologies. With the help of digital technology, businesses may use digital transformation to improve their ability to innovate and operate technologies more efficiently. This helps businesses to better understand market demands and encourage iterative product and service innovation. Internally, the enterprise structure will alter somewhat as a result of digital transformation, and this will encourage the enterprise to adapt to the external environment's structure. In order for businesses to develop new methods of value creation, digital transformation

*Corresponding author: Anandkumar.naorem@icar.gov.in

Kuldeep Singh and Prasanna Kolar (eds.) *Digital Agricultural Ecosystem: Revolutionary Advancements in Agriculture*, (175–190) © 2024 Scrivener Publishing LLC

requires a more effective and open organizational structure as the carrier [1]. Digital transformation is the driving force behind enterprise technological innovation since it results from the interaction between technical advancement and operational requirements of businesses [2]. It can serve as an external incentive to encourage business technical innovation, which is a requirement for organizations to realize digital transformation. As part of the digital transformation, businesses modernize and transform their industries and carry out technological innovation more successfully. This forces businesses to switch from the old innovation mode of traditional development to the new innovation mode of digital-driven development.

10.2 Importance of Soil Health Management

Soil is a 4D dynamic natural entity, existing at the boundary between the lithosphere, hydrosphere, biosphere, and atmosphere. In soil, liquid, gaseous, and solid phases interact at various sizes to produce a variety of ecosystem products and services. As a heterogeneous media, soil is home to a complex network of plants and bacteria and can be identified by a number of its characteristics. Four essential soil processes—carbon transformations, nutrient cycles, soil structure preservation, and pest and disease control—are all maintained through maintaining soil health [3].

As a living system, healthy soil performs a number of ecosystem services, such as preserving water quality, promoting plant growth, recycling nutrients from the soil, decomposing organic matter, and removing greenhouse gases from the atmosphere [4]. According to Doran and Zeiss [5], soil health is the ability of the soil to "function as a vital living system to sustain biological productivity, maintain environment quality, and promote plant, animal, and human health." Soil quality is another property used interchangeably with soil health; however, both are completely different. Soil health is an intrinsic soil property, whereas soil quality is an extrinsic characteristic of soils and changes with the way it is used by humans. While soil quality primarily emphasizes the physical and chemical qualities of the soil, microbial diversity and activity are significant contributors to soil health. "Soil health" refers to both the soil's short-term state and its long-term quality [4].

The assessment of soil health is based on factors related to soil quality that ensure the viability of crop production in agricultural areas [4]. Although it is very difficult to determine soil health directly, it can be inferred from measurements of certain soil characteristics related to it, such as the amount of organic matter present, soil fertility, etc. Therefore, changes in such soil properties are clear signs of the state of soil health. The condition of the soil directly affects human health. Since the beginning of civilization, the connection between soil and human health has long been understood. As a result, the "One Health concept" is evolving, according to which the health of planet Earth, animals, and humans are all interconnected. Soil health terminology and the idea of nutritional security are related.

There are four main soil ecosystem services considered during soil health management (Figure 10.1):

1. *Sustainable plant production*: A healthy soil is built on its biodiversity. Some management techniques, such as extensive tillage techniques and the exclusive use of inorganic fertilizers in intensive agriculture, are bad for soil

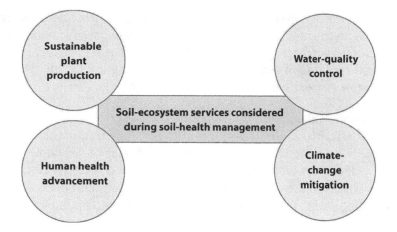

Figure 10.1 Soil ecosystem services considered during soil health management.

biodiversity and, consequently, worsen soil health. Thus, the adoption of regenerative farming which restores microbial diversity in topsoil must be made to maintain sustainable plant production as it maintains SOM, nutrient cycling, and microbial count.

2. *Water quality control*: As rain and snowmelt pass through the soil, it can act as a source [6] or sink of contaminants. The migration of nitrate, phosphate, or pesticide and their contamination to water can be slowed by vegetative filter strips around agricultural regions or artificial wetlands [7]. The common hydrocarbon toluene is one organic contaminant that soil biota can safely convert into other chemicals [8].

3. *Human health advancement*: Optimal micronutrient availability in soils is associated with lower malnutrition [9], and increased soil organic matter enhances the nutritional value of crops [10]. Antibiotics utilized in the medical sector, including streptomycin, are made by soil microorganisms [11]. The nutritional value of crops can also be increased by reducing soil-borne plant diseases and increasing the bioavailability of micronutrients to crops, both of which are influenced by a healthy soil biodiversity. Soils may have a harmful effect on human health.

10.3   Soil Health Monitoring and Assessment

10.3.1   Soil Sensors and Internet of Things (IoT) Devices

In many different applications, including agricultural, environmental monitoring, and smart cities, soil sensors and Internet of Things (IoT) devices are frequently used in conjunction to monitor and control soil conditions. Devices called soil sensors are made to measure several aspects of the health and condition of the soil. The IoT can be defined as "An open and comprehensive network of intelligent objects that have the capacity to auto-organize, share information, data and resources, reacting and acting in face of situations and changes in the environment" [12]. The sensors can be deployed in the ground and offer real-time information on soil moisture, temperature, pH levels, nutrient content, salinity, and other pertinent variables. Making informed judgments about the timing of irrigation applications, fertilizer applications, and crop management in general may require the use of data gathered by soil sensors [13]. For monitoring soil health, the following IoT gadgets and soil sensors are used:

Soil Moisture Sensors: The amount of irrigation used in agriculture is strongly correlated with soil moisture, which also affects crop productivity. As a result, a soil moisture sensor is a crucial piece of equipment for determining the amount of soil moisture at different depths. They provide farmers with up-to-date data on soil moisture levels, empowering them to optimize their irrigation schedules and prevent both under- and overwatering [14]. For effective water management and sustaining ideal soil conditions, this knowledge is essential.

Soil pH Sensors: Unquestionably, one of the most important environmental factors affecting soil biology and biogeochemistry is soil pH [15]. Additionally, pH levels have an effect on the nutrients that are available to plants. Measurement of soil pH in situ is challenging though. As opposed to this, IoT-based soil pH sensors can assess the soil's acidity or alkalinity, allowing farmers to modify the pH for the best crop nutrient uptake [16]. Maintaining the proper nutritional balance and avoiding toxicities or deficits requires regular pH monitoring of the soil.

Soil Temperature Sensors: The physical, chemical, and biological processes in soil that are crucial for plant growth are all significantly influenced by soil temperature, which can range from −10°C to 50°C [17]. Soil temperature plays a vital role in agriculture as it impacts various plant growth processes like germination, blooming, root growth, composting, and other essential aspects, along with influencing microbial activity. By monitoring the soil temperature, IoT sensors can assist farmers in making crop selections, scheduling planting times, managing frost-prone areas, and managing soil moisture [18].

Soil Nutrient Sensors: Among the soil nutrients, the most crucial nutrients for crop productivity are nitrogen (N), phosphorus (P), and potassium (K). Fertilizers containing N, P, and K are mostly used in agriculture to increase crop productivity. However, too much anthropogenic fertilizer input has negative economic and environmental repercussions. For the advancement of precision agriculture and environmental sustainability, accurate and efficient nutrient component detection in soil is crucial for plants to adapt to nutrient-deficient situations. Sensing data may now be transmitted globally more quickly, stably, and economically due to advances in communications and technology. This procedure aids farmers in identifying nutrient excesses or shortfalls, enabling them to apply fertilizer precisely and strategically. Farmers can enhance crop health and decrease nutrient runoff by maximizing nutrient management [19]. Optical and/or electrochemical techniques make up the majority of *in-situ* soil sensing methods out of all those that are accessible.

Soil Erosion Sensors: IoT-based erosion sensors can measure and track the rate of soil erosion. To determine the risk of erosion, these sensors monitor variables such as soil moisture, slope, and rainfall intensity [20]. Farmers can put conservation practices and erosion control measures in place to safeguard the health of their soil by identifying areas that are prone to erosion.

Soil Pollutant Sensors: Undesirable heavy metal buildup, pesticides, industrial waste, herbicides, and hydrocarbon pollutants improperly contaminating soil will result in soil pollution, which poses serious threats to the ecosystem and human health. Electrochemical, colorimetric-based soil sensors, bioassays sensors, and β-galactosidase-based colorimetric paper sensors are used for the monitoring of soil pollutants [21].

Soil Organic Matter (SOM) Sensors: IoT devices are able to assess SOM content, which is a crucial sign of the fertility and health of the soil [22]. By analyzing the reflectance spectrum of soil samples across both the infrared and visible wavelength ranges, it becomes feasible to identify the optimal wavelengths for predicting the SOM content [23]. Farmers can better understand soil structure, water-holding capacity, nitrogen cycling, and microbial activity by monitoring organic matter levels. Making informed decisions on techniques for managing organic matter and enhancing soil health is made easier with the help of this knowledge.

Soil Pest/Insect Sensors: Plant roots and bulbs may be directly harmed by soil-borne illness or pest, which may initially grow and flourish in the soil before becoming aboveground phytophagous disease. Moths, butterflies, beetles, flies, and other pests of equal importance are the main soil pests that cause agriculture loss. Sensors like optoelectronic, acoustic, impedance, and nanostructured biosensors are a few promising sensor-based techniques to identify soil pests [24].

Soil Compaction Sensors: Root development and nutrient uptake are hampered by compacted soil. IoT sensors can assess soil compaction levels, allowing farmers to see compacted regions and take remedial action [25]. Implementing suitable soil tillage techniques, controlling traffic patterns, and preserving ideal soil structure are made easier with the aid of this knowledge.

IoT-Enabled Soil Monitoring Systems: Multiple soil sensors and devices can be integrated via IoT platforms to enable thorough soil health monitoring. These systems gather data from multiple sensors, analyze it, and then offer farmers insightful advice [26]. These platforms frequently provide simple user interfaces for displaying and analyzing the data.

Farmers may make informed decisions regarding irrigation, fertilization, and overall soil management by using IoT devices for monitoring soil health. This improves soil resilience over the long term, conserves resources, lessens environmental impact, and maximizes agricultural yields.

10.3.2   Remote Sensing and Imaging Techniques

For the goal of monitoring soil, which is essential for sustainable development, remote sensing (RS) techniques can help more directly, cheaply, and quickly estimate crucial indicators. Here are several popular remote sensing and imaging methods for keeping track of soil health:

Satellite Imagery: In satellite-based remote sensing, sensors on the satellites are used to take pictures of the Earth's surface. The topic of spectroscopic imaging holds great promise for large-scale field monitoring and is attracting growing research interest. The health of the plant, soil moisture, and soil composition can all be determined from multispectral and hyperspectral satellite pictures [27]. Farmers and academics are able to spot possible problems with soil health and decide on the best methods for soil management by analyzing these photos.

Hyperspectral Imaging: Images are captured using hyperspectral imaging, which uses many small spectral bands. As a result, soil composition, nutrient content, and organic matter may be precisely characterized [28]. It also offers thorough information about the spectrum reflectance characteristics of the Earth's surface. Besides being utilized in laboratory settings, soil reflectance spectroscopy has found applications in diverse scenarios, including satellite sensors, aircraft, and unmanned aerial systems. The visible near-infrared (vis-NIR) spectrum, which has a wavelength range of 400 to 2,500 nm, can reveal details about the mineralogy, texture, organic content, and color of soil. Mid-infrared (MIR) spectroscopy on soil measures wavelengths between 250 and 25,000 nm. When a soil sample is exposed to MIR radiation, the fundamental vibrations of its molecular bonds give rise to the MIR absorption curve [29]. Numerous soil physical, chemical, and biological parameters have been successfully predicted using the MIR spectra [30]. The MIR spectra display a greater number of robust absorption characteristics when contrasted with the vis-NIR spectra, resulting in enhanced accuracy for predicting soil properties [31]. Thus, targeted soil analysis and property mapping are made possible with hyperspectral imaging.

Aerial Imagery: Recent years have seen a fast increase in the use of near-earth aerial imagery in soil health monitoring due to rapid advancements in unmanned aerial systems (UAVs), which enable low-cost data capture at high spatial, spectral, and temporal resolutions [32]. High-resolution data from aerial imaging can be used to monitor crop health, measure soil erosion, and find variations in the soil. Farmers can use it to sample soil from particular locations or apply site-specific soil management techniques [33].

Thermal Imaging: Thermal imaging can identify variations in surface temperatures and reveal information about water stress and soil moisture. In essence, a thermal camera functions as a heat sensor that gathers infrared radiation from objects and builds an image using its knowledge of temperature differences. Farmers may optimize irrigation practices and avoid overwatering or underwatering by using thermal image analysis to detect variations in soil moisture levels. Additionally, compacted soil or regions with poor drainage can be found using thermal imaging.

Electromagnetic Induction (EMI): Indirect contact sensors like EMI can detect the temporal and geographical variations in electrical conductivity of soil in real time [34]. Electromagnetic fields are generated by EMI sensors, which then gauge the soil's reaction. The soil texture, salinity, and moisture content can all be mapped using these data. When characterizing soil variability and locating regions with various soil qualities, EMI is especially helpful.

Ground Penetrating Radar (GPR): GPR is an environmentally friendly geophysical technique that employs radar pulses to analyze soil layers. It involves the collaborative functioning of an antenna-transmitter and an antenna-receiver to emit and capture electromagnetic waves in the ground. In essence, there are two primary categories of GPR units and antennas: air-coupled horn antennas, tailored to collect data from a distance ranging from a few tens of centimeters to over 1 m above the surface, and ground-coupled shielded antennas, which maintain direct contact with or remain a few centimeters above the surface being studied while data are being acquired [35]. The presence of subsurface layers or structures that affect the health of the soil can be determined by GPR, as well as the depth and compaction of the soil. It is frequently employed for determining soil compaction problems and soil profiling.

Light Detection and Ranging (LiDAR): LiDAR creates three-dimensional maps of the Earth's surface by measuring distances with laser pulses. Terrain characteristics, vegetation structure, and erosion patterns can all be evaluated using LiDAR data. Using LiDAR data in conjunction with additional data, such as soil moisture or nutrient levels, farmers can learn more about the health of their soils and use the best management techniques.

Spatial mapping and analysis of soil health indicators are made possible through the integration of remote sensing and imaging methods with geographic information systems (GIS) and data processing tools. These methods support farmers in making well-informed decisions on soil management, crop selection, fertilization, and irrigation. Farmers can maximize resource use, increase crop output, and improve agricultural practices' sustainability by remotely monitoring soil health.

10.3.3   Data Analytics and Modeling for Soil Health Assessment

In order to integrate and interpret different data sources, data analytics and modeling approaches are effective tools for assessing soil health. Here are some popular methods for assessing the health of soil that employ data analytics and modeling.

Statistical Analysis: To analyze soil data and find patterns, trends, and connections among various soil health indicators, statistical approaches can be used. Techniques including descriptive statistics, regression analysis, correlation analysis, and multivariate analysis aid in revealing patterns and clarifying the connections between different soil properties.

Data Integration: Combining data from several sources, such as soil sensor readings, satellite imaging, climate data, and historical records, is a common practice in soil health assessment. Utilizing data integration techniques, it is possible to combine and harmonize several datasets to provide a complete picture of the soil conditions.

Geostatistics: Geostatistical approaches are a significant component of spatial statistics, which is one of the main methodologies used in environmental statistics and has numerous applications in environmental surveys (such as soil science). For spatial interpolation and soil property prediction, geostatistical approaches like kriging are helpful. To estimate values at unmeasured places, these approaches take into account the spatial correlation between soil samples. With the aid of geostatistics, continuous soil property maps may be created, enabling a more thorough evaluation of the state of the soil across a landscape.

Soil Health Indices: Multiple soil health indicators are combined into a single numerical value called a "soil health index" that describes the overall state of the soil. These indices offer a comprehensive evaluation of soil health by using weighted combinations of different soil factors, including organic matter, pH, nutrient levels, and compaction. They can be obtained using statistical techniques like principal component analysis or professional knowledge-based procedures [36].

Machine Learning: Recently, numerous general statistical and data mining methodologies using digital soil mapping (DSM) have been used to estimate the spatial soil quality based on large datasets. These algorithms are able to find intricate patterns and connections in the data, allowing for the prediction of soil characteristics and conditions based on different inputs [37]. For applications like soil categorization, nutrient prediction, and disease detection [38], supervised learning techniques such as decision trees, random forests, support vector machines, and neural networks can be used.

Modeling of Soil Processes: Process-based models simulate soil dynamics and processes and offer insights into the health of the soil through time. These models take into account variables including microbial activity, carbon sequestration, nutrient cycling, and water flow. These models enable scenario analysis and aid in assessing the effects of various management practices on soil health by simulating soil processes.

It is crucial to remember that determining soil health is a challenging endeavor that calls for careful consideration of a number of variables, such as regional circumstances, crop requirements, and management objectives. Therefore, to gain a thorough understanding of soil health and make wise management decisions, a combination of data analytics, modeling, and expert knowledge is frequently used.

10.4 Precision Irrigation Management

Irrigation is one of the largest consumers of freshwater globally. Due to the growing scarcity of water, there is a need for the precise use of freshwater without compromising crop quality and yield through the development of more effective irrigation approaches [39]. Hedley and Yule (2009) [40] reported the possibility of about 25% of water savings through improvements in application spatially with varied irrigation applications. In this direction, precision irrigation has emerged as a promising solution, demonstrating noteworthy advancements. Precision irrigation is defined as "the application of right amount of water at right time and at right location, optimized to the specific needs of each plant or part of the field" [41]. However, in order to fully exploit the potential benefits of precision irrigation, the integration and implementation of supplementary technologies are imperative. Hence, smart precision irrigation considers the spatial and temporal heterogeneity of soil parameters, weather conditions, and hydraulics of the irrigation system. The field-specific conventional irrigation method is associated with overirrigation and less water saving, whereas precision irrigation takes care of variability in the field providing the advantages of water saving and productivity [42]. By effectively monitoring soil–plant–atmosphere factors, precision irrigation enables informed decision-making, leading to significant water conservation and enhanced crop yields.

Precision irrigation involves the integration of various components to achieve accurate and efficient water application. It incorporates smart information (sensor-based field data), smart communication (IOT-based functioning), smart control system (controller- and distributor-based allocation), and smart response (AI-based decision support) into the irrigation process [43]. These smart systems help to achieve optimal utilization of water resources while minimizing the negative effects on the environment [44]. In general, the precision or smart irrigation system consists of the following components:

10.4.1   Components of Precision Irrigation System

Precise Information

Moisture Measuring Unit: This acts as a primary monitoring device in the soil to record the soil moisture level. In the field, the point-based or network-based soil moisture monitoring is performed. The point-based monitoring records value at a single location only, while the network-based system facilitates the high-resolution moisture status by capturing variability in the field [45]. However, the cost involved could be increased with the increase in the number of sensors. Soil moisture sensors, tensiometers, or capacitance sensors are commonly used to collect data on soil moisture content.

Weather Monitoring Unit: For tracking of the local weather, recording devices are used. These provide data on weather conditions such as temperature, humidity, wind speed, and solar radiation. The collected weather data are utilized to estimate the water requirement of the crop/plant. This information is crucial for adjusting irrigation schedules and determining the appropriate irrigation amounts.

Precise Communication:

IoT Unit: IoT-enabled systems utilize the interconnected sensor network. The IoT system transmits the data collected from the sensors (soil moisture and weather) to a data storage device (local database or cloud server). This central data system creates the database to be used by advanced algorithms and analytics (Data Management and Decision Support Systems). Furthermore, the smart decision taken by the decision support system or analytics is transmitted to the central control system to deploy smart irrigation scheduling and water management accordingly. Moreover, with IoT in irrigation systems, the users can remotely monitor and control their irrigation operations using smartphones/computers. By analyzing historical data, IoT systems can provide valuable insights and optimize irrigation strategies for improved water efficiency and crop health.

Precise Control:

Irrigation controllers act as the central control unit for precision irrigation systems. They receive instructions from a server based on sensor and weather data inputs and automatically control irrigation operations smartly, including location, timing, duration, and water flow rates.

Positioning Systems: Positioning technologies such as global positioning system (GPS) enable accurate mapping and tracking of the location of irrigation. This information is also used to create spatially variable irrigation plans and ensure targeted water application.

Flow Control Devices: Flow control devices, such as valves and flow meters, coupled with the Arduino system regulate and measure the water flow in irrigation systems. They allow for precise control and monitoring of water distribution.

Variable Rate Sprinklers/Emitters: These sprinklers/emitters have adjustable water flow rates and can distribute water according to specific spatial requirements. They allow for precise water application, ensuring that each plant or section of the field receives the appropriate amount of water.

Precise Response:

Data Management and Decision Support Systems: These systems collect and analyze data from various sources (sensors, weather stations, crop models, etc.). The collected data are then processed with an AI-based decision system, and accordingly, the irrigation operation is performed [46]. Furthermore, this component (enabled with IoT) allows users to get valuable insights aiding in the supervision of irrigation operation (irrigation scheduling, water allocation, and resource optimization). They can receive alerts and notifications about critical parameters, enabling them to take immediate action when necessary.

Table 10.1 Sensors used in IoT-based irrigation systems (sources: [41, 47]).

IoT system	Sensors	Reference
Smart system to predict the irrigation requirements	• Soil moisture • Temperature • Relative humidity • Radiation	[50]
Intelligent approach for efficient plant irrigation	• Soil moisture (HL-69 hygrometer) • Humidity sensor (DHT22) • Temperature • Light sensor (BH1750 FVI)	[51]
Cloud-based AI for water stress detection	• Modified Canon • MAPIR Survey II cameras	[52]
Autonomous IoT-based irrigation system	• Soil moisture (LM393) • Temperature and humidity (DHT 11 digital) • pH sensors	[53]
IoT-based machine learning for the control of hydroponics	• Water level • Temperature • Humidity • Light • pH	[54]
IoT smart irrigation	• Humidity • Temperature • Soil moisture • Light	[42]
Irrigation monitoring system using IoT with data logging and analysis	• Humidity • Temperature • Soil moisture	[55]

10.4.2   Precision and Automation in Irrigation: Sensors and IoT

Sensor and IoT-based smart systems are promising in predicting real-time irrigation requirements in particular and significantly transforming the whole agricultural system in general [47]. Sensors are used to measure the data, and IoT technologies are used to communicate these data between sensors/controllers and data servers. For efficient irrigation, minimum water loss, and higher crop water productivity, the efficient real-time measurement of several soil–plant–atmosphere variables is crucial [41]. The sensor devices sense these related parameters as per their accuracy and precision. For example, soil moisture (real time) is a very important parameter to be measured accurately for irrigation decision and scheduling [48]. The wired or wireless network placed in the field at different locations continuously monitors the soil water status. Mostly, the low-cost capacitance-based (works on dielectric device principle) sensors of reasonable accuracy are used with the probe inserted in the soil [49], whereas for more accuracy, time domain reflectometry (TDR) sensors are used. The weather sensors measure the weather parameters (temperature, relative humidity, sunlight hours, wind speed, etc.). The main objective of real-time weather monitoring is to estimate evapotranspiration (ET) happening in the soil–plant system indicating the water loss to be replaced. Generally, the automatic weather station or wireless sensor network devices are used to measure all these parameters simultaneously in the surrounding environment [41]. Similarly, the plants' temperature and other related parameters (normalized difference vegetative index, leaf area index, stomatal conductance, etc.) are recorded by a corresponding sensor network (Raspberry Pi camera, unmanned aerial vehicle, plant canopy imager, porometer, etc.). Now the measured field data are transmitted to the server in real time using IoT devices like Raspberry Pi, Arduino prototyping boards, GSM network, etc. [41]. The sensor network and the IoT system together enable continuous data collection, transmission to storage device/cloud, and storage of gathered data. Hence, their integration with the irrigation system makes it automatic in operation with high accuracy and less human intervention. Table 10.1 presents some IoT-based irrigation systems and sensors used in the automation of precision irrigation.

10.5   AI-Based Models and Irrigation Scheduling

Precision irrigation systems and its components have gained widespread acceptance and implementation globally. The agriculture sector and other organizations have engaged in the automation of irrigation activities to reduce costs and enhance operational efficiency in irrigation practices. Several cases could be identified demonstrating acceptance, implementation, and benefit of automation of precision irrigation using digital technologies such as AI and IoT.

Pramanik et al. [56] developed an automated surface irrigation system based on basin layout, using soil moisture data. The system encompassed the establishment of wireless communication between soil moisture sensors (capacitance-based) and automatic check gates through IoT technology including employing the (Long-Range) LoRa wireless network protocol and GSM. The study tested three different irrigation schedules for three moisture deficit conditions (40%, 30%, and 20%). The system's efficacy was assessed through nine

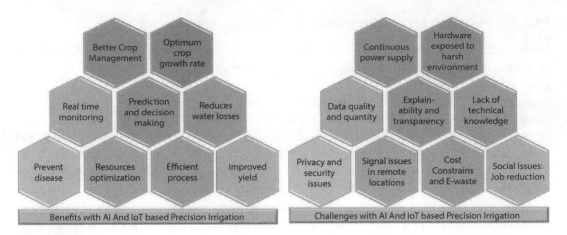

Figure 10.2 Pyramids of the benefits and challenges with AI- and IoT-based precision irrigation systems (compiled from [47]).

irrigation events conducted on bare soil. This integration of automation led to a substantial enhancement in irrigation application efficiency, reaching up to 86.6% for basin irrigation.

Zhang *et al.* [57] developed and evaluated an IoT (LoRaWAN)-based precision irrigation system for tomato production. The automation of irrigation for four different irrigation schedules based on ET, soil metric potential levels (MP60, MP40), and GesCoN-fertigation DSS was evaluated for irrigation water use efficiency (iWUE), system feasibility, and crop yield. The study reported overall iWUE of 22.2, 26.5, 27.9, and 28.4 kg·m^{-3} for ET, MP60, MP40, and GesCoN, respectively. The study found the LoRaWAN-based IoT system suitable in terms of overall performance and suggested that it can be implemented for precision and automatic irrigation operations to enhance crop water use efficiency and sustainability.

AgriSens, an IoT-based dynamic irrigation scheduling system for irrigation water management, was developed by Roy *et al.* [58]. The IoT-based AgriSens automatically monitors real-time water dynamics in the field and provides remote access of manual irrigation to the farmer. The system uses cost-effective water level sensors and is customized for automation in dynamic-cum-manual irrigation as per the farmer's requirements. The study shows improved crop productivity by 10.21% using AgriSens for irrigation over the traditional manual irrigation method.

The study exhibited promising possibilities of AI- and IoT-assisted irrigation systems to achieve precision; however, there are several challenges and obstacles that require attention (Figure 10.2).

10.6 Conclusions

The integration of AI-based models, data analytics, imaging techniques, Internet of Things (IoT) devices, irrigation scheduling, modeling for soil health assessment, precision irrigation management, remote sensing, soil health monitoring and assessment, and soil sensors represents a significant leap forward in modern agriculture. These digital innovations have the potential to revolutionize the way we manage soil health and optimize agricultural practices. By harnessing the power of advanced technologies and tools, farmers and researchers can gather real-time data, analyze it effectively, and make informed decisions to enhance crop productivity, optimize irrigation practices, and ensure sustainable land management. The combination of precision technologies, data-driven approaches, and remote sensing capabilities allows for a more precise and efficient allocation of resources, leading to improved soil health, reduced environmental impact, and increased yields. As we continue to explore the possibilities offered by these advancements, it is clear that they hold immense promise for transforming agriculture and paving the way toward a more sustainable and productive future.

References

1. Hrustek, L., Sustainability driven by agriculture through digital transformation. *Sustainability*, 12, 20, 8596, 2020. https://doi.org/10.3390/su12208596.
2. Mueller, A., Frolova, O., Makarychev, V., Yashkova, N., Kornilova, L., Akimov, A., Digital transformation of agricultural industry. *IOP Conf. Ser. Earth Environ. Sci.*, IOP Publishing, 346, 1, 012029, October 2019. https://doi.org/10.1590/1678-6971/eRAMR230055.en.
3. Lal, R., Soil health and carbon management. *Food Energy Secur.*, 5, 4, 212–222, 2016. https://doi.org/10.1002/fes3.96.
4. Tahat, M., Alananbeh, K.M., Othman, Y.A., Leskovar, D.I., Soil health and sustainable agriculture. *Sustainability*, 12, 12, 4859, 2020. https://doi.org/10.3390/su12124859.
5. Doran, J.W. and Zeiss, M.R., Soil health and sustainability: Managing the biotic component of soil quality. *Appl. Soil Ecol.*, 15, 1, 3–11, 2000.
6. Zimnicki, T., Boring, T., Evenson, G., Kalcic, M., Karlen, D.L., Wilson, R.S., Blesh, J., On quantifying water quality benefits of healthy soils. *BioScience*, 70, 4, 343–352, 2020. https://doi.org/10.1093/biosci/biaa011.
7. Tournebize, J., Chaumont, C., Mander, Ü., Implications for constructed wetlands to mitigate nitrate and pesticide pollution in agricultural drained watersheds. *Ecol. Eng.*, 103, 415–425, 2017. https://doi.org/10.1016/j.ecoleng.2016.02.014.
8. Hanson, J.R., Macalady, J.L., Harris, D., Scow, K.M., Linking toluene degradation with specific microbial populations in soil. *Appl. Environ. Microbiol.*, 65, 12, 5403–5408, 1999. https://doi.org/10.1128/AEM.65.12.5403-5408.1999.
9. Barrett, C.B. and Bevis, L.E., The self-reinforcing feedback between low soil fertility and chronic poverty. *Nat. Geosci.*, 8, 12, 907–912, 2015. https://doi.org/10.1038/ngeo2591.
10. Wood, S.A., Tirfessa, D., Baudron, F., Soil organic matter underlies crop nutritional quality and productivity in smallholder agriculture. *Agric. Ecosyst. Environ.*, 266, 100–108, 2018. https://doi.org/10.1016/j.agee.2018.07.025.
11. Schatz, A., Bugle, E., Waksman, S.A., Streptomycin, a substance exhibiting antibiotic activity against gram-positive and gram-negative bacteria.*. *Proc. Soc. Exp. Biol. Med.*, vol. 55, pp. 66–69, 1944, https://doi.org/10.3181/00379727-55-14461.
12. Madakam, S., Lake, V., Lake, V., Lake, V., Internet of Things (IoT): A literature review. *J. Comput. Commun.*, 3, 05, 164–173, 2015. https://doi.org/10.4236/ jcc.2015.35021.
13. Karlen, D.L., Veum, K.S., Sudduth, K.A., Obrycki, J.F., Nunes, M.R., Soil health assessment: Past accomplishments, current activities, and future opportunities. *Soil Tillage Res.*, 195, 104365, 2019. https://doi.org/10.1016/j.still.2019.104365.

14. Soulis, K.X., Elmaloglou, S., Dercas, N., Investigating the effects of soil moisture sensors positioning and accuracy on soil moisture based drip irrigation scheduling systems. *Agric. Water Manage.*, 148, 258–268, 2015. https://doi.org/10.1016/j.soilbio.2022.108862.

16. Yin, H., Cao, Y., Marelli, B., Zeng, X., Mason, A.J., Cao, C., Soil sensors and plant wearables for smart and precision agriculture. *Adv. Mater.*, 33, 20, 2007764, 2021. https:// doi.org/10.1002/adma.202007764.

17. Jackson, R.D. and Sterling, A.T., Ch. 39 Thermal conductivity and diffusivity, in: *Methods of Soil Analysis: Part 1 Physical and Mineralogical Methods 5*, A. Klute (Ed.), pp. 945–956, American Society of Agronomy, Inc./Soil Science Society of America, Inc., Madison, WI, USA, 1986, https://doi.org/10.2136/sssabookser5.1.2ed.c39.

18. Wang, H., Gao, S., Yue, X., Cheng, X., Liu, Q., Min, R., Qu, H., Hu, X., Humiditysensitive PMMA fiber Bragg grating sensor probe for soil temperature and moisture measurement based on its intrinsic water affinity. *Sensors*, 21, 21, 6946, 2021. https://doi.org/10.3390/ s21216946.

19. Rossel, R.A.V. and Bouma, J., Soil sensing: A new paradigm for agriculture. *Agric. Syst.*, 148, 71–74, 2016. https://doi.org/10.1016/j.agsy.2016.07.001.

20. Liu, C., Li, H., Xu, J., Gao, W., Shen, X., Miao, S., Applying convolutional neural network to predict soil erosion: A case study of coastal areas. *Int. J. Environ. Res. Public Health*, 20, 3, 2513, 2023. https://doi.org/10.3390/ijerph20032513.

21. Yin, H., Cao, Y., Marelli, B., Zeng, X., Mason, A.J., Cao, C., Soil sensors and plant wearables for smart and precision agriculture. *Adv. Mater.*, 33, 20, 2007764, 2021. https:// doi.org/10.1002/adma.202007764.

22. Wu, Q., Liang, Y., Li, Y., Wang, X., Yang, L., Wang, X., Factors acquisition and content estimation of farmland soil organic carbon based upon Internet of Things. *Chin. Geogr. Sci.*, 27, 431–440, 2017. http://dx.doi.org/10.1007/s11769-017-0875-9.

23. Krishnan, P., Alexander, J.D., Butler, B.J., Hummel, J.W., Reflectance technique for predicting soil organic matter. *Soil Sci. Soc Am. J.*, 44, 6, 1282–1285, 1980. https://doi.org/10.2136/sssaj19 80.03615995004400060030x.

24. Vittum, P.J., *Insecticide Series, Part VII: Insect Monitoring Techniques and Setting Thresholds*, TurfGrass Trends, Cleveland, OH, USA, 1997.

25. Serrano, J., Marques, J., Shahidian, S., Carreira, E., Marques da Silva, J., Paixão, L., Paniagua, L.L., Moral, F., Ferraz de Oliveira, I., Sales-Baptista, E., Sensing and mapping the effects of cow trampling on the soil compaction of the montado mediterranean ecosystem. *Sensors*, 23, 2, 888, 2023. https://doi.org/10.3390/s23020888.

26. Sudharson, K., Alekhya, B., Abinaya, G., Rohini, C., Arthi, S., Dhinakaran, D., February 2023. Efficient soil condition monitoring with IoT enabled intelligent farming solution, in: *2023 IEEE International Students' Conference on Electrical, Electronics and Computer Science (SCEECS)*, IEEE, pp. 1–6.

27. Babaeian, E., Sadeghi, M., Jones, S.B., Montzka, C., Vereecken, H., Tuller, M., Ground, proximal, and satellite remote sensing of soil moisture. *Rev. Geophys.*, 57, 2, 530–616, 2019. https:// doi.org/10.1117/12.2572395.

28. Chabrillat, S., Ben-Dor, E., Cierniewski, J., Gomez, C., Schmid, T., van Wesemael, B., Imaging spectroscopy for soil mapping and monitoring. *Surv. Geophys.*, 40, 361–399, 2019. https://link.springer.com/article/10.1007/s10712-019-09524-0.

29. Stenberg, B., Rossel, R.A.V., Mouazen, A.M., Wetterlind, J., Visible and near infrared spectroscopy in soil science. *Adv. Agron.*, 107, 163–215, 2010. https://doi.org/10.1016/ S0065-2113(10)07005-7.

30. Soriano-Disla, J.M., Janik, L.J., Viscarra Rossel, R.A., Macdonald, L.M., McLaughlin, M.J., The performance of visible, near-, and mid-infrared reflectance spectroscopy for prediction of soil

physical, chemical, and biological properties. *Appl. Spectrosc. Rev.*, 49, 2, 139–186, 2014. https://doi.org/10.1080/05704928.2013.811081.

31. Hutengs, C., Seidel, M., Oertel, F., Ludwig, B., Vohland, M., *In situ* and laboratory soil spectroscopy with portable visible-to-near-infrared and mid-infrared instruments for the assessment of organic carbon in soils. *Geoderma*, 355, 113900, 2019. https://doi.org/10.1016/j.geoderma.2019.113900.

32. Adak, S., Mandal, N., Maity, P.P., Mukhopadhyay, A., Drones: A modern breakthrough for smart farming. *Food Sci. Rep.*, 3, 9, 54–57, 2022.

33. Ge, X., Ding, J., Jin, X., Wang, J., Chen, X., Li, X., Liu, J., Xie, B., Estimating agricultural soil moisture content through UAV-based hyperspectral images in the arid region. *Remote Sens.*, 13, 8, 1562, 2021. https://doi.org/10.3390/rs13081562.

34. Doolittle, J.A. and Brevik, E.C., The use of electromagnetic induction techniques in soils studies. *Geoderma*, 223, 33–45, 2014. https://doi.org/10.1016/j.geoderma.2014.01.027.

35. Wang, F., Yang, S., Wei, Y., Shi, Q., Ding, J., Characterizing soil salinity at multiple depth using electromagnetic induction and remote sensing data with random forests: A case study in Tarim River Basin of southern Xinjiang, China. *Sci. Total Environ.*, 754, 142030, 2021. https://doi.org/10.1016/j.scitotenv.2020.142030.

36. Rinot, O., Levy, G.J., Steinberger, Y., Svoray, T., Eshel, G., Soil health assessment: A critical review of current methodologies and a proposed new approach. *Sci. Total Environ.*, 648, 1484–1491, 2019. https://doi.org/10.1016/j.scitotenv.2018.08.259.

37. Adak, S., Bandyopadhyay, K.K., Sahoo, R.N., Purakayastha, T.J., Shrivastava, M., Mridha, N., Assessment of soil health parameters using proximal hyperspectral remote sensing. *J. Agric. Phys.*, 18, 1, 88–98, 2018.

38. Mandal, N., Adak, S., Das, D.K., Sahoo, R.N., Mukherjee, J., Kumar, A., Chinnusamy, V., Das, B., Mukhopadhyay, A., Rajashekara, H., Gakhar, S., Spectral characterization and severity assessment of rice blast disease using univariate and multivariate models. *Front. Plant Sci.*, 14, 1067189, 2023. https://doi.org/10.3389/fpls.2023.1067189.

39. Adeyemi, O., Grove, I., Peets, S., Norton, T., Advanced Monitoring and management systems for improving sustainability in precision irrigation. *Sustainability*, 9, 3, 353, 2017. https://doi.org/10.3390/su9030353.

40. Hedley, C.B. and Yule, I.J., Soil water status mapping and two variable-rate irrigation scenarios. *Precis. Agric.*, 10, 4, 342–355, 2009. https://doi.org/10.1007/s11119-009-9119-z.

41. Abioye, E.A., Abidin, M.S.Z., Mahmud, M.S.A., Buyamin, S., Ishak, M.H., II, Rahman, M.K., II, Otuoze, A.O., Onotu, P., Ramli, M.S.A., A review on monitoring and advanced control strategies for precision irrigation. *Comput. Electron. Agric.*, 173, 105441, 2020. https://doi.org/10.1016/j.compag.2020.105441.

42. Kumar, A., Surendra, A., Mohan, H., Valliappan, K.M., Kirthika, N., Internet of things based smart irrigation using regression algorithm. *2017 International Conference on Intelligent Computing, Instrumentation and Control Technologies (ICICICT)*, pp. 1652–1657, 2017, https://doi.org/10.1109/ICICICT1.2017.8342819.

43. Bitella, G., Rossi, R., Bochicchio, R., Perniola, M., Amato, M., A novel low-cost open-hardware platform for monitoring soil water content and multiple soil-air-vegetation parameters. *Sensors*, 14, 10, 19639–19659, 2014. https://doi.org/10.3390/s141019639.

44. Shibusawa, S., Precision farming approaches for small scale farms. *IFAC Proc. Volumes*, 34, 11, 22–27, 2001. https://doi.org/10.1016/S1474-6670(17)34099-5.

45. Hamouda, Y.E.M., Smart irrigation decision support based on fuzzy logic using wireless sensor network. *2017 International Conference on Promising Electronic Technologies (ICPET)*, pp. 109–113, 2017, https://doi.org/10.1109/ICPET.2017.26.

46. Rajeswari, S., Suthendran, K., Rajakumar, K., A smart agricultural model by integrating IoT, mobile and cloud-based big data analytics. *2017 International Conference on Intelligent Computing and Control (I2C2)*, pp. 1–5, 2017, https://doi.org/10.1109/I2C2.2017.8321902.

47. Patel, A., Kethavath, A., Kushwaha, N.L., Naorem, A., Jagadale, M., Sheetal, K.R., Renjith, P.S., Review of artificial intelligence and internet of things technologies in land and water management research during 1991–2021: A bibliometric analysis. *Eng. Appl. Artif. Intell.*, 123, 106335, 2023. https://doi.org/10.1016/j.engappai.2023.106335.

48. Rajalakshmi, P. and Devi, M., IOT based crop-field monitoring and irrigation automation. *2016 10th International Conference on Intelligent Systems and Control (ISCO)*, pp. 1–6, 2016, https://doi.org/10.1109/ISCO.2016.7726900.

49. Shigeta, R., Kawahara, Y., Goud, G.D., Naik, B.B., Capacitive-touch-based soil monitoring device with exchangeable sensor probe. *2018 IEEE Sensors*, pp. 1–4, 2018, https://doi.org/10.1109/ICSENS.2018.8589698.

50. Goap, A., Sharma, D., Shukla, A.K., Krishna, C.R., An IoT based smart irrigation management system using Machine learning and open source technologies. *Comput. Electron. Agric.*, 155, 41–49, 2018.

51. Munir, M.S., Bajwa, I.S., Naeem, M.A., Ramzan, B., Design and implementation of an iot system for smart energy consumption and smart irrigation in tunnel farming. *Energies*, 11, 12, 3427, 2018. https://doi.org/10.3390/en11123427.

52. Freeman, D., Gupta, S., Smith, D.H., Maja, J.M., Robbins, J., Owen, J.S., Peña, J.M., de Castro, A. I., Watson on the farm: Using cloud-based artificial intelligence to identify early indicators of water stress. *Remote Sens.*, 11, 22, 2645, 2019. https://doi.org/10.3390/rs11222645.

53. Abba, S., Namkusong, J.W., Lee, J.A., Crespo, M.L., Design and performance evaluation of a lowcost autonomous sensor interface for a smart iot-based irrigation monitoring and control system. *Sensors*, 19, 17, 3643, 2019. https://doi.org/10.3390/s19173643.

54. Mehra, M., Saxena, S., Sankaranarayanan, S., Tom, R.J., Veeramanikandan, M., IoT based hydroponics system using Deep Neural Networks. *Comput. Electron. Agric.*, 155, 473–486, 2018. https://doi.org/10.1016/j.compag.2018.10.015.

55. Rajkumar, M.N., Abinaya, S., Kumar, V.V., Intelligent irrigation system—An IOT based approach. *2017 International Conference on Innovations in Green Energy and Healthcare Technologies (IGEHT)*, pp. 1–5, 2017, https://doi.org/10.1109/IGEHT.2017.8094057.

56. Pramanik, M., Khanna, M., Singh, M., Singh, D.K., Sudhishri, S., Bhatia, A., Ranjan, R., Automation of soil moisture sensor-based basin irrigation system. *Smart Agric. Technol.*, 2, 100032, 2022. https://doi.org/10.1016/j.atech.2021.100032.

57. Zhang, H., He, L., Gioia, F.D., Choi, D., Elia, A., Heinemann, P., LoRaWAN based internet of things (IoT) system for precision irrigation in plasticulture fresh-market tomato. *Smart Agric. Technol.*, 2, 100053, 2022. https://doi.org/10.1016/j.atech.2022.100053.

58. Roy, S.K., Misra, S., Raghuwanshi, N.S., Das, S.K., Agrisens: Iot-based dynamic irrigation scheduling system for water management of irrigated crops. *IEEE Internet Things J.*, 8, 6, 5023–5030, 2021. https://doi.org/10.1109/JIOT.2020.3036126.

Part 3

SMART FARMING AND SUSTAINABLE AGRICULTURE

Blockchain Technology—Adoption, Opportunities, and Challenges for a Sustainable Agricultural Ecosystem

Sweta Kumari[1]* and Vimal Kumar Agarwal[2]

[1]ATLAS SkillTech University, Mumbai, Maharashtra, India
[2]University of Technology & Applied Sciences (UTAS), Shinas, Sultanate of Oman

Abstract

This study makes an all-inclusive and comprehensive effort to include the applications and difficulties of blockchain in the agricultural sector. It begins by investigating how the blockchain functions, including its data structures, smart contracts, digital encryption methods, and procedures. It also gives an overview of recent improvements in agricultural practices. Second, it looks at several blockchain-based agricultural applications, such as those that deal with the supply chain, the accuracy of production records, product tracing, intelligent farming, sustainable water management, and index-based crop insurance systems. It also reflects on the possible applications of smart contracts in agriculture. The report is based on secondary research using a range of academic research papers found through Google Scholar and a range of articles released by research and consulting firms. Implications are drawn with regard to the feasibility of using blockchain in the farming sector. The chapter concludes by indicating future directions of research in this field and offers various stakeholders, including academicians, policymakers, and farmers, insightful material about how blockchain technology can reform the agricultural sector.

Keywords: Blockchain, agriculture, food safety, sustainability, supply chain

11.1 Introduction

The agricultural sector occupies a very important place in any economy. With an ever-increasing world population, the market demand for almost all agricultural products is growing rapidly. Consumers are also becoming more aware and are looking for details about breeding techniques and cultivation. They want healthy options and high-quality products. In such a scenario, technological innovations can play a dynamic role and actively support in meeting all the challenges faced by the agricultural sector. In fact, precision agriculture, Industry 4.0, and other upcoming technologies all aim at the integration of

Corresponding author: sweta.kumari@atlasuniversity.edu.in

Kuldeep Singh and Prasanna Kolar (eds.) Digital Agricultural Ecosystem: Revolutionary Advancements in Agriculture, (193–210) © 2024 Scrivener Publishing LLC

technology in the agricultural sector. Technology can help to elevate productivity besides developing novel business models [1].

The growth and development of any sector may depend on numerous factors, among which continuous research and investment in advanced technologies are significant. The same also holds true for the agricultural sector. The use of technology can favorably increase the productivity of the sector [2]. With precision agriculture, artificial intelligence, and Industry 4.0 coming in and driving all sectors, there is a greater need to use these emergent technologies in agriculture. Prominent among these developing technologies are blockchain and artificial intelligence. The use of these technologies and the digital revolution of the agricultural sector represents a complete transformation of procedures and processes in agriculture toward flexibility, automation scalability, increased quality, and greater productivity [3].

Of all the growing technologies, blockchain is considered to be disruptive, and its importance and use are growing continuously. Beyond the usual financial applications of blockchain, many other sectors are making extensive use of this disruptive technology. Blockchain applications are being used heavily in areas such as accounting, finance, manufacturing, security and information, data storage, supply chain, supervision, digital purchasing, and transaction recording, to name just a few [4].

11.1.1   What is Blockchain?

Blockchain technology is the "next big thing," being used all over to create new models of business. A blockchain contains blocks, nodes, and master nodes all connected through a chain. Nodes basically take care of the network's blocks. Creating a blockchain by adding blocks requires mathematical problem-solving and is a difficult task. The blockchain's capacity to increase is controlled by the solving of complex mathematical puzzles. Hacking or varying the blockchain network is not possible due to the distinctiveness of codes [5]. A blockchain stores data in the form of unique codes in such a manner that it is not possible to hack or deceive the network. Diverse sets of data known as blocks are interconnected through a chain, thus deriving its name, blockchain. Blockchain is nothing but a distributed ledger, and a copy of the ledger is made available on all connected computers. A blockchain is thus a network that photocopies and dispenses copies of a transaction record [6]. A blockchain is basically a distributed ledger, and agents in the chain take turns in the recording. This distributed ledger is jointly managed by all the participating parties, together with the help of a peer-to-peer network. Any addition of a new record is first verified and only on verification that it is added to the blockchain. Similarly, modification in the already recorded and existing data should have consent from all parties. It should also be noted that any alteration to a record will alter all the subsequent records in the chain. Therefore, it is nearly impossible to modify or alter the data logged in any of the blockchains [7].

> Blockchain is a transactional ledger but in the digital form

Blockchain is regarded as "an open, distributed ledger that can record transactions between two parties efficiently and in a verifiable and permanent way." Blockchain is thus capable of transforming and bringing about a complete revolution of data capture in any sector, and the agricultural sector is not an exception. Decentralized applications (Dapps) are prominent features of the blockchain and enable people to interact and connect directly. They are applications existing in a decentralized form and can be run and stored on all the computers that are in a blockchain instead of a centralized single server. The fundamental idea is to have a global and comprehensive computer that is distributed and facilitates the blockchain where everything is recorded and kept unquestionably. One copy of the blockchain will be available to all the parties [8].

In the current scenario, consumers' expectations concerning the origin and quality of food are high, and this has resulted in an increased inclination to spend a sufficient amount of monetary resources on high-quality and certified food products. Notwithstanding the technologies that are already in use, in most of the cases, traceability and tracking structures are completely obsolete, especially with regard to data sharing. Existing systems also lack transparency and safety because of the non-availability of quick, trustworthy, or reliable means to recover required information on the origin or source of food products. Considering all these factors, along with speedy technological innovations, distributed ledger technologies (DLT), commonly known as blockchain, offers unique solutions to many of the prevailing problems in the agricultural sector but simultaneously may also pose some challenges [9].

In the last few years, a significant increase in the practical use and application of blockchain in the supply chains of the agricultural ecosystem has been noticeable. Traceability addresses a wide range of questions on food fraud, compliance with regulations, food security, and consumer awareness. Tracking of agricultural products can lead to amplified value and increased profit, in addition to a significant reduction in costs in the agricultural sector [10].

Figure 11.1 shows the exceptional features of blockchain technology in agricultural sector. Blockchain in agriculture can be used to improve food safety and record transaction times. The agricultural sector, together with the food sector, is considered to be one of the major global employers. The supply chain of the agricultural sector is complicated, and its management includes coordination among a large number of stakeholders, farmers,

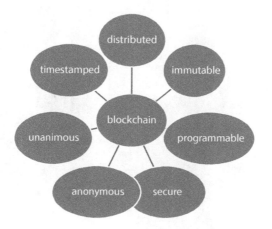

Figure 11.1 Features of blockchain.

customers, retailers, and distributors. The use of blockchain can accurately identify the origin or the source of the food and contribute to constructing dependable supply chains while also increasing customer confidence [11]. Blockchains make farming smart and also allow timely payouts to all the stakeholders with the help of smart contracts. The ever-increasing interest in the adoption of blockchain technology in agriculture requires a systematic outline. Blockchain has great potential in the agricultural space as it offers solutions to all stakeholders [12]. Trustworthy data are made easier through blockchain, and it offers transparency among all the parties. Blockchain makes it convenient for sellers and buyers to communicate directly through a decentralized system and decide on a fair price, guaranteeing that the farmers are paid well. Blockchain technology can also be used to reduce losses due to human error [13].

11.1.2   Recent Developments and Investments in Indian Agriculture and Food Industry

Investment and development in India's agricultural industry have increased significantly as the government has made steps to raise crop and animal production and improve market infrastructure. The industry has attracted huge funds in foreign direct investment (FDI) and private investment in the recent past. The global processed food industry sector is projected to reach Rs. 3,451,352.5 crores (US$ 470 billion), with a compound annual growth rate (CAGR) of 10%, due in large part to the organic food category. Furthermore, by 2025 (source: IBEF), US$ 30–35 billion would have been invested in Indian aggrotech firms.

The sustainability of India's agricultural industry and its exports is mixed, as shown by the statistics in Figure 11.2. The fast growth of India's population is one of the main forces

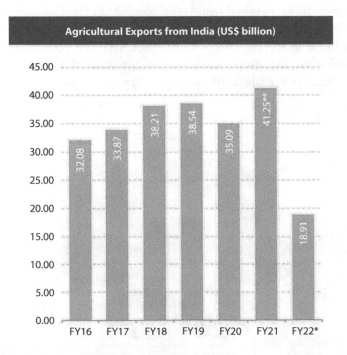

Figure 11.2 Agriculture exports from India (source: www.ibef.org).

propelling the agriculture sector which is anticipated to reach US$ 24 billion by the year 2025. This emphasizes the need for environmentally friendly farming methods that can keep up with the rising demand for food without compromising on either front.

The efficiency and production of agriculture can be increased through the use of pioneering tools such as artificial intelligence (AI), blockchain, geographic information systems (GIS), remote sensing technologies, and drones. It is critical, however, that these technologies be deployed in a way that does not compromise ecological balance or exacerbate global warming.

Climate variations and change is a key problem for the agricultural industry in India. Droughts and floods are only a few instances of the kinds of extreme weather that may wreak havoc on agricultural output and threaten food supplies. Therefore, sustainable practices that may assist in lessening the impact of climate change must be implemented immediately. Renewable energy sources, such as solar electricity, could assist in reducing emissions of greenhouse gases and fighting climate change. India's agriculture industry has the ability to contribute to sustainable development, as seen by the country's export statistics for commodities, including marine products, rice, buffalo meat, sugar, tea, and coffee. Exports may be beneficial, but only if they are generated in a way that does not harm the environment or cause social inequity. The export of marine goods, for instance, may have a major effect on aquatic environments and ecosystems. Therefore, it is crucial to maintain sustainable fishing methods that do not add to overfishing or damage marine environments.

There are social and environmental costs associated with producing rice, buffalo meat, sugar, tea, and coffee. Chemical fertilizers and pesticides, for instance, can harm soil quality and contaminate water supplies. Therefore, it is crucial to advocate for environmentally friendly and socially fair farming methods.

Increased investments in infrastructure, including irrigation facilities, warehousing, and cold storage, are anticipated to propel India's agricultural industry to new heights in future years. Increasing agricultural yields is another reason why farmers are interested in genetically modified crops. Investments in the fisheries industry are also part of the government's plan to double fish output to 220 lakh tons by 2024–2025. There will be many positive outcomes as a result of the food processing sector's implementation of safety and quality assurance methods like total quality management and good manufacturing practices. The PMKSY plan, funded with an allocated Rs. 4,600 crores from the Ministry of Food Processing Industries through March 2026, is an initiative aimed at increasing investment

Uttar Pradesh
West Bengal
Madhya Pradesh
Karnataka
Maharashtra
Punjab
Rajasthan

Figure 11.3 Agri-cluster of India (source: www.ibef.org).

in India's food processing sector. Increased investment and government backing have created favorable conditions for the expansion of India's agricultural sector (IBEF). Some areas within the different Indian states are particularly well-known for their agricultural output and are hence recognized as important agricultural clusters. Uttar Pradesh, Madhya Pradesh, Rajasthan, West Bengal, Karnataka, Punjab, Maharashtra, and Assam are all examples of such states (see Figure 11.3).

11.2   Blockchain in the Agriculture Ecosystem

Blockchain has plenty of applications in diverse fields, and the agricultural sector is one of the sectors where its implementation can bring very promising results. In fact, blockchain can bring about breakthroughs in this sector with its ever-increasing potential. Blockchain technology facilitates the availability of information throughout the supply chain, thereby promoting sustainability in the sector. It also helps to enhance food safety as it can store data that allow for the traceability of agricultural products. Also, the use of blockchain in the area of smart farming or intelligent farming is assuming importance. Crop insurance systems are being increasingly based on decentralized finance systems using blockchain and smart contracts. Blockchain can provide information about the quality of plants, crop growth, and seed quality. It can even record the journey of the product once it leaves the fields. These data can dramatically bring about the required transparency in the supply chain and eliminate any concerns arising from unethical procedures. It also allows for tracking of any contamination back to the original source [14]. Blockchain application in the agri-sector thus includes food safety, traceability of supply chains, management of information, crop certification, agro-trade, finance, and insurance, to name a few. Thus, this digital and disruptive technology promotes sustainability and growth, and when the consumers get increased transparency, they make informed decisions and, in turn, use the information to reward producers and farmers who implement digital farming methods using blockchain. The application in agriculture has a very wide scope and it includes food safety through traceability of provenance, agro-trade, information system, crop certification, agri-finance and insurance, etc. [15].

China has been at the forefront of developing its rural and countryside economy as an elementary nationwide policy, and it has widely and successfully used blockchain to provide the required technical backing for the growth of its rural economy. Investigational data show that sustainable agriculture and digital farming using technologies like blockchain bring greater scope of farm sales, increasing such by an average minimum of 25% [16].

The Indian state and the central government together ensure food security through the "Public Distribution System" (PDS). The Indian ASC (Agricultural Supply Chain) is semi-integrated, complex, and unorganized. It involves numerous intermediaries, resulting in an incompetent agri-environment. Furthermore, food security plans are vulnerable to losses in ASC due to scarce infrastructure, inappropriate handling, and lack of marketing facilities, making it difficult to guarantee sustainable food security. Further wastage and corruption often result in unproductive food distribution. Thus, technology upgrade through blockchain is considered essential for developing countries like India. Blockchain can be combined with PDS to monitor and ensure sustainable agriculture [17].

Furthermore, diversification into different agricultural supplies, typically fruits and vegetables, has assumed momentous policy attention in most of the developing countries. The drive for diversification is to ensure a growing demand for fresh and organic food by the consumers, besides reducing farm poverty. Food safety is often the key concern for consumer welfare, but at the same time, the producer's ability to standardize the global supply chain is important to increase income and reduce risks and uncertainty in the existing supply chain. Also, postharvest loss and wastage of farm products at the fields, throughout the storage points, and at retail and wholesale markets, are challenging concerns and also result in the decline of export competitiveness. These challenges can be overcome by the use of blockchain which can provide direct marketing platforms, ensuring food safety, traceability, high quality, and transparency. Pre- and postharvest management are challenging issues, and food manufacturers have shown increased interest in using blockchain [18].

11.2.1 Cases of Blockchain Use in Agriculture

Blockchain in agriculture can result in increased transparency, reinforce trustworthiness, eradicate redundant intermediaries from the agricultural supply chain, and increase customers' confidence and willingness to pay higher prices for quality products.

11.2.2 Management of Supply Chains

A supply chain is the journey of goods from suppliers to customers. The flow of goods has a major impact on quality and cost. While all the food products in the agriculture business pass through several players from the fields to the plate, there is a strong desire on the part of the consumers to understand what they are eating and where is it coming from. Supply chains in this sector have also become lengthier and more complex, involving many players and further increasing concerns about the origin and flow of food products. Here, blockchain serves to bring traceability of the food product to its original source. Sensors are now being used by aggrotech companies, and in this context, blockchain can be successfully used to compile data on various issues, like crop tracking, seed quality, and the exact path of food crops from the fields to the final market.

Besides bringing transparency to the entire supply chain, blockchain can result in improved security by elimination of unethical practices of crop production, enabling consumers to make better and informed decisions. Comprehensive data collection using blockchain may also help the farmers [19].

Figure 11.4 shows stakeholders of the agricultural supply chain. Supply chains are always managed by centralized systems, such as enterprise resource management systems, which are susceptible to hacking, errors, or corruption. Blockchain helps in managing these issues as it is not only digital but also decentralized. This disruptive technology allows for the tracking of the flow of food products from their source throughout the entire supply chain on a real-time basis. It also gives the operators of the supply chain relevant information on what was done by whom and at the exact time when it was done [20]. It is also easy and convenient to effectively communicate throughout the entire supply chain using this technology as it is decentralized and does away with intermediaries providing reliable and accurate info to the stakeholders in the supply chain. The use of the technology thus leads to the sustainability of the agricultural sector. The use of blockchain in this sector also increases

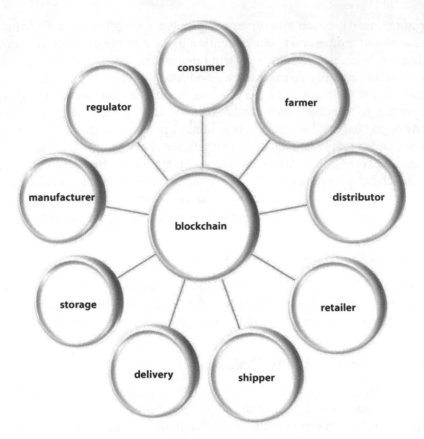

Figure 11.4 Stakeholders of the agricultural supply chain.

transparency as it makes it possible and easy to track the product precisely from farms to its final delivery to the consumer [21].

11.2.3   Smart Contracts and Agriculture

Smart contracts help in discarding the intermediaries. All the contributing parties can directly interact with each other through a smart contract. This is very similar to traditional contracts, in the sense that it is also a collection of rules and regulations that control the trust factor between all the parties involved. All the parties have to function within the scope of the contract [22, 23]. The difference between a traditional contract and a smart contract is that it is coded with the help of a programming language. All the rules and conditions are executed through coding, thus representing the precise agreement as approved and accepted by all the parties concerned [24].

Smart contracts using blockchain have invaded all the other sectors, but the agricultural sector is still catching up. Most of the time, postharvest and preharvest processes are carried out using traditional methods. Smart contracts can improve the process of storing, tracing, and publishing of agri-data to a great extent, resulting in farmers getting payment in time and consumers getting authentic information before purchase. This also discourages intermediaries from increasing the retail prices. Using smart contracts, the entire process is automated, as well as it creates complete trust between all the parties concerned [25].

Smart contracts can thus be used between different parties for the sale of agri-goods, as well as for managing the agricultural supply chain, giving small farmers an opportunity to stay on top in the agriculture sector [26].

> The most popular platform for smart contracts is Ethereum. It is fundamentally a blockchain with an in-built program that facilitates the working of the smart contracts and their applications, which are completely decentralized. The digital code is written in "Ethereum virtual machine code".
>
> Frequently, smart contracts are required to access real world data and the data is made available by the oracles [27].

11.2.4   Agricultural Finance

The agricultural sector and farmers, especially in developing economies, are financially excluded from the formal financial system. Identifying these technologies such as blockchain can help in reaching these farmers and providing them with the required finance. This of course requires a strong understanding of these technologies and their features and benefits. Only a few innovations have created the hype as blockchain, and this evolving technology could allow for a broader market for agricultural finance [28].

Access to financial services is a challenge in developing countries. Steps to tackle the challenges are part of the financial inclusion initiatives of each country. The aim is to give affordable access to financial services to all, and with the agricultural sector being predominant in developing economies, blockchain can be very useful in meeting the financial needs of the agricultural sector. Financial inclusion is not optimal, especially for remote communities normally dependent on agriculture. The difficulty is that farmers are not able to access financial services because they do not have assets that banks normally accept as collateral. Most of the farmers have assets such as land, livestock, and harvests, which cannot be used as collateral. Technology, like blockchain, can be used to improve the manner in which farmers can benefit. The potential of applying blockchain technology lies in facilitating the transfer of value of such assets which farmers cannot take advantage of in the present financial scenario [29]. Agricultural finances may also include cross-border settlements between countries, including sellers, farmers, buyers, and traders. The traditional model of payment is complicated and requires a lot of paperwork, thereby reducing the effectiveness of the whole transaction.

Blockchain can facilitate quick and real-time payments in the sector. Elimination of all intermediaries can greatly reduce the costs as well as risks. They also help in increasing the cash flow, leading to a better working capital position. Ripple, based on blockchain, can be successfully used in solving the majority of cross-border settlement problems. Ripple basically makes use of virtual money, such as Ethereum or Bitcoin for settling the transactions. The use of virtual cryptocurrencies, with the help of a blockchain as a universal currency, in the supply chain of the agricultural sector can eliminate unnecessary costs, reduce exchange and transaction fees, and save time as well.

Thus, blockchain allows for speedy and safe payouts at a very reduced cost. Traditional models of payment may take up to 3–5 days, and a lot of time goes by, with many banks posing as middlemen, leading to increased transaction charges and increasing the burden on farmers and agri-food workers. This is especially true with regard to developing economies. Payments through blockchain could greatly reduce costs, irrespective of the amount of the transactions. Transactions made on the blockchain can be settled in a matter of minutes. Neither bank sanction is required nor any checks are needed, and in turn, more effective financial transactions can lead to improved financial inclusion and a better agro-sector [30].

11.2.5   Controlling the Weather Crisis

Farmers must deal with unpredictable weather conditions which have an impact on the various crop varieties. For the preservation of crops and vegetables, weather forecasting is essential. For instance, because of the intense spring rains, some of the plants grown in the US were unable to withstand feeding as there was more oxygen than there should be. Additionally, due to a lack of openness, the current food chain platforms see a hazy and significant price increase in the event of bad weather conditions. When crops get spoiled due to bad weather and prices rise, consumers suffer, unaware of the whole situation. Farmers and stakeholders would be in a better position to learn about price variations in food products with the help of blockchain which can offer complete traceability and transparency [31].

The use of blockchain requires three essential steps for weather control and forecasting.

1. The weather station sends relevant data to the specified blockchain; thereafter, the application of smart and digital agriculture assists farmers in recognizing the behavior of the crops with the help of sensors or mapping areas. Weather stations using blockchain can provide all relevant information—rainfall, soil temperature, wind direction, wetness in the leaves, air temperature, wind intensity, atmospheric pressure, and relative humidity. All this information is precalculated and stored in the blockchain, thereby helping the farmers immensely.
2. Precautionary measures can be taken with the help of collected and stored data, and accurate decisions can be made accordingly. For example, if the farmers are aware in advance about heavy rains in the coming days, they can plan their farming activities accordingly or make arrangements for saving their crops.
3. Blockchain technologies eliminate the intermediaries and help in the speedy allocation of subsidies for agriculture. In case of a loss due to a weather crisis, farmers can claim their insurance instantly with the help of blockchain. Insurance companies and authorized organizations can safely access the data as collected by the weather stations, thanks to the blockchain's clear and irretrievable operation. They might use smart contracts to ask the blockchain directly for essential information. The farmers get the necessary funds

directly from the relevant accounts after submitting and having an insurance claim acknowledged. A blockchain-based technology can help farmers get payments quickly and easily [32].

11.2.6   Agricultural Insurance

Being an agricultural nation, a large portion of India's population is dependent directly on agriculture. This is true with all developing economies. In the recent past, farmer suicides in India happened at an alarming rate, the primary reason being crop failures as a result of natural disasters like floods, droughts, and hurricanes. Crop insurance is therefore of prime importance in all countries dependent on farming. Crop insurance provides farmers with several benefits, such as income stability and low debts. The traditional systems of insurance are entirely centralized and farmers are required to follow set terms or conditions to get a crop insured. Most of the time, since farmers are not literate enough to thoroughly comprehend numerous and complex terms or conditions, they end up not getting an insurance secured, leading to loss of crops being devastated in case of natural calamity. The farmer may lose his entire savings after the crop failure, further resulting in loan repayment default. Loan exemption by the government may be an option, but it puts the economy under a lot of pressure and may not always be a feasible solution. The viable solution is getting the farmers to purchase crop insurance [33].

All industries need to be updated and are required to keep up with the changing market dynamic, especially in terms of technology in order to sustain. The insurance sector is one of the most important segments of the financial sector, and it has actively adopted new-age technologies [31]. Decentralized insurance, commonly referred to as DeFi insurance, is a type of insurance that utilizes decentralized platforms and blockchain technology and runs on decentralized systems that are not governed by any central authority, as opposed to traditional insurance, which is run by centralized institutions like insurance firms [34].

The use of blockchain promises to offer new and improved categories of agricultural insurance, as well as risk minimization and fraud prevention through the implementation of smart contracts. For the customer or the policy holder, the management of the insurance claim will be completely automated and be much faster [35].

In the traditional form of insurance, the farmers have to work with the help of insurance brokers. Policies are handled through paper contracts, and claims and payments require human intervention, leaving them prone to bias and error. To add to this, there is the uncertainty of damage identification and claim verification. Each phase in this joint process involving the brokers, farmers, insurers, and reinsurers leads to a greater possibility of multiple failure points, where data may be lost, policies may be misunderstood, and settlement times may be extended. In this context, blockchain offers a simpler yet sophisticated way to reduce risks, costs, and the time involved in the entire process [36].

As policyholders, farmers can acquire insurance policies directly from the platform in a decentralized insurance system using blockchain, without the aid of an intermediary such as an insurance firm. Before the claim is filed, the premiums paid by the farmers are combined and held in a smart contract. If the terms of the policy are satisfied, the smart contract will automatically make payments of the claim to the affected policyholder. The category of coverage, the insurer, and the length of the contract are some of the variables that affect the cost of decentralized financial insurance. There may be set guidelines in the smart contract, for example, if in 12 months, a heavy rainfall condition lasts for more than 10 days in a particular location and the rice crop is in the sowing season, it may automatically lead to payment of 100% of the insured amount without any verification. Similarly, there may be other conditions, such as if the condition of heavy rainfall exists for 6 days or less, the farmer is entitled to get only 30% of the amount insured [37]. Traditional agricultural insurances are different from the ones based on blockchain with regard to loss assessment and the way in which payments are made. Traditional forms of insurance cover the farmers on the basis of actual damage which is sometimes difficult to assess. They are commonly called indemnity-based insurance, and they generally face the problem of damage assessment. Information about the risk involved in the production practices is unevenly circulated between the concerned parties. Farmers are not trained as to the proper selection of the different insurance policies available. Therefore, indemnity-based insurance involves costly and time-consuming damage assessment and other problems as a result of asymmetric information [38].

Index-based insurance using blockchain is a suitable alternative to meeting these challenges. The payout here is based not on the assessment of loss but on a quantifiable index, such as the degree of rainfall as measured by the weather department. Thus, there is no disparity in the information available, and there is uniformity and clarity about the amount of payment and when and how it is to be made. Payments may take less time and may be automatically transferred immediately after the announcement and measurement of a bad weather event.

Blockchain can thus improve crop insurance in two different ways. First, the payments are made on time and are automated as they are dependent on the weather data as specified in the smart contract. Secondly, relevant information about weather can be integrated with the help of a smart oracle, making the whole process of index determination as well as the payout process more efficient [39].

11.2.7   Mitigation of Food Fraud

Food fraud is frequently caused by erroneous labeling; therefore, the traceability and consequent responsibility of blockchain models are crucial in preventing it. Misleading advertising is pervasive as the demand for antibiotics, herbal remedies, and genetically modified foods increases. However, the complete supply chain may be successfully tracked and monitored, thanks to IoT and blockchain technology. Using IoT devices, radiofrequency identification (RFID) tags, and sensors, even minor payments in factories, fields, or warehouses could be followed, and the same information is sent all over the supply chain. By avoiding multiple interactions in the supply chain, blockchain ensures that productivity increases and fraud cases are reduced [40].

11.2.8   Maintaining the Quality of Raw Materials

Grain and seed quality play a significant major role in developing healthy crops. Furthermore, low-quality seeds and grain may severely impact the farmers' business and may also lead to unnecessary expenditures. It is important that both small and big farmers buy only quality products; the use of the blockchain system plays a very important role here. In the case of suppliers providing inferior or poor quality seeds, the data are directly mirrored and shown in the chain for all the stakeholders including the farmers and the consumers. It helps the

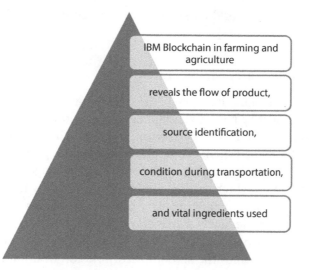

Figure 11.5 IBM applications of the blockchain technology in the agri-sector.

customers to identify the errors or the black spots of the food products on which they spend money. It empowers the agriculturalists to make improved and knowledgeable purchase decisions.

Figure 11.5 shows IBM applications of the blockchain technology in the agri-sector. For example, the IBM blockchain technology platform is successfully used to predict transparency, helping the farmers by revealing the flow of their products in real time. It also helps by showing records that reflect the conditions of the product at various stages of transportation, as well as identifying the source of the product and the ingredients used [41].

11.2.9   Decentralized Smaller Organizations

With growing competition, small businesses are replaced by big corporations which control a larger part of the agri-market. Big companies command and dictate everything, from what to grow and how to cultivate, to the price at which they should sell, and the farmers have no choice but to listen to them. The petty farmers agree to all terms and conditions as they rely on these big companies as their clients. Even the suppliers work according to the conditions and terms set by these companies as they do not want to lose out on big orders. Blockchain technology allows for complete decentralization, and farmers can directly negotiate favorable terms with the parties concerned. The use of blockchain allows them to obtain finances and also allows them to work on their own conditions of operation. In turn, consumers may receive high-quality food products at more realistic prices [42].

11.2.10   The Quality Controls

Blockchain technology provides for a protected and safe storage of information about seeds, crops, raw materials, and livestock. Quality of soil, types of pests affecting the crops, irrigation facilities, and many other relevant factors can be supervised on phones using sensors. The development team of an Israeli company, Flux, has worked on Eddy—a blockchain platform, and developed the world's first Growbot, explicitly designed to guarantee fruitful harvests and improved yields [43].

11.2.11   Sustainable Water Management

Given that irrigation uses more than 70% of the water sources available, water management in the agriculture sector may have a substantial socioeconomic influence that extends far beyond the advantages to end users or service providers. This necessitates more environmentally friendly water management practices, and companies providing services are forced to develop accurate systems to gauge their customers' water usage. However, these systems have centralized structures, which are frequently administered by the service provider, and they limit the players' capacity to participate in the water management process directly.

IoT and blockchain immediately enhance numerous corporate processes, including accounting, billing, and distribution, for managing scarce resources such as water or energy. Additionally, the system enables the smooth incorporation of a number of other players that can reward or verify specific user behaviors on the actual usage of the resources being monitored, especially in the case of water management for agriculture [44].

11.3   Cases of Blockchain in Agriculture

Walmart is one of the forerunners to install blockchain on the traceability of food products. It operates in collaboration with IBM and has arranged two pilot studies. These studies are on tracing for mangoes in the American market and pork products in the Chinese market. The log files contain all of the e-certificates, along with agricultural treatments, the manufacturers' details, security concerns, ID numbers, and safety-related records. With blockchain technology, procurement managers can track all the data online in real time, making it simple to identify certain contaminated products without having to recall the entire batch. The solutions enable for item-level traceability rather than batch-level traceability, which not only speeds up safety traceability but also lowers recall costs [45].

The Swiss food and beverage processing corporation Nestle collaborated with a third party, the Rainforest Alliance, to offer data independently above and beyond what the company typically discloses. In order to launch Zoégas whole beans and ground roast coffee in Sweden, Nestle extensively made use of IBM's blockchain technology named Food Trust. The IBM Food Trust blockchain platform makes the information provided by the Rainforest Alliance about the traceability of the coffee available to everyone [46]. Microsoft, IBM, SAP-SE, Ambrosus, OriginTrail, AgriDigital, Rip.io, ChainVine, Provenance, and Arc-net are the major companies using blockchain technology in the agriculture sector [47].

Table 11.1 shows the list of Startups renovating the agricultural sector through blockchain with an astonishing compound annual growth rate (CAGR) of 47.3% globally, the market for blockchain in agriculture and the food supply chain increased from $0.28 billion (2022) to $0.41 billion (2023) (source: blockchain in agriculture and food supply chain, Global market report 2023). At least briefly, the Russia–Ukraine conflict hindered any expected rebound of the global economy hit by COVID-19. With sanctions on a number of countries and the subsequent increase in prices followed by severe disturbances in the supply chain as a result of the war, inflation has increased, and in such circumstances,

Table 11.1 Startups renovating the agricultural sector through blockchain.

AgriChain	A platform bringing together different stakeholders in the supply chain, thereby helping them make informed decisions
AgriDigital	Digitalize grain management
AgriLedger	Tracking and tracing of food products, assessing financial services
Demeter	Facilitates easy renting of farms and microfields all over the world without any middlemen
Etherisc	Offers farmers decentralized crop insurance policies saving on time and expenses
Ripe	Helps in developing and building digital and **transparent supply chain** and provides adequate data to create food mapping throughout the food journey
TE-FOOD	Facilitates transportation of fresh food packages and tracks the items in the supply chain
WorldCover	Provides protection through decentralized crop insurance and also uses satellites to predict weather conditions so that payments can be triggered automatically

blockchain can bring about a rapid revival of the economy, lowering the prices of products. At a CAGR of 47.1%, the marketplace for this disruptive technology is anticipated to reach $1.92 billion in 2027 [48].

11.4   Challenges and Future Implications

The supply chain in the agricultural sector is very complex, and there are certain informal rules and regulations in the sector making it difficult to adopt blockchain technology. The stakeholders lack technological expertise, the products go through numerous changes over the supply chain cycle, and a supply chain is disseminated across a wide geographic area [49].

The advantages of blockchain technology vary depending on how big the farms are. Smaller farms can easily adopt blockchain-based insurance if they are able to collect and synthesize farming data, but most of them lack the structure required for it. There is also an absence of awareness about these procedures among small farmers. Therefore, future work should focus on ensuring that both small and large farms can equally access blockchain technology [49].

Additionally, gathering data to be transferred to the distributed ledger may be an expensive process, creating a huge barrier to the industry's adoption of blockchain technology. The setting up of the blockchain ledger is not very expensive, but assembling a huge amount of data in order to make it completely functional can be very expensive. Sampling may definitely control the costs. In any case, smaller farms have higher data-gathering costs than larger farms, which widens the revenue difference. Also, creating awareness and educating farmers and other stakeholders on the technicalities and usage of blockchain technology are very important [49].

Part of its essence and a factor in Bitcoin's success is the idea of an unregulated blockchain. As can be seen, there are a lot of legal disputes surrounding blockchain, particularly in the context of virtual currencies. Permissioned, private, and consortium blockchains have been used to meet the need or opportunity to add controls to the network.

Blockchain technology has multiple benefits for the agricultural sector, but there are challenges as well. Prominent among these challenges are policy risk and regulation, privacy, data storage and integration, and lack of technical know-how among the farmers and other stakeholders. If these challenges are successfully met, blockchain can truly revolutionize the entire agricultural sector. The technology has special implications for all rural-based economies, and the policymakers and governments should work toward educating the farmers about the technology in addition to developing a legal framework of regulation.

References

1. Trivelli, L., Apicella, A., Chiarello, F., Rana, R., Fantoni, G., Tarabella, A., From precision agriculture to Industry 4.0: Unveiling technological connections in the agrifood sector. *Br. Food J.*, 121, 8, 1730–1743, 2019.
2. Rocha, G.D.S.R., de Oliveira, L., Talamini, E., Blockchain applications in agribusiness: A systematic review. *Future Internet*, 13, 4, 95, 2021.
3. Sott, M.K., Furstenau, L.B., Kipper, L.M., Giraldo, F.D., Lopez-Robles, J.R., Cobo, M.J., Imran, M.A., Precision techniques and agriculture 4.0 technologies to promote sustainability in the coffee sector: State of the art, challenges and future trends. *IEEE Access*, 8, 149854–149867, 2020.
4. Kuzior, A. and Sira, M., A bibliometric analysis of blockchain technology research using VOSviewer. *Sustainability*, 14, 13, 8206, 2022.
5. Grover, P., Kar, A.K., Vigneswara Ilavarasan, P., Blockchain for businesses: A systematic literature review, in: *Challenges and Opportunities in the Digital Era: 17th IFIP WG 6.11 Conference on e-Business, e-Services, and e-Society, I3E 2018*, Kuwait City, Kuwait, vol. Proceedings 17, Springer International Publishing, pp. 325–336, 2018October 30–November 1, 2018.
6. Javaid, M., Haleem, A., Singh, R.P., Suman, R., Khan, S., A review of blockchain technology applications for financial services. *BenchCouncil Trans. Benchmarks Stand. Eval.*, 6, 17, 100073, 2022.
7. Xiong, II., Dalhaus, T., Wang, P., Huang, J., Blockchain technology for agriculture: applications and rationale. *Front. Blockchain*, 3, 7, 2020.
8. Iansiti, M. and Lakhani, K.R., The truth about blockchain. *Harv. Bus. Rev.*, 95, 1, 118–127, 2017.
9. Demestichas, K., Peppes, N., Alexakis, T., Adamopoulou, E., Blockchain in agriculture traceability systems: A review. *Appl. Sci.*, 10, 12, 4113, 2020.
10. Mirabelli, G. and Solina, V., Blockchain and agricultural supply chains traceability: Research trends and future challenges. *Procedia Manuf.*, 42, 414–421, Procedia Manuf, 2020.
11. Sylvester, G., *E-Agriculture in Action: Blockchain for Agriculture, Opportunities and Challenges*, FAO, Italy, 2019.
12. Torky, M. and Hassanein, A.E., Integrating blockchain and the internet of things in precision agriculture: Analysis, opportunities, and challenges. *Comput. Electron. Agric.*, 178, 105476, 2020.
13. Niknejad, N., Ismail, W., Bahari, M., Hendradi, R., Salleh, A.Z., Mapping the research trends on blockchain technology in food and agriculture industry: A bibliometric analysis. *Environ. Technol. Innov.*, 21, 101272, 2021.

14. Yadav, V.S. and Singh, A.R., A systematic literature review of blockchain technology in agriculture, in: *Proceedings of the International Conference on Industrial Engineering and Operations Management*, IEOM Society International, Southfield, MI, USA, pp. 973–981, July 2019.

15. Casino, F., Dasaklis, T.K., Patsakis, C., A systematic literature review of blockchain-based applications: Current status, classification and open issues. *Telemat. Inform.*, 36, 55–81, 2019.

16. Li, X., Wang, D., Li, M., Convenience analysis of sustainable E-agriculture based on blockchain technology. *J. Clean. Prod.*, 271, 122503, 2020.

17. Nayal, K., Raut, R.D., Narkhede, B.E., Priyadarshinee, P., Panchal, G.B., Gedam, V.V., Antecedents for blockchain technology-enabled sustainable agriculture supply chain. *Ann. Oper. Res.*, 327, 3, 1–45, 2021.

18. Saurabh, S. and Dey, K., Blockchain technology adoption, architecture, and sustainable agri-food supply chains. *J. Clean. Prod.*, 284, 124731, 2021.

19. Srivastava, A. and Dashora, K., Application of blockchain technology for agrifood supply chain management: A systematic literature review on benefits and challenges. *Benchmarking: An Int. J.*, 29, 10, 3426–3442, 2022.

20. Ronaghi, M.H., A blockchain maturity model in agricultural supply chain. *Inf. Process. Agric.*, 8, 3, 398–408, 2021.

21. Rana, R.L., Tricase, C., De Cesare, L., Blockchain technology for a sustainable agrifood supply chain. *Br. Food J.*, 123, 11, 3471–3485, 2021.

22. Kosior, K., The importance of blockchain technology in the development of agricultural insurance–a review of applications and solutions. *Ubezpieczenia W Rolnictwie*, 137, 1–75, 2021.

23. Sajja, G.S., Rane, K.P., Phasinam, K., Kassanuk, T., Okoronkwo, E., Prabhu, P., Towards applicability of blockchain in agriculture sector. *Mater. Today Proc.*, 80, 23, 3705–3708, 2021.

24. Pranto, T.H., Noman, A.A., Mahmud, A., Haque, A.B., Blockchain and smart contract for IoT enabled smart agriculture. *PeerJ Comput. Sci.*, 7, e407, 2021.

25. Pranto, T.H., Noman, A.A., Mahmud, A., Haque, A.B., Blockchain and smart contract for IoT enabled smart agriculture. *PeerJ Comput. Sci.*, 2, 21, 1–11, 2021. arXiv e-prints, arXiv-2104.

26. Frank, J., Blockchain functionality: How smart contracts can save small farms, in: *NYLS Legal Studies Research Paper, 3662648*, 2020.

27. Zhang, F., Cecchetti, E., Croman, K., Juels, A., Shi, E., Town crier: An authenticated data feed for smart contracts. *Proceedings of the 2016 ACM SIGSAC Conference on Computer and Communications Security*, 2016, ACM, Vienna, Austria, pp. 270–282, 2016.

28. Mattern, M., Consultative Group to Assist the Poor, *Exploring Blockchain Applications To Agricultural Finance*, 7, 18, 1-19, Washington, DC, 2018.

29. Chinaka, M., *Blockchain technology–applications in improving financial inclusion in developing economies: Case study for small scale agriculture in Africa*, Doctoral dissertation, Massachusetts Institute of Technology, 2016.

30. Xu, J., Guo, S., Xie, D., Yan, Y., Blockchain: A new safeguard for agri-foods. *Artif. Intell. Agric.*, 4, 153–161, 2020.

31. Anand, A., McKibbin, M., Pichel, F., Colored coins: Bitcoin, blockchain, and land administration, in: *Annual World Bank Conference on Land and Poverty*, p. 6, 20162017.

32. Blockchain–can this new technology really revolutionize the land registry system? In Responsible land governance: Towards an evidence based approach. *Proceedings of the Annual World Bank Conference on Land and Poverty*, pp. 1–13.

33. Jha, N., Prashar, D., Khalaf, O., II, Alotaibi, Y., Alsufyani, A., Alghamdi, S., Blockchain based crop insurance: A decentralized insurance system for modernization of Indian farmers. *Sustainability*, 13, 16, 8921, 2021.

34. Srivastava, R., Prashar, A., Iyer, S.V., Gotise, P., Insurance in the Industry 4.0 environment: A literature review, synthesis, and research agenda. *Aust. J. Manage.*, 23, 22, 1–8, 03128962221132458, 2022.

35. Shuaib, K., Abdella, J., Sallabi, F., Serhani, M.A., Secure decentralized electronic health records sharing system based on blockchains. *J. King Saud Univ.-Comput. Inf. Sci.*, 34, 8, 5045–5058, 2022.

36. Roriz, R. and Pereira, J.L., Avoiding insurance fraud: A blockchain-based solution for the vehicle sector. *Proc. Comput. Sci.*, 164, 211–218, 2019.

37. Shetty, A., Shetty, A.D., Pai, R.Y., Rao, R.R., Bhandary, R., Shetty, J., Dsouza, K.J., Blockchain application in insurance services: A systematic review of the evidence. *SAGE Open*, 12, 1, 21582440221079877, 2022.

38. Dominguez Anguiano, T. and Parte, L., The state of art, opportunities and challenges of blockchain in the insurance industry: A systematic literature review. *Manag. Rev. Q.*, 2, 23, 1–22, 2023.

39. Vroege, W., Dalhaus, T., Finger, R., Index insurances for grasslands–a review for Europe and North-America. *Agric. Syst.*, 168, 101–111, 2019.

40. Deshpande, A., Stewart, K., Lepetit, L., Gunashekar, S., *Distributed Ledger Technologies/ Blockchain: Challenges, Opportunities and the Prospects For Standards. Overview Report*, vol. 9, F. Tian, (Ed.), pp. 1–34, The British Standards Institution, UK, (BSI, 20172017.

41. Xiong, H., Dalhaus, T., Wang, P., Huang, J., Blockchain technology for agriculture: Applications and rationale. *Front. Blockchain*, 3, 7, 2020.

42. Shi, X., An, X., Zhao, Q., Liu, H., Xia, L., Sun, X., Guo, Y., State-of-the-art internet of things in protected agriculture. *Sensors*, 19, 8, 1833, 2019.

43. Alobid, M., Abujudeh, S., Szűcs, I., The role of blockchain in revolutionizing the agricultural sector. *Sustainability*, 14, 7, 4313, 2022.

44. Pincheira, M., Vecchio, M., Giaffreda, R., Kanhere, S.S., Cost-effective IoT devices as trustworthy data sources for a blockchain-based water management system in precision agriculture. *Comput. Electron. Agric.*, 180, 105889, 2021.

45. Banafa, A., *Secure and smart Internet of Things (Iot): Using Blockchain and artificial intelligence (AI)*, Stylus Publishing, LLC, Sterling, VA, United States, 2019.

46. Kamath, R., Food traceability on blockchain: Walmart's pork and mango pilots with IBM. *JBBA*, 1, 1, 2–15, 2018.

47. *Blockchain in Agriculture and Food Supply Chain Global Market Report 2023*, [Online]. Available at: https://www.reportlinker.com/p06246504/Blockchain-In-Agriculture-And-Food-SupplyChain-Global-Market-Report.html?utm_source=GNW#summary.

48. LB, K., Survey on the applications of blockchain in agriculture. *Agriculture*, 12, 9, 1333, 2022.

49. Jothikumar, R., Applying blockchain in agriculture: A study on blockchain technology, benefits, and challenges, in: *Deep Learning and Edge Computing Solutions for High Performance Computing*, pp. 167–181, Springer, Cham, 2021.

12

Fostering Agriculture Ecosystem for Sustainability

Batani Raghavendra Rao[1]*, Anusha R. Batni[2] and Preeti Shrivastava[3]

[1]Faculty of Management Studies, Jain (Deemed-to-be University), Bengaluru, India
[2]Audit and Assurance, Deloitte, Dublin, Ireland
[3]Muscat College, Muscat, Oman

Abstract

The agriculture ecosystem comprises the farmers, inputs, weather, financial institutions, government, value-addition facilitators (distribution channels, supply chain, grading, branding, marketing, etc.), commodity exchanges, and consumers. Strengthening each and every unit of the agriculture ecosystem for the sustainable development of agriculture cannot be overemphasized. The chapter dwells on the role of technology, digitization, policy framework, corporate intervention in the Indian context across the agriculture value chain (popularly described as farm to fork), and the global outlook.

Keywords: Agriculture ecosystem, agriculture value chain, policy intervention, SDG 2, sustainability, growth drivers, agriculture tech investments

12.1 Introduction

The United Nations' Sustainable Development Goal 2 (SDG 2) is "zero hunger." SDG 2 aims at creating a world free of hunger by 2030 [1]. To achieve SDG 2, sustained performance in agriculture is imperative. Agriculture contributes 4% to the world's GDP. In the case of least developed countries (LDCs), the share of agriculture in the GDP is over 25%. Agriculture is the mainstay for LDCs [2].

As far as India is concerned, agriculture is a critical sector of the country's economy. It is multidimensional. Agro-based industries thrive on agriculture. Agriculture has a noteworthy contribution to India's exports. During 2021–2022, agricultural exports reached USD 50.2 billion, which is an all-time high [3]. Appendix 1 provides data on the exports of various agricultural products from 2020–2021 through 2022–2023. The allied sectors of agriculture play a significant role in supplementing and augmenting the farmers' income. The growth in agriculture and its allied sectors is presented in Figure 12.1.

Sustainable agriculture is the key as agriculture accounts for 20% of India's GDP and engages about 48% of the nation's workforce [4]. It is both a challenge and an opportunity to transform the Indian farming community. The enablers are policy push,

*Corresponding author: br.rao@jainuniversity.ac.in; ORCID: https://orcid.org/0000-0003-0663-2394

Kuldeep Singh and Prasanna Kolar (eds.) *Digital Agricultural Ecosystem: Revolutionary Advancements in Agriculture*, (211–228) © 2024 Scrivener Publishing LLC

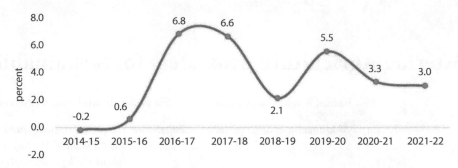

Figure 12.1 Growth in agriculture and its allied sectors. Source: [3].

technology, overhauling of agriculture infrastructure, education, and skill building. The start-ups and the incumbent corporate houses play a critical role in making a sustainable agriculture.

12.2 Agriculture Ecosystem and Agriculture Value Chain

12.2.1 Agricultural Ecosystem

The Indian agriculture ecosystem encompasses the constituent elements that make up the agriculture sector. It includes the farming community, government (Ministry of Agriculture and other allied ministries), farmer-producer organizations (FPOs), vendors of agri-inputs, food processing units, banks, insurance companies, transport and logistics facilitators, other value-added facilitators contributing value to the agri-produce, customers, consumers, and the organized and unorganized agriculture market.

The India Digital Ecosystem of Agriculture (IDEA) framework, the Indian government initiative, has constituted the architecture for the digitization of farmers' database. Under IDEA, numerous agritech enterprises are identified and curated. These agritech companies and the government of India collaboratively undertake to develop the proof of concepts (PoCs). The PoC will be developed on the federated farmers' database [5].

12.2.2 Agriculture Value Chain

Value chain essentially is a series of activities, stages, and processes that add up to the value of the product or service. Agricultural value chain mainly comprises stages like pre-production, production, and post-production stages. Figure 12.2 depicts the agriculture value chain in detail.

Agricultural value chain is extensive and its analysis provides the opportunity to spot the bottlenecks and paves the way for increasing the operational efficiency at each stage. The important levers that equip and strengthen the agriculture value chain are building on the capabilities and skills of farmers and farming, leveraging technology, data analytics, and conducive policy framework.

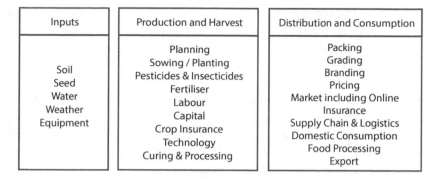

Inputs	Production and Harvest	Distribution and Consumption
Soil Seed Water Weather Equipment	Planning Sowing / Planting Pesticides & Insecticides Fertiliser Labour Capital Crop Insurance Technology Curing & Processing	Packing Grading Branding Pricing Market including Online Insurance Supply Chain & Logistics Domestic Consumption Food Processing Export

Figure 12.2 Agriculture value chain (farm to fork). Source: authors' own.

Educating and upskilling the farmers and workforce engaged in agriculture is of crucial importance for superior performance. In this regard, the Agriculture Skill Council of India (ASCI) assumes a pivotal role. ASCI administers and imparts skill-building modules in emerging areas of agriculture for the people engaged in agriculture.

The Open Network for Digital Commerce (ONDC), the government-backed open-protocol e-commerce venture, is yet another revolutionary initiative. ONDC provides an online platform for the agriculture ecosystem, and one of its earlier investors is the National Bank of Agriculture and Rural Development (NABARD). The ONDC facilitates for onboarding of the entire agriculture value chain with the formation of the NABARD-ONDC grand challenge. As per T. Koshy, the Managing Director and CEO of ONDC, "nearly 400 farmer organizations are in various stages of integration with ONDC" [6].

Farm mechanization is a key to boost agriculture productivity. In order to recognize the significance of farm mechanization in bolstering agricultural productivity, the McKinsey report highlights the potential of digital technologies to enhance production at every stage. From the optimization of high-quality agriculture inputs to achieve world-class agriculture outputs, farm mechanization emerges as a pivotal factor in the context of agricultural productivity [7].

The supply chain is also another critical element in the value chain of agriculture. In order to enhance the efficacy of the agriculture supply chain, the circular economy concept has drawn the attention and consideration of many researchers and practitioners. It is believed that the circular economy is a potential solution for social, economic, and environmental challenges [8].

The role of the government of India in terms of minimum support price (MSP), promotion of crop diversification, and developing market infrastructure is noteworthy [3].

The Committee on Doubling Farmers' Income (DFI) considers dairying, livestock, poultry, fisheries, and horticulture as high-growth engines. Consequently, a focused policy with a concomitant support system for the allied sector is recommended by the DFI Committee. The DFI Committee identifies three variables, namely, (i) productivity gains, (ii) reduction in the cost of cultivation, and (iii) remunerative price, for working its strategy for doubling farmers' income [4, 9].

The budget allocation for the Ministry of Agriculture & Farmers Welfare was only Rs. 25,460.51 crore in the year 2015–2016. This went up in 2022–2023 by more than 5.44 times to Rs. 138,550.93 crore [10].

Although the Green Revolution in India helped achieve food security, agricultural production was resource-intensive, cereal-centric, and regionally biased. As a consequence, sustainability concerns like loss of biodiversity, increase in greenhouse gas emissions, deforestation, land degradation, and increasing strain on water resources of the country cropped up [11, 12].

Yield gap is an important metric to appreciate the significance of the role of enablers in agriculture as it examines the gap between the actual yield obtained versus the potential or benchmark yield under ideal conditions. A study by the Planning Commission (Planning Commission, 2007) estimated these yield gaps: (i) between 6% and 300% in cereals, (ii) between 5% and 185% in oilseeds, and (iii) between 16% and 167% in sugarcane [13].

12.3   Growth Drivers for Sustainable Agriculture

12.3.1   Growth Drivers

The term "drivers" refers to the independent variables that drive the dependent variable upward or downward. The drivers cause growth or degrowth in the independent variable. In the context of agriculture, the chief drivers are weather, policy framework, irrigation, quality of inputs, mechanization, demand management, innovation, infrastructure, aggregation of farmers into the Farmer Producer Organization (FPO), and so on.

Weather is external, and due to the advent of technology, agriculture practices can be tuned to weather conditions to a considerable extent. Crop insurance is one of the options to guard against weather. Regenerative agriculture and natural farming are the other solutions to combat weather challenges.

The policy framework plays a significant role in the sustainable performance of agriculture. The government has embarked on and laid out projects and schemes to enable the farmers. Appendix 2 provides the list of government initiatives in this regard. A detailed discussion on the role of government and policy interventions is provided in the next section of the chapter.

Irrigation is a critical variable in the agriculture industry. Rainwater harvesting, increasing storage capacity, and drip and microirrigation are some of the ways to improve irrigation infrastructure [14].

The drivers like quality of inputs, mechanization, demand management, innovation, and infrastructure are well managed due to the state policy intervention and the role played by the institutions (NABARD, Ministry of Agriculture and Farmers Welfare, ONDC, banks, cold storage and logistics, insurance companies, ASCI, Food Corporation of India, DFI measures, etc.) and the corporates (both incumbent and start-ups).

Agriculture infrastructure is the institutional framework and the marketplace which empowers and endows the value chain for the superior performance of agriculture. The government of India's Agriculture Infrastructure Fund scheme with the collaboration of the participating lending institutions provides a single window facility in converging all schemes of the central and state government.

12.4   Role of the Government and Policy Interventions

The role of the government is crucial in terms of policy framework, digitization, budget allocation, reforms across the value chain of agriculture, enriching the farmers, capacity building in the agriculture infrastructure, and ensuring a robust agriculture ecosystem for sustainable performance in agriculture.

The National Mission for Sustainable Agriculture (NMSA) was initiated in the year 2014–2015. It aims at making agriculture a sustainable venture. NMSA's sustainable agriculture strategy has 10 pointers. It is explained in Figure 12.3.

In the realm of the role of government in the agriculture space, the National Food Security Act, 2013 (NFSA) is a path-breaking enactment. The "Right to Food" is secured by the NFSA. It is an Act of Parliament. In India, agriculture is a state subject. As agriculture is a multidimensional subject, the central government has a ministry of agriculture.

Market intelligence is the key for farmers to understand the demand and supply dynamics. The Agricultural and Processed Food Products Export Development Authority (APEDA) provides market intelligence reports for the pulses, cereals, fruits, animal husbandry products, dairy products, vegetables, etc. [16].

Value addition to the agricultural produce is very important. In this direction, the government has set up special economic zones (SEZs) and food parks. SEZs foster the creation of (i) an enabling business environment, (ii) improved policies, (iii) infrastructure, and (iv) competitive transactions, hence resulting in enhanced agricultural transformation [17]. In India, eight SEZs are approved for the agro and food processing sector [18].

The list of SEZs is provided in Table 12.1.

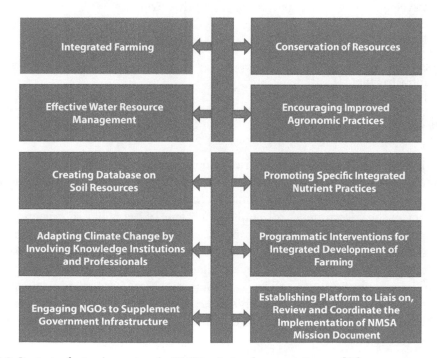

Figure 12.3 Strategies for implementing the NMSA mission document. Source: [15].

Table 12.1 Agro and food processing SEZs in India.

Sl.	Developer name	Type of SEZ	Location	SEZ status
1	Kerala Industrial Infrastructure Development Corporation (KINFRA)	Agro-based food processing	Malappuram, Kerala	Operational
2	Parry Infrastructure Company Private Limited	Food processing	Kakinada, Andhra Pradesh	Operational
3	CCCL Pearl City Food Port SEZ Ltd.	Food processing	Tuticorin, Tamil Nadu	Operational
4	Nagaland Industrial Development Corporation Limited	Agro and food processing	Dimapur, Nagaland	Notified
5	Ansal Colours Engineering Limited	Agro and food processing products	Sonepat, Haryana	Notified
6	CCL Products (India) Limited	Agro-based food processing	Chittoor, Andhra Pradesh	Notified
7	Tripura Industrial Development Corporation Limited	Agro-based food processing	South Tripura, Tripura	Notified
8	Akshaypatra Infrastructure Private Limited	Food processing	Mehsana, Gujarat	Formal approval

Source: [19].

The Ministry of Food Processing Industries came up with the scheme of "Mega Food Park." This scheme is based on the cluster approach, wherein a link is provided between agriculture production and the market with the outcome of a robust agriculture infrastructure [20].

The efficacy of the government's role and the outcome of the policy intervention must be assessed. As the subject matter is agriculture, measuring the performance of agriculture is the key. Niti Ayog is working on the Agriculture Transformation Index for measuring the performance of states. This is based on seven pillars: (i) inputs, (ii) sustainability, (iii) productivity and diversification, (iv) policy, (v) preservation, (vi) processing and exports, and (vii) farmers' income and welfare [21]. This index, on the one hand, helps to evaluate the impact of the agricultural policies and, on the other hand, to revisit the policy framework, in the light of the performance review.

12.5   Technology Initiatives of Corporates and Start-Ups

12.5.1   Role of Incumbent Corporates

Technology plays a crucial role in transforming agriculture. Artificial intelligence (AI) provides a plethora of applications for the agriculture industry [22]. Leveraging technology across the value chain of agriculture empowers the individuals and institutions that make up the value chain. The technology investment calls for know-how, capability, capital investment, and the gestation period to recover the investment. Several listed corporate houses have taken up the initiatives in this regard. Select real examples of the listed companies are presented in the ensuing paragraphs.

Jain Irrigations Systems

In line with technological innovations, Jain Irrigation Systems has spearheaded a revolution in water resource management. This company has introduced a range of innovative equipment and tools, particularly in the field of microirrigation. Their innovations include gravity and solar-powered drip irrigation systems, sprinklers, boom irrigation, hose reel irrigation, and more. Jain Irrigation Systems has played a pivotal role in advancements to efficient water utilization and sustainable agricultural practices [23].

Finolex

Finolex's agronomy cell also plays a key role in microirrigation. It helps in offering know-how about the specific needs of cropping to the farmers. It leverages on microirrigation application technologies. It helps in land productivity and enhances water and fertilizer use efficiency [24]. The final outcome is sustainable and profitable agriculture.

Marico

Marico's cluster farming program is a great success. This program is targeted for the coconut growers in Kerala. Under this program, a cluster of farmers is formed. The farm productivity initiatives are discussed and promoted jointly by the farmers of the cluster. The sequels are the rise in farmers' income by 20% and productivity gain of 20% for Marico [25].

ITC

ITC's e-Choupal is a landmark initiative that has established backward linkages with the farmers. It has empowered 4 million farmers over the last two decades. The competitiveness of Indian agriculture is enhanced through the e-Choupal. The value-added services like integrating farmers, input vendors, and government agencies have enabled the farmers [26].

Britannia

Britannia has embarked on several dairy farming initiatives and technology-enabled solutions to help farmers augment their incomes from the dairy vertical. The outcomes are reduced incidence of lameness in cattle, reduced instances of bacterial infection, rise in milk yield, drop in silage cost, drop in calves' mortality, better reproductive management and breeding, higher cattle productivity, etc. [27].

Nestle

Nestle brought out an agricultural framework underscoring the significance of the implementation of regenerative agriculture. The company has developed Farm Assessment Tools (FATs) to assess the maturity level of regenerative agriculture implementation. As each crop is unique and specific, FAT is tailored to meet crop specificities. There are three levels of classification to assess the journey and progress of regenerative agriculture.

Level 1: Engaged
Level 2: Advanced
Level 3: Leading

The criteria for the classification are soil tillage, crop rotation, manure management, herbicide management, water usage, technology used, etc.

John Deere

John Deere is a well-known agri equipment manufacturer, established in 1837 as a tool manufacturer for agriculture. It develops automated farm vehicles to plow and sow. It leverages the global positioning systems (GPS). Its FarmSight system is calibrated and designed to enable data-driven insights, based on shared user data, enabling informed decision-making for the farmers [28].

12.5.2 Role of Start-Ups

The agritech start-ups are playing a significant role in strengthening the agricultural value chain. There are over 1,000 agritech start-ups in India. These start-ups support and anchor the farmers in improving farming techniques [3]. The Union Budget 2023–2024 made a provision for setting up an agritech start-up fund and providing farmer-centric solutions, and the budget proposed a digital public infrastructure for agriculture [29].

Cropin is an agritech company. Its farm monitoring and management solution helps to geotag the farm plots and digitize farm/farmer records. Its connect app provides seamless communication among growers, field officers, and agri-business firms. Its trace app tracks the farm-to-fork journey [30].

DeHaat is one of the rapidly growing start-ups in the agritech sector. It builds AI-enabled technologies helping the forming community in the areas of supply chain and production efficiency. Its "Farmer App" is a one-stop platform for frequent crop reminders, weather reports, crop advisories, sharing local mandi rates, etc. It is catering to over 1.4 million farmers in 12 major agri-based states in India [31].

Other start-up companies like Ninjacart and BharatAgri are empowering the farmers with tech-enabled services. The snapshot of the initiatives of the incumbent companies and start-ups is outlined in Table 12.2.

Table 12.2 Summary of technology initiatives of corporates and start-ups.

Companies	Initiatives
Jain Irrigation	Microirrigation
Finolex Industries	Agronomy cell
Marico	Cluster farming program
ITC	e-Choupal
Britannia	Dairy farming welfare program
Nestle	Regenerative agriculture
John Deere	AI to transform farming
Start-ups	*Initiatives*
Cropin	Digital agri app
DeHaat	DeHaat farmer app

Source: authors' own.

12.6   Agritech Investment

Investing in technology is the way to sustainable performance in agriculture. Technology enables easy access, convenience, speed, cost optimization, democratization, inclusion, connectivity, and other related benefits. As the investment involves a huge capital and is risky, venture capitalists play the dominant role. The investment must be across the value chain of agriculture for the overall and all-round development. The McKinsey Report provides insights into venture capital investment in agriculture. The report states that the investment is widespread, spanning from farm to fork, with a total deal size of 114. The total investment was USD 1,155 million in 2022.

The details are available in Tables 12.3 and 12.4.

12.7   Global Outlook

Global policies will play an important role in the biofuel, agriculture, and fisheries market and affect the market structure. Though policies will remain unchanged, the introduction of digital innovation will affect sustainability in the long run. There was a free trade agreement signed by the Regional Comprehensive Economic Partnership (RCEP) in November 2020 which included 10 ASEAN countries basically from Asia and the Pacific (Japan, China, Korea, New Zealand, and Australia). It has accounted for 30% of the world's population which is 2.2 billion people and 30% of the global GDP which is 26.2 billion USD. The main aim of this cooperation is to lower trade barriers and ensure market access for goods and services [32].

Table 12.3 Venture capital investments in Indian agtech companies by description, 2022.

Description	Deals number
Creating sustainable financing options for rural agriculture stakeholders	1
Solutions that offer machineries as a service or provide other automation technologies for use on the farm	5
B2C platform for input linkages, for categories including seeds, nutrition, agrochemicals, etc.	8
Direct-to-consumer brands or platforms that link the farmers to the end consumers and make an impact on improving farming practices	13
Biotech/materials such as bio-inputs, alternative ingredients, etc.	16
Supply chain solutions (e.g., logistics, warehousing, infrastructure, etc.) offered for agri-produce	7
Providers of digital, advisory, Internet of Things, and mobile- or sensor-based solutions to farmers	40
Platforms having a significant presence in multiple segments (such as inputs and outputs)	4
B2B business or B2C platforms for output linkages, between farmers, businesses, and/or consumers	20
Total	114

Source: [7].

Table 12.4 Venture capital investments in Indian agtech companies by category, 2022.

Category	Funding in $ million
Agriculture fintech	8
Agriculture mechanization/automation	45
Upstream agtech	47
Farm-to-fork brands	63
Agriculture biotech	80
Midstream agtech	92
Digital solutions and precision agtech	113
End-to-end ecosystem	158
Downstream agtech	549
Total	1,155

Source: [7].

The OECD/FAO (2021) Report has also highlighted the impact of agriculture on climate change. The impact of agricultural production on carbon intensity is expected to lower down over the decade, and it is a positive step toward sustainability. Agricultural global greenhouse gas (GHG) projections will also have lower growth. However, global GHG emissions will increase by 4% over the next 10 years. The major contribution will be from livestock, accounting for more than an 80% increase. There is a need for policy efforts that will help reduce GHG emissions. This shows the way for climate smart productions at a large scale to handle the issues of GHG [32]. The pertinent question is what should be done to support production and lower the negative impact of climate on livestock and agriculture. The debate for using smart technologies in agriculture for increasing production and lower GHG emissions requires a major shift in mindset and investments. All the new features and adoptions will also require strong government, public, and community support and conducive policies and guidelines to fulfill the targets.

One of the studies by McKinsey named Global Farmer Insights (2022) covered seven countries, namely, India, EU, China, USA, Canada, Argentina, and Brazil. Around 5,500 farmers were surveyed, and the results were fascinating and promising. Seventy percent of the surveyed farmers agreed that they are willing to innovate despite external uncertainties. It is motivating to see that they are ready to experiment and try new products to increase productivity and curtail costs. The opportunities identified were higher crop prices due to higher yields, lower input prices, favorable consumer demand shifts, and demand from other countries, whereas the risks were increased overhead costs and processing, supply chain disruptions, extreme weather conditions, and farmers' shortages. It was evident from the response about digital commerce adoption that only 50% of the farmers have experienced online purchases. South America (66%) was leading the trend followed by North America (53%) and Europe (54%) and then Asia (24%). It is anticipated that equipment and technology products are expected to be purchased online. Globally, only 60% of farmers use cash and only 30% use digital payments. China is leading the trend, followed by Canada and Europe. Argentina and Asia were far behind the league. Western countries will lead in agtech adoption majorly in farm management software as compared with Asian countries [2].

The global outlook on agriculture uncovers many megatrends. As per the Deloitte's report on "Transforming Agriculture through Digital Technologies," the trends or developments are noteworthy for the overhaul and rejig of the agriculture ecosystem. The stakeholders of agriculture can exploit these megatrends to accomplish sustainable development in agriculture. The summary version of the reflections is as follows [33]:

> There is a need for developing an integrated common agriculture policy to serve the growing population of the world, which is expected to reach 9.5bn by 2050.
> Technology (AI, drones, blockchain, IoT, robotics) plays a pivotal role to increase productivity and mitigate risks, costs, and weather.
> The global agritech market size is expected to cross USD 1 trillion by 2023.
> The agricultural industry needs to align with SDGs (more importantly with SDGs like no poverty, zero hunger, good health and well-being, responsible consumption, and production).

12.8   Conclusion

Agriculture in India is at a crossroads. Agriculture plays a crucial role as far as food security, growth of agro-based industries, SDG 2, breeding employment and entrepreneurship prospects, and contribution to the nation's GDP. Lower agriculture yield, lack of demand and supply equilibrium, fragmented and small farm holdings posing a challenge for implementing mechanization, weather playing spoilsport, education, skilling, digital and financial inclusion of farmers, etc. are the challenges. However, these challenges throw up opportunities as well. The stakeholders should demonstrate orchestrated performance for the common good. The multifunctionality concept needs to be explored and defined clearly. A balance for new technologies with economic, social, and environmental aspects is needed. Developing countries must be self-sufficient and need a comprehensive system to balance technology, markets, sustainability, and agriculture policies for green revolution. Sustainable agriculture takes cognizance of the limited resources and the growing needs of the burgeoning population of the globe. In this backdrop, fostering the agriculture ecosystem for sustainability is a prerequisite and imperative.

Appendix 1: Three-year export statement of products by the Agricultural and Processed Food Products Export Development Authority (APEDA) [qty in MT; value in Rs. lacs].

	2020–2021		2021–2022		2022–2023	
Product	Qty	Rs. lacs	Qty	Rs. lacs	Qty	Rs. lacs
Floriculture						
Floriculture	15,695.29	57,598.4	23,597.22	77,141.49	21,024.41	70,780.53
Fruits and vegetable seeds	17,177.18	80,840.15	11,549.89	75,067.04	13,605.72	82,713.24
Total	32,872.47	138,438.55	35,147.11	152,208.53	34,630.13	153,493.77
Fresh fruits and vegetables						
Fresh onions	1,578,016.58	282,653.44	1,537,496.85	343,216.34	2,525,258.36	452,279.14
Other fresh vegetables	682,085.8	214,320.11	770,233.22	216,073.66	827,288.05	244,304.25
Walnuts	1,069.66	2,978.69	2,482.56	7,397.8	717.64	2,583.26
Fresh mangoes	21,033.56	27,187.82	27,872.77	32,745.14	22,963.76	37,849.39
Fresh grapes	246,107.37	229,845.05	263,075.62	230,216.4	267,950.39	254,342.12
Other fresh fruits	609,612.92	223,331.33	761,031.2	290,069.58	674,291.7	273,698.88
Others (betel leaves and nuts)	10,151.6	13,778.78	14,056.58	21,522.65	17,205.45	53,472.77

Total	3,148,077.49	994,095.22	3,376,248.8	1,141,241.57	4,335,675.35	1,318,529.81
Processed fruits and vegetables						
Cucumber and gherkins	223,515.51	165,181.82	217,521.38	148,729.95	227,699.04	176,109.84
Processed vegetables	403,355.38	371,862.95	460,621	398,645.35	410,415.99	498,735.56
Mango pulp	98,369.75	71,440.84	123,476.71	92,454.25	109,501.38	118,965.81
Processed fruits, juices, and nuts	306,990.51	317,342.41	374,260.06	362,607.6	388,207.95	475,482.93
Pulses	296,169.8	211,669.06	410,375.86	283,428.87	775,024.48	539,785.58
Total	1,328,400.95	1,137,497.08	1,586,255.01	1,285,866.02	1,910,848.84	1,809,079.72
Animal products						
Buffalo meat	1,085,619.93	2,346,038.3	1,175,193.02	2,461,323.96	1,175,869.13	2,564,810.15
Sheep/goat meat	7050.55	32,996.37	8,695.97	44,757.7	9,592.31	53,717.68
Other meat	894.04	1,805.59	1,946.95	4,551.71	701.8	1,692.65
Processed meat	774.11	1,191.99	462.58	1,055.83	331.57	1,171.78
Animal casings	13,887.74	41,654.25	13,826.91	47,403.67	12,577.04	32,601.59
Poultry products	255,686.92	43,552.91	320,240.46	52,980.3	664,753.46	108,161.6
Dairy products	54,762.31	149,165.91	108,711.21	292,879.67	67,572.99	226,985.03
Casein	3,401.65	18,041.48	8,768.48	59,278.39	8,843.53	81,631.9
Natural honey	59,999.25	71,613.29	74,413.06	122,117.59	79,929.17	162,277.34
Albumin (eggs and milk)	2,278.28	9,497.02	1,464.97	8,981.58	2,219.94	26,688.47
Total	1,484,354.78	2,715,557.11	1,713,723.61	3,095,330.4	2,022,390.94	3,259,738.19
Other processed foods						
Groundnuts	638,582.92	538,161.35	514,163.87	469,710.06	668,885.4	673,525.24
Guar gum	234,871.29	194,907.32	321,394.92	333,477.27	406,513.53	494,460.48
Jaggery and confectionery	631,895.81	265,957	551,716.73	279,784.8	761,640.19	433,006.63
Cocoa products	25,768.04	110,838.43	27,318.76	114,547.65	34,249.85	124,212.83
Cereal preparations	403,267.68	470,580.91	415,544.58	486,219.39	480,432.62	605,159.93

Milled products	392,935.4	151,343.89	695,779.69	228,611.38	629,253.46	222,393.76
Alcoholic beverages	247455.66	238691.21	197868.31	207,091.55	230,903.46	254,644.26
Miscellaneous preparations	624257.36	586644.08	946537.37	740,698.21	826,382.62	888,918.4
Prepared animal feeder	0	0	0	0	796,462.12	358,704.22
Other oil cake/ solid residues	0	0	0	0	583,387.18	93,965.57
Total	3,199,034.16	2,557,124.19	3,670,324.23	2,860,140.31	5,418,110.43	4,148,991.32
Cereals						
Basmati rice	4,630,463.14	2,984,988.97	3,948,161.03	2,641,653.86	4,558,972.23	3,852,410.55
Non-Basmati rice	13,095,130.2	3,547,661.45	17,262,235.1	4,565,235.31	17,786,092.8	5,108,872.03
Wheat	2,088,487.66	403,760.45	7,239,366.77	1,584,033.53	4,693,264.09	1,182,690.44
Maize	2,879,202.94	467,578.24	3,690,469.1	761,541.72	3,453,680.58	898,713.04
Other cereals	2,425.31	778.26	2,227.41	722.4	2,841.94	1,344.23
Millet	147,501.08	44,317.17	159,332.15	47,957.71	170,008.45	62,206.7
Total	22,843,210.3	7,449,084.54	32,301,791.5	9,601,144.53	30,664,860.1	11,106,237
Cashew						
Cashew kernels	70,087.59	311,222.38	75,422.6	337,740.44	59,575.83	286,872.45
Cashewnut shell liquid	429.82	145.29	1,368.06	692.03	10,641.81	5,638.61
Cardanol	3,306.09	1,826.87	3,575.59	2,558.95	6,607.05	5,708.32
Total	73,823.5	313,194.54	80,366.25	340,991.42	76,824.69	298,219.38
Grand total	32,109,773.7	15,304,991.2	42,763,856.6	18,476,922.8	44,463,340.5	22,094,289.2

Source: [34].

Appendix 2: Government initiatives and policy intervention.

Schemes	Thrust areas/objectives
National Mission on Sustainable Agriculture (NMSA)	Sustainability in agriculture
Paramparagat Krishi Vikas Yojana (PKVY)	Soil health management

Bharatiya Prakritik Krishi Paddhati (BPKP)	Natural farming: promoting traditional indigenous practices
Rashtriya Krishi Vikas Yojana (RKVY)	Innovation and agri-entrepreneurship development
National e-Governance Plan in Agriculture (NeGP-A)	Funding to the state(s)/UT(s) for projects involving artificial intelligence (AI), machine learning (ML), blockchain, robotics, drones, data analytics
National Agriculture Market (e-NAM) Scheme	Creating an online transparent competitive bidding system to facilitate farmers with remunerative prices for their produce
FARMS- Farm Machinery Solutions	Multi-language mobile app platform to facilitate local farmers to connect with vendors of agricultural machinery and equipment for renting or buying
Modified Interest Subvention Scheme (MISS)	Affordable farm credit
Negotiable Warehouse Receipts (NWRs)	Postharvest loans on par with interest subvention scheme for small and marginal farmers
National Disaster Response Force (NDRF) assistance	Assistance to farmers affected by severe natural calamities
Electronic Kisan Credit Cards (KCCs)	Farmers' financial needs of agriculture
National Agricultural Insurance Scheme (NAIS)	Covers food crops (cereals, millets, and pulses), oilseeds, and annual commercial horticultural crops
Open Network for Digital Commerce (ONDC)	Digital commerce for agricultural products

Sources: [35–43].

References

1. United Nations, Goal 2: Zero hunger-united nations sustainable development, United Nations Sustainable Development. *United Nations Report*, 1, 23, 1-5, 2023. Available: https://www.un.org/sustainabledevelopment/ hunger/.
2. World Bank, Overview. *World Bank Report*, 1, 23, 1-5, 2023, Available: https://www.worldbank.org/en/topic/agriculture/overview#:~:text=Agriculture%20is%20also%20crucial%20to.
3. Ministry of Finance, Department of Economic Affairs, *Economic Survey 2022-23*, Jan. 2023, Available: file:///C:/Users/staff95/Downloads/Economic%20Survey%20Complete%20PDF.pdf.
4. Committee on Doubling Farmers' Income, *March of Agriculture since Independence and Growth Trends*, Ministry of Agriculture & Farmers' Welfare, India, Aug. 2017. Available: Ministry of Agriculture & Farmers' Welfare.

5. Digitalisation of Agricultural Sector. pib.gov.in. *Ministry of Agriculture & Farmers Welfare*, 1, 21, 1-5, 2021, Available: https://pib.gov.in/PressReleasePage. aspx?PRID=1777684.

6. Nearly 400 farmer organisations in various stages of integration with ONDC: T Koshy, *ONDC Report*, 1, 23, 1-5, Apr. 15, 2023. www. thehindubusinessline.com. Available: https://www.the-hindubusinessline.com/info-tech/nearly-400-farmer-organisations-in-various-stages-of-integration-with-ondc-tkoshy/article66737932.ece.

7. How agtech is poised to transform India into a farming powerhouse. *McKinsey*. 1, 23, 1-5, 2023, www. mckinsey.com. Available: https://www.mckinsey.com/industries/agriculture/our-insights/how-agtech-is-poised-to-transform-india-into-a-farming-powerhouse.

8. Mehmood, A., Ahmed, S., Viza, E., Bogush, A., Ayyub, R.M., Drivers and barriers towards circular economy in agri-food supply chain: A review. *Bus. Strategy Dev.*, 6, 21, 1-7, Jun. 2021. doi: https://doi.org/10.1002/bsd2.171.

9. Goa State Coordination Committee, Indian Council of Agricultural Research, *Doubling of Farmers Income by 2022 Strategy Document for Goa*, India, Jan. 2018.

10. Doubling of Farmers' Income. pib.gov.in. *Ministry of Agriculture & Farmers Welfare*, 1, 23, 1-5, 2023, Available: https://pib.gov.in/PressReleaseIframePage.aspx?PRID=1896136#:~:text=As%20compared%20to%20previous%20year.

11. Patel, N., Athura, S., Sethi, T., Meena, S. (Eds.), *Compendium of Success Stories of Natural Farming*, NITI Aayog, India, 2022, Available: https://www.niti.gov.in/sites/default/files/2022-04/Compendium_of_Success_Stories_of_Natural_Farming_English_19042022.pdf.

12. *Natural Farming: NITI Initiative*, NITI Aayog, India, 2020, www.niti.gov.in. Available: https://www.niti. gov.in/natural-farming-niti-initiative.

13. Planning Commission, *Working Group on Risk Management in Agriculture for XI Five Year Plan (2007–2012)*, Government of India, Available: https://pmfby.gov.in/compendium/General/2007%20-THE%20WORKING%20GROUP%20ON%20Risk%20Management%20Agriculture.pdf.

14. Jain, R., Kishore, P., Singh, D.K., Irrigation in India: Status, challenges and options. *J. Soil Water Conserv.*, 18, 4, 354, 2019, doi: https://doi.org/10.5958/24557145.2019.00050.xDr.

15. National Mission for Sustainable Agriculture. nmsa.dac.gov.in. *National Mission for Sustainable Agriculture*, 1, 23, 1-5, 2023, Available: https://nmsa.dac. gov.in/frmStrategy.aspx.

16. News of, *agriexchange.apeda.gov.in. Agricultural and Processed Food Products Export Development Authority*, 1, 23, 1-5, 2023, Available: https://agriexchange.apeda.gov.in/news/NewsSearch.aspx?newsid=48209. [Accessed: Jun. 20, 2023].

17. Tinarwo, J., Transforming African agriculture through special economic zones: Opportunities and challenges, in: *Building a Resilient and Sustainable Agriculture in Sub-Saharan Africa*, pp. 241–255, 2018, doi: https://doi.org/10.1007/978-3-319-76222-7_11.

18. Kumar, C.M.S., Solar energy: A promising renewable source for meeting energy demand in Indian agriculture applications. *al.Sustain. Energy Technol. Assess.*, 55, 102905, Feb. 2023. doi: https://doi.org/10.1016/j.seta.2022.102905.

19. Special Economic Zones. pib.gov.in. *Ministry of Commerce & Industry Report*, 1, 23, 1-7, 2023, Available: https://pib.gov.in/PressReleasePage.aspx?PRID=1779402. [Accessed: Jun. 20, 2023].

20. Mega Food Park | Ministry of Food Processing Industries | GOI, *GOI Report*, 1, 12, 1-5, 2012. Mofpi.gov.in Available: https://www.mofpi.gov.in/Schemes/mega-food-parks.

21. Sharma, Y.S., Niti Aayog preparing index for agri transformation now. *Economic Times*, 1, 23, 1-5, Jan. 11, 2023. Available: https://economictimes.indiatimes.com/news/economy/agriculture/niti-aayog-preparing-index-for-agri-transformation-now/articleshow/96892573.cms. [Accessed: Jun. 20, 2023].

22. AI in Agriculture: The Future of Farming. *nasscom Off. Community Indian IT Industry.* 1, 23, 2-5, 2023, Available: https://community.nasscom.in/communities/agritech/ai-agriculture-future-farming. [Accessed: Jun. 20, 2023].

23. Micro Irrigation. *JAIN IRRIGATION SYSTEMS LIMITED Report*, 1, 23, 1-7, 2023, www.jains.com. Available: https://www.jains.com/Segment/Irrigation.htm#4.

24. Finolex Drip I Agronomy. *FInolex Plasson.* 1, 23, 1-5, 2023, Available: https://www.finolexdrip.com/agronomy.

25. Marico – make a difference. www.marico.com. Available: https://www.marico.com/html/sustainability.html

26. *Nation First: Sab Saath Badhein Report and Accounts 2022*, Available: https://www.itcportal.com/about-itc/shareholder-value/annual-reports/itc-annual-report-2022/pdf/ITCReport-and-Accounts-2022.pdf.

27. Britannia.co.in, *Britania Report*, 1, 17, 1-5, 2017. Available: https://www.britannia.co.in/article/britannia-enhances-farmers-livelihood-with-tech-enabled-and-sustainable-dairy-farming-solutions.

28. Marr, B., The incredible ways John Deere is using artificial intelligence to transform farming. *Forbes.*, 1, 18, 1-5, 2018, Available: https://www.forbes.com/sites/bernardmarr/2018/03/09/the-incredible-ways-john-deere-is-using-artificial-intelligence-to-transform-farming/.

29. *Government of India Nirmala Sitharaman Minister of Finance*, India Budget, India, 2021, Available: https://www.indiabudget.gov.in/doc/Budget_Speech.pdf.

30. Scale your farmer enablement with crop apps. www.cropin.com. *Cropin Report*, 1, 23, 1-3, 2023, Available: https://www.cropin.com/intelligent-agriculture-cloud/cropin-apps.

31. Farmer application-agricultural solution for farmers | Download now. agrevolution.in. *Agrevolution Report*, 1, 23, 1-5, 2023, Available: https://agrevolution.in/solution-for-farmers.

32. *OECD-FAO Agricultural Outlook 2021-2030*, OECD, Paris, France, 2023, www.oecd-ilibrary.org. https://www.oecd-ilibrary.org/agriculture-and-food/oecd-fao-agricultural-outlook-2021-2030_19428846-en.

33. Transforming agriculture through digital technologies. *Deloitte Report*, 1, 20, 1-5, 2020. Available: https://www2.deloitte.com/content/dam/Deloitte/gr/Documents/consumer-business/gr_Transforming_Agriculture_through_Digital_Technologies_noexp.pdf.

34. Three Year Export Statement of APEDA Products. *Ministry of Agriculture & Farmers Welfare*, 1, 21, 1-5, 2021, agriexchange.apeda.gov.in. Available: https://agriexchange.apeda.gov.in/indexp/exportstatement.aspx.

35. National Mission for Sustainable Agriculture. nmsa.dac.gov.in. *National Mission for Sustainable Agriculture*, 1, 23, 1-5, 2023, Available: https://nmsa.dac. gov.in/frmStrategy.aspx.

36. The Nestlé Agriculture Framework Measuring progress and performance. *Nestle Report*, 1, 23, 1-5, 2023, Available: https:// www.nestle.com/sites/default/files/2022-12/nestle-agriculture-framework-measures.pdf. [Accessed: Jun. 20, 2023].

37. *Paramparagat Krishi Vikas Yojana (PKVY)*, Govt. of India, India, 2023, pib.gov.in. Available: https://pib.gov.in/ PressReleaseIframePage.aspx?PRID=1739994.

38. Digitalisation of Agricultural Sector. pib.gov.in. *Ministry of Agriculture & Farmers Welfare*, 1, 21, 1-5, 2021, Available: https://pib.gov.in/PressReleasePage. aspx?PRID=1777684.

39. *FARMS (Farm Machinery Solutions) Mobile App | Govt of India*, agrimachinery.nic.in. Govt. of India, India, 2023, Available: https://agrimachinery.nic.in/Index/farmsapp.

40. *Agriculture Credit Overview*, Govt. of India, India, 2023, Available: https://agricoop.gov.in/Documents/AgricultureCredit-Overview_23_03_2023.pdf.

41. Master Circular-Kisan Credit Card (KCC) Scheme. *RBI Report*, 1, 17, 1-5, 2017. Available: https://www.rbi.org.in/commonman/Upload/English/Notification/PDFs/04MCKCC03072017.

42. Agriculture Insurance, . agricoop.nic.in. *Ministry of Agriculture & Farmers Welfare*, 1, 21, 1-5, 2021, Available: https://agricoop.nic.in/sites/ default/files/AGRICULTURE%20INSURANCE-Credits.pdf.

43. NABARD-National Bank for Agriculture and Rural Development, Nabard.org, *Nabard Report*, 1, 22, 1-3, 2022. Available: https://www.nabard.org/news-article.aspx?id=25&cid=552&NID=489.

13

Design of Smart Digital Crop Harvester Monitoring Cluster

Aditi Oak[1]*, Ishwari Patil[1], Aarya Phansalkar[1], Ashwini M. Deshpande[1] and Shounak Sharangpani[2]

[1]Department of Electronics and Telecommunication Engineering, MKSSS's Cummins College of Engineering for Women, Pune, India
[2]Twintech Control Systems Pvt. Ltd., Pune, India

Abstract

In this work, we propose a smart digital crop harvester monitoring cluster designed to aid farmers and agricultural workers in keeping track of essential agricultural vehicle information. The proposed system monitors and displays the vehicle's real-time data for essential parameters. Monitoring the fuel levels is important for avoiding downtime and delays in operations. Tracking of engine oil pressure becomes pivotal as low oil strain can demonstrate potential engine issues. The cluster provides real-time data on radiator water temperature, to avert potential issues with the engine cooling system. Threshing RPM (speed) is useful since different crops require different RPMs for the effective separation of grain from straw. Data thus acquired are sent to the cloud allowing live monitoring and predictive analysis. Currently, in the market, similar devices are imported into India, leading to heavy import duties and a significant increase in cost. This puts a financial strain on Indian consumers creating a gap in the accessibility of the latest agricultural technologies. Our market survey confirms that this integrated solution can address multiple parameters simultaneously, reducing production and testing costs while streamlining the installation process. Hence, the cluster is an easy-to-operate, cost-effective, and indigenous product-based design to promote a modern digital agriculture ecosystem.

Keywords: STM32, ATMEGA, embedded systems, crop harvester monitoring

13.1 Introduction

In recent years, there have been a lot of technological advancements in the agriculture sector, which make a big contribution to the production of food worldwide. The introduction of technology has made agriculture more productive and cost-effective, but agricultural apparatus and hardware can be costly to keep up with and maintain. One of the primary causes of these breakdowns is a lack of real-time monitoring and analysis of vital agricultural vehicle data. In this work, we aim to resolve this issue by proposing a digital instrument cluster

*Corresponding author: aditioak02@gmail.com

Kuldeep Singh and Prasanna Kolar (eds.) *Digital Agricultural Ecosystem: Revolutionary Advancements in Agriculture*, (229–258) © 2024 Scrivener Publishing LLC

involving an intuitive and comprehensive dashboard for live data of agricultural vehicles offering continuous observation and investigation of their pivotal information.

The device will provide all of the following features:

i) Display and track the fuel consumption of the machine
ii) Radiator water temperature sensor to track the cooling of the engine
iii) Battery voltage and engine oil pressure tracking
iv) Engine and threshing RPM measurement
v) Engine running and threshing hours
vi) Comprehensive calibration options: provides flexibility in the choice of sensors as long as they are resistive
vii) Personalized user interface: allows for customization of the user interface to meet individual needs
viii) Improved safety features: incorporates enhanced safety measures to ensure maximum safety

With the above features, this dashboard is easy to operate and simple to introduce and decreases the gamble of free time or breakdowns. Figure 13.1 shows the design of the UI of the cluster. As seen in the figure, the dashboard will be intuitive and easy for the layman to operate and analyze.

13.2   Literature Survey

As an essential step of the design and development of a product, we executed a product survey which included a detailed comparative study of products that could be potentially similar to ours. "MTA Smart" and "Murphy Powerview PV380-R2" have a close resemblance to that of ours.

Murphy Powerview provides a grayscale monochrome display along with all the tell-tale signs on the single screen itself. This has made it difficult for the users to interpret and monitor the crucial parameters. Our device provides tell-tale signs for alerts and indications outside the screen in a structured fashion, and the continuously changing values are displayed in terms of progressive bars on the screen. This allows the user to differentiate

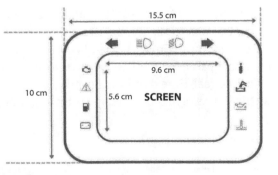

Figure 13.1 Cluster model with dimensions.

between the alerts so that those do not get ignored and corrective action can be taken immediately while still monitoring the real-time values of other parameters.

MTA Smart offers a color display along with 10 tell-tale LED signs. The added advantages and functionalities provided by our device include 12 tell-tale LED signs and a more intuitive and easier-to-read dashboard. Additionally, two CAN ports are provided for the smooth transmission of the vehicle's vital data to and fro. Both products mentioned cater to a wide range of applications in vehicles like earth-moving trucks and similar heavy machinery along with agricultural vehicles. Our product focuses on agricultural thresher and keeps the thresher as a central idea while designing and developing the cluster. This reduces generalization in the design, and a parameter-specific monitoring system can be developed. While some parameters monitored are common for every vehicle, threshing RPM and threshing hours need to be considered separately, especially for a thresher, and built into the monitoring system accordingly.

Studies offered in [1] assisted in elevating the understanding of how sensor data are to be collected from multiple sources and transmitted to the microcontroller STM32. It also discusses various approaches to building robust STM32-based systems and effective interfacing of multiple sensors for their simultaneous working to be faster.

Testing the system is a crucial step before the product is declared as efficient and accurate. In [2], the authors have presented some insights on how testing for results is performed to eliminate any errors that might have been ignored during the design and development stages. Both [1] and [2] include an STM32-based monitoring system design which provided an initial direction on how to go about the design and articulate our product for a flawless user experience.

13.3   Methodology

Our device development comprises two essential components, namely, hardware and software. The hardware design incorporates the capability to monitor and measure significant parameters of your vehicle such as fuel level, radiator water temperature, battery voltage level, engine oil pressure, engine running hours, and threshing hours, whereas the software design involves programming the microcontrollers and developing an intuitive dashboard user interface that is user-friendly and easy to navigate. With this holistic approach, we ensure seamless integration of hardware and software for efficient functioning and maximum performance of our device.

13.3.1   Working

Figure 13.2 shows the block diagram of the electrical circuit inside the cluster. The sensors seen in the figure will sense the parameters from the surroundings and then transfer all these physical values of signals to their specific conditioning units for further processing.

The signal conditioning unit will convert the received signals into the desired form. For sending the signals to the microcontroller, we require them to be in voltage form. All sensors (excluding the RPM sensor) are of resistive type, meaning their output is resistance value. Thus, voltage dividers are used as signal conditioners to convert resistance values to voltages.

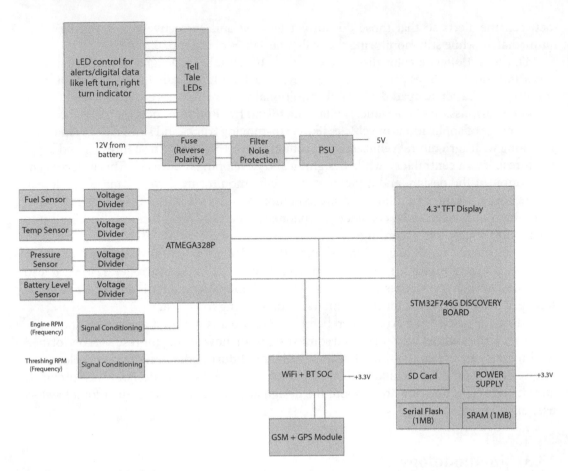

Figure 13.2 System block diagram.

The microcontroller chosen (STM32) has an inbuilt ADC present to convert signals from an analog domain to a digital domain. Apart from that, the STM32 microcontroller is used to display the acquired data by controlling the TFT display, and the ATMEGA328 microcontroller is used for interfacing all the sensors. As a final step, the acquired data are sent using Wi-Fi/Bluetooth over to the cloud platform for further analysis, storage purposes, and ease of accessibility.

13.3.2 Design of Fuel Level Measurement Circuit

A fuel-level measurement circuit is necessary to provide accurate information about the amount of fuel in a vehicle's fuel tank. There are several reasons why such a circuit is important:

    i. Fuel management: Agricultural vehicles, such as tractors, combines, and harvesters, often operate in remote locations, and refueling can be a challenge. Knowing the fuel level allows farmers to plan their operations efficiently and avoid running out of fuel in the field, which can be costly and time-consuming.

ii. Maintenance: The fuel system's performance can be affected by the harsh conditions that agricultural vehicles are subjected to, such as dust, dirt, and debris. Observing the fuel level can assist farmers with distinguishing potential issues early and plan upkeep on a case-by-case basis.

- *Input:* The input to a float-type fuel level sensor is the physical level of fuel in the tank that causes the float to move and change the resistance of the variable resistor.
- *Output:* Voltage varying from 0 to 5 V proportional to the amount of fuel in the tank
- *Application requirement range:* 0 to full range
- *Working:* A voltage divider is used to convert the output obtained from the resistive fuel sensor to a value between 0 and 5 V which can be then sensed by the microcontroller pins [3]. Figure 13.3 shows the circuit which consists of a 240-Ω resistor which forms a voltage divider with the resistive fuel sensor. FUEL_IN is the output of the voltage divider circuit which gives the voltage value corresponding to the fuel level that can be given to the microcontroller.
- *Calculations:* A voltage divider circuit shown in Figure 13.3 is used for fuel sensor measurement, and the calculations are given in Equations (13.1), (13.2), and (13.3).

Following the design equations with reference to [3], the calculations are as follows:

i. When the fuel level is minimum, the output voltage is as follows:

$$Vo = \frac{R_{fuel}}{R_{fuel} + R_7} \times V_{in} = \frac{345}{345 + 240} \times 5 = 2.94V \tag{13.1}$$

ii. When the fuel level is maximum, the output voltage is as follows:

$$Vo = \frac{R_{fuel}}{R_{fuel} + R_7} \times V_{in} = \frac{7}{7 + 240} \times 5 = 0.141V \tag{13.2}$$

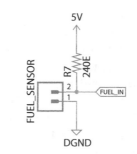

Figure 13.3 Voltage divider circuit for the fuel sensor.

iii. Power dissipation

$$P = \frac{V^2}{R_7 + R_{fuel}(min)} = \frac{5^2}{240 + 7} = 0.101W \qquad (13.3)$$

The fuel sensor outputs higher resistance when the fuel is minimum and lower resistance when the fuel is maximum. When the fuel varies from 0 to full, there is a change in the voltage from 2.94 to 0.141 V and a power dissipation of 0.101 W. This signal is now fit to be given to the microcontroller.

13.3.3   Design of the Temperature Measurement Circuit

Radiator water temperature refers to the temperature of the coolant fluid that circulates through the engine cooling system and passes through the radiator to dissipate heat. The cooling system in a vehicle is designed to regulate the engine temperature by circulating coolant fluid through the engine block to absorb heat, then transferring that heat to the radiator, where it is dissipated into the surrounding air.

Radiator water temperature measurement is crucial in agricultural vehicles for several reasons:

i. Engine performance: The temperature of the engine coolant affects the engine's performance and efficiency. If the engine runs too hot or too cold, it can impact the vehicle's power output and fuel economy. Monitoring the coolant temperature allows the operator to adjust the engine's operation as necessary to maintain optimal performance.

ii. Engine protection: Overheating can damage the engine, leading to costly repairs or even engine failure. Monitoring the coolant temperature allows the operator to detect potential overheating issues early and take corrective action before significant damage occurs.

- *Input:* The input to a temperature sensor is the temperature of the coolant fluid circulating through the engine cooling system.
- *Output:* Voltage varying from 0 to 5 V proportional to the radiator water temperature
- *Application requirement range:* 40°C–140°C
- *Working:* As seen in Figure 13.4, a voltage divider is used to convert the output obtained from the resistive temperature sensor to a value between 0 and 5 V which can be then sensed by the microcontroller pins. TEMP_IN is the output of the voltage divider circuit which gives the voltage value corresponding to the radiator water temperature that can be given to the microcontroller.
- *Calculations:* Figure 13.4 indicates a voltage-divided circuit used for temperature sensor measurement. The design calculations done are given in Equations (13.4), (13.5), and (13.6).

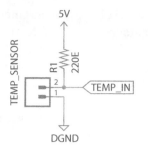

Figure 13.4 Voltage divider circuit for temperature sensor.

i. When the temperature is minimum, the output voltage is as follows:

$$Vo = \frac{R_{temp}}{R_{temp} + R_1} \times V_{in} = \frac{115.54}{115.54 + 220} \times 5 = 0.345V \qquad (13.4)$$

ii. When the temperature is maximum, the output voltage is as follows:

$$Vo = \frac{R_{temp}}{R_{temp} + R_1} \times V_{in} = \frac{153.58}{153.58 + 220} \times 5 = 0.411V \qquad (13.5)$$

iii. Power dissipation

$$P = \frac{V^2}{R_1 + R_{temp}(min)} = \frac{5^2}{220 + 115.54} = 0.074W \qquad (13.6)$$

When the temperature varies from the minimum to maximum value, there is a change in the voltage from 0.345 to 0.411 V and a power dissipation of 0.074 W.

13.3.4 Design of the Battery-Level Measurement Circuit

Battery voltage estimation is fundamental in light of the fact that:

The state of charge and health of a battery can be determined from its voltage. Regularly measuring the voltage of the battery can help determine when it needs to be charged or replaced before it fails.

If the battery voltage is too high or too low, it can damage electrical devices like motors and electronics. The equipment's safe voltage range can be confirmed by measuring the battery voltage.

Temperature and load can have an impact on the performance of batteries. Estimating the battery voltage can assist with advancing battery execution by distinguishing the best temperature and burden conditions for the battery.

- *Input:* The input for battery voltage measurement is the voltage across the battery terminals. This battery voltage is directly measured from the battery and then given to the signal conditioning unit to convert its range to one sensed by a microcontroller. The voltage measurement works as an indicator of the state of charge or discharge of the battery and is an important parameter for monitoring its efficiency and health.
- *Output:* The output of the battery voltage measurement circuit is the battery voltage between 0 and 5 V that will be sensed and processed by the microcontroller.
- *Application requirement range:* 8 to 16 V maximum
- *Working:* A sensor is not needed in this circuit since battery voltage is already in volts, but a voltage divider is needed to convert the battery voltage of 0–12 V to 0–5 V which can be given to the microcontroller. As seen in Figure 13.5, two resistors of values 10 and 2.7 kΩ are used in the voltage divider circuit.
- *Calculations:* The voltage divider arrangement for the battery sensor is shown in Figure 13.5, followed by design calculations in Equations (13.7), (13.8), and (13.9).

i. When battery level is maximum, the output voltage is as follows:

$$Vo = \frac{R_2}{R_2 + R_1} \times V_{battery} = \frac{2.7}{2.7 + 10} \times 12\,V = 2.55\,V \tag{13.7}$$

ii. When battery level is minimum, the output voltage is as follows:

$$Vo = \frac{R_2}{R_2 + R_1} \times V_{battery} = \frac{2.7}{2.7 + 10} \times 0\,V = 0\,V \tag{13.8}$$

Hence, as the battery voltage changes from 0 to 12 V, the signal conditioning circuit output changes from 0 to 2.55 V. The output of the signal conditioning labeled as BATTERY_IN can now be given as input to the microcontroller for further processing.

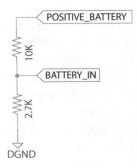

Figure 13.5 Voltage divider circuit for the battery sensor.

13.3.5   Design of the Oil Pressure Measurement Circuit

Oil pressure observation in a vehicle is fundamental since it guarantees that the motor is appropriately greased up and running effectively. Oil is essential for lubricating the engine's moving parts, reducing wear and friction, and dissipating heat. The engine may experience a variety of issues if there is not enough oil pressure, such as increased wear and tear on engine parts, decreased fuel economy, or even engine failure.

A gauge or warning light and a sensor that measures the oil's pressure as it flows through the engine are typically the components of an oil pressure monitoring system. The driver will be informed of the issue by the gauge or warning light if the oil pressure falls below a predetermined level. This lets the driver do things like add more oil or stop the car to protect the engine from damage.

- *Input:* The input of an oil pressure sensor in an engine is the actual oil pressure in the engine's lubrication system. The sensor, which is typically located in the oil pump or the engine block, measures the pressure of the engine oil as it moves through the engine. An electrical signal proportional to the actual measured pressure is produced by the sensor when it detects changes in oil pressure brought on by engine speed, temperature, and load.
- *Output:* The output of an oil pressure sensor in an engine is a voltage between 0 and 5 V which is proportional to the oil pressure measured by the sensor.
- *Application requirement range:* 0–392 kPa
- *Working:* As shown in Figure 13.6, a resistor of 100 Ω is used in the voltage divider circuit which is used to convert the output obtained from the resistive pressure sensor to a value between 0 and 5 V which can be sensed by the microcontroller pins.
- *Calculations:* A voltage divider circuit for the pressure sensor shown in Figure 13.6 considers component values as per the design steps followed in Equations (13.9), (13.10), and (13.11).

i.   When pressure is minimum, the output voltage is as follows:

$$Vo = \frac{P}{P + R_1} \times V_{in} = \frac{83}{83 + 100} \times 5\,V = 2.26\,V \qquad (13.9)$$

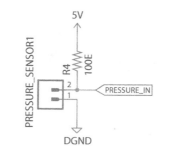

Figure 13.6 Voltage divider circuit for the pressure sensor.

ii. When pressure is maximum, the output voltage is as follows:

$$Vo = \frac{P}{P + R_1} \times V_{in} = \frac{43}{43 + 100} \times 5\,V = 1.503\,V \qquad (13.10)$$

iii. Power dissipation

$$P = V \times I = 5 \times 0.02 = 0.1\,W \qquad (13.11)$$

When the pressure varies from the minimum to maximum value, there is a change in the voltage from 2.26 to 1.503 V and a power dissipation of *0.1*.

13.3.6   Design of the RPM Measurement Circuit

The RPM (revolutions per minute) of an engine refers to how many times the engine's crankshaft rotates in a minute. It is an important parameter to know because it can affect the performance, fuel efficiency, and durability of the engine. Hence, this circuit is needed to measure the engine RPM and threshing RPM of the harvester.

- *Input:* The RPM sensor is attached to the teeth of the engine or more specifically to its flywheel. The sensor senses the frequency and gives an output which is in the form of a sinusoidal wave whose amplitude is 80 V peak to peak under open circuit conditions.
- *Output:* The sinusoidal wave from the RPM sensor is converted to a square wave with amplitude ranging from $V_{ce} = 90$ mV to $V_{cc} = 5$ V using which the threshing and engine RPMs are measured.
- *Application requirement range:* 0–10 kHz
- *Working:* Figure 13.7 below shows the signal conditioning needed for the RPM measurement circuit. The output of the RPM sensor which is a

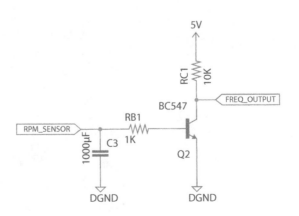

Figure 13.7 RPM sensor transistor circuit.

sinusoidal wave is converted to a square wave which can then ensure accuracy in the measurement of the frequency of the signal, which is proportional to the engine speed. Conversion of sine wave to square wave is done using an NPN transistor used as a switch. Resistors RB1 and RC1 are used for biasing of the transistor, and a capacitor is used for noise cancellation.

- **Design steps:**

i. Selection of biasing resistors R_b and R_c referring to [3] and [4]:

$$V_{cc} = 5V \tag{13.12}$$
$$V_{ce} = 0.2 \text{ V}$$
$$R_c = \frac{V_{cc} - V_{ce}}{I_{cc}}$$

$$I_c = \frac{5 - 0.2}{10} = 0.48mA \tag{13.13}$$

$$I_b = \frac{I_c}{\beta} = \frac{0.48 * 10^{-3}}{455} = 0.001mA \tag{13.14}$$

Using modeling of the circuit using h-parameters,

$$Zout = 800 \ to \ 1,500 \ ohms$$

According to Thevenin's theorem, to maximize the power transfer through the circuit, impedance matching is done as,

$$Zin = 1,000 \ to \ 1,200 \ ohms$$

Hence, values of $Rb = 1\,k\Omega$ and $Rc = 10\,k\Omega$

ii. Protection from noise:

A 0.01-µF capacitor is placed in the circuit to filter out all frequencies above 15 kHz since the desired signal has a frequency of up to only 10 kHz, and frequencies above this value need to be filtered out.

iii. Calculations:

$$R_b = 1\,k\Omega$$
$$C = 0.01\,\mu F$$
$$f_c = \text{cutoff frequency}$$

$$f_c = \frac{1}{2\times pi \times R_b \times C} = \frac{1}{2\times 3.14\times 1\times 10^3 \times 0.01\times 10^{-6}} = 15.91\,\text{kHz} \qquad (13.15)$$

Hence, the capacitor filters out all signals above 15 kHz and allows only frequencies under 15 kHz to pass.

iv. Power dissipation of circuit:

$$P = V_{cc} \times Ic = 0.48\,mA \times 5V = 2.4\,mW$$

$$(13.16)$$

v. Accuracy of the RPM measurement: ±1 RPM

13.3.7   Design for the Threshing RPM Measurement Circuit

Threshing is the process of separation of grain from unwanted straw. For this effective separation, different crops may require different threshing speeds. Strong and sturdy crops require higher threshing RPM, whereas soft and fragile crops require lower threshing RPM. Incorrect threshing RPM can lead to overthreshing which can lead to grain damage or grain loss while underthreshing can result in the threshing process remaining incomplete. Hence, for the optimization of threshing, tracking of this parameter is crucial.

All design considerations are the same as the RPM measurement circuit.

13.3.8   Design of the Power Supply

The power supply unit (PSU) is an integral part of the cluster. The PSU is responsible for delivering stable and reliable power to the various components and peripherals for them to function effectively. It is thus important to choose a PSU that has sufficient wattage and appropriate connectors to power all the components in the cluster. Overloading or underpowering the PSU can lead to system instability or even damage to the components [5].

- *Requirement:*
Different components have different requirements of operating ranges like the following:

    i. Microcontroller—3.3 V
    ii. Peripherals—5 V

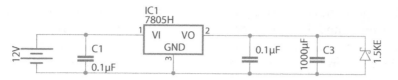

Figure 13.8 Power supply circuit.

    iii. TFT display—18 V (480 pixels × 272 pixels)
    iv. Tell-tale LED—8.4 V (6 LEDS with 1.4 V drop each)

- *Design/calculations for 12 to 5V conversion*

A 5-V supply is needed for the working of all the sensors in the circuit; hence, the 12 V coming from the battery needs to be stepped down to 5 V. As seen in Figure 13.8, a regulator, three capacitors, and a transorb are used in this step-down circuit.

    i. Mornsun 7805 DC/DC Switching Regulator—A switching regulator can convert input direct current (DC) voltage to the desired direct current (DC) voltage. By turning a switching element ON and OFF, a switching regulator enables high-efficiency electricity conversion as it supplies the required amount of electricity only when needed.
    ii. Capacitors—0.1 µF (2), 1,000 µF—They are used to suppress electrical noise coming from the power supply line. There are many sources of power line noise that make the power supply voltage fluctuate at various frequencies. Some noise sources like large loads introduce voltage spikes when they are switched on and off.
    iii. 1.5KE Transorb—Transorb (or transient voltage suppressor, TVS) is an electronic component used in electrical circuits to protect sensitive electronic devices from voltage spikes, transients, or surges.

Referring to [6], a TVS is designed to absorb the energy from voltage spikes and transients and divert it away from sensitive electronic components, such as integrated circuits, by shorting the voltage surge to the ground or other protective devices. This helps prevent the voltage surge from damaging or destroying sensitive electronic devices. For 12 to 18 V, 12 to 3.3 V, and 12 to 1.8 V: converted by STM32.

13.3.9   Design of Reverse Polarity Circuit

Reverse polarity protection is essential, particularly in automotive and battery-operated devices. In battery-operated devices like this cluster, reverse polarity protection is essential

Figure 13.9 Reverse polarity protection circuit.

to prevent damage to the cluster components and peripherals. If unintentionally the battery connects incorrectly and the voltage gets applied in reverse, it can cause current to flow in the wrong direction, which can lead to overheating and possibly cause a short circuit or damage to the components. To ensure protection from any damages caused due to reverse polarity, a diode is used.

- *Component used:* 1N4007 Rectifier diode
- *Working:* A diode is primarily a P–N junction semiconductor device. It acts as a one-way switch that allows the current to flow in one direction and halts in the other direction. When the anode is connected to a higher potential than the cathode (forward biasing), the current flows from the anode to a cathode terminal, whereas reverse biasing will restrict the flow of current [3]. Hence, as seen in Figure 13.9, if the battery is incorrectly connected to the diode, the diode will be reverse-biased and will ensure that the battery is not connected to the load, hence preventing electrical damage to the circuit, while if the battery is properly connected to the circuit, the diode will be forward-biased and hence will act as a closed switch between the battery and load.

13.3.10   Microcontrollers

In the device, we are using two microcontrollers, STM32 and ATMEGA328. These microcontrollers serve the purpose of interfacing with the various sensors used and to read, acquire, and display data in a minimalistic and user-friendly UI.

- *STM32*

i.   Based on the ARM Cortex-M processor architecture, the STM32 family of 32-bit microcontrollers provide high efficiency, processing power, clock speeds up to 480 MHz, and flash memory capacities of up to 2 MB.

ii. This microcontroller is preferred over others due to its low power consumption, which increases device uptime and extends battery life.

iii. Additionally, this controller provides a comprehensive development ecosystem, including STMCubeIDE and the TouchGFX designer, which will be utilized for UI development.

iv. A wide variety of development tools, such as the STM32CubeIDE, STM32CubeMX, and STM32CubeProg, make it simple for developers to create, debug, and program STM32-based applications.

v.   The display of the sensor data is done with STM32. It has a TFT LCD display inside that measures 480 pixels by 272 pixels.

vi. Our device dashboard's main screen will be this LCD display.

vii. STM32 microcontrollers provide excellent support for developers by providing comprehensive documentation, a lively community, specialized development tools, a robust hardware ecosystem, and ongoing updates. This ensures that developers have the resources they require for projects that are successful.

viii. The STM32 microcontroller family upholds I2C correspondence through its equipment I2C fringe. Involving I2C in STM32 microcontrollers includes empowering and arranging the I2C fringe, starting and ending correspondence utilizing start and stop conditions, and sending/getting information utilizing the DR register.

ix. Interrupts can also be used to deal with events that happen during I2C communication.

- **ATMEGA328**

i. The ATMEGA328 is a member of the AVR family of microcontrollers. It has 1 KB of EEPROM for non-volatile data storage, 2 KB of SRAM for data storage, and 32 KB of flash memory for storing program code.

ii. It also has various digital and analog input/output pins that can be used to interface with other devices or sensors.

iii. The ATMEGA328 microcontroller has been used in our project to establish communication and exchange data between all the sensors and the system.

iv. The ability of the ATMEGA328 to effectively process and manage data from multiple sensors and to facilitate the system's overall operation is the primary factor in its selection as the sensor interface.

v. The ATmega328 microcontroller also supports I2C communication through its hardware I2C peripheral. Using I2C in Atmega328 microcontrollers involves enabling and configuring the I2C peripheral, setting the slave address (for slave mode), initiating and terminating communication using start and stop conditions, and sending/receiving data using the TWDR register.

- **Need for the usage of two microcontrollers**

i. The STM32 microcontroller is used to display the acquired data, and the ATMEGA328 microcontroller is used for interfacing all the sensors.

ii. The STM32 TFT LCD display is 480 pixels × 272 pixels, and hence, it requires a fast refresh rate. This displaying process is task-intensive and requires a lot of energy.

iii. Adding to the load of the sensor interfacing on this microcontroller would not be feasible, as for example even if 1 frequency count is missed due to over loading, the RPM readings would go wrong.

iv. To remove this load from STM32, we are using ATMEGA328 for interfacing the sensors, i.e., hard real-time tasks.

13.3.11   ESP32

i. ESP32 is a low-cost, low-power system on a chip (SoC) microcontroller with integrated Wi-Fi and Bluetooth capabilities, developed by Espressif Systems. It is a popular choice for Internet of Things (IoT) projects due to its small size, low power consumption, and wireless connectivity.

ii. The ESP32 features a dual-core processor with up to 240 MHz clock speed, up to 520 KB of SRAM, and up to 16 MB of flash memory. It also has a wide range of peripherals including analog-to-digital converters (ADCs), digital-to-analog converters (DACs), UART, SPI, I2C, and PWM.

iii. ESP32 microcontrollers provide integrated Wi-Fi capabilities, low power consumption, and a rich peripheral set, making them an excellent choice for our Wi-Fi-enabled projects with easy development and strong community support.

iv. The ESP32 can be programmed using the Arduino IDE. Overall, the ESP32 is a versatile and powerful microcontroller with integrated Wi-Fi and Bluetooth capabilities that is well-suited for a wide range of IoT applications.

v. ESP32 was interfaced to Wi-Fi utilizing Arduino, using the ESP32 Wi-Fi library, which gives capabilities to design and lay out a wireless association and then se.t up the SSID and password.

13.3.12   API—Application Programming Interface

i. A collection of protocols, routines, and tools for building software applications is known as an API (application programming interface).

ii. The goal was to create an API [14] that would send data to the cloud, allow for live data monitoring and analysis, and aid in device management, predictive maintenance, and equipment efficiency as a whole. The POST method, which is a common HTTP (Hypertext Transfer Protocol) method used to send data to a web server, was used here.

iii. An API must be tested [15, 16] before it can be used to make sure it works as intended and meets its requirements. Tools for testing APIs like JMeter, Postman, and SoapUI can be utilized, and they can assist in automating and streamlining the testing procedure.

iv. During the underlying phases of programming interface improvement, Mailman was used as a testing device to guarantee that the programming interface was working accurately and satisfying its necessities. Developers can use Postman, a well-known API testing tool, to create and run test cases, send requests to endpoints, and validate responses.

v. In the later stages, a programming interface testing device given by the client was used for the end goal of testing with spurious qualifications to test the working of the programming interface.

vi. The next step was to use real credentials to run a real-time test of the API in real time to make sure that the data flowed as expected and that the API was working properly. Because it allows for the identification of any issues that may not have been detected during the previous stages of testing, this stage of the testing is crucial because it simulates the actual usage of the API.

vii. The next step is to connect the API to the ESP32 device and push data over Wi-Fi after the testing of the API is finished and it works as intended. The ESP32 device will be able to push data to the API in real time once the integration is finished. This will make it possible to transfer data quickly and monitor the device's sensors or other parts from afar.

viii. The data must first be formatted in a way that is compatible before being pushed via the API using the ESP32. In this instance, the data were converted into the JSON format, which is a popular data format for APIs that makes it simple to communicate with other systems.

ix. Data can be viewed in real time on a dashboard after the pipeline for data transfer via ESP32 over Wi-Fi has been set up and the JSON-formatted data have been sent to the API. This considers constant checking of the information and can give bits of knowledge into the exhibition and conduct of the associated gadget.

Figure 13.10 shows the algorithmic programming of ATMEGA328. It shows the reset (zero conditions) along with the threshold levels above or below which the system should generate alerts. Additionally, it shows the EEPROM and LED control conditions. The EEPROM is used for a timer or clock, and the LED control will decide when to turn the LED on/off based on the values received from the actual sensors.

13.3.13   TouchGFX Designer

TouchGFX Designer is a software tool that allows developers to design and create user interfaces (UIs) for embedded systems using the TouchGFX framework [7]. It is a visual editor that enables developers to create UIs by dragging and dropping prebuilt widgets, images, and other graphical elements. It assists in the acceleration of the HMI-of-things revolution through the creation of smartphone-like graphic user interfaces. The main advantage of TouchGFX Designer is its ability to run on a wide range of hardware platforms, including ARM Cortex-M microcontrollers. As the microcontroller used is STM32, which is ARM Cortex-M, TouchGFX Designer provides optimal support in frontend UI building as well as integration with the STM32CubeMX compiler.

Installation and development of TouchGFX Designer [10]:

1. Installation can be done from the official ST website by downloading "X-CUBE-TOUCHGFX" and then extracting it on a local machine.
2. The ".msi" installer will install a zip with the following
   a. TouchGFX Designer which is the GUI builder tool
   b. TouchGFX Generator which creates HAL compatible with STM32CubeMX
   c. TouchGFX Engine which is a C++ framework
3. Once installation is complete, now the GUI building can be started using the Windows-based Designer.
4. Within the Designer application, choose the desired micro controller board and TouchGFX will simulate the TFT display for the specified board to show how the designed UI will work on actual hardware.
5. Once the UI is ready, the generator will generate a STMCubeMX compatible code which can be exported and loaded into the microcontroller.

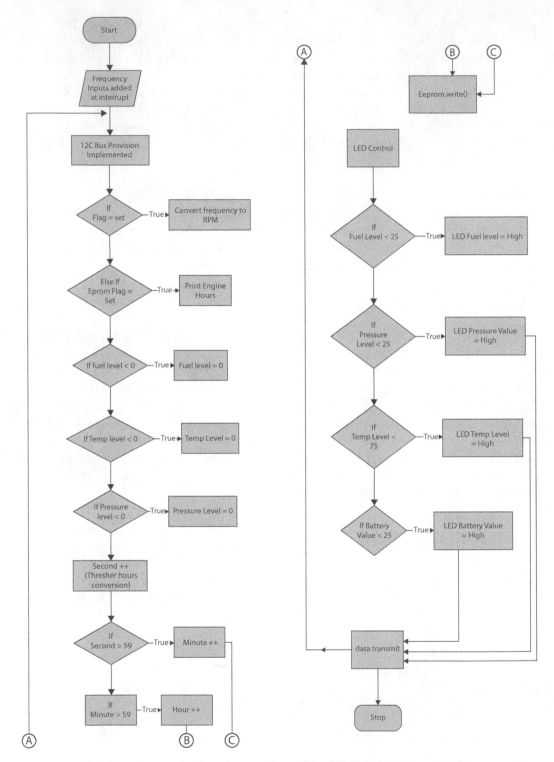

Figure 13.10 Flowchart showing the algorithmic working of the ATMEGA328 microcontroller.

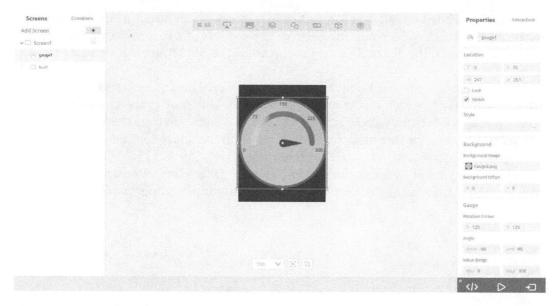

Figure 13.11 Typical TouchGFX screen UI along with its major components [7].

Figure 13.11 shows how the entire TouchGFX software screen is primarily divided:

1. Main screen: The screen represents a full-screen drawable area. This is the copy of the actual physical screen corresponding to the hardware board chosen. The elements on this screen will be displayed on a physical TFT display.
2. Widget options: Highly customizable high-fidelity UI components like buttons, images, containers, progress bars [9], and gauges are already provided which can be further calibrated for ranges.
3. Properties sidebar: These functionalities provided by TouchGFX Designer are used to calibrate, style, and fix the locations of widgets on the main screen. Setting of the background images [8], arc angles, style components, min–max value ranges, etc. can be done easily with real-time reflection of changes on the main screen components.

13.3.14   STM32CubeMX and STM32CubeIDE

1. **STM2CubeIDE:**

It is a C/C++ development platform [11] that offers peripheral configuration, generation of code, compilation of code, and debugging for STM32 microcontrollers. Microcontrollers or processors used in embedded systems specifically require programs to be compact and well-optimized. STM32CubeIDE provides HAL (hardware abstraction layer) closer to that of the actual hardware and generates smaller binaries at a faster speed. The key advantage of using STM32CubeIDE is that after the required microcontroller board is selected if the user wants any changes to be done to the peripherals, RTOS, or clock configurations, the user can return to the initialization and configuration screen, make necessary updates, and then regenerate the code with all the changes reflecting in the initial code.

Figure 13.12 shows a typical STM32CubeIDE screen with file structure in the left panel along with the "main.c" code file. The file structure consists of a root project along with its binary files, drivers, the TouchGFX application code, the SM32CubeMX-generated code, and the IOC file.

The code generation is structured in such a way that even if the code gets regenerated multiple times, the user-written blocks remain unchanged. This code generation is supported by HAL libraries which provide APIs. The HAL and LL (low level) form the lowest layers of software architecture and are used to communicate with the upper application layers. HAL provides basic functions like HAL_GPIO_Init, HAL_ADC_Start, and HAL_MAX_DELAY. It provides two types of APIs for development, namely, generic and extension. Figure 13.13 shows some HAL functions for GPIO (general purpose input output) which are used to

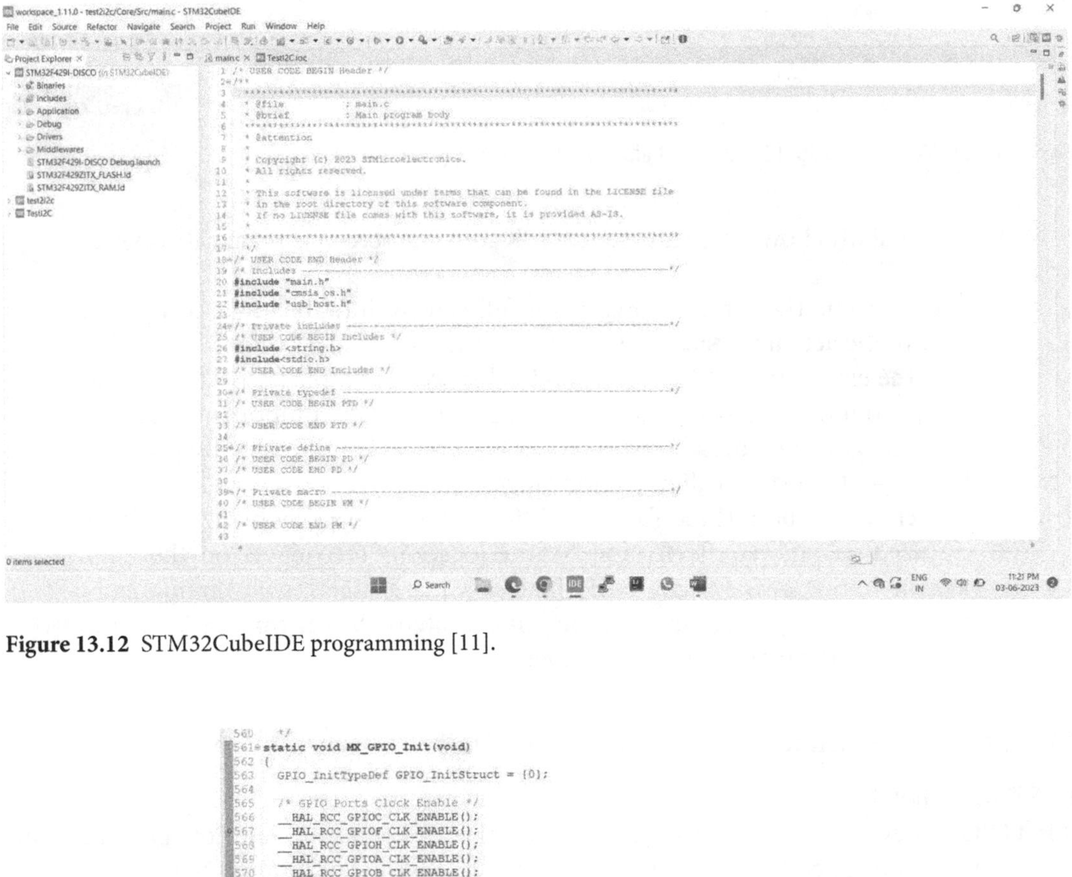

Figure 13.12 STM32CubeIDE programming [11].

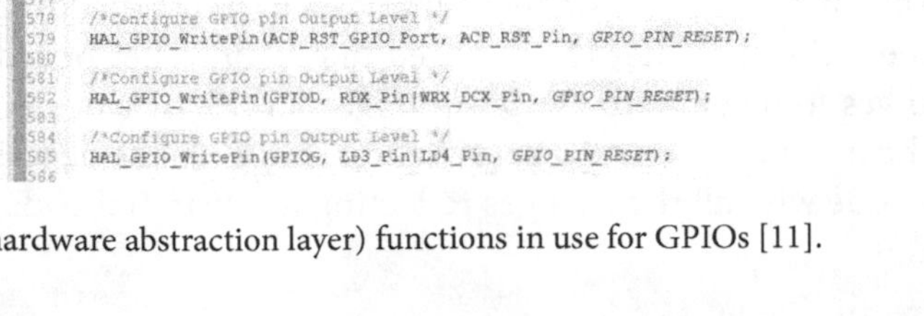

Figure 13.13 HAL (hardware abstraction layer) functions in use for GPIOs [11].

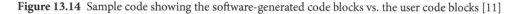

```
18  /* Includes ----------------------------------------------------*/
20  #include "main.h"
21  #include "cmsis_os.h"
22  #include "usb_host.h"
23
24  /* Private includes ----------------------------------------------*/
25  /* USER CODE BEGIN Includes */
26  #include <string.h>
27  #include<stdio.h>
28  /* USER CODE END Includes */
29
30  /* Private typedef -----------------------------------------------*/
31  /* USER CODE BEGIN PTD */
32
33  /* USER CODE END PTD */
34
35  /* Private define ------------------------------------------------*/
36  /* USER CODE BEGIN PD */
37  /* USER CODE END PD */
38
39  /* Private macro -------------------------------------------------*/
40  /* USER CODE BEGIN PM */
41
```

Figure 13.14 Sample code showing the software-generated code blocks vs. the user code blocks [11]

enable clocks using HAL_RCC_GPIOXX_CLK_ENABLE() and configure pins as input or output as required using HAL_GPIO_WritePin(). Each GPIO is multi-configurable, meaning a single pin can have more than one configurable functionality.

Figure 13.14 shows a sample code snippet generated in the STM32CubeIDE which shows the "#include" preprocessor directives which prove to be a starting point of any C/C++ program in two different bocks. Lines 20–22 in the figure illustrates the code generated automatically by the IDE as per the initial settings, whereas lines 26 and 27 are added inside the "USER CODE BEGIN" and "USER CODE END" blocks, which means they are added by the user according to the requirements.

2. STM32CubeMX:
It is a graphical tool [12] that simulates the actual microcontroller or microprocessor board input/output pins and their peripheral functions including the following:

i. A system core that provides settings for GPIOs, ADC and DAC, RTC (real-time clock), and other timer configurations
ii. Connectivity options like SPI, I2C, USART, USB, and CAN
iii. Supplementary media options like the LTDC (LCD-TFT display controller) display screen

All the abovementioned functionalities are customizable as per the user and application requirements. Furthermore, this tool is integrated automatically with the STM32CubeIDE. Figure 13.15 shows the pinout of STM32F429 along with all the setting control options in the left panel.

Figure 13.16 shows the software flowchart of our application which is programmed stepwise as given below:

i. Once the visual is ready in TouchGFX Designer, the code generated is exported in STM32CubeMX IDE through which it is actually loaded into the microcontroller.
ii. TouchGFX tasks are scheduled for the display of real-time sensor values with calibrations in the respective progress bar formats or as numeric values in

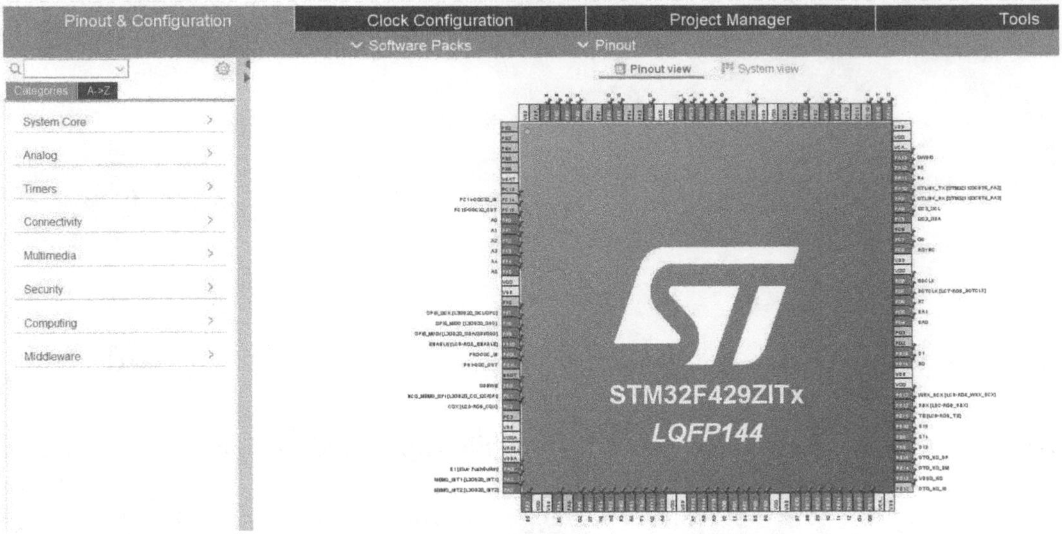

Figure 13.15 STM32CubeMX with the pinout view of STM32F429 [12, 13].

text boxes. The use of wildcards is for the purpose of dynamic value updates after a specified delay.

iii. Transmission and reception of sensor data takes place using I2C (inter-integrated circuit). I2C uses a master slave format with the STM32 microcontroller acting as the master and can request for data or send required data from/to peripherals. FreeRTOS tasks are scheduled for this purpose.

iv. Once the design is complete in TouchGFX, the code is generated, and the same is imported in STM Cube ID, a "ScreenView.cpp" file is imported, which contains functions to change specific settings for the widgets and allocate wildcards with real-time sensor data. Default tasks for RTOS are also scheduled in Cube IDE.

v. The entire code is then loaded into the microcontroller.

13.4 Results and Discussion

This section presents the results of the entire system. The tabular results show the various sensors with the respective sensor readings, the bar graph results, their resistance values, and LED conditions. The display images show the actual physical cluster in action along with the testing jig. The following are the implementation results:

13.4.1 Temperature Sensing Results

Table 13.1 shows the temperature with its corresponding LED indicator conditions. It also shows what value is displayed on the bar graph on the actual cluster screen. Additionally, the respective resistance values for temperatures are also included.

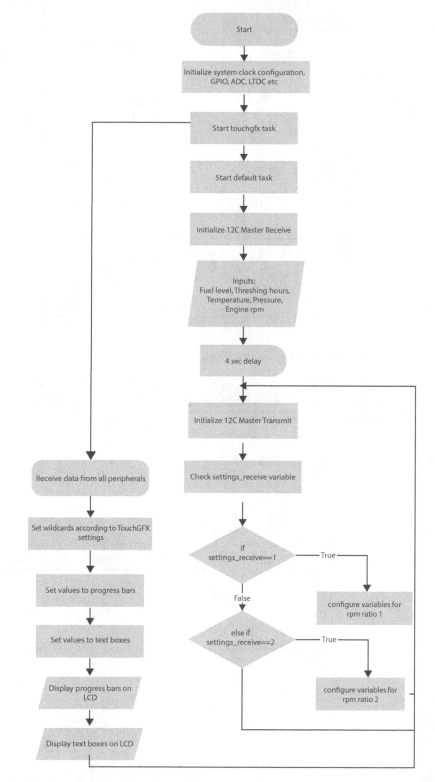

Figure 13.16 Flowchart showing the working of the STM32 microcontroller.

Table 13.1 Temperature sensor results.

Sr. no.	Sensor input	Temperature condition	Resistance set on the jig (Ω)	Observed on the display bar graph	Red LED indicator
1	Temperature	35°C	670	0	OFF
2		80°C	118	1/2	OFF
3		140°C	22	High	ON

13.4.2 Battery Voltage Measurement Results

Table 13.2 shows the battery voltage conditions. It also shows what value is displayed on the bar graph on the actual cluster screen and the values on the power supply device vs. the values on the digital multimeter.

Table 13.2 Battery voltage sensor results.

Sr. no.	Sensor input	Voltage set on power supply	Voltage observed on DMM	Observed on the display bar graph
1	Battery voltage	8	7.98	0
2		12	12.04	1/2
3		16	16.05	Full

13.4.3   Fuel Level Sensing Results

Table 13.3 shows the fuel level with its corresponding LED indicator conditions. It also shows what value is displayed on the bar graph on the actual cluster screen. Additionally, the respective resistance values for fuel levels are also included.

13.4.4   Pressure Level Results

Table 13.4 shows the pressure level with its corresponding LED indicator conditions. It also shows what value is displayed on the bar graph on the actual cluster screen. Additionally, the respective resistance values for pressure are also included.

Table 13.3 Fuel level sensor results.

Sr. no.	Sensor input	Level condition	Resistance set on the jig (Ω)	Observed on the display bar graph	Yellow LED indicator
1	Fuel level	0	330	0	ON
2		1/4th	205	1/4	ON
3		1/2 half	118	1/2	OFF
4		4/4 full	98	FULL	OFF

Table 13.4 Pressure sensor results.

Sr. no.	Sensor input	Pressure condition	Resistance set on the jig (Ω)	Observed on the display bar graph	Red LED indicator
1	Pressure	0 Pa	82.4	0	While giving negative its LED will glow
2		392 Pa	43	Full 4 bar	OFF

13.4.5   Engine Running Hours Sensing Results

Table 13.5 shows the running hours of the engine with its corresponding hours displayed on the cluster screen conditions. Additionally, it shows the starting and stopping times of the engine from which further calculations are made.

13.4.6   RPM and Indicator Results

Table 13.6 shows the frequency values supplied to the cluster using the frequency generator. The table shows the desired RPM value and the actual observed RPM value for two different RPM ratios. The last table shows the actual and observed LED signals for various parameters like high/low beam, indicators, and grain tank level check.

Figure 13.17(a) shows the monitoring system in action when all the input parameters are provided via the test jig. It shows the screen with all the progress bar values based on the input from the test jig. All the LED indicators are at the *ON* condition. The test jig has multiple potentiometers to change the values and see the results changing in real time. When the

Table 13.5 Engine running hours results.

Sr. no.	Engine running hours	Start time	Blinking	Stop time	Display shows (h)
1	0.50	12:00:00	Start	01:30:00	02:20:00
2	Threshing hours to given + 12V DC	12:00:00	Start	01:30:00	02:20:00

Table 13.6 RPM values and indicator results.

			RPM1 ratio: 5.25
Sr. no.	Frequency	Desired engine RPM	Cluster observed RPM on display tolerance (±80 RPM)
1	185	970	969
2	217	1,147	1,142
3	267	1,403	1,399
4	317	1,669	1,661
5	367	1,930	1,923
6	392	2,060	2,054
			RPM2 ratio: 1
Sr. no.	Frequency	Desired engine RPM	Cluster observed RPM on display
1	185	185	185
3	217	217	217
5	267	267	268
7	317	317	316
9	367	367	366
10	392	392	392
Sr. no.	Icon name	Given supply	Indicator color	Observed color visually
1	ENG check	12V.DC (+)	Yellow	Yellow
2	Air restriction	12V.DC (+)	Yellow	Yellow
3	LOW battery	Negative	Red	Red
4	Left turn	12V.DC (+)	Green	Green
5	High beam	12V.DC (+)	Blue	Blue
6	Low beam	12V.DC (+)	Green	Green
7	Right turn	12V.DC (+)	Green	Green
8	Thressure Auagar	12V.DC (+)	Yellow	Yellow
9	Grain tank full	12V.DC (+)	Yellow	Yellow

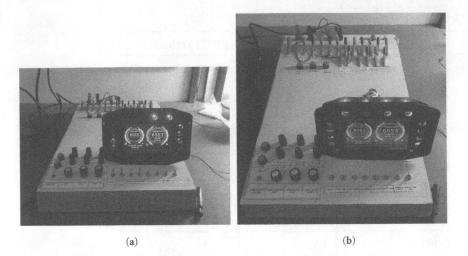

(a)   (b)

Figure 13.17 (a) Final product—smart digital crop harvester monitoring cluster. (b) Top view of the final product with the testing jig.

values of parameters like pressure, fuel level etc go beyond the allowed threshold, the corresponding alerts are activated showing the need to take corrective actions. Additionally, it has switches like low beam, high beam, and left and right indicators that simulate vehicle functionalities. Figure 13.17(b) shows the test jig used for testing the cluster working for various conditions and calibrating it as required. The bottom right corner has eight switches that can be turned on and off to check the working of the parameters as given in Table 13.6.

13.5   Conclusion

The development of this product has resulted in the creation of an integrated dashboard that enables real-time monitoring of crucial parameters in agricultural operations. The dashboard incorporates the use of both the STM32 microcontroller and the ATMEGA328 microcontroller to provide a comprehensive solution. The integrated dashboard's ability to monitor the fuel level, battery level, threshing hours, radiator water temperature, and engine oil pressure is one of its main features. The smooth and effective operation of agricultural machinery depends on these parameters. Operators can gain valuable insights into the condition of their equipment and make informed decisions as a result of continuously monitoring these metrics.

The STM32 microcontroller is connected to the sensors through the ATMEGA328 microcontroller. ATMEGA328 sends the acquired data to the STM32 microcontroller for display and facilitates communication between the various sensors, such as the fuel level sensor, the temperature sensor, and the pressure sensor. The simplicity and effective interfacing capabilities of the ATMEGA328 microcontroller were chosen to guarantee seamless communication between the display system and the sensors. The STM32 microcontroller is an essential component of this system as it controls the display of the acquired data. It processes the sensor readings before displaying them on the integrated dashboard in a format that is easy to understand. This microcontroller is excellent for handling the difficult task of data visualization because of its performance and adaptability.

To improve the convenience of the coordinated dashboard, different demonstrating signs are consolidated. Operators are made aware of any potential problems or abnormal readings by these signs, which provide them with visual cues and warnings. This component expands the usability and openness of the item, empowering administrators to rapidly recognize and resolve any issues that might emerge during farming tasks. In conclusion, this product's development has resulted in the design of a cluster that gives operators access to useful information, makes it easier for them to make quick decisions, and makes agricultural processes work better in general on the driving vehicle.

Although this product offers several notable strengths, it also has a few limitations like small screen size and lack of adjustable screen brightness. By addressing these limitations and focusing on improving screen size and brightness adjustability, the product can enhance the overall user experience and usability. The functionalities of the developed device can be further expanded to the following: android application for remote real-time monitoring; indicator of grain tank level; reverse sensors; and integration of cameras, odometer, and speedometer.

References

1. Ren, L. and Yu, X., Hardware implementation of STM32 microcontroller-based indoor environment monitoring system. *Open J. Appl. Sci.*, 11, 999, January 2021.
2. Visconti, P., Sbarro, B., Primiceri, P., de Fazio, R., Lay-Ekuakille, A., Design and testing of an electronic control system based on STM X-Nucleo board for detection and wireless transmission of sensors data applied to a single-seat formula sae car. *Int. J. Electron. Telecommun.*, 11, 999, 2019.
3. Floyd, T.L., *Electronic Devices*, Pearson, New York, 2018.
4. International, Fairchild Semiconductor Inc, BC546/547/548/549/550 NPN Epitaxial Silicon Transistor, Nov. 2014. https://www.mouser.com/datasheet/2/149/BC547-190204.pdf.
5. Texas Instruments, How to Approach a Power-Supply Design-Part 1, March 2023. https://www.ti.com/lit/ pdf/slvafj2.pdf.
6. STMicroelectronics, 1.5KE, Feb. 2002 [Revised 12-March-2012. https://www.farnell.com/datasheets/2307452.pdf.
7. Installation, *TouchGFX Documentation 4.15*, [Online]. Available at: https://support.touchgfx.com/4.15/docs/introduction/installation (Accessed: 19 February 2023).
8. Scalableimage, *TouchGFX Documentation 4.15*, [Online]. Available at: https://support.touchgfx.com/4.18/docs/development/ui-development/ui-components/images/scalable-image,(Accessed: 12 February 2023).
9. Circleprogress, *TouchGFX Documentation 4.15*, [Online]. Available at: https://support. touchgfx.com/docs/development/ui-development/ui-components/progress-indicators/circleprogress, (Accessed: 12 February 2023).
10. UI Development Introduction, *TouchGFX Documentation 4.15*, [Online]. Available at: https://support.touchgfx.com/4.21/docs/development/ui-development/ui-development-introduction, (Accessed: 12 February 2023).
11. STMicroelectronics, *UM2609 User manual STM32CubeIDE user guide*, February 2023, Available:https://www.st.com/resource/en/user_manual/um2609-stm32cubeide-ser-guide-stmicroelectronics.pdf.

12. STMicroelectronics, *UM1718 User manual STM32CubeMX for STM32 configuration and initialization C code generation*, February 2023, Available: https://www.st.com/resource/en/user_manual/um1718-stm32cubemx-for-stm32-configuration-and-initialization-c-code-generation- stmicroelectronics.pdf.

13. STMicroelectronics, *UM1670 User manual Discovery kit with STM32F429ZI MCU*, Sep. 10, 2013 [Revised 26-Aug-2020, Available: https://www.st.com/resource/en/user_manual/um1670-discovery-kit-with- stm32f429zi- mcu-stmicroelectronics.pdf.

14. Tanenbaum, A., Wetherall, D., Feamster, N., *Computer Networks*, Prentice-Hall, United States, 2022.

15. Ministry of Electronics and Information Technology, Government of India | Home Page, *IoT Policy*, 5, [Online]. Available at: https://www.meity.gov.in/sites/upload_files/dit/files/Draft-IoT-Policy% 20(1).pdf (Accessed: 23 January 2023).

16. IoT System Certification Scheme (IoTSCS) | STQC | Standardisation Testing and Quality Certification Directorate, *IoT System Certification Scheme*, 1, [Online]. Available at: https://www.stqc.gov.in/node/614 (Accessed: 23 January 2023).

14

Exploring the Prospects and Challenges of Digital Agriculture for Food Security—A Case Study of the "Hands Free Hectare" Digital Farm in the UK

Arnab Chatterjee

Department of Humanities (Basic Sciences & Humanities), Budge Budge Institute of Technology, Kolkata, India

Abstract

Digital technology can have an impact on agricultural trade in new countries through private sector suppliers with new standard compliance and flexible border processes for agricultural goods. This study looks at the first completely functional digital farm system, a ground-breaking digital farm that garnered international attention. In the UK, Harper Adams University and Precision Divisions founded this farm "Hands Free Hectare" in 2016, and it has since become a showcase for innovative practices used around the British Isles. With just a small amount of government funding and one Iseki tractor, the team was able to transform the entire conventional agricultural system into an autonomous one that was run by lasers, GPS, and robotic arms. This novel system's intricacy and any potential long-term repercussions are thoroughly investigated.

Keywords: Digital technologies, sustainable agriculture, robotic arms, autonomous farming, case study

14.1 Introduction

Digital technologies have played a crucial role in facilitating tasks that are mundane and challenging for human labor. Robotic arms in assembly line systems have been employed to handle repetitive tasks with precision and efficiency [1]. Recently, frontier technologies, such as artificial intelligence, robotics, and biotechnology, have exhibited immense potential for sustainable development. As the global population continues to grow, the agricultural sector faces the daunting challenge of meeting increasing food demands, making the integration of digital technologies imperative for long-term success. While digital technologies have shown promise in fostering sustainable agriculture, their widespread adoption in the farming industry appears to be a recent phenomenon. Nevertheless, their proliferation is essential to achieving sustainable agricultural practices.

Email: carnab393@kluniversity.in

Kuldeep Singh and Prasanna Kolar (eds.) Digital Agricultural Ecosystem: Revolutionary Advancements in Agriculture, (259–268) © 2024 Scrivener Publishing LLC

The steady proliferation of digital technologies is rapidly changing people's lives. AI, or artificial intelligence, has significantly contributed to making tasks easier. From smarter Google searches to applications that ensure timely completion of work, humans now surpass deadlines rather than merely meeting them. This transformation extends to various sectors, including agriculture. Although farming has been practiced since the Neolithic era, the recent surge in the adoption of smart technologies is particularly notable. Smart farms embrace cutting-edge advancements like robotics, AI, and a fusion of human and non-human technologies to enhance production and minimize human intervention [2, 3]. Although the realization of a fully "smart" farm may still be distant, there have been tangible experiments in this field.

14.1.1   The Need for Smart Farms

Smart farms have become a necessity in the present time. This truth stems from two primary reasons. Firstly, these farms utilize viable technology to minimize human toil and enhance food production, a crucial aspect considering the rising global population. Ensuring food production within feasible time frames becomes imperative as the world's population continues to grow steadily. Smart farming has been described in various ways, and according to the Internet of Things (IoT) for all, it is defined as follows [4].

Smart farming refers to managing farms using modern information and communication technologies to increase the quantity and quality of products while optimizing the human labor required. Among the technologies available for present-day farmers are as follows:

- Sensors: soil, water, light, humidity, temperature management
- Software: specialized software solutions that target specific farm types or applications agonistic to IoT platforms
- Connectivity: cellular, LoRA
- Location: GPS, satellite
- Robotics: autonomous tractors, processing facilities
- Data analytics: standalone analytics solutions, data pipelines for downstream solutions

As depicted in the picture (see Figure 14.1), smart farms incorporate a multitude of technologies to enhance digital advancements, thereby improving the overall quality of life. For instance, the integration of robotics with tractors has been highlighted as a means to enhance the food production process. According to Food Tank (foodtank.com), the use of assistive robots is gaining momentum not with the intention to disrupt but to support farmers in meeting the escalating demand for food. Figure 14.2 shows that, one such robot, named "Oz," developed by the French company Naio Technologies, aids farmers in carrot fields, providing valuable assistance throughout the production process [6].

According to the article titled "Robotics in Agriculture: New Era of Smart Farming," Badwal and Bhardwaj offer a crucial insight into how smart technologies are revolutionizing the agricultural industry. Their work serves as a stark reminder of the daunting fact that the human population is projected to reach a staggering nine billion by the year 2050 AD [8].

Artificial intelligence (AI) is gaining significant momentum within the agricultural industry, and its integration with robotics is becoming increasingly prevalent in this sector.

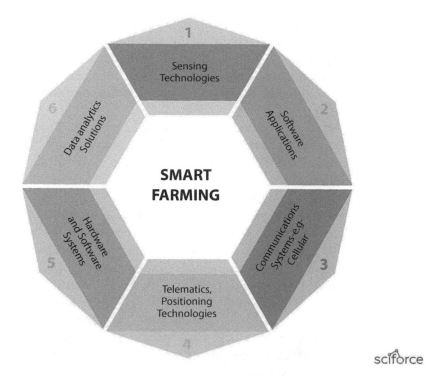

Figure 14.1 The mechanics of smart farming [5] (source: www.iotforall.com).

Figure 14.2 Oz the robot assists a farmer [7] (source: foodtank.com).

The global demand for food is on the rise, particularly with the projected world population expected to reach nine billion by 2050. In a 2020 report commissioned for the World Resources Institute, it was asserted that agriculture must increase production by approximately 25% to meet this growing demand. Given such prospects, one would naturally expect farmers to thrive in this environment [8].

Robotics and smart technologies are progressively transforming the agricultural landscape. Robots are finding utility in a wide range of tasks, including soil testing and monitoring crop coloration and ripeness, as well as advanced farming techniques like weeding and fruit picking. The implementation of these diverse applications relies on cutting-edge technologies such as cloud computing, the IoT, and sensor technology to facilitate these advancements (see Figure 14.3).

In the article titled "Smart Farming: A Better Technological Option for Modern Farming Society under Theme of Doubling of Farmer's Income," Neeta Mahawar *et al.* examine the numerous ways in which smart farming is gradually reshaping the agricultural landscape. The authors highlight how the widespread adoption of modern information systems is revolutionizing the perspective on agricultural production [9].

Smart farming embodies the incorporation of modern information and communication technologies (ICT) into agriculture, marking a significant advancement referred to as the Third Green Revolution. Building upon the successes of plant breeding and genetics revolutions, this new era is revolutionizing agriculture through the synergistic application of ICT solutions. These solutions encompass precision equipment, the IoT, sensors and actuators, geopositioning systems, big data, unmanned aerial vehicles (UAVs or drones), and robotics, among others. The advent of smart farming holds immense potential to revolutionize agricultural production, offering a more efficient and sustainable approach. By leveraging precise and resource-efficient methodologies, smart farming aims to enhance productivity while promoting environmental sustainability.

In addition to an array of facilities offered by smart farming, including helicopter sowing, aerial photography, and the use of drones for pesticide application, weeding, spraying, and

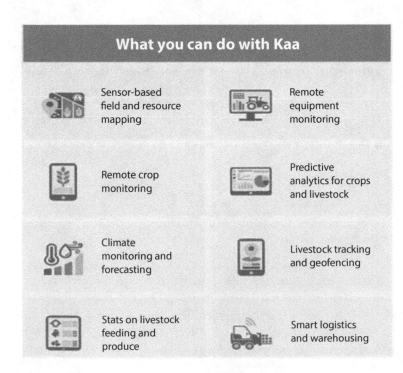

Figure 14.3 IOT-based open source (source: https://www.kaaiot.com/).

crop health monitoring, the authors also highlight the significance of IoT-based sensors for soil moisture estimation, as well as the integration of self-controlled and robotic labor. Furthermore, they draw attention to the application of KAA (www.kaaiot.com/), an open-source platform software, which they consider a critical middleware technology enabling safe entry into the agriculture IoT domain by interconnecting various sensors, connected devices, and farming facilities [10]. As the authors affirm, KAA opens up new possibilities and allows for remarkable achievements in the field of smart farming.

As evident from the mentioned aspects, smart farming technologies are reshaping traditional perceptions of agricultural production. In the current era, the labor force in farming is facing shortages, with more individuals diverting to the tertiary sector. Smart technologies not only aim to minimize human toil significantly but also explore diverse methods to increase yields with minimal human labor input. Consequently, farming is gradually embracing mechanization through the implementation of smart technologies capable of achieving precision comparable to human capabilities in tasks that were once solely dependent on manual labor. As a result, the cost of human involvement will be minimized, although some level of human intervention will remain essential in the agricultural production process. This dynamic gives rise to intense debate concerning the extent to which smart technologies should be integrated into activities that were historically reliant on human effort alone. The matter of how far smart technologies should be allowed to penetrate these areas will be a topic for future commentators to deliberate upon.

14.1.2   The Case of the Hands-Free Farm in the UK

The hands-free farm stands as one of the pioneering experiments aimed at eliminating human intervention entirely and entrusting the fields to automated machines. This groundbreaking project, jointly undertaken by the Precision Divisions, Harper Lee University, and FramScan AG, was initiated in 2019 to create the world's first fully automated farm. Securing funding from Innovate UK, the farm was established on the University of Shropshire's campus, which was extended to cover an impressive 35 hectares and utilized a

Figure 14.4 The hands-free farm team (source: https://www.agriland.co.uk).

fleet of autonomous vehicles, thereby materializing the concept of a hands-free farm. The decision to embark on this experiment was prompted by the declining wheat yields in the UK, attributed to the use of heavy machinery and the soil-leveling practices that adversely affected agricultural production (see Figure 14.4). The hands-free farm emerged as one of the few experiments that sought to eliminate the usage of large and cumbersome machinery, which had been identified as bottlenecks impeding sustained agricultural production. In doing so, the project aimed to enhance production through improved methods, harnessing the potential of technology to achieve this goal.

Having completed 6 years of existence, the hands-free farm has successfully navigated all challenges on its path to becoming the world's first fully automated farm, operating with the aid of smart technology. However, the hurdles faced during the journey to forefront automation are elaborated in the subsequent section.

14.1.3   The Challenges

The hands-free farm originated as a project in 2019, initially planned to span 3 years. As previously mentioned, the project aimed to address the issue of declining agricultural production in the UK caused by the adverse effects of larger vehicles, which led to the gradual flattening of land. To tackle this problem, the decision was made to utilize smaller vehicles for implementing this innovative farming technique. The chosen land for the project was undulating, and it was suggested that the original Iseki tractor and a Claas combine be employed. For vehicle and data management, Precision Divisions took charge, utilizing the "MiFarm platform." The farm, situated within a university campus, was designed to replicate real-world conditions, and the application of smart farming technology was to be explored to devise solutions for countering such challenges. The project aimed to understand how smart farming techniques could effectively address real-world farming conditions, using smaller and more adaptable vehicles to optimize production and minimize the negative impact on agricultural yields. By employing cutting-edge technology and innovative approaches, the hands-free farm sought to pave the way for more efficient and sustainable agricultural practices.

One of the significant achievements of the farm stemmed from the successful implementation of unconventional technology and the strategic use of smaller equipment. As previously discussed, the detrimental impact of larger and cumbersome machinery had been hindering the goal of increasing crop yield and optimizing soil utilization. By adopting a different approach, the hands-free farm managed to overcome these challenges. The utilization of smaller, more adaptable equipment allowed for the effective implementation of innovative technologies, leading to improved agricultural practices and enhanced productivity. Through this creative and forward-thinking approach, the farm demonstrated the potential of employing smart farming solutions to address longstanding issues in traditional farming methods.

14.1.4   The Key People

As mentioned, the success of the project was the outcome of a collaborative effort, involving individuals from various fields of technology and innovation who recognized the urgency to improve the agricultural sector. Key contributors to this remarkable endeavor, as stated in the blog Technology [11], include the following:

(i) Jonathan Gill, Mechatronics Researcher at the university, expressed, "This time, we're planning to grow three different combinable crops across 35 hectares. We're moving past the feasibility study which the hectare provided us with, to a vision of the future of farming. We want to prove the capability and ability of these systems in reducing the levels of soil compaction and precision application."

(ii) Martin Abell, Mechatronics Engineer for Precision Decisions, added, "With the farm, we're looking to solve problems like fleet management and swarm vehicle logistics and navigation. We still believe that smaller vehicles are best, so we'll be using up to three small tractors for the project, including our original Iseki tractor and a Claas combine will be joining our old Sampo. This time, we're moving away from the perfect hectare and to real-world situations. The fields will be irregular, there'll be obstacles, undulating land, and pathways. Precision Decisions will be handling vehicle and data management through our MiFarm platform."

(iii) Kit Franklin, Senior Agricultural Engineering Lecturer, explained, "We want the farm to become a testbed for agricultural innovation. Once the farm's established, we'll be encouraging companies to come and test and evaluate their technologies. It's also great that the project will remain on the university campus, so that students will be able to learn from it, watch our progress and see how dynamic and innovative the agricultural engineering industry is."

(iv) Callum Chalmers, Business Development Manager for Farmscan AG, stated, "We're hoping to expand on the great foundations the HFHa laid by integrating our existing industry-proven technology with a developing autonomous platform to provide precision control across the farm. Our goal is to have multiple small unmanned vehicles working together seamlessly in the same fields, all remotely monitored and completing all the tasks you would expect in a commercial farm. Navigating roads and pathways between fields is a new challenge; we want to face real-world conditions, where fields aren't often in one place and it's a necessity to travel between them."

(v) Additional elements of the project include Professor James Lowenberg-DeBoer, the Elizabeth Creak Chair of Agri-Tech Economics at Harper Adams, conducting an economic outputs study in relation to the project. Moreover, in the final year of the project, in addition to being run at the university, the system will be evaluated by partner farmer David Blacker. The diverse expertise and dedication of these individuals have been pivotal in shaping the success and progress of the hands-free farm project.

14.1.5 Appraisal of the Hands-Free Farm

The hands-free farm has been operational for over 6 years, and its success in augmenting agricultural production is a testament to the remarkable efforts of brilliant minds behind its conception. As reported by Harper Adams University, the farm sought to create a unique space where agricultural production could thrive without human intervention. However, in real-life farming, field farmers face numerous obstacles such as roads, poles, and ditches before they can effectively sow crops. The hands-free farm addressed this challenge admirably by utilizing smaller machines that could navigate these obstacles without compromising productivity [11]. Working in a perfect hectare, which was flat and fenced off, provided an initial setting for the project. However, the real-world fields where farmers operate daily present a different set of challenges, including telegraph poles, hills, ditches, and public footpaths. To address these practical concerns, the new 35-hectare farm was designed to mimic real-world conditions and to withstand unpredictable weather conditions, as any farmer is accustomed to.

During the project's development, various aspects of the site were examined, ranging from soil quality to insect life and biodiversity. Collaborating academics from Harper Adams University and beyond joined forces with the hands-free team to conduct comprehensive evaluations. The preparation for spring crops to be harvested in early 2023 signaled the culmination of the project's progress. However, unforeseen challenges emerged, such as weather-related delays that pushed winter drilling plans to the following spring. Subsequently, an entirely different challenge arose with the onset of the coronavirus pandemic. Despite these obstacles, the dedication and ingenuity of the team persisted, leading to significant achievements in smart farming technology.

During a presentation, attendees had the opportunity to explore some of the hands-free farm machines and engage with team members. The event culminated with an observation of the farm's autonomous vehicles in action, showcasing the practical application of the hands-free approach to agricultural operations. The continuous pursuit of innovation and adaptation to real-world conditions have been central to the ongoing success of the hands-free farm project.

14.2 Conclusion

The hands-free farm represents a pioneering effort to enhance agricultural production by embracing innovative machinery and minimizing human intervention. It stands as one of the few global initiatives employing such inventive practices in farm operations. As the world's population continues to grow, the demand for food will increase significantly, necessitating the widespread adoption of smart technologies for augmented food production. The traditional means of production alone will prove inadequate to meet this surge in demand. Embracing smart technologies in agriculture will become the new norm, enabling us to address the impending challenges of food scarcity and hunger effectively. The future of agriculture lies in harnessing the potential of smart technologies to optimize food production and ensure equitable distribution of resources. By leveraging these advanced tools, we can substantially eradicate hunger and foster a world where everyone has access to sufficient food. Smart technologies are undeniably the need of the hour, and their pervasive presence will dominate the agricultural landscape, shaping a more sustainable and food-secure future for all.

References

1. United Nations Conference on Trade and Development, UNCTAD, *Technology and Innovation Report: Catching technological waves: Innovation with equity*, Geneva, Switzerland, 2021, https://unctad.org/publication/technology-and-innovation-report-2021.

2. Leider, S. and Schroter-Schlaak, C., Smart farming technologies in arable farming: Towards a holistic assessment of opportunities and risks. *Sustainability*, 13, 12, 1–20, 2021. https://doi.org/10.3390/su13126783.

3. OECD, Technology and digital in agriculture. *Organisation for Economic Co-operation and Development*, 1, 23, 1-5, 2023. https://www.oecd.org/agriculture/topics/technology-and-digital-agriculture/ Accessed 13 June 2023.

4. IoT for all, Smart farming: The future of agriculture. 2023. https://www.iotforall.com/smart-farming-future-of-agriculture. Accessed 23 May 2023.

5. Neeta, M., Jitendra, S.B., Swetha, D., Kumar, C., Sai, S.N., Tirunagari, R., Somdutt, B., Pratishtha, D., Smart farming: A better technological option for modern farming society under theme of doubling of farmers' income. *Int. J. Curr. Microbiol. Appl. Sci.*, 20, 11, 976–992, 2020.

6. Food Tank, Rise of the small farm robots. *Foodtank*, 1, 23, 1-4, 2023. https://foodtank.com/news/2016/09/rise-ofthe-small-farm-robots-part-2/ Web. Accessed 13 May, 2023.

7. IoT, Oz the robot assists a farmer. *Foodtank*, 1, 23, 1-2, 2022. www.foodtank.com. Accessed 13 May, 2023.

8. Badwal, D. and Bharadwaj, M., Robotics in agriculture new era of smart farming. *Just Agric.*, 11, 20, 1–4, 2020.

9. Neeta, M., Jitendra, S.B., Swetha, D., Smart farming: A better technological option for modern farming society under theme of doubling of farmers' income. *Int. J. Curr. Microbiol. Appl. Sci.*, 20, 11, 976–992, 2020.

10. Technology, UK project aims to develop hands-free farm model. *Ag Equipment Intelligence*, 1, 19, 1-5, 2019. https://www.agequipmentintelligence.com/articles/2941-uk-project-aims-to-develop-hands-free-farming-model Accessed May 21, 2019.

11. Harper Adams University, Six years of autonomous agriculture-the hands-free farm team look back. *Harper Adams University Report*, 1, 23, 1–5, 2023. https://www.harper-adams.ac.uk/news/207995/six-years-of-autonomous-agriculture-the-hands-free-farm-team-look-back. 5 April 2023.

15

Smart Farming—A Case Study from India

Vedantam Seetha Ram[1]*, Kuldeep Singh[2] and Bivek Sreshta[3]

[1]Faculty of Management Studies, CMS Business School, Jain (Deemed-to-be-University), Bengaluru, Karnataka, India
[2]School of Management, Gati Shakti Vishwavidyalaya, Vadodara, India
[3]Nepal Electronic Payment Systems Ltd., Kathmandu, Nepal

Abstract

Agricultural output improved along with irrigation land increase on one side and population increase on the other. So, innovative means are invented to improve yield through the introduction of new varieties and the adoption of new technologies and farmer-friendly policies. Current exploratory research has brought out changes that happened over two decades selected for the study from 2001–2002 to 2020–2021 fiscal years' data. Literature helped in finding out divergent technologies introduced in the farming sector during the period, their use by farmers under divergent conditions, and policies formulated for the same by governments such that the yield of agriculture output has increased or not. For the present research, apart from published research work in journals, researchers have gone through reports published by the World Bank, Indian Council of Agriculture Research, Reserve Bank of India, Government of India-Ministry of Finance, Ministry of Agriculture and Farmers Welfare, and National Bank for Agriculture and Rural Development showing the state of India adopting and applying modern technology in farming that proved to be a dominant contributor as gross value addition to India's gross domestic product which increased over the years consistently.

Keywords: Artificial intelligence, blockchain, data analysis, gross value addition, laser land leveling, precision agriculture, smart farming, sustainability

15.1 Introduction

The agriculture sector in India has seen tremendous changes over the decades due to the adoption of technology making it possible for the yield to increase and costs to decline helping policymakers revise output targets, work on subsidies, and create a conducive environment for farmers and the farming community in eliminating disparities in agricultural and allied sectors across regions of India. Being a geographically diverse country, India practices different types of farming procedures depending on soil type, climatic conditions, crops grown, rainfall, monsoon, and so on [1, 2].

*Corresponding author: vedramphd@gmail.com; ORCID: https://orcid.org/0000-0002-6375-1501
Kuldeep Singh: ORCID https://orcid.org/0000-0002-8180-4646

Kuldeep Singh and Prasanna Kolar (eds.) Digital Agricultural Ecosystem: Revolutionary Advancements in Agriculture, (269–290) © 2024 Scrivener Publishing LLC

15.1.1   Types of Farming

In India, multiple types of farming take place depending on the nature of the soil, the cultivation mechanism adopted, types of food grains produced, climatic conditions that prevail at different places based on monsoon conditions [3], water and irrigational facilities available, government support to diversified geographical area, and scientific advancement achieved, adopted, and implemented by farmers. The following section describes the different types of farming mechanisms prevailing in India over centuries that changed due to technological advancement, climatic conditions, and availability of water and other resources for higher and sustainable yields.

15.1.1.1   Subsistence Farming

Another farming practice followed in India is subsistence farming which offers the benefits of lesser or almost zero use of chemical fertilizers, insecticides, and pesticides, as a large portion of their produce is either consumed by their families or sold in the local market. Subsistence farming is popular in the northeast part of India, Southeast Asia, Africa, and the Amazon basin. This method of farming helps communities live together through the farming process since all the family members are involved in the cultivation or they help fellow farmers without any monetary transactions, reflecting the old trade concept of the barter system in a different manner, i.e., farmers help each other on their respective fields whenever cultivation happens on their fields. Conventional methods are practiced in subsistence farming like dependency on monsoon and the use of local varieties of seeds, organic fertilizers, and chemicals due to the farmers' very small portions of cultivable landholding, and this makes the use of machine or technology in subsistence farming costly; thus, developing economies have adopted the restricted use of machines or technology in farming activity, apart from high rates of unemployment. Government policies helped India move from subsistence farming to commercial farming [3, 4].

15.1.1.2   Dryland Farming

Israel, one of the world's advanced technology-adopted farming countries, follows the dryland farming technique. For centuries, nations such as the USA and the Russian Federation have followed dryland farming that requires less water resources. So, dryland farming is highly practiced in regions of adverse weather conditions, low water resource, low rainfall, or frequent drought. In India, Rajasthan, Gujarat, Uttar Pradesh, parts of Madhya Pradesh, Tamil Nadu, and Andhra Pradesh follow this dryland farming (ICAR) technique. Due to advancements in mechanization and technology, deep tillage, counter or cross plowing, mulching, rotation of crops, mixed cropping or strip cropping, low weed varieties of seed, weed management, and green manure help increase tillage area, crop yield, and farmers' income. Engineering measures such as the construction of check dams or farm ponds help improve dryland farming [5].

15.1.1.3   Arable Land Farming

Arable land is the most prominent and fertile land used for agricultural purposes, mainly dependent on natural as well as human-induced minerals and water facilities. Due to its nature, almost all types of food grains as well as commercial crops can be grown on these lands. As per literature, India uses 52.26% of its land for cultivation purposes [6].

15.1.1.4   Aquaculture

India, with its vast sea coast spanning 4,670.6 miles, is the third largest fish producer in the world, the second largest in aquaculture, and the first in inland fish supply, having huge potential with 10% of the world's species. The schemes such as the Prime Minister Fish Wealth Scheme known as Pradhan Mantri Matsya Sampada Yojana (PMMSY) offered by the Government of India generate 20.05 billion Indian National Rupee (INR). The Prime Minister Fish Farmer Support Sub-Scheme (Pradhan Mantri Matsya Kisan Samridhi Sah-Yojana, PM-MKSSY) is floated as a subplan under PMMSY to boost 100% foreign direct investment to help in enhancing the livelihood of all the stakeholders of the fisheries sector [7].

15.1.1.5   Dairy Farming

The dairy industry is one of the fastest-growing sectors in India. From an importer in 1951 to a global exporter of 23% of global requirements for the year 2022 of milk and milk solids, India is the largest milk producer in the world [8]. This is possible due to the "White Revolution" that was initiated with the name "Operation Flood" in the year 1970 through a cooperative movement. With the use of modern technology, new breeds of cattle are reared by farmers which helped them improve milk yield that contains high fat content. This was possible with the support of government schemes such as the National Programme for Dairy Development (NPDD), Pradhan Mantri Kisan Sampada Yojana (Prime Minister Farmer Wealth Scheme, PMKSY), Kisan Credit Cards to Livestock Farmers (KCCLF), Rashtriya Gokul Mission [9], Rashtriya Pashudan Vikas Yojna, and National Livestock Mission [10], and all these schemes are floated as standalone or sub-schemes of the existing ones, such that the benefit continues to the farmers and help them improve their livelihood through enhanced income apart from contributing to the growth and development and preserving indigenous cattle breeds that are known for their vigor and high yield across the globe.

Figure 15.1 shows the total agriculture produce in India in both the Rabi and Kharif seasons for the time period 2012–2013 to 2022–2023 indicating growth in total production of food grain in India that has improved both in Rabi and Kharif seasons [11].

Technology helps compete with other players in the global market by exporting quality output, earning foreign exchange, and maintaining standards in cultivation that ease the job of farming [12, 13]. Figures 15.2 and 15.3 depict keyword search for research on

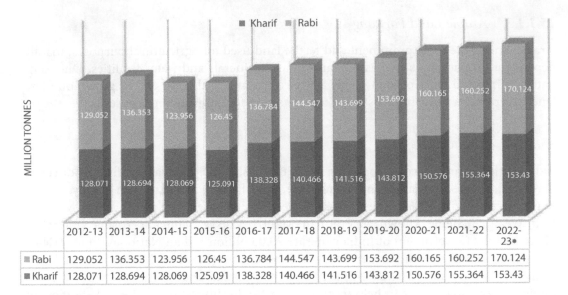

	2012-13	2013-14	2014-15	2015-16	2016-17	2017-18	2018-19	2019-20	2020-21	2021-22	2022-23*
▪ Rabi	129.052	136.353	123.956	126.45	136.784	144.547	143.699	153.692	160.165	160.252	170.124
▪ Kharif	128.071	128.694	128.069	125.091	138.328	140.466	141.516	143.812	150.576	155.364	153.43

2022-23*: Estimates

Figure 15.1 Foodgrain production in India during the two seasons for the time period 2012–2013 till 2022–2023. Source: Ministry of Agriculture and Farmers Welfare, Department of Agriculture and Farmers Welfare, Second Advance Estimates of Production of Food Grains for 2022–2023 accessed at https://agricoop.nic.in/Documents/Time%20Series%20%28English%29%20PDF.pdf

16,023 Agriculture Multidisciplinary	4,364 Biotechnology Applied Microbiology	4,188 Chemistry Apple	1,849 Computer Science Interdisciplinary Applications
	4,364 Energy Fuels		
7,792 Agricultural Engineering		1,433 Agronomy	731 Environmental Sciences
	4,274 Food Science Technology	836 Biology	

Figure 15.2 Technology in agriculture (WoS search for keywords by the authors). Source: Web of Science database.

technology in agriculture and agriculture technology on the Web of Science database which in turn helps in understanding the researcher's orientation in the dynamic environment. Multidisciplinary research dominated (16,023) for technology use in the agriculture sector, while food science (49,333) research is leading in agriculture technology, followed by multidisciplinary research (16,231), then chemistry applied (10,175), and agricultural engineering (8,158). Hence, a large chunk of research is happening on understanding the modern means followed in agriculture practices [14–17].

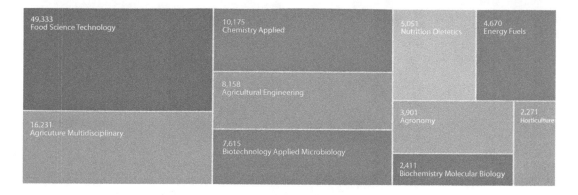

Figure 15.3 Agriculture technology (WoS search for keywords by the authors). Source: Web of Science database.

Literature-based research on smart farming for the search word smart farming gave 330 reference documents from the Web of Science database downloaded in RIS format and ran in VOSviewer software showing that research on agriculture is closely associated with the word technology. Algorithm, blockchain [18–23], image technology [24–30], artificial neural network [31], artificial intelligence [29, 30, 32, 33], Internet of Things (IoT) [34–43], machine vision [44–50], networking, design methodology approach, precision agriculture [51–58], wireless sensor network [43, 59–66], communication technology, and support vector machine (SMV) mechanism are integral to technology and are also associated to agriculture during different time periods between 2012 and 2018, but the research on blockchain and artificial intelligence has been conducted since 2016 as seen in the Figure 15.4. Other words linked with agriculture are season, food, food security, farmer, plant, yield, and sustainability, where research was carried out to a considerable level from 2012. The density of research topics selected by researchers is depicted in the Figure 15.5, and technology is highly researched compared with the keyword of the study, i.e., farming. Algorithm and image technology follow the keyword in the progression of research compared with others.

For the same research, bibliographic information was analyzed to determine the number of authors that contributed to smart farming research with the help of literature, and depicted in Figure 15.6, and based on the analysis, there were 1,238 authors found with eight authors making the maximum number of contributions. Full counting was applied

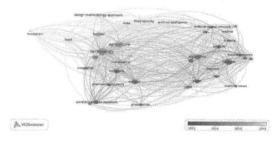

Figure 15.4 Text research survey on smart farming using the VOSviewer software. Source: compiled by the authors based on RIS data files downloaded from WoS.

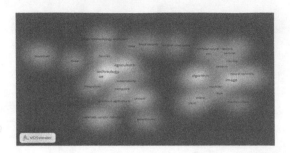

Figure 15.5 Density mapping of a text research survey on smart farming using the VOSviewer software. Source: compiled by the authors based on RIS data files downloaded from WoS.

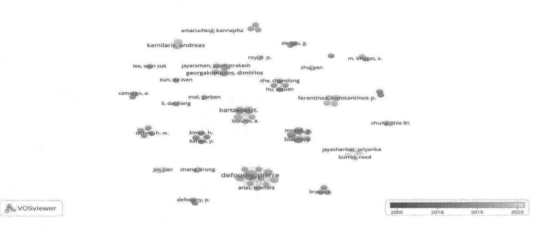

Figure 15.6 Network research chart of bibliographic research study on smart farming using the VOSviewer software. Source: compiled by the authors based on RIS data files downloaded from WoS.

and researchers who made a minimum of two contributions were included. Results show that 75 researchers have worked in clusters since 2005 till 2020 and published their work in different journals.

However, the pace of mechanization in the agriculture sector is not as anticipated in developing economies compared with developed ones due to opposition from farmers which has impacted the pace of mechanization and technology adoption; however, this scenario changed over the decades due to the benefits realized by farmers across the globe. One of the key factors that influenced the use of technology in developing economies is landholding by farmers, which is 1.08 hectares in India as revealed by the agriculture census in 2015 [67], boosting intensive farming using high resources for a small landholding compared with extensive farming, which though consumes high resources, has the advantage of large landholding, which negates the disadvantages of intensive farming, making it more conducive in the adoption of technology that paves the way to precision agriculture practices.

Figure 15.7 depicts the smart farming dimensions that are identified based on a literature survey organized by the researchers during the study.

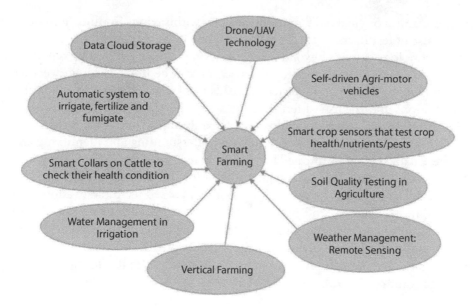

Figure 15.7 Dimensions of smart farming. Source: compiled by the authors based on conceptual learning from multiple sources.

Smart farming is a combination of sensor technology, remote sensing, irrigation techniques followed, automatic system prevailing, drone or UAV technology [30, 68–72] prevailing, soil quality testing mechanism adopted, modern means of farming like vertical farming [73, 74], smart collar for cattle [75], etc. that help in the exchange of information on the cloud computing [39, 76–79] process such that this information can be used by multiple agencies or people involved in farming activities.

15.2   Technology in Farming

The use of technology tools such as artificial neural networks, artificial intelligence, blockchain, robotics, cloud computing, and data analytics helps bring change in production, processing, and distribution mechanisms such that the agricultural sector can sustain, thus benefiting all stakeholders. Applications such as predictive intelligence and predictive analytics help in analyzing weather, soil quality and its testing, seed selection, fertilizer and agrochemical use, yield estimation, the right time to collect the produce, market price movement, selection of the right market to sell the produce, cost-effectiveness, and so on [80–82]. In India, in the last 20 to 25 years, farming has seen changes in the form of introduction of new high-yielding varieties and pest- or climate change-resistant seeds; the use of machines to plow or sow, water the fields, weed out the crop, cut the produce, or clean the field; or effectively marketing the produce. However, the recent changes in the use of large-scale machinery with the help of advanced technology such as artificial intelligence, cloud computing, data analytics, and advanced intelligent farm equipment like driverless tractors and self-guided drone technology have changed conventional farming and helped change the market dynamics of yield of farm produce along with savings in time, human resource cost, and the use of fertilizers or agrochemicals [27, 83–87].

Current technology extends beyond mechanization and helps in finding out soil quality, such that the selection of the right crop for a season can be done, through weather management technology, and the right variety of seeds can be selected that sustains change in weather conditions and the use of fertilizers and agrochemicals that provides better yield [45, 88–91]. The use of drone technology does not only apply to water, fertilizer, and agrochemical sprinkler management but also involves understanding and identifying crop deficiencies. These data are communicated to the server, measures are suggested, and these are stored for future purposes. There is a huge demand for the Internet of Things, blockchain technology, artificial intelligence, networking tools, and allied technology adoption as part of smart farming techniques, and not only wastage can be minimized but also production cost, and improved distribution mechanism and green agriculture are attained as part of meeting Sustainable Development Goal-02 (SDG2) of the United Nations apart from attaining the nation's increased gross value addition that contributes to the gross domestic product of the country [26, 92].

15.2.1   Laser Land Leveling Technology

Laser land leveling (LLL) technology has become a game changer in the process of adoption of technology in farming that helped large farmers in reducing costs of maintaining the farmland such that cultivation becomes easy since resource consumption is equally distributed apart from saving resources such as water consumption by more than 35%, chemical fertilizer distribution across the field that saves 20% to 25% than the present consumption, and minimum or almost zero weed presence apart from increasing yield up to 25% [93–99]. Once land leveling is done, farmers can reap the benefits for at least 8 to 10 years. This modern agriculture tool helped farmers as staple food suppliers in gaining benefits compared with the conventional land leveling process which uses unscientific mechanism to estimate the high and low places in a farmland, is labor-intensive, and involves huge costs. LLL is a scientifically proven method as it uses global positioning system attached to a hydraulic high-power tractor that picks mud from a high-level area and needs to be set at a low-land level area in the farm. However, the initial investment on this equipment costs US$1,650 to US$4,300 apart from the tractor cost. So, marginal to large farmers would be able to benefit much from this method compared with small farmers. However, in cases of subsistence farming, farmers can come together to hire the equipment, since it takes 5 to 6 h to level 1 hectare of land compared with 10 to 12 days in case of manual leveling with the help of animals [99]. Apart from leveling land, LLL is helpful in increasing cultivable land area, bringing forest land or uncultivable land or uneven terrains under cultivation with nominal or minimum cost (see Fig. 15.8). So, governments can take measures in providing this equipment on a lease basis through farmer cooperative societies or outsource services of leveling at a nominal price.

15.2.2   Watershed Technology

More than 68% of India's agriculture is dependent on rainfall, and in arid and semiarid regions of India, rainwater plays an important role. So, to preserve excess rainwater during

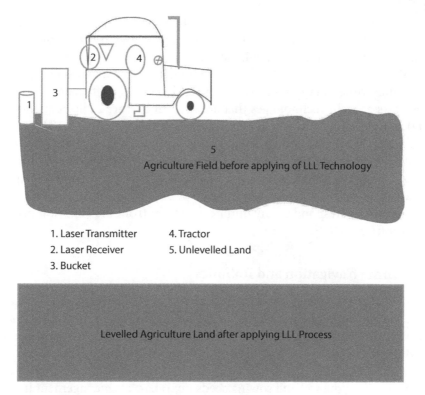

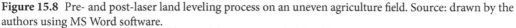

Figure 15.8 Pre- and post-laser land leveling process on an uneven agriculture field. Source: drawn by the authors using MS Word software.

the on-season or during downpour, farmers, cooperatives, and the government have come forward in managing the rainwater resource. Excess rainwater can damage the crops if the rainfall happens when it is not required for the crops or during the off-season. So, rainwater management through the applications of technology offers higher benefits [5, 71]. Hence, watershed technology was introduced in 2002–2003 in India, but it gained momentum in 2009–2010 with a target of providing water management facilities to 55 million hectares by the year 2027 [100, 101]. Watershed management involves draining of excess water into a pool or lake through canals such that it does not harm crops. One more advantage of watershed management is that excess water collected in ponds improves groundwater level apart from using the ponds for freshwater aquaculture by villagers without harming the environment. Moreover, it generates revenue for village administration.

15.2.3 Internet of Things

Popularly known as IoT, this technology helped farmers in choosing data from across the globe to understand new, innovative, and modern technologies in cultivating diversified varieties of food grains, helping to move toward sustainability. Precision agriculture involves the use of drone technology in farming for water, fertilizer, weed, pesticide, and overall crop management. IoT uses sensors in identifying the predefined algorithm-based program software, and any deviation in plant or crop health on the field information is provided as feedback to the server computer at the farmer's place with the help of satellite technology such that the farmer can take corrective measures from time to time. This process is highly applied in modern cultivation methods such as greenhouse farming and vertical farming by farm enthusiasts who are computer literate adopting the latest technology such that their time, energy, and farm resources are utilized efficiently, which motivates other enthusiasts as well. Technologies that are used in IoT are radiofrequency identification (RFID) [43, 102, 103], near-field communication (NFC) [33, 72, 104, 105], and low-power wide area (LPWA) technologies depending on the distance of the field to the server computer such that the data can be stored with accuracy. IoT technology is used in drones that are used in place of sprinklers for water management, pest and weed management, and fertilizer management. Sensors are used in place of physical verification of plants or crops to observe their and to respond to any minute deviation from the common process loaded as a program software [104].

15.2.4   Machine Navigation and Robotics

Remote control mechanisms are dominating every field of activity, and the same is happening with the agriculture sector as well. Advancement in geo positioning system (GPS) compared with previous times has paved the way for technology to navigate automated vehicles and devices like tractors and drones to detect any kind of obstacles and self-guide their path in meeting targets set beforehand. This helps reduce or even minimize the use of labor force in tilling the soil and sowing seeds up to harvest management independently such that farmers benefit independently as well as collectively since this technology not only motivates other farmers but also encourages them as farm and automation subsidies are offered through banks as per the recommendations of the Ministry of Agriculture and Farmers Welfare, Government of India [94, 104, 106–108].

Robotics extends to the modern farming process, which is helpful in farm agriculture like fruit cultivation, processing, and packaging activities improving the quality of farming in its own way. In staple crops like paddy and wheat, robots are helpful in weed management that uses image processing technology to find out the type of weed, and the extent of damage caused by the weed to the crop based on which the use of weedicide can be determined without damaging the prime crop, apart from storing the data for future requirements in analyzing and mitigating the risk of loss of yield to the farmer. Apart from weed management, farmers can use robots in fertilizer and pest management. In fruit farms, the use of robots and robotic technology is beneficial, especially for vast farms, such as in identifying ripe fruits and performing other farm jobs, saving time, money, and labor for the farmers and farm owners.

15.2.5   Drone Technology

Field surveillance is the prime activity undertaken with the help of drone technology. In farming, drones are used to observe, collect, process, evaluate, and analyze data collected at different time intervals to identify anomalies if any, such that causes for such anomalies are found out to take corrective measures such that farming takes place smoothly and farm yield is improved. In India, through the Mahalanobis National Crop Forecasting Centre (MNCFC), the government has conducted a survey that helped in mitigating agriculture disputes, risk assessment of districts for forecasting the groundwater levels such that drought or drought-like conditions can be estimated prior hand to suggest alternative crops to farmers or to take counter measures against forecasted data. In India, the government through its Ministry of Agriculture provides benefits in different means to agriculture cooperatives or Krishi Vigyan Kendra (KVK) members by offering training, providing trial operations of drones on the fields of farmers based on the requests they make as a society through agriculture universities, state or central agricultural agencies or institutions or KVKs. Subsidy is offered to hire drones from private or government agencies or to buy if coming forward through a registered society. This subsidy ranges from 40% to 50% of the total cost of a drone which at present is US$12,000 to US$15,000 depending on the farmers' choice. However, the subsidy can be availed once a farmer or society is recognized based on the skills they possess in operating a drone. So far, more than US$5.5 million is allocated to 100 KVKs, 75 research institutions under the Indian Council for Agriculture Research (ICAR), and 25 state agriculture universities for training and demonstration activities, and an amount of US$8.65 million is provided to state governments and customized hiring centers that offer training to farmers as well as the purchase of drones [109].

15.2.6   Data Analytics

Cloud computing is helping data scientists in collecting, collating, and making available loads of information in soft format that can be accessed from anywhere in the world. India to a greater extent is an agricultural economy with more than 45% of its population working in the field, and 86% of agriculture land is in the hands of small or marginal farmers. Through the application of Internet of Things technology, available data can be analyzed even if a meager 10% farmland data are collected for analysis [110]. KRISHI, a portal developed and launched by India's agriculture research agency ICAR in the year 2014, acts as a repository for large sets of data covering scientific, experimental, weather, remote sensing, academic, commodity, and market data including price aside from the government schemes or social media and internet-based information through its open platform. Data collected by agriculture agencies help farmers in identifying sustainable varieties available in the market under different weather conditions and determining excess or shortage of rain before the harvesting process, weed management or pest control varieties, market conditions for different agricultural products, and market price prevailing during different seasons such that they could decide about the sale of their agriculture produce at the nearest market. Apart from agriculture activities, data relevant to dairy, fisheries, and agriculture processing industries with detailed assessments in the language that the farmers understand easily are also available although the reports are published in the English language, and translation opportunities are also available for individuals to understand easily. Farmers can also consult KVK representatives or district, state, or central government agency representatives to explain in detail in a vernacular language such that they reap higher benefits with minimum effort.

15.2.7   Government Schemes in Smart Farming

The Union Government in India through its Ministry of Agriculture and Farmers Welfare is operating multiple schemes that offer training, skill enhancement, and adoption and adaptation techniques apart from monetary benefit schemes that enrich farmers with knowledge as well as equip them financially. The agency has also initiated "Digital Agriculture Mission (DAM)" under "India Digital EcoSystem of Agriculture (IDEA), Farmers Database, Unified Farmers Service Interface (UFSI)" along with some more funding schemes to states in meeting technology adoption targets of the nation applying artificial learning or machine learning, Internet of Things, blockchain technology, and others. Schemes such as Pradhan Mantri Krishi Sichai Yojana (PMKSY-PDMC) help improve groundwater resources and the use of effective water resources through micro-irrigation technologies. Kisan Dairy helps farmers by providing them with an audio-visual training kit through a village agriculture officer (VAO) who helps farmers in villages by trying to solve minor problems based on local environmental conditions and by approaching agriculture field officers or universities or research institutes for help so that major problems can be resolved at a faster pace [9, 10, 111, 112, 118].

Climate smart agriculture (CSA) is one of the goals of smart agriculture strategies formulated to counter and regulate greenhouse gas emissions without compromising on output. As per the United Nations Office for Disaster Risk Reduction (UNSIDR) 2018 report, disasters have created an economic loss of US$2,908 billion during the period 1997–2017 with a major contribution due to changes in climatic conditions across the globe [113]. For this, the government has adopted the crop yield prediction model, the AI sensor scheme, and the drone-based agriculture scheme, i.e., SENSAGRI, with the help of AI tools. Also, the government in its 2022–2023 budget has allocated, sanctioned, and disbursed US$26.4 billion apart from start-up funding to the agriculture sector. eNAM, an online national agriculture market, helps in understanding the market networking system where price variations in nearby markets are observed and a decision to sell or hold can be made by the farmers. ICAR launched a system-based application called "KISAAN" under the government's initiative of "Farm, Innovations, Resources, Science and Technology (FIRST)," a farmer–scientist interface, to operate beyond production and productivity [110].

Other schemes that are operated by the government for the benefit of farmers include "KISAN Credit Cards" in which credit benefits can be availed starting from the purchase of seeds until the crop reaches the farmer's home. These also include Pradhan Mantra Fasal Bima Yojana (PMFBY), Weather-Based Crop Insurance Scheme (WBCIS), Coconut Palm Insurance Scheme (CPIS), Pilot Unified Package Insurance Scheme (UPIS), Agriculture Infrastructure Fund (AIF), Credit Facility for Farmers (CFF), Crop Insurance Schemes (CIS), Group Accident Insurance Scheme for Fishermen (GAISFF), Interest Subvention for Dairy Sector (ISDS), Krishi UDAN Scheme (KUS), Mission Amrit Sarovar (MAS), National Bee Keeping and Honey Mission (NBHM), National Mission on Edible Oils (NMEO), National Mission on Natural Farming (NMNF), National Scheme of Welfare of Fishermen (NSWF), PM Kisan Maan Dhan Yojana (PMKMDY), Pradhan Mantri Kisan Samman Nidhi (PMKSN), Pradhan Mantri Krishi Sinchai Yojana (PMKSY), Primary Agriculture Credit Societies (PACS), Unique Package for Farmers (UPF), Vibrant Villages Program (VVP), Agri Clinics and Agri Business Centers Scheme (ACABC), National Horticulture Mission (NHM), National Livestock Mission-Entrepreneurship Development and Employment Generation (NLM-EDEG), and Dairy Entrepreneurship Development Scheme (DEDS) [10, 114–116]. All the mentioned schemes are in operation and are meant for different farmers based on their needs and all farmers are eligible irrespective of state or farming activity they are involved in.

15.3   Discussion

15.3.1   India's Agriculture Journey from 2001–2002 to 2020–2021

The last two decades have seen a robust growth in the agricultural and allied sectors with the government and its agencies catering to the needs of the sector with trends in technological advancement that gave a free hand to farmers in cultivating hybrid and strengthened varieties of seed.

India's gross domestic product has increased throughout the study periods, i.e., 2001–2002 till 2021–2022, except in 2008–2009 and 2021–2022 that reached three trillion globally (Figures 15.9 and 15.10), but the percentage of value addition of agriculture, forestry, and fisheries sectors to GDP stands at 2,670 billion US$ from 485.44 billion US$ and the percentage estimates show a decline to 18.65% in 2020–2021 from 21.62% in 2001–2002, and this decline in percentage is attributed to the migration of labor force from agriculture and allied activities to manufacturing and service sectors. However, the yield per agriculture laborer has ranged between 3.14 tons per hectare and 8.76 tons per hectare (Figure 15.10). It can be observed, post-2010–2011, that growth in yield per hectare per laborer declined in 2014–2015 but recovered the following year and continued to grow continuously till 2019–2020 due to changes in engineering and technology applications adopted by farmers apart from irrigational facilities and fertilizer availability [117].

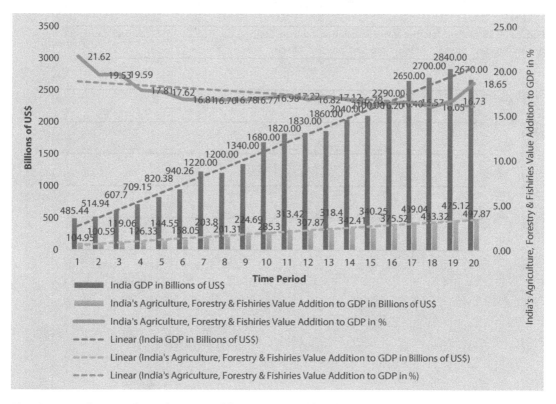

Figure 15.9 India: agriculture, forestry, and fisheries value addition to GDP. Source: compiled by the researchers based on the World Bank indicators database.

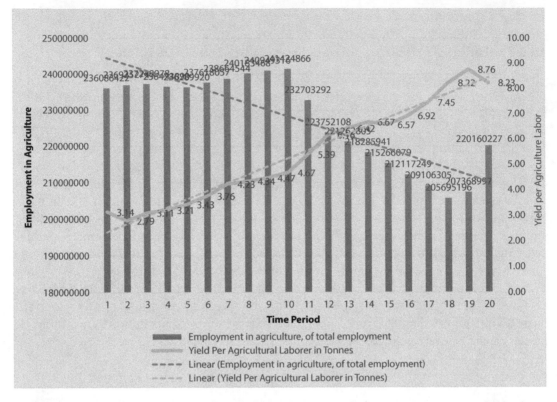

Figure 15.10 India: yield per agriculture laborer during 2001–2002 till 2020–2021. Source: compiled by the researchers based on the World Bank indicators database.

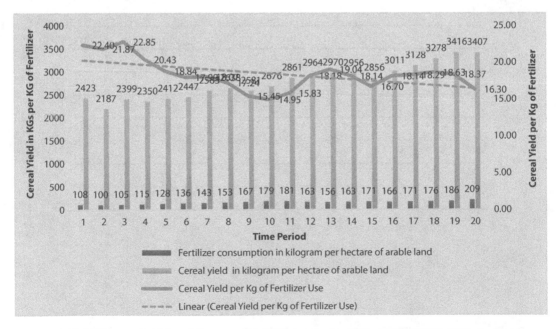

Figure 15.11 India: cereal yield per kilogram of fertilizer use during 2001–2002 till 2020–2021. Source: compiled by the researchers based on the World Bank indicators database.

Fertilizers that play a primary role in the yield of agricultural produce are classified as natural and chemical fertilizers. The availability of natural fertilizers, i.e., manure, is meager because animal manure is used for biogas plants set up by farmers, and the extracts from biogas plants alone are used as manure for agricultural fields, apart from using them as feed by other allied fields like poultry and fisheries sectors. So, farmers use chemical fertilizers in greater quantity, which are imported from countries like Iran, China, and the USA and involve higher costs. Hence, the government is offering subsidies on chemical fertilizers used by farmers making its availability a concern to farmers from time to time. Figure 15.11 shows the dwindling trends of yield of cereals per kg of fertilizer used by farmers on their land. Consumption of fertilizers has increased from 108 kg in 2001–2002 to 209 kg per hectare in 2020–2021, which is almost double the previous consumption along with increased farm yield over the years. However, the use of fertilizers alone is not sufficient to increase yield. So, farmers started employing modern technological machines such as drone sprinklers that help distribute fertilizers aside from using sensors and drones in identifying the extent of weed, plant health, and need for water.

Image technology helped farmers in finding out crop health, where drones are used to fly over the crop land to capture images of the crop field from different dimensions such that the data are stored and shared with cloud computers which in turn are shared with field scientists who recommend an appropriate mix of pesticides which once again is sprinkled using drones. In India, small and marginal farmers are provided subsidies or financing

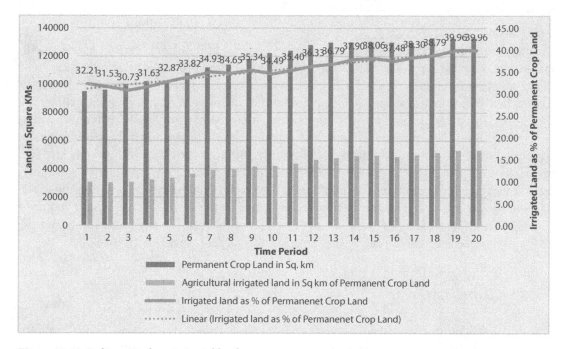

Figure 15.12 India: agriculture irrigated land to permanent cropland during 2001–2002 till 2020–2021.

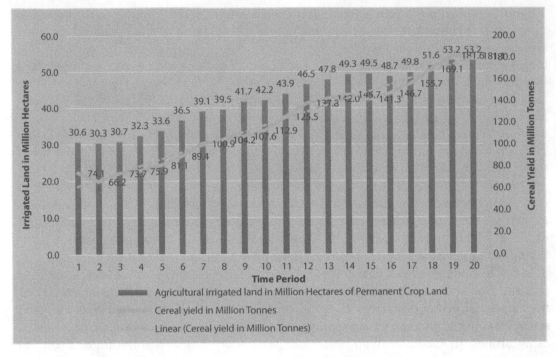

Figure 15.13 India: cereal yield to irrigated land during 2001–2002 till 2020–2021. Source: compiled by the researchers based on the World Bank indicators database.

through banks and cooperatives, which helps to increase and improve cereal yield that will encourage other farmers to participate in diversified farming processes to help increase irrigated land to permanent cropland. Since land is a scarce resource, other forms of cultivation like vertical farming also started gaining momentum in India in cities along with villages.

Figures 15.12 and 15.13 show that there is an increase in permanent cropland as well as irrigated land that in turn has increased cereal yield in India during the study periods which is possible with the adoption of technology and advanced computing tools such as artificial intelligence, machine learning tools, blockchain technology, and image processing techniques. Modern technology in computing, i.e., cloud computing, has made it possible to securely store data and access them from anywhere in the world so that similar requirements by multiple stakeholders are met at once. Hence, technology is an intermediary that caters to the needs of the desired parties so that their targets are met with ease.

15.4 Conclusion

Farming has changed dimensions over the decades in which technology has played an important role such that farming is smart enough to increase yield, minimize cost, secure resources, and maximize benefits. Drone technology, artificial intelligence, machine learning, blockchain, image processing, cloud computing, data monitoring, and analysis have helped change farming and helped increase farmers' income apart from yield improvement. Agriculture-allied activities of farmers like dairying, maintaining fisheries, and honey bee and poultry farming also are generating income for farmers which the farmer can take simultaneously with the help of several of the government schemes apart from the subsidies they receive. Hence, one can conclude that smart farming leads to better income and higher standards of living.

References

1. Krujia, H., Various types of agriculture farming in India, 2018, [Online]. Available: https://krishi.icar.gov.in/jspui/bitstream/123456789/39702/1/Various types of agri culture farming in India The Morung Express.html.

2. Taro Pumps, Types of agriculture in India, 2021, [Online]. Available: https://www.taro-pumps.com/blog/types-of-agriculture-in-india.

3. Pathak, T. M. P. R. H., Indian Agriculture: Achievements and Aspirations, in: *Indian Agriculture after Independence*, pp. 1–26, 2022.

4. Mohapatra, T., Doubling farmers income, *Indian Counc. Agric. Res.*, New Delhi, pp. 1–102, 2022.

5. Vijayan, R., Dryland agriculture in India – problems and solutions. *Asian J. Environ. Sci.*, 11, 2, 171–177, 2016.

6. University of Oxford, Our World in data-share of land area used for arable agriculture, ourworldindata.org, 2018, [Online]. Available: https://ourworldindata.org/grapher/share-of-land-area-used-for-arable-agriculture.

7. Sensarma, S., Fisheries & aquaculture, Invest India, 2023, [Online]. Available: https://www.investindia.gov.in/sector/fisheries-aquaculture.

8. G. @ of I. Press Information Bureau, Milk production in India, National Informatics Centre, 2022, [Online]. Available: https://pib.gov.in/FeaturesDeatils.aspx?NoteId=151137&ModuleId=2.

9. Department of Animal Husbandry & Dairying, Rashtriya Gokul Mission, National Informatics Centre, New Delhi, 2023, [Online]. Available: https://dahd.nic.in/schemes/programmes/rashtriya_gokul_mission.

10. C-DAC, Government schemes, Vikaspedia, 2023, [Online]. Available: https://vikaspedia.in/schemesall/schemes-for-farmers.

11. G. Ministry of Finance, Economic survey 2022-23, pp. 1–414, 2023.

12. Jayashankar, P., Johnston, W.J., Nilakanta, S., Burres, R., Co-creation of value-in-use through big data technology- a B2B agricultural perspective. *J. Bus. Ind. Mark.*, 35, 3, 508–523, 2020.

13. N. Academy, O. Agricultural, N. E. W. Delhi, *Big data analytics in agriculture*, National Academy of Agricultural Sciences, New Delhi, 2021.

14. Rumpf, T., Mahlein, A.K., Steiner, U., Oerke, E.C., Dehne, H.W., Plümer, L., Early detection and classification of plant diseases with Support Vector Machines based on hyperspectral reflectance. *Comput. Electron. Agric.*, 74, 1, 91–99, Oct. 2010.

15. Singh, A. and Sharma, A., Deep tech & national security, 2022.

16. Liu, Y., Liu, C., Zhou, M., Does digital inclusive finance promote agricultural production for rural households in China? Research based on the Chinese family database (CFD). *China Agric. Econ. Rev.*, 13, 2, 475–494, 2021.

17. Chandra, P., Bhattacharjee, T., Bhowmick, B., Does technology transfer training concern for agriculture output in India? A critical study on a lateritic zone in West Bengal. *J. Agribus. Dev. Emerg. Econ.*, 8, 2, 339–362, 2018.

18. Pearson, S. *et al.*, Are Distributed Ledger Technologies the panacea for food traceability? *Glob. Food Secur.*, 20, 145–149, Mar. 2019.

19. Krause, M.J. and Tolaymat, T., Quantification of energy and carbon costs for mining crypto-currencies. *Nat. Sustain.*, 1, 11, 711–718, Nov. 2018.

20. Creydt, M. and Fischer, M., Blockchain and more - Algorithm driven food traceability. *Food Control*, 105, 45–51, Nov. 2019.

21. Kumar, M.V. and Iyengar, N.C.S.N., A framework for blockchain technology in rice supply chain management plantation, Nov. 2017, pp. 125–130.

22. Li, X., Wang, D., Li, M., Convenience analysis of sustainable E-agriculture based on blockchain technology. *J. Cleaner Prod.*, 271, 122503, Oct. 2020.

23. Thompson, B.S. and Rust, S., Blocking blockchain: Examining the social, cultural, and institutional factors causing innovation resistance to digital technology in seafood supply chains. *Technol. Soc.*, 73, 102235, May 2023.

24. Kim, J., Kim, S., Ju, C., Il Son, H., Unmanned aerial vehicles in agriculture: A review of perspective of platform, control, and applications. *IEEE Access*, 7, 105100–105115, 2019.

25. Maheswari, Precision farming technology, adoption decisions and productivity of vegetables in resource-poor environments. *Agric. Econ. Res. Rev.*, 21, 415–424, 2008.

26. Munir, K., Ghafoor, M., Khafagy, M., Ihshaish, H., AgroSupportAnalytics: A cloud-based complaints management and decision support system for sustainable farming in Egypt. *Egypt. Inform. J.*, 23, 1, 73–82, 2022.

27. Partel, V., Charan Kakarla, S., Ampatzidis, Y., Development and evaluation of a low-cost and smart technology for precision weed management utilizing artificial intelligence. *Comput. Electron. Agric.*, 157, January, 339–350, 2019.

28. Regan, Á., Smart farming' in Ireland: A risk perception study with key governance actors. *NJAS - Wageningen J. Life Sci.*, 90–91, 100292, 2019.

29. Selvaraj, M.G. *et al.*, AI-powered banana diseases and pest detection. *Plant Methods*, 15, 1, 1–11, 2019.

30. Talaviya, T., Shah, D., Patel, N., Yagnik, H., Shah, M., Implementation of artificial intelligence in agriculture for optimisation of irrigation and application of pesticides and herbicides. *Artif. Intell. Agric.*, 4, 58–73, 2020.

31. Karimi, Y., Prasher, S.O., Patel, R.M., Kim, S.H., Application of support vector machine technology for weed and nitrogen stress detection in corn. *Comput. Electron. Agric.*, 51, 1–2, 99–109, Apr. 2006.

32. Kozai, T. and Fujiwara, K., Moving toward self-learning closed plant production systems, in: *LED Light. Urban Agric.*, pp. 445–448, Jan. 2016.

33. Wolfert, S., Ge, L., Verdouw, C., Bogaardt, M.J., Big data in smart farming – A review. *Agric. Syst.*, 153, 69–80, May 2017.

34. Vallejo-Gómez, D., Osorio, M., Hincapié, C.A., Smart irrigation systems in agriculture: A systematic review. *Agronomy*, 13, 2, 342–367, Feb. 2023.

35. Doshi, J., Patel, T., Bharti, S.K., Smart farming using IoT, a solution for optimally monitoring farming conditions. *Proc. Comput. Sci.*, 160, 746–751, Jan. 2019.

36. Kakamoukas, G.A., Sarigiannidis, P.G., Economides, A.A., FANETs in agriculture – A routing protocol survey. *Internet Things (Netherlands)*, 18, 100183, May 2022.

37. Ma, J., Zhou, X., Li, S., Li, Z., Connecting agriculture to the internet of things through sensor networks. *Proc. - 2011 IEEE Int. Conf. Internet Things Cyber, Phys. Soc. Comput. iThings/CPSCom 2011*, pp. 184–187, 2011.

38. Chen, M., Mao, S., Liu, Y., Big data: A survey. *Mob. Netw. Appl.*, 19, 2, 171–209, Apr. 2014.

39. Yong, W. *et al.*, Smart sensors from ground to cloud and web intelligence. *IFAC-PapersOnline*, 51, 17, 31–38, Jan. 2018.

40. Kodali, R.K. and Sahu, A., An IoT based soil moisture monitoring on Losant platform. *Proc. 2016 2nd Int. Conf. Contemp. Comput. Informatics, IC3I 2016*, pp. 764–768, 2016.

41. Talavera, J.M. *et al.*, Review of IoT applications in agro-industrial and environmental fields. *Comput. Electron. Agric.*, 142, 283–297, Nov. 2017.

42. Oruganti, R.K. *et al.*, Artificial intelligence and machine learning tools for high-performance microalgal wastewater treatment and algal biorefinery: A critical review. *Sci. Total Environ.*, 876, 162797, Jun. 2023.

43. Tzounis, A., Katsoulas, N., Bartzanas, T., Kittas, C., Internet of Things in agriculture, recent advances and future challenges. *Biosyst. Eng.*, 164, 31–48, Dec. 2017.

44. Camargo, A. and Smith, J.S., Image pattern classification for the identification of disease causing agents in plants. *Comput. Electron. Agric.*, 66, 2, 121–125, May 2009.

45. Kurtulmus, F., Lee, W.S., Vardar, A., Immature peach detection in colour images acquired in natural illumination conditions using statistical classifiers and neural network. *Precis. Agric.*, 15, 1, 57–79, Feb. 2014.

46. De Rainville, F.M. *et al.*, Bayesian classification and unsupervised learning for isolating weeds in row crops. *Pattern Anal. Appl.*, 17, 2, 401–414, 2014.

47. Chen, X., Xun, Y., Li, W., Zhang, J., Combining discriminant analysis and neural networks for corn variety identification. *Comput. Electron. Agric.*, 71, SUPPL. 1, S48–S53, Apr. 2010.

48. Ahmed, F., Al-Mamun, H.A., Bari, A.S.M.H., Hossain, E., Kwan, P., Classification of crops and weeds from digital images: A support vector machine approach. *Crop Prot.*, 40, 98–104, Oct. 2012.

49. Wang, P., Liu, N., Qiao, J., Application of machine vision image feature recognition in 3D map construction. *Alexandria Eng. J.*, 64, 731–739, Feb. 2023.

50. Athani, S.S. and Tejeshwar, C.H., Support vector machine-based classification scheme of maize crop. *Proc. - 7th IEEE Int. Adv. Comput. Conf. IACC 2017*, Jul. 2017, pp. 84–88.

51. Bauer, S.D., Korč, F., Förstner, W., The potential of automatic methods of classification to identify leaf diseases from multispectral images. *Precis. Agric.*, 12, 3, 361–377, Jun. 2011.

52. Córdoba, M., Bruno, C., Costa, J., Balzarini, M., Subfield management class delineation using cluster analysis from spatial principal components of soil variables. *Comput. Electron. Agric.*, 97, 6–14, 2013.

53. Larsolle, A. and Hamid Muhammed, H., Measuring crop status using multivariate analysis of hyperspectral field reflectance with application to disease severity and plant density. *Precis. Agric.*, 8, 1–2, 37–47, Apr. 2007.

54. Mohd Kassim, M.R., Mat, I., Harun, A.N., Wireless sensor network in precision agriculture application. *2014 Int. Conf. Comput. Inf. Telecommun. Syst. CITS 2014*, 2014.

55. Waheed, T., Bonnell, R.B., Prasher, S.O., Paulet, E., Measuring performance in precision agriculture: CART—A decision tree approach. *Agric. Water Manage.*, 84, 1–2, 173–185, Jul. 2006.

56. Dinh Le, T. and Tan, D.H., Design and deploy a wireless sensor network for precision agriculture. *Proc. 2015 2nd Natl. Found. Sci. Technol. Dev. Conf. Inf. Comput. Sci. NICS 2015*, Oct. 2015, pp. 294–299.

57. Tan, L., Cloud-based decision support and automation for precision agriculture in orchards. *IFAC-PapersOnLine*, 49, 16, 330–335, 2016.

58. De Lima, G.H.E.L., Silva, L.C.E., Neto, P.F.R., WSN as a tool for supporting agriculture in the precision irrigation. *6th Int. Conf. Netw. Serv. ICNS 2010, Incl. LMPCNA 2010; INTENSIVE 2010*, pp. 137–142, 2010.

59. Gubbi, J., Buyya, R., Marusic, S., Palaniswami, M., Internet of Things (IoT): A vision, architectural elements, and future directions. *Future Gener. Comput. Syst.*, 29, 7, 1645–1660, 2013.

60. De La Concepcion, A.R., Stefanelli, R., Trinchero, D., A wireless sensor network platform optimized for assisted sustainable agriculture. *Proc. 4th IEEE Glob. Humanit. Technol. Conf. GHTC 2014*, pp. 159–165, Dec. 2014.

61. Bhargava, K., Ivanov, S., Donnelly, W., Internet of nano things for dairy farming. *Proc. 2nd ACM Int. Conf. Nanoscale Comput. Commun. ACM NANOCOM 2015*, Sep. 2015.

62. Shiravale, S. and Bhagat, S.M., Wireless sensor networks in agriculture sector-implementation and security measures. *Int. J. Comput. Appl.*, 92, 13, 25–29, 2014.

63. Ojha, T., Misra, S., Raghuwanshi, N.S., Wireless sensor networks for agriculture: The state-of-the-art in practice and future challenges. *Comput. Electron. Agric.*, 118, 66–84, 2015.

64. Barrenetxea, G., Ingelrest, F., Schaefer, G., Vetterli, M., The hitchhiker's guide to successful wireless sensor network deployments. *SenSys'08 - Proc. 6th ACM Conf. Embed. Networked Sens. Syst.*, pp. 43–56, 2008.

65. Asikainen, M., Haataja, K., Toivanen, P., Wireless indoor tracking of livestock for behavioral analysis. *2013 9th Int. Wirel. Commun. Mob. Comput. Conf. IWCMC 2013*, pp. 1833–1838, 2013.

66. Kwong, K.H. *et al.*, Practical considerations for wireless sensor networks in cattle monitoring applications. *Comput. Electron. Agric.*, 81, 33–44, Feb. 2012.

67. P. I. Bureau, *Categorisation of farmers*, pp. 1–3, 2019.

68. Freeman, P.K. and Freeland, R.S., Agricultural UAVs in the U.S.: Potential, policy, and hype. *Remote Sens. Appl. Soc. Environ.*, 2, 35–43, Dec. 2015.

69. Nogueira Martins, R. *et al.*, Digital mapping of coffee ripeness using UAV-based multispectral imagery. *Comput. Electron. Agric.*, 204, 107499, Jan. 2023.

70. Fornace, K.M., Drakeley, C.J., William, T., Espino, F., Cox, J., Mapping infectious disease landscapes: Unmanned aerial vehicles and epidemiology. *Trends Parasitol.*, 30, 11, 514–519, Nov. 2014.

71. Huuskonen, J. and Oksanen, T., Soil sampling with drones and augmented reality in precision agriculture. *Comput. Electron. Agric.*, 154, 25–35, Nov. 2018.

72. Rejeb, A., Abdollahi, A., Rejeb, K., Treiblmaier, H., Drones in agriculture: A review and bibliometric analysis. *Comput. Electron. Agric.*, 198, 107017, Jul. 2022.

73. Hinnell, A.C., Lazarovitch, N., Furman, A., Poulton, M., Warrick, A.W., Neuro-Drip: Estimation of subsurface wetting patterns for drip irrigation using neural networks. *Irrig. Sci.*, 28, 6, 535–544, 2010.

74. Sivamani, S., Bae, N., Cho, Y., A smart service model based on ubiquitous sensor networks using vertical farm ontology. *Int. J. Distrib. Sens. Netw.*, 9, 12, 161495, 2013.

75. Huircán, J.I., *et al.*, ZigBee-based wireless sensor network localization for cattle monitoring in grazing fields. *Comput. Electron. Agric.*, 74, 2, 258–264, Nov. 2010.

76. Savitha, C. and Talari, R., Mapping cropland extent using sentinel-2 datasets and machine learning algorithms for an agriculture watershed. *Smart Agric. Technol.*, 4, 100193, Aug. 2023.

77. Cai, Y. *et al.*, A high-performance and in-season classification system of field-level crop types using time-series Landsat data and a machine learning approach. *Remote Sens. Environ.*, 210, 35–47, Jun. 2018.

78. Zamora-Izquierdo, M.A., Santa, J., Martínez, J.A., Martínez, V., Skarmeta, A.F., Smart farming IoT platform based on edge and cloud computing. *Biosyst. Eng.*, 177, 4–17, Jan. 2019.

79. Botta, A., De Donato, W., Persico, V., Pescapé, A., Integration of cloud computing and Internet of Things: A survey. *Future Gener. Comput. Syst.*, 56, 684–700, Mar. 2016.

80. Keesstra, S.D. *et al.*, The significance of soils and soil science towards realization of the United Nations sustainable development goals. *Soil*, 2, 2, 111–128, 2016.

81. Granitto, P.M., Verdes, P.F., Ceccatto, H.A., Large-scale investigation of weed seed identification by machine vision. *Comput. Electron. Agric.*, 47, 1, 15–24, Apr. 2005.

82. Granitto, P.M., Navone, H.D., Verdes, P.F., Ceccatto, H.A., Weed seeds identification by machine vision. *Comput. Electron. Agric.*, 33, 2, 91–103, 2002.

83. Gackstetter, D. *et al.*, Autonomous field management – An enabler of sustainable future in agriculture. *Agric. Syst.*, 206, 103607, Mar. 2023.

84. Valdés-Vela, M., Abrisqueta, I., Conejero, W., Vera, J., Ruiz-Sánchez, M.C., Soft computing applied to stem water potential estimation: A fuzzy rule based approach. *Comput. Electron. Agric.*, 115, 150–160, Jul. 2015.

85. Batchelor, W.D., McClendon, R.W., Adams, D.B., Jones, J.W., Evaluation of SMARTSOY: An expert simulation system for insect pest management. *Agric. Syst.*, 31, 1, 67–81, 1989.

86. Alibabaei, K., Gaspar, P.D., Campos, R.M., Rodrigues, G.C., Lopes, C.M., Evaluation of a deep learning approach for predicting the fraction of transpirable soil water in vineyards. *Appl. Sci.*, 13, 5, 2815, Mar. 2023.

87. Vesper, H. and Gartner, B., Executive forum measuring progress education in. *J. Bus. Ventur.*, 12, 403–421, 1997.

88. Chlingaryan, A., Sukkarieh, S., Whelan, B., Machine learning approaches for crop yield prediction and nitrogen status estimation in precision agriculture: A review. *Comput. Electron. Agric.*, 151, 61–69, Aug. 2018.

89. Amaruchkul, K., Multiobjective land–water allocation model for sustainable agriculture with predictive stochastic yield response. *Int. Trans. Oper. Res.*, 30, 4, 1647–1672, 2023.

90. Johannes, A. *et al.*, Automatic plant disease diagnosis using mobile capture devices, applied on a wheat use case. *Comput. Electron. Agric.*, 138, 200–209, Jun. 2017.

91. Lim, K.K., Chong, Z.K., Khoshdelniat, R., Sim, M.L., Ewe, H.T., Paddy growth monitoring with wireless sensor networks. *2007 Int. Conf. Intell. Adv. Syst. ICIAS 2007*, pp966–970, 4658529, 2007.

92. Pathmudi, V.R., Khatri, N., Kumar, S., Abdul-Qawy, A.S.H., Vyas, A.K., A systematic review of IoT technologies and their constituents for smart and sustainable agriculture applications. *Sci. Afr.*, 19, e01577, Mar. 2023.

93. Pal, B.D., Kapoor, S., Saroj, S., Jat, M.L., Kumar, Y., Anantha, K.H., Adoption of climate-smart agriculture technology in drought-prone area of India – implications on farmers' livelihoods. *J. Agribus. Dev. Emerg. Econ.*, 12, 5, 824–848, 2021.

94. Fan, J., Zhang, Y., Wen, W., Gu, S., Lu, X., Guo, X., The future of Internet of Things in agriculture: Plant high-throughput phenotypic platform. *J. Cleaner Prod.*, 280, Part-1, 123651, Jan. 2021.

95. Kanannavar, P.S., Premanand, B.D., Subhas, B., Anuraja, B., Bhogi, P.B., Laser land levelling- an engineering approach for scientific irrigation water management in irrigation command areas of Karnataka, India. *Int. J. Curr. Microbiol. Appl. Sci.*, 9, 5, 2393–2398, 2020.

96. Ali, A., Hussain, I., Rahut, D.B., Erenstein, O., Laser-land leveling adoption and its impact on water use, crop yields and household income: Empirical evidence from the rice-wheat system of Pakistan Punjab. *Food Policy*, 77, February, 19–32, 2018.

97. Chilur, R., Kanannavar, P.S., Ravindra, Y., Kumar, M., Laser land levelling: Its impact on slope variation in verisols of Karnataka. *Environment and Ecology*, 34 (2A), June, 740–744, 2016.

98. Chandiramani, M., Kosina, P., Jones, J., Laser land leveling: A precursor technology for resource conservation. Rice-Wheat Consortium, p. 48, 2007.

99. ML Jat, M.G., Chandana, P., Gupta, R., Sharma, S.K., Laser land leveling: A precursor technology for resource conservation, 2006.

100. G. @ of India, Watershed Management, GoI, New Delhi, 2023, [Online]. Available: https://www.mygov.in/group/watershed-management-0/.

101. World Bank, Use of cutting edge technology for watershed development, The World Bank Group, 2011, [Online]. Available: https://www.worldbank.org/en/news/feature/2011/08/02/india-cutting-edge-watershed-development.

102. Li, X., Peng, L., Sun, C., The application and forecast of geospatial information technology in agriculture Internet of Things. *2012 2nd Int. Conf. Remote Sensing, Environ. Transp. Eng. RSETE 2012 - Proc.*, 2012.

103. Matharu, G.S., Upadhyay, P., Chaudhary, L., The Internet of Things: Challenges & security issues. *Proc. - 2014 Int. Conf. Emerg. Technol. ICET 2014*, Jan. 2014, pp. 54–59.

104. Dhanaraju, M., Chenniappan, P., Ramalingam, K., Pazhanivelan, S., Kaliaperumal, R., Smart farming: Internet of Things (IoT)-based sustainable agriculture. *Agric.*, 12, 10, 1–26, 2022.

105. Verdouw, C.N., Beulens, A.J.M., van der Vorst, J.G.A.J., Virtualisation of floricultural supply chains: A review from an internet of things perspective. *Comput. Electron. Agric.*, 99, 160–175, 2013.

106. Wakchaure, M., Patle, B.K., Mahindrakar, A.K., Application of AI techniques and robotics in agriculture: A review. *Artif. Intell. Life Sci.*, 3, 100057, Dec. 2023.

107. Hassoun, A. *et al.*, Food processing 4.0: Current and future developments spurred by the fourth industrial revolution. *Food Control*, 145, 109507, Mar. 2023.

108. Mylonas, N., Malounas, I., Mouseti, S., Vali, E., Espejo-Garcia, B., Fountas, S., Eden library: A long-term database for storing agricultural multi-sensor datasets from UAV and proximal platforms. *Smart Agric. Technol.*, 2, 100028, Dec. 2022.

109. P. I. Bureau, Use of drones in agriculture sector, GoI, 2022, [Online]. Available: https://pib.gov.in/PressReleasePage.aspx?PRID=1884233.

110. P. I. Bureau, Smart farming. *NAAS*, GoI, 2022, [Online]. Available: https://www.pib.gov.in/PressReleasePage.aspx?PRID=1848720.

111. MAFW, *A farmer friendly handbook schemes & programmes*, Dep. Agric. Coop. Farmers Welf. (DAC&FW), Minist. Agric. Farmers Welf. (MAFW), Gov. India, 2019.

112. M. O. F. Agriculture, F. Welfare, F. Welfare, Output-outcome monitoring framework (for the schemes with financial outlays 500 crore and more than 500 crore, 2022.

113. R. Parliament Library and Reference and D. A. I. Service, Climate smart agriculture: A key to sustainability, 2022.

114. VIkaspedia, Schemes for farmers, Vikaspediia GoI, 2023, [Online]. Available: https://vikaspedia.in/schemesall/schemes-for-farmers.

115. NABARD, Government schemes for farmers, NABARD, 2023, [Online]. Available: https://www.nabard.org/content1.aspx?id=23&catid=23&mid=530.

116. N. B. for A. and R. Development, Farmers' welfare in India a state-wise analysis, 2021.

117. MoSPI, Contribution of agricultural sector in GDP, PIB, 2023, [Online]. Available: https://www.pib.gov.in/PressReleasePage.aspx?PRID=1909213.

118. Social Statistics Division, Women and Men in India (A statistical compilation of Gender related Indicators in India), vol. March 2018, no. 20, Minist. Stat. Program. Implementation, Gov. India, p. 131, 2018.

16

Frugal Innovation in Developing a Fertilizer Sprayer—A Case of an Ingenious Design in Maharashtra

Madhavi R.[1]*, Urmila Itam[1], Harold Andrew Patrick[1], Ravindran Balakrishnan[2], Chaya Bagrecha[1], Shalini R.[1] and V. Y. John[1]

[1]CMS Business School, Jain (Deemed-to-be University), Bengaluru, Karnatka, India
[2]Omnicom Media Group, Lagos, Nigeria

Abstract

India, for long, has been known as an agricultural country. While the country prides itself on its rich heritage and long-standing consistency in agricultural commodities, its woes are growing by the day. A key requirement for every farmer is spraying adequate and necessary fertilizer to protect and promote crop output from time to time. The right usage of fertilizers is known to enhance the nutrient constituents in the soil apart from positively impacting the output. Even in cases where farmers have access to the right fertilizer, spraying the same has its unique set of challenges—the equipment required, even spraying, time consumption, and the labor required for this. What is the status of a humble farmer who cannot afford expensive equipment for this purpose? Tired of the above-described scenario, a young farmer—proud of his profession, a native of Maharashtra—has developed an ingenious solution that can address the problem and offer visible improvement to such farmers. This research effort presents a case study on this specific *fertilizer sprayer* which is affordable and reduces the huge effort for farmers due to its design, sense, and efficiency in delivering value on the farmland.

Keywords: Fertilizers, agriculture, farmers, shark tank

16.1 Introduction

India is a country with diverse climatic conditions, which makes it suitable for cultivating a wide range of crops. The nation is renowned for producing major food grains like rice, wheat, jowar, bajra, and maize, among others. Additionally, pulses, various lentils, and oilseeds including groundnut, rapeseed, soybean, and sunflower, as well as other crops like sugarcane, jute, cotton, and vegetables, are prominent in India. These statistics are reported by the Government of India (GOI) and recorded by the Directorate of Economics and Statistics (DA&FW), which maintains an open-source document for stakeholders to access [1].

*Corresponding author: dr.madhavi@cms.ac.in; madhu4ratna@gmail.com

Kuldeep Singh and Prasanna Kolar (eds.) Digital Agricultural Ecosystem: Revolutionary Advancements in Agriculture, (291–306) © 2024 Scrivener Publishing LLC

According to the compiled data, the cultivated land area in India has consistently increased over the years. Starting from just over 97 million hectares in 1951, it has now surpassed 129 million hectares as of 2021 [1]. The Department of Agriculture and Farmers Welfare, under the Government of India, is responsible for compiling information on the financial assistance provided to farmers on a state-wide basis. These data are considered crucial by the government as it aims to support the farming community. These statistics reveal the consistent need for fertilizer usage and its growing needs.

16.2   Fertilizers and Their Usage

Timely irrigation and appropriate use of fertilizers are two vital factors essential for the healthy growth of crops. Fertilizers are composed of ingredients that provide essential nutrients to crops, maintaining their health and promoting their growth. These fertilizers are widely used worldwide. It is crucial for fertilizers to be soil-friendly in order to preserve the natural health of the soil, which is often supported by specific microorganisms present in the soil. The estimated value of the fertilizer market in India is approximately INR 900 billion (Indian Fertilizer Market Size, Share, Growth, Report 2023–2028, 2022) [2].

While India holds the second position globally and ranks first among the SAARC nations in terms of total fertilizer usage, the average amount of fertilizer applied per hectare in India is significantly lower compared with other SAARC nations. This lower utilization of applied nutrients can be attributed to factors such as overuse, misuse, or imbalanced application of fertilizer nutrients, as well as a lack of attention toward secondary and micronutrients. Consequently, there has been an accumulation of fertilizer nutrients in the soil and potential leakage into the environment, leading to environmental degradation and climate change [4]. A study by Praveen et al. (2022) analyzed patterns in fertilizer use at the national and state levels. They employed interrupted time series analysis to examine the impact of significant policies on fertilizer consumption. In addition, bibliometric analysis was conducted to identify current research priorities in the field. The study specifically focused on the impact of important policies on fertilizer use in India. Time series data from 1972 to 2017 were utilized, considering both national and state levels. While it is widely recognized that the usage of chemical fertilizers has been increasing, the study revealed that the growth in fertilizer nutrient usage during the decade from 2010 to 2020 was either low or negative, representing a new national-level trend. Significantly, the analysis indicated a gradual increase in the intensity of fertilizer use across states, with a shift from areas where usage has peaked to regions where it can have a more beneficial impact. The study concluded that the main initiatives implemented have successfully influenced fertilizer consumption [3].

The introduction of the Nutrient-Based Subsidy (NBS) in 2010 played a crucial role in ensuring the availability of affordable fertilizers to farmers. This subsidy program aims to benefit farmers nationwide, particularly small and marginal farmers who often face challenges in affording fertilizers at market prices. The disadvantages of imbalanced fertilization include reduced crop yields and quality, soil degradation, environmental pollution, and health risks. To address these concerns, the recommendations put forward emphasize the importance of promoting the use of organic and biofertilizers. It also advocates for practices such as soil testing and balanced fertilization to optimize nutrient application. The study conducted by Arvind Kumar Shukla, Sanjib Kumar Behera, S. K. Chaudhari, and Gajendra

Singh (2022) emphasizes the urgent need for India to establish a clear and comprehensive system that enforces strict regulations on balanced fertilizer use. Furthermore, it advocates for integrated nutrient management, which involves utilizing locally available organic manures and crop residues and cultivating crop genotypes with high yields [4].

16.3 Role of Technology in Agriculture

In recent years, machine learning techniques have been employed to optimize the careful selection of the best fertilizer for each crop, as it plays a crucial role in increasing agricultural yield. Findings from an experimental study revealed that the combination of recursive feature elimination and the proposed heterogeneous stacked ensemble classifier (HSEC) offers a higher prediction rate compared with other methods [5].

Furthermore, another study explores the implementation of agricultural sensors as part of smart farming in India. Advancements in communication technology have made smart farming feasible in the country. Sensors play a vital role in helping farmers monitor and optimize crops based on environmental conditions and constraints. Wireless sensors serve various purposes, such as precise location detection, airflow measurement, nutrient identification, and analysis of soil composition and moisture content. By leveraging sensors, farmers can apply fertilizers more efficiently while reducing chemical usage and labor resources. This process enables farmers to maximize their yields as well as conserve natural resources. The adaption of technology in agriculture addresses challenges such as a decline in cultivable land and food wastage in production and distribution [6].

Integrating technology with conventional framing methods makes agriculture look smarter and effective in meeting the demands of the global population. The adaption of communication technology and sustainable IoT-based sensors plays an important role in enhancing crop yields and controlling environmental pollution. On the other hand, the inappropriate and excessive usage of fertilizers can lead to soil health deterioration, nutritional imbalances, and environmental hazards such as excessive water consumption by the farmers. To address this issue, the Government of India launched the "Soil Health Card Scheme" aimed at reducing input costs and increasing productivity and profitability while ensuring the sustainability of agriculture. Technological interventions facilitate the precise utilization of agricultural inputs based on crop, soil, and weather requirements, optimizing fertilizer usage for maximum productivity [7].

Brichi *et al.* analyzed the state-of-the-art application of organic residues in agricultural production systems. This is done by examining trends and findings from published research on the use of organic residues for soil health and crop productivity. A bibliographic analysis was conducted with 81 papers from the Web of Science database. The analysis reveals that there is a growing trend of research being conducted on this subject from China, India, and the United States. The application of compost, animal manure, crop residues, municipal solid waste, and biochar was analyzed. This analysis shows that applying organic residues improves soil health and increases the productivity of crops [8].

Joshi *et al.* talked about serious concerns about the sustainability of natural resources due to inappropriate application of fertilizers in agricultural fields. The absence of proper application will lead to deterioration of soil health, nutritional imbalance, and other environmental hazards. Excessive use of inorganic fertilizers has led to increased water consumption.

To address the inappropriate use of fertilizers, the Government of India launched the "Soil Health Card Scheme" to reduce input costs and increase productivity and profitability which is affecting the sustainability of agriculture. Technology intervention facilitates the precise utilization of agricultural inputs depending on the crop, soil, and weather requirements to optimize the use of fertilizers for maximum productivity [9].

16.4   Research Gap and Objective

While the literature above provides valuable insights into the potential of fertilizers and technology for healthy farming, there are still research gaps and needs that researchers should address. Some studies have mentioned that cellulose modification can alter the release of fertilizers and more insights are needed to understand the mechanism for precise nutrient release control. By achieving better control over nutrient release, farmers can optimize fertilizer application rates and reduce nutrient losses. Effective incorporation of technology into precision agriculture systems, which includes sensor technologies and fertilizer spraying techniques, needs the attention of the researchers. These kinds of integrations have the capacity in optimizing nutrient use in crop productivity. The outcomes of such research understanding will facilitate the adoption of efficient methods in agriculture and farming to meet the challenges posed by the growing population demands.

In order to address the above gaps, researchers considered a case research design to understand the technology invented by a young farmer from the state of Maharashtra, India, who named it Bharath K2 under the fertilizer spraying segment. By focusing on a real-world case, researchers can gain insights into the practical implementation and effectiveness of the technology in the agriculture sector.

Another important research gap identified from the literature is the need to assess the economic viability of fertilizer spray devices. Using affordable and environmental protection technologies is crucial for sustainable agriculture. Therefore, further research should focus on the evaluation and assessment of production cost, scalability, and cost-effectiveness of cellulose-based CRF/SRF fertilizers compared with conventional chemical fertilizers. This understanding will promote the adoption of cellulose-based fertilizers by farmers.

16.5   Research Design

This research work adopts a qualitative approach to present the case study. A checklist of open-ended questions was used to interact with the farmer over the phone. The questions were carefully drafted aligning them toward the development of the said invention. The farmer was approached and requested to be a part of this case study by explaining the modalities. Any queries raised by the farmer were addressed, and with complete clarity and transparent communication, the farmer was asked to provide informed consent. On receiving the informed consent, the farmer was interviewed. Thus, in-depth interviews have been conducted to collect data on the subject matter with the inventor-farmer. The responses were noted and the case narrative was developed. Data sources include both primary and secondary bases. Secondary data were collected from relevant government websites, research articles, and newspaper articles.

16.6   Jugadu Kamlesh—The Inventor-Farmer Turned Agripreneur and His Fertilizer Sprayer

Mr. Kamlesh Nanasaheb Ghumare, a young farmer from the state of Maharashtra, is the mastermind behind this simple, yet novel equipment. In his explanations, he happily speaks about tackling each gap and replacing it with convenience and functionality. Small farmers have perennial challenges, and this is an important piece of equipment in reducing a few of those challenges. A farmer by choice, he thinks beyond his comforts and highlights the utility value this simple design can provide to thousands of small and marginal farmers. Hailing from a farmer's family, he took to the profession out of choice and passion. He dropped out of formal education during graduation realizing the mismatch in the learning and the lack of utility value as a farmer.

Mr. Kamlesh Ghumare, self-proclaimed as *Jugadu Kamlesh* in his own words, describes the journey of the fertilizer sprayer since the year 2014. The word "*Jugadu*" in the Hindi language refers to ingenious ideas. This informal suffix is attached to his name due to his problem-solving attitude toward farming challenges. As a farmer's son, he is well aware of the problems pertaining to the usage of fertilizers such as skin problems developed over a period of time due to repeated contact with fertilizers; problems connected to vision, often ignored till they get too late; etc. His father experienced skin problems; including but not limited to itching, burning, etc. The inspiration was to rid his family and other small farmers of these problems. Figure 16.1 shows the evidence of the first ingenious effort in putting together the idea. Figure 16.2 shows the evidence of the first ingenious effort in putting together the idea (Side view)

Figure 16.1 Screenshot from his first YouTube post (image source: adopted from the farmer's video post on his YouTube channel with his permission).

Figure 16.2 The working model—first version (side view) (image source: adopted from the farmer's video post on his YouTube channel with his permission).

16.7   The Design Journey

The abovementioned intention compelled him to put together the first version of his fertilizer sprayer by using scrap material. The idea was to bring the thought to a working physical shape. This was a phase filled with confusion and a lot of inside dialogue for the farmer. He would go to fetch scrap material and then come back to use that to bring some usable shape to his ongoing thoughts. This phase is often referred to as ideation in new product development. This went on for years. After years of struggle, some questioning, and criticism, he was able to build the first working model. Excited, he decided to test the prototype by using it first on his farm to spray the fertilizer. This helped his father at the first level. Mr. Kamlesh knows clearly that small farmers are suffering on this account as most of them cannot afford costly equipment.

This is the first YouTube video posted (screenshot on the left) by the farmer that went viral proclaiming the idea and the working design to the farming community in particular and the entire world in general. Bringing a thought to life is never an easy task.

This first model was low on flexibility and heavy to operate. This increases the efforts of the user. The farmer posted a video in shorts and it was well received. This first model helped him identify changes to better the machine on multiple counts.

Following are a few images shared by the farmer as part of the new product development process. The farmer highlighted the relentless thinking and discussions about the equipment along the way.

These iterations helped enhance the features to bring it to the present version in terms of reducing heaviness and improving functionality.

16.8   The Shark Tank: India Experience

Mr. Ghumare applied to be on the reality TV show Shark Tank, India (Season 1). This show is the replica of the original series launched in the USA under the aegis of the Former

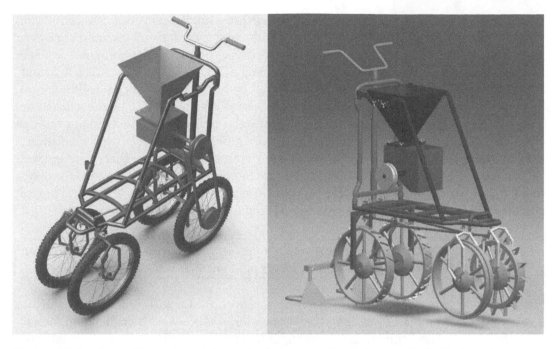

Figure 16.3 Iterations of the equipment during the design stage. (Images' source: Used with farmer's permission)

President of the USA—Mr. Barack Obama. Obama envisioned to develop the entrepreneurial spirit of the masses in the USA and strengthen the SMEs (small and medium enterprises) as they contribute over 25% of the GDP collectively as mentioned by the sharks in their conversations in the show. However, such small enterprises face a myriad of problems: scaling issues, operational inefficiency, teamwork challenges, lack of connections, constraints in financial matters, no professional guidance in managerial decision-making, etc. The show is designed exclusively for entrepreneurs seeking VC funding and participation to bolster their entrepreneurial ideas at different stages. This show has been instrumental in developing real-life changing stories for entrepreneurs from varied backgrounds—small and tired. Shark Tank is a premium platform for such enterprises and for such budding entrepreneurs to seek funding and have an expert on board. Most sharks are successful entrepreneurs in at least one sector or are serial entrepreneurs themselves. Such sharks have the knowledge of failure and success parameters to guide the ventures that they choose to fund. After a brief standard presentation, each shark often interacts by asking questions to learn more about the presented venture and then decide to either invest or stay out. Often, there is a negotiation that occurs before the investment—often known as the DEAL—is finalized. This platform offers incentives to the sharks who have monetary resources, business connections, and managerial skill sets that they may share with budding business owners for an equity stake, helping them expand their entrepreneurial empire. This is usually followed up by a thorough due diligence of the invested business to evaluate its current situation to take the conversation ahead and begin the actual work. Figure 16.3 shows the evidence of the iterations that the farmer went through in the design stages.

After a few rounds of filtering, each of the shortlisted applicants gets a chance to be on the final stage where they can interact directly with the sharks. Such interactions are woven into a TV show. The episode aired in India revealed that the farmer presenting his fertilizer sprayer—just as a working model—sought funding of Rs. 40 lakhs. He sought the funding, as he wanted to produce the sprayers himself by setting up a plant in his hometown. There were about seven sharks present who listened to his presentation and evaluated the costs involved. These sharks come from different walks of life. Most sharks found the idea endearing and appreciated the farmer's initiative and enthusiastic approach wholeheartedly, but they failed to find it investible. The key reason was that the sharks are not well acquainted with the agricultural world to be able to bolster the kind of push and progress they can promise in other sectors. However, Mr. Peyush Bansal, CEO of Lenskart.com, sat quietly till the last, pondering, and then announced to make an offer as follows:

> *Equity capital of Rs. 10 lakhs for 40% stake in the business and an interest free loan of Rs. 30 lakhs (totaling to Rs. 40 lakhs) to be paid gradually at the farmer's ease.*

This matches the desire of the farmer who was overjoyed that he was able to convince a shark to come on board. Reaching this destination was filled with challenging interactions. Some questions pointed at approaching banks to seek the desired financial assistance instead. If funding is the key element in his case, why wait for a shark when there are many financial institutions in India? The farmer opined that the traditional financial institutions may not support such an idea and consider it not viable. Throughout the interaction, Mr. Ghumare exhibited unclenching confidence and conviction in farming and his proposal. He teamed up with his relative Mr. Naru who provides absolute support round the clock in all his endeavors. This cousin (Mr. Naru) joined him for the pitch on Shark Tank (Etimes, 2023). He topped it with a convincing thought that he will not stop with just this one equipment but work incessantly to design and develop solutions to the unending problems that require addressing in farming, particularly in India for small farmers. As part of the conversation, Mr. Ghumare presented evidence from social media interactions that his idea and product are not just problem-solving in nature but are marketable. His first video upload of the working prototype of the product has garnered lakhs of views. This was followed by farmers in the fraternity reaching out to him with queries and willingness to buy in thousands on WhatsApp as a result of watching the video.

After the Shark Tank experience, a team of engineers was hired to undo the flaws identified during the testing phase, apart from working on the value-enhancing features. The inventor felt the design was a failure for a long-run effective usage. Bringing in professionals was only the logical thing to do. This led to productive discussions to enhance the prototype from a functional perspective. This was repeated a few times with constant and rigorous testing on the field to arrive at the current version. The farmer also explains that when the prototype works well on one farm, it need not be so on another. The nature and type of the crop and related factors determine if the sprayer serves these typical needs. For example, when one designs a cycle or a motorcycle, it is well known that its usage is on the street built for it. Such "streets" have a standard understanding and are often stable in their build and usage. If the motorcycle is used on any other platform, its performance cannot be optimum.

Similarly, the fertilizer sprayer needs to run on the field which presents many challenges—wet land, uneven floor, watered portions, pebbles, sprouting seeds, thin sections of lanes to ride through, etc. None of these conditions can be avoided. It is safe to say that such aspects need to be factored in at varying levels for different crops with changing seasons and geographical aspects.

Testing is a crucial phase. He looks at his prototype as his brainchild and does not anticipate trouble. With a smile, Mr. Ghumare says "How can you find fault with your child?" So, he employs the idea by testing it on other farmers' lands to get the required reality check by reaching out to experienced farmers across crops. Farmers are the right audience in this regard. They experience many challenges and this is just one equipment that can solve a small fraction of the pie. Large companies do not focus on this as it is not profit-driven. Crops need nourishment without being hurt or disturbed while the pesticides are being sprayed. Such testing also helped the team factor in that some crops have a height as a challenge and some the lack of it. Can the same equipment serve these diverse crops?

The final slim design allows the machine to maneuver across different types of crops. The farmer is confident that the testing done across various fields has benefitted their decision-making at all stages and helped them remove amateur errors.

(Source: images used with the permission of the inventor).

The above images are from a variety of crops—sugarcane, pulses, and cotton—and the machine is capable of being used on all of them. This instills the confidence that this can be used across crops—regardless of their height, strength, and nature of the soil and land features. The testing phase also uncovered new requirements for flexibility and ease of functioning. For example, the sugarcane crop is essentially tall as compared with pulses or cotton and the farmer must be able to reach the top of the yield to use adequate pesticide.

For this reason, height adjustments and flexi-bending were incorporated to enhance the functionality of the model. The following pictures depict the same [10, 11].

The four-arm design at two levels is the basic design feature. This is further enhanced by allowing the back arms to reach a height of up to 10 feet or bend down to the ground level and at any desirable variations in between.

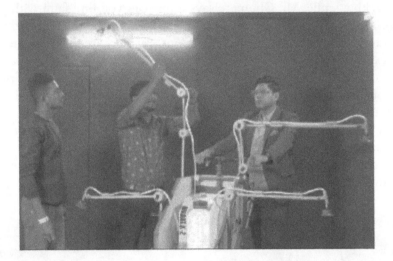

The bending of the spraying arm is demonstrated here. The red nozzle at the spraying end also has flexi-bending features at its level.

Here, it further bends down (left arm) to touch the ground level. This reduces human effort and the user need not come in contact with the actual fertilizer.

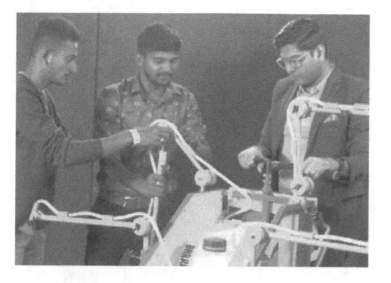

This is the front portion with switches to regulate the pressure of the sprayer and the on/off buttons for ease of usage.

The strong nozzle is fixed firmly to the metal connector which does the spraying and has flexi-rotating features.

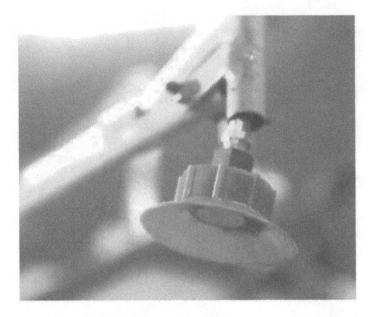

The angular look of the finished product is ready to hit the market and serve the farmers. The pesticide can is firmly held in the central section with a maximum capacity of 25 kg.

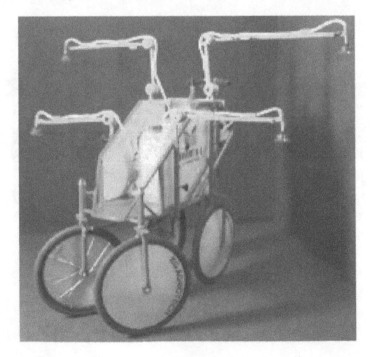

The side view of the machine ready with finishing touches including painting, brand name, and the company name printed with a logo.

(Source: images used with the permission from the inventor-farmer).

The proposed MRP of the sprayer with all its multifunctional features is about Rs. 25,000, while it is costing the new agripreneur about Rs. 20,000 per unit to manufacture as announced by him in conversation with his investor for an article in Business Insider in early 2023 [10].

"I'm delighted to share the first significant update on Kamlesh and his startup KG Agrotech (now a Pvt. Ltd. firm). It took a lot of hard work, research, travel, failures, learnings, and four-iterations to get here. Our first go-to-market version is ready and we are calling it Bharat-K2 (to signify the second version as the original was what was presented in the tank). We are hitting production with this version and the first batch of saleable carts will be on the ground within 60 days," shared Mr. Bansal on LinkedIn [11].

16.9 Design Thinking

The framework on design thinking as given by Darden School of Business (University of Virginia, USA) was brought into action in the development of this fertilizer sprayer.

Briefly, the framework speaks about four elements of design thinking:

What is?	What if?	What wows?	What works!

1. **What Is?**
   This is the first step that asks: "How things are?" This key phrase recommends clearly uncovering the existing reality, the problem that needs to be addressed in all its certainty. So, bringing out the set of challenges, what is the actual problem faced—defining the same clearly with its core on the forefront—is considered important. A deep understanding of the current situation is vital to take the journey in the right direction.

2. **What If?**
   This question asks for a vital change/augmentation in the existing scenario/problem aspiring to add value in solving the problem or to enhance the performance of the questioned product/service or idea.
3. **What Wows?**
   This focuses on the best or the highest possible change/augmentation derived from the process to better things. The best or the highest idea here need not necessarily be easy to achieve. The thinking here is to not be limited by possibilities alone as it can restrict the free flow of thoughts.
4. **What Works?**
   This strives to strike a balance between what is amazing and what actually is possible. The objective here is the retain as many best features as possible that work in the real world to deliver value to the identified stakeholders.

   Mr. Ghumare's aspiration has gone through these stages through an iterative process to reach the level of sophistication and functionality that are now visible in the sprayer's working abilities.

16.10 The Path Ahead

The Government of India has announced subsidies on drones for farmers. During the interaction, the farmer pointed out the facts and some concerns are listed here:

- Are farmers educated and ready for advanced technology when many lack or cannot afford education?
- While drones are problem-solving in nature and can do a better job than their previous counterparts, will anybody focus on checking the preparedness of the farming community itself, not just the farmer?
- What are the prerequisites for the successful implementation of such technology from infrastructure and environment perspectives?
- Are subsidies really problem-solving in themselves? This question naturally presents itself at this point. The farmer also states that many farmers still follow age-old methods of farming. So, to bring in advanced technology on many aspects of farming, farmers need support beyond just subsidy.

16.11 Conclusion

Integrating further features or higher-tech initiatives into the current model is not an immediate requirement for the farmer. Mr. Ghumare opines that providing a solution-driven idea, tested and accepted by the farmers, allows them to not just accept the idea but also be eager to use the same on their crops. The young farmer aspires to develop many ingenious solutions keeping it affordable and solution-driven to empower the small farmers of this country. In his conversations, he emphasizes that farming is a profession that is facing a myriad of challenges and very few solutions to keep the small farmer motivated on the ground.

Conflict of Interest

The authors have no conflict of interest in developing and publishing this case study.

Acknowledgments

The authors are very thankful to Mr. Kamlesh Ghumare (the inventor-farmer) for his interest, patience, and cooperation toward this case development, joining calls for in-depth interviews, responding to queries in his busy schedule, and sharing the relevant images required in this regard.

References

1. Agricultural Statistics at a Glance, Official website of Directorate of Economics and Statistics, Department of Agriculture and Farmers Welfare, Ministry of Agriculture and Farmers Welfare, Government of India (desagri.gov.in), 2021.
2. Fertilizer Sector in India, 2022, https://www.civilsdaily.com/fertilizer-sector-of-india/.
3. Praveen, K.V., Singh, A., Kumar, P., Jha, G.K., Kingsly, I., Advancing with fertilizers in Indian Agriculture: Trends, challenges, and research priorities. *Agric. Econ. Res. Rev.*, 33, Conference Number, 49–60, 2020, DOI: 10.5958/0974-0279.2020.00017.8.
4. Shukla, A.K., Behera, S.K., Chaudhari, S.K., Singh, G., Fertilizer Use in Indian Agriculture and its Impact on Human Health and Environment. *Indian J. Fertilizers*, 18, 3, 218–237, March, 2022.
5. Mariammal, G., Suruliandi, A., Segovia-Bravo, K.A., Raja, S.P., Predicting the suitable fertilizer for crop based on soil and environmental factors using various feature selection techniques with classifiers. *Expert Syst.*, e13024. 7, 22, 1–8, 2022, https://doi.org/10.1111/exsy.13024.
6. Role of modern technology in Agriculture, Sehgal Foundation, Mar 2023, https://www.smsfoundation.org/role-of-modern-technology-in-agriculture/.
7. Dhanaraju, M., Chenniappan, P., Ramalingam, K., Pazhanivelan, S., Kaliaperumal, R., Smart Farming: Internet of Things (IoT)-Based Sustainable Agriculture. *Agriculture*, 12, 10, 1745, 2022, https://doi.org/10.3390/agriculture12101745.
8. Brichi, L., Fernandes, J.V.M., Silva, B.M., Vizu, J.D., Junior, J.N.G., Cherubin, M.R., Organic residues and their impact on soil health, crop production and sustainable agriculture: A review including bibliographic analysis. *Soil Use Manage.*, 39, 2, 686–706, 2023.
9. Joshi, P.K. and Varshney, D., Agricultural Technologies in India: A Review. NABARD Research and Policy Series No. 5, Department of Economic Analysis and Research, National Bank for Agriculture and Rural Development, Mumbai, 2022, https://www.nabard.org/auth/writereaddata/tender/1507223612Paper-5-Agricultural-Tech-in-India-Dr.Joshi-&-Varshney.pdf.
10. Etimes, *Shark Tank Report*, 2023, Source https://timesofindia.indiatimes.com/tv/news/hindi/shark-tank-indias-jugadu-kamlesh-shows-his-upgraded-product-model-to-investor-peyush-bansal-shares-first-year-revenue-target-is-rs-5-crore/articleshow/97372986.cms.
11. Magan, S., 'Jugaadu' Kamlesh from Shark Tank India S1 is ready with the go-to-market version of the pesticide spraying cart, 2023, https://www.businessinsider.in/business/startups/news/jugaadu-kamlesh-from-shark-tank-india-s1-is-ready-with-the-go-to-market-version-of-the-pesticide-spraying-cart/articleshow/98083509.cms.

17

For Sustainable Farming in India: A Data Analytics Perspective

Shanta Pragyan Dash[1*] **and K. G. Priyashantha**[2]

[1]Centre for Socio-Architectural Studies, Manipal School of Architecture and Planning, Manipal Academy of Higher Education, Karnataka, India
[2]Department of Human Resource Management, Faculty of Management and Finance, University of Ruhuna, Matara, Sri Lanka

Abstract

The farming industry in India is a significant contributor to the country's economy, providing livelihoods to millions of people and supplying food to a large population. The farming industry faces significant challenges such as low productivity, fragmented landholdings, climate change, lack of irrigation facilities, poor market access, and changing consumer demands. The research aims to review the challenges faced by the farming industry in India and the potential scope of change or improvement for the farming industry. It highlights the importance of data analytics and its ability to provide light on a wide range of agricultural phenomena, including crop yields, soil quality, weather patterns, and market trends. Through a review analysis, it is found that using data analytics by optimizing inputs, detecting crop diseases and pests, and giving real-time information could contribute toward enhancing the potential scope of improving the future of the farming industry. The review findings also summarize how capacity building through data analytics in the farming industry is essential to help farmers adopt new technologies and practices that can improve productivity, reduce costs, and increase profitability.

Keywords: Consumer demands, data analytics, future farming, capacity building, farming practice, SDG-2, SDG-12, SDG-13

17.1 Introduction

The farming industry has shown a significant emphasis on India's agricultural contribution, where the country is securing second position in global foot grain, vegetable, and fruit production along with a dominating market in the industry as a larger producer of milk, sugarcane, and tea [1, 3]. However, this industry has faced multiple challenges that need attention including low productivity significance, the impact of climate change, and fragmented land ownership, with inadequate irrigation facilities and marketing strategies [4]. Considering all of these challenges, a sustained effort from the government and other stakeholders is

*Corresponding author: shanta.dash@manipal.edu

Kuldeep Singh and Prasanna Kolar (eds.) Digital Agricultural Ecosystem: Revolutionary Advancements in Agriculture, (307–318) © 2024 Scrivener Publishing LLC

needed to promote a sustainable and productive farming practice in the current setting. Emphasis is also needed on various key challenges which demand attention, including climate change water scarcity, soil degradation, and limited access to modern technology and best practices [5]. Therefore, adopting such data-driven approaches in the farming sector is becoming crucial in overcoming such challenges. The successful implementation of these approaches is possible if they rely on improved digital infrastructure and access, especially in rural India [1, 2]. Since the country is already experiencing the various adverse effects of global warming and climate change and its frequent weather events such as floods and droughts, enabling sustainable practices like conservation in agriculture and integrated pest management becomes indispensable toward preserving the soil health and mitigating the impact of climate change [3, 6]. Likewise, it is also significant to consider the evolving needs of the consumers toward shaping the farmers' future and the farming industry in India, as there is always a rising demand for safe and high-quality products in the market [2, 7].

This article aims to comprehensively review the need for data analytics in India's farming industry and its future, which is imperative to effectively address the prevailing challenges and secure its long-term sustainability targeting the SDGs. It also addresses adopting data-driven approaches and sustainable practices to meet the evolving demands of consumers. It reviews the various government initiatives as well as the challenges during their execution and the requirement to have a self-sustainable as well as a capacity-building attribute of implementing data analytics in the farming sector to contribute toward the farming industry in India, which can thrive and continue to be a pillar of economic growth and employment opportunities as well as food security for the nation.

17.1.1 Current Status of the Farming Industry in India

In India's economy, the farming industry plays a significant role in employing a major portion of the workforce and substantially contributing to the country's GDP. However, the crucial factor faced is the challenges that impede its growth and progress in the market (Figure 17.1). One of the major challenges is the persistent issue that despite vast land and a considerable agricultural workforce, the country's agricultural productivity falls behind many other countries due to its low productivity. Such discrepancies can be attributed to various factors such as poor soil quality, inefficient access to reliable irrigation facilities, and the lack of awareness of modern and best sustainable agricultural practices and technologies to optimize productivity in farming [8, 9, 11]. The second major crucial challenge is climate change, which seriously threatens Indian farmers throughout the year regarding their productivity [12–14]. The increase in the erratic weather pattern and the frequent occurrences of extreme natural events such as floods and droughts create an atmosphere and a vulnerability factor of unpredictability and uncertain circumstances that adversely affect the yield of the crops leaving the farmers vulnerable to the consequences of these adverse climatic disruptions [10, 15, 18]. Small-scale farmers who consistently face resource constraints have to bear these challenges and find it extremely difficult to recover from such setbacks over a period of years [15, 19]. The Indian farmers also encounter difficulty in assessing the credit and identifying a suitable market for securing fare prices for their agricultural products to enhance their productivity along with the low productivity challenges and climatic-related concerns [11, 19]. Due to a lack of capital and an inadequate understanding of market dynamics, it has always been difficult for farmers to expand their

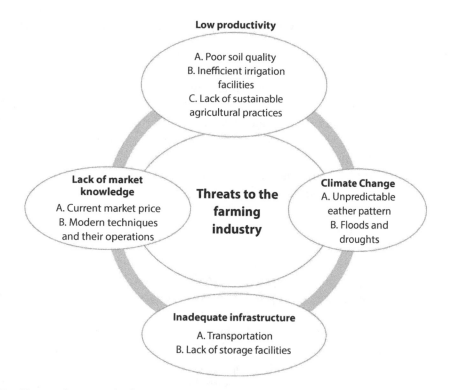

Figure 17.1 Various threats to the farming industry (source: authors).

businesses and invest in contemporary inputs to improve their living standards through agricultural techniques [16, 20]. Additionally, inadequate infrastructure, as well as transportation networks, storage facilities, and poll chains, also contributes to a significant challenge toward the market of agricultural products and reducing post-harvest losses [10, 20, 24]. Nonetheless, the Government of India acknowledges the significance of supporting the farming industry. It has taken several initiatives to address these challenges, such as subsidies for agricultural inputs for seeds and fertilizers, which have been implemented to alleviate the financial burdens borne by the farmers [6, 13, 17]. Also, significant efforts have been strategized to improve the irrigation infrastructure and promote water saving and sustainable water techniques to enhance water availability and optimize efficiency in terms of best practices in the farming industry [4, 15, 19]. Moreover, the government also succeeded in introducing innovative agricultural technologies and practices to enhance the sustainability as well as productivity of the farming sector, where there has been a growing emphasis on promoting organic farming as well as implementing renewable energy resources in agriculture, which is considered to be a part of the government's commitment to foster sustainable farming practices and to mitigate the climatic change and environmental impact [20, 22]. Therefore, by prioritizing the research toward adapting innovative technologies and methods in farming, India may thrive on cultivating a more resilient and strengthened farming sector, which can substantially contribute to the food security of the nation contributing toward the economic growth and the farmers and the farming industry and the community engaged in the agricultural farming sector.

17.1.2   Data Analytics and Its Applied Methods in Current Farming Practices

Data analytics has been looked upon as a transformative tool toward the potential for revolutionizing the farming industry in the Indian context [21, 23]. Farmers can get valuable insights by harnessing the power of data to make decisions to optimize resource allocation and enhance agricultural productivity (Figure 17.2). One of its most significant implementations is the precision agriculture practice, where the farmers can analyze data on soil quality, level of moisture, and nutrient content with crop health, which are the essential information required to enhance the field's productivity [2, 25]. Once equipped with this information, Indian farmers can customize the cultivation technique and plan their irrigation schedules with precision in terms of applying fertilizers resulting in optimal resource utilization to improve crop yields over time [25, 26]. Additionally, the data analytic knowledge also facilitates crop prediction and risk assessment by analyzing the historical and real-time data of the weather patterns. It helps in identifying the pest and disease prevalence as well as the growth rate of the crops [5, 16, 27]. This, in turn, will help the farmers to plan their plantings by implementing the targeted pace management strategies and consider the measures toward mitigating the impact of adverse weather conditions. Market analysis is another significant area where data analytics plays a significant role. Farmers can get various insights into the market trends along with consumer preferences and demand patterns through the analysis of the market data. This, in turn, will empower the farmer to make informed decisions toward the crop selection harvesting time as well as the sales strategies aligning their cultivation practices with the market demands optimizing the price

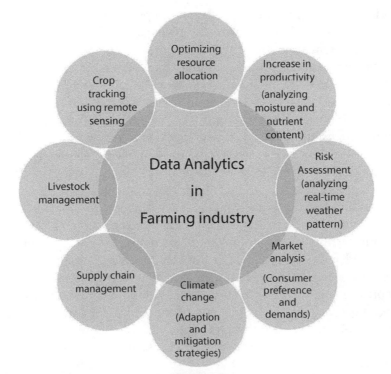

Figure 17.2 Data analytics in the farming industry (source: authors).

strategies and enhancing the profitability in contributing to the overall GDP of the nation [26]. Furthermore, data analysts also contribute to climate change adaptation and mitigation strategies. It includes historical weather data as well as the soil moisture levels and other relevant factors which can be analyzed through data analytics to help the farmer make an informed decision and knowledge about the suitable crop varieties, irrigation methods, and land management practices [28]. By proactively adjusting their farming practices, farmers can also mitigate the impact of climate change and maintain a sustainable agricultural system toward optimizing agricultural productivity and contributing toward economic growth over the years. Data analytics also enhances the supply chain management in the agricultural system by analyzing the data related to the transportation routes logistics as well as the storing conditions and the market demands, and these optimizations reduce the post-harvest losses as well as improve inventory management and efficient crop transportation from the market [25, 27]. Data analytics also contributes toward livestock management practices, which increase productivity and enhance animal welfare and farm profitability, embracing its potential to revolutionize the industry by data-driven decision-making, improving resource efficiency, and reducing risks, contributing toward overall agricultural productivity.

Data analysis methods can potentially optimize farming practices in different regions of India. Soil mapping enables a detailed assessment of soil fertility and helps to make an informed choice of crop and precise fertilizer. Indian start-ups have used electromagnetic induction and gamma radiometry techniques to create soil maps [25, 29]. Accurate weather forecasting plays a vital role in successful farming, and by analyzing data from weather stations and satellites, farmers can make informed decisions about seeding and harvest schedules [9, 30]. In India, several companies offer weather forecasts tailored to the needs of farmers. Pest and disease management is a major challenge; data analysis can monitor diseases and take timely actions. Indian start-ups use artificial intelligence and machine learning algorithms to detect and predict pest and disease outbreaks. Crop tracking using remote sensing and satellite imagery helps monitor crops and identify areas that need attention, which helps make decisions about irrigation and fertilization. Indian companies offer tracking services using satellite imagery, drones, and ground sensors [18, 30]. Data analysis can optimize agricultural practices, leading to higher yields, lower costs, and better sustainability. However, ensuring access to information and technology to smallholders is crucial for widespread adoption and equitable benefits.

17.1.3 Capacity Building through Data Analytics in the Farming Industry

The capacity-building process enables farmers to embrace new technology and practices to enhance productivity, reduce cost, and increase profitability in the agricultural and farming industry (Figure 17.3). There are various approaches that have been found in the literature emphasizing the capacity-building approach toward data analytics execution in the farming industry [28, 29]. First is the development of training programs specifically designed for the farmers [29, 30]. Such programs not only educate the farmers regarding the collection and analysis of relevant data related to their crops along with the soil conditions as well as weather patterns but also, by learning how to analyze these data effectively, they get a scope to explore the areas for improvement and optimize resource allocation. It makes them informed about the inputs as well as the prevailing agricultural practices [2, 31].

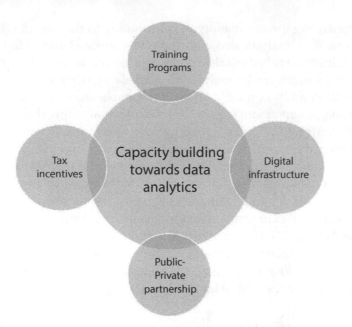

Figure 17.3 Capacity building toward the implementation of data analytics in the farming industry (source: authors).

Such training programs must be conducted through workshops and extensive services and in farmer field schools, ensuring widespread access to the knowledge and skills of the farmer group. Secondly, establishing the digital infrastructure is equally important to provide farmers with easy access to analytic tools and platforms, which can be achieved through mobile applications, web-based platforms, and other technologies that help the farmers leverage data-driven insight [8, 12, 32]. These tools are designed to be accessible, intuitive, and tailored to the specific needs and capabilities of the farmers so as to make the data analytic tool readily available for the driven decision-making process by the farmers for their farms. Thirdly, the significant aspect is the public–private partnership which greatly supports the capacity-building effort in data analytics for farming [21, 32, 33]. Collaboration with universities, research institutions, and technology companies can also provide valuable expertise and resources toward knowledge enhancement of the farmers. Search partnerships also provide the farmers with an excess of data analytics experts who can offer training, mentor them, and support their knowledge and understanding of the best sustainable practices in the field [34]. This enables the farmers to develop their expertise in terms of their knowledge and apply them in their farming operations. Moreover, government policies and incentives also play a critical role in promoting the adoption of data analytics in farming. The government develops policies and incentives for the farmers to invest in the digital infrastructure by offering subsidies and financial support. It also adds tax incentives, providing a surplus opportunity for farmers to adopt data analytics techniques to foster innovation in the farming industry [31, 34]. The need for capacity building through data analytics in the farming industry is toward empowering the farmer to embrace new technology and practices to boost productivity, reduce costs, and increase the profitability of their business [31, 33, 34]. Therefore, by implementing such programs toward establishing digital infrastructure posting public and private partnerships as well as supportive government policies, farmers can be well equipped with the necessary tools and resources and can be informed about the data-driven decisions in their agricultural operations, which eventually contribute toward overall advancement in the agricultural sector.

17.1.4   Future Scope of India with Data Analytics in the Farming Industry

Data analytics poses a significant potential toward increasing farm yield by providing farmers with valuable insights and recommendations driven from diverse data sources, one of the major advantages being the capacity to optimize the utilization of crucial requirements like water fertilizer and pesticides. Through the analysis of soil data, weather patterns, and crop growth, the farmers cannot determine the optimal quality and quantity with the timings for applying these inputs, which contribute toward increasing the crop yield and reducing the cost. Data analytics also plays a significant role in the detection of crop diseases and infection from pests, which enables the farmers to take preliminary action toward the prevention of crop damage and mitigate the yield losses across the period. Significantly for a country like India, where the crop losses are mostly due to pest and disease infections, it poses a strong challenge toward agricultural productivity by reducing the crop yield. Furthermore, the data analytics also strengthened farmers with real-time information on the weather pattern and crop growth, which can be utilized to make informed decisions toward the schedule of irrigation as well as optimal harvesting schedule and other farming practices, which ultimately results in a high-quality yield. It also exists that farmers identify the underperforming areas within their form and implement the targeted improvement to enhance the overall productivity in their farming where the farmers by leveraging the data analytics can identify the crop-specific suitability for different areas of their farms based on the prevailing conditions and the soil characteristics. This information and knowledge allow them to select the crop best suited to specific areas, optimizing resource allocation and maximizing productivity. Therefore, data analytics holds a strong potential to increase farm yield with suitable insights and recommendations derived from the comprehensive data analysis and optimizing the input utilization detecting and managing crop diseases and pests, thereby increasing higher yields and greater profitability. Embracing the concept of data analytics in agriculture has shown a significant way forward toward sustainability, productivity, and resilience in the farming and agricultural industry nationwide. The future of India's farming industry holds a promising and strong scope toward data analytics.

As the country's population grows continuously, food production demand rises while limited resources are available. In this context, data analytics always plays a significant power tool to address these challenges with the driven agricultural success, and by harnessing their potential, Indian farmers can enhance their efficiency, and this leads toward optimizing resource utilization. Risk management is another crucial area where data analytics plays a significant role. Climate change and unpredictable weather patterns have led to crop failure fluctuation and natural disasters. It enables them to identify the potential risks, and analyzing the historical data and real-time information helps them to develop effective strategies to mitigate such challenges. Farmers can identify new crops and innovative products with high market potential by analyzing market trends and consumer demand. This enables farmers to adapt their farming practices and seize new market opportunities both domestically and internationally, contributing to the growth and profitability of the agricultural sector. In addition, data analytics provides real-time information about crops and weather conditions, helping farmers become more self-sufficient. This information allows farmers to make informed decisions about irrigation schedules, optimal harvest times, and crop protection measures. This timely decision will result in better crop quality, higher yields, and ultimately, higher profitability. Overall, the increasing adoption of data analytics holds great potential for Indian agribusiness. By using data to optimize resource use, manage risk, diversify crops, and achieve self-sufficiency, farmers can achieve long-term success and contribute to national food security goals. Moreover, integrating data analytics into agriculture will create new business opportunities and boost economic growth and prosperity in rural areas, thereby transforming the agricultural landscape in India.

17.1.5   Urge Toward Adapting Data Analytics for Rural Areas in India

In the agricultural sector of rural India, the application of data analytics has a strong potential impact and benefit in long-term sustainability. Since agriculture is a vital contributor to the country's economy, data analytics also plays a pivotal role in driving the growth in agriculture and farming for the nation. The primary advantage of data analytics in rural areas is its potential to enhance resource utilization. Farmers can optimize using crucial resources such as water fertilizers and pesticides by leveraging the data analytic technique, which optimizes and reduces the cost and improves the yield in farming operations. Farmers can also enhance their economic viability by efficiently managing resources and contributing to the development of rural areas. Also, a vital role in risk management is a crucial factor in agricultural sectors in rural areas. Therefore, data analytics can enable farmers to maintain stable incomes, protect their agricultural investments, and enhance economic security through effective risk management. Precision agriculture is another key area where data analytics plays a significant role in effectively using weather data and water management practices and techniques. This is particularly important for rural farmers who often have limited resources and need to maximize agricultural production. By analyzing the data, rural farmers can diversify their crops and find new ways to produce value-added products. Market trend analysis and insights into consumer demand allow growers to identify niche crops and unique products with high market potential. This diversification increases income and revitalizes the rural economy by creating new business opportunities and expanding agricultural value chains. In addition, data analysis improves rural farmers' access to credit and financial services. Accurate and reliable information about crops, production methods, and market information helps farmers prove their creditworthiness to lenders. This leads to more favorable credit conditions and encourages investment in agricultural enterprises, which increases productivity in rural areas and boosts overall economic growth. The potential impact of data analytics in rural India is significant. Harnessing the power of data to optimize resource use, manage risk, diversify crops, and improve financial inclusion will help farmers achieve long-term success and contribute to India's food security goals. Moreover, the adoption of data analytics can create new business opportunities, stimulate economic growth, promote rural prosperity, and ultimately change the landscape of agriculture and rural development in India.

17.1.6   Mapping the Future of Data Analytics in Farming and Linking to SDGs

Agricultural data analysis helps achieve sustainability goals by addressing different aspects of sustainability (Figure 17.4). Firstly, in SDG 2: zero hunger, data analysis enables farmers to increase crop production and strengthen food security. By analyzing data on soil conditions, weather conditions, and crop health, farmers can make informed decisions about planting schedules, irrigation methods, and pest control. This knowledge allows them to improve productivity, minimize crop losses, and ensure consistent nutrition, helping to end hunger. Secondly, data analysis contributes to achieving Sustainable Development Goal 12: responsible consumption and production by promoting sustainable agricultural practices. Farmers can reduce the excessive use of water, fertilizers, and pesticides by using precision farming techniques. By using these inputs accurately based on data knowledge, farmers can reduce waste, prevent environmental degradation, and promote efficient resource management. This approach promotes responsible consumption and production models and ensures the sustainability of agriculture. In addition, data analysis supports SDG 13: climate action by facilitating climate-resilient agricultural practices. By analyzing weather data and historical trends, farmers can anticipate climate-related risks and adjust their strategies accordingly. For example, they can optimize irrigation practices during droughts to conserve water or adjust planting schedules to meet changing rainfall patterns. Data analytics enables farmers to mitigate the impact of climate change on agriculture, improve their adaptive capacity, and contribute to climate action.

In summary, it can be stated that agricultural data analytics plays a key role in achieving sustainable development goals. By optimizing crop production, encouraging responsible consumption of resources, and improving resilience to climate change, farmers can use data-driven insights to actively advance sustainability goals related to hunger, responsible consumption and production, and climate action. These advances in agricultural practices

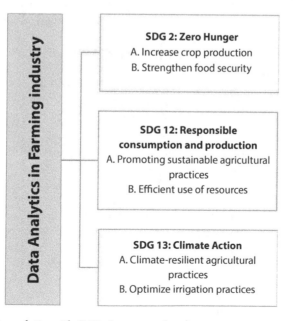

Figure 17.4 Mapping data analytics with SDGs (source: authors).

promote sustainability, ensure the long-term viability of agricultural systems, and support global efforts toward a more sustainable future.

17.2   Conclusion

The chapter analyzes the various perspectives of sustainable farming in the Indian context, the role of data analytics in addressing farming issues, and the prospects of using data analytic techniques in the agricultural sector. Firstly, it summarizes the challenges faced by the farming industry and the various improvement prospects suggested in past research. Secondly, it emphasizes the need for sustainability and capacity building to boost the industry's productivity, economic growth, job opportunities, and food security in line with incorporating data analytics in the farming industry. The chapter also reviews the role of data analytics in addressing the challenges for long-term sustainability and SDGs, as agricultural data analysis is instrumental in achieving sustainability goals by addressing various aspects of sustainability. The future scope of research should intend to orient the focus toward incorporating artificial intelligence to propose the best practices to the farmers to enhance agricultural productivity and also to incorporate innovative technologies toward proposing sustainable farming, keeping in mind the sustainability attributes and the global climatic change for future generations.

References

1. Ramesh, P., Panwar, N.R., Singh, A.B., Ramana, S., Yadav, S.K., Shrivastava, R., Rao, A.S., Status of organic farming in India. *Curr. Sci.*, 98, 1190–1194, 2010.
2. Gandhi, V., Kumar, G., Marsh, R., Agroindustry for rural and small farmer development: issues and lessons from India. *Int. Food Agribus. Manage. Rev.*, 2, 3-4, 331–344, 1999.
3. Chand, R. and Srivastava, S.K., Changes in the rural labour market and their implications for agriculture. *Econ. Political Wkly.*, 49, 47–54, 2014.
4. Golait, R., *Current issues in agriculture credit in India: An assessment*, Reserve Bank of India, Mumbai, Maharasta, India, 2007.
5. Evenson, R.E. and Jha, D., The contribution of agricultural research system to agricultural production in India. *Indian J. Agric. Econ.*, 28, 902-2018-2255, 212–230, 1973.
6. Mahadevan, R., Productivity growth in Indian agriculture: the role of globalisation and economic reform. *Asia Pac. Dev. J.*, 10, 2, 57–72, 2003.
7. Rangarajan, C., *Agricultural growth and industrial performance in India*, vol. 33, *Intl. Food Policy Res. Inst.*, India, 1982.
8. Mundhe, F., Agricultural productivity in India: trends during five-year plans. *Bus. Manage. Rev.*, 5, 4, 175, 20152015.
9. Von Blottnitz, H. and Curran, M.A., A review of assessments conducted on bio-ethanol as a transportation fuel from a net energy, greenhouse gas, and environmental life cycle perspective. *J. Cleaner Prod.*, 15, 7, 607–619, 2007.
10. Manjula, M., The smallholder in the agriculture market reforms in India. *Econ. Political Wkly.*, 56, 15, 22–26, 20212021.
11. Ellis, F. and Freeman, H.A., Rural livelihoods and poverty reduction strategies in four African countries. *J. Dev. Stud.*, 40, 4, 1–30, 2004.

12. Guiteras, R., *The impact of climate change on Indian agriculture*, Department of Economics, University of Maryland, College Park, Maryland, 2009.

13. Singh, D.K. and Singh, A.K., Groundwater situation in India: Problems and perspective. *Int. J. Water Resour. Dev.*, 18, 4, 563–580, 2002.

14. Powell, D., Agnew, D., Trexler, C., Agricultural Literacy: Clarifying a Vision for Practical Application. *J. Agric. Educ.*, 49, 1, 85–98, 2008.

15. Sharma, B.R., Gulati, A., Mohan, G., Manchanda, S., Ray, I., Amarasinghe, U., *Water productivity mapping of major Indian crops*, NABARD and ICRIER, New Delhi, 2018.

16. Tripp, R., Biodiversity and modern crop varieties: sharpening the debate. *Agric. Hum. Values*, 13, 48–63, 1996.

17. Uphoff, N., Higher yields with fewer external inputs? The system of rice intensification and potential contributions to agricultural sustainability. *Int. J. Agric. Sustainability*, 1, 1, 38–50, 2003.

18. Barik, A.K., Organic farming in India: Present status, challenges and technological breakthrough, in: *3rd Conference on Bio-Resource and Stress Management International*, pp. 101–110, 2017.

19. Behera, B.S., Panda, B., Behera, R.A., Nayak, N., Behera, A.C., Jena, S., Information communication technology promoting retail marketing in agriculture sector in India as a study. *Proc. Comput. Sci.*, 48, 652–659, 2015.

20. Sanjeev, K., Bhatt, B.P., Dey, A., Ujjwal, K., Idris, M., Mishra, J.S., Santosh, K., Integrated farming system in India: current status, scope and future prospects in changing agricultural scenario. *Indian J. Agric. Sci.*, 88, 11, 1661–1675, 2018.

21. Mehta, C.R., Chandel, N.S., Jena, P.C., Jha, A., Indian agriculture counting on farm mechanisation. *Agric. Mech. Asia Afr. Lat. Am.*, 50, 1, 84–89, 2019.

22. Som, S., Burman, R.R., Sharma, J.P., Padaria, R.N., Paul, S., Singh, A.K., Attracting and retaining youth in agriculture: challenges and prospects. *J. Community Mobilization Sustain. Dev.*, 13, 3, 385–395, 2018.

23. Kumar, V., Wankhede, K.G., Gena, H.C., Role of cooperatives in improving livelihood of farmers on sustainable basis. *Am. J. Educ. Res.*, 3, 10, 1258–1266, 20152015.

24. Mahul, O. and Stutley, C.J., *Government support to agricultural insurance: challenges and options for developing countries*, World Bank Publications, Washington, D.C., United States, 2010.

25. Tiwari, R., Chand, K., Bhatt, A., Anjum, B., Thirunavukkarasu, K., Agriculture 5.0 in India: Opportunities and Challenges of Technology Adoption, in: *A Step Towards Society 5.0*, pp. 179–198, 2021.

26. Sagar, B.M. and Cauvery, N.K., Agriculture data analytics in crop yield estimation: a critical review. *Indones. J. Electr. Eng. Comput. Sci.*, 12, 3, 1087–1093, 2018.

27. Kolipaka, V.R.R., Predictive analytics using cross media features in precision farming. *Int. J. Speech Technol.*, 23, 1, 57–69, 2020.

28. Aditya Shastry, K. and Sanjay, H.A., Data analysis and prediction using big data analytics in agriculture, in: *Internet of Things and Analytics for Agriculture*, vol. 2, pp. 201–224, 2020.

29. Raj, E.F.I., Appadurai, M., Athiappan, K., Precision farming in modern agriculture, in: *Smart Agriculture Automation Using Advanced Technologies: Data Analytics and Machine Learning, Cloud Architecture, Automation and IoT*, pp. 61–87, Springer Singapore, Singapore, 2022.

30. Bendre, M.R., Thool, R.C., Thool, V.R., Big data in precision agriculture: Weather forecasting for future farming, in: *2015 1st International Conference on Next Generation Computing Technologies (NGCT)*, IEEE, pp. 744–750, 2015.

31. Rogito, O., Maitho, T., Nderitu, A., Capacity Building in Participatory Monitoring and Evaluation on Sustainability of Food Security Irrigation Projects. *J. Eng. Proj. Prod. Manage.*, 10, 2, 94–102, 2020.

32. Gautam, R.S., Bhimavarapu, V.M., Rastogi, D.S., Impact of Digitalization on the Farmers in India: Evidence Using Panel Data Analysis. *Int. J. Manage. Humanit.*, 6, 1, 5–12, 2021.

33. Zhao, G., Olan, F., Liu, S., Hormazabal, J.H., Lopez, C., Zubairu, N., Zhang, J., Chen, X., Links between risk source identification and resilience capability building in agri-food supply chains: a comprehensive analysis. *IEEE Trans. Eng. Manage.*, 99, 1–18, 2022.

34. Kajwang, B., Capacity building for agriculture insurance: lessons from developed economies. *Am. J. Agric.*, 4, 1, 89–109, 20222022.

Part 4

MODELING AND ANALYSIS OF AGRICULTURAL SYSTEMS

Modeling Barriers to Access Credit from Institutional Sources in Rural Areas Using the ISM Approach

Priyanka Yadav[1]*, Bhartrihari Pandiya[1] and Alok Kumar Sharma[2]

[1]*School of Management Studies, National Forensics Sciences University, Gandhinagar, India*
[2]*Department of Information Management, Chaoyang University of Technology, Taichung, Taiwan*

Abstract

Despite several efforts by the government in the past, lending to the rural sector in India is inadequate. Informal credit markets are still prevalent at large in rural India. In this context, this research is an attempt to 1) identify barriers to access institutional credit in rural India and 2) model these barriers to understand how they interact with each other. Eleven relevant barriers to access credit from institutional sources in India have been identified from the literature, and contextual relationships among these have been identified after seeking experts' opinions. Interpretive structural modeling (ISM) was employed to establish a hierarchical model that reveals the interrelationships among these barriers, and MICMAC analysis was conducted to classify the barriers based on their dependence and driving power. The findings reveal six barriers as "key barriers," which are primarily responsible for poor access to institutional credit in rural India. The novel contribution of this study lies in unveiling the systematic relationships among barriers and presenting how working on key barriers will lead to the removal of other barriers in the system.

Keywords: Barriers, rural India, credit, interpretive structural modeling, MICMAC analysis

18.1 Introduction

Agriculture in India is more than an occupation. It employs more than 80% of the rural population in India. The availability of institutional credit has obtained an important position in the development process planning of India for several past decades. Better access to credit leads to increased agricultural production and promotes rural development. Besides several efforts, the prevalence of non-institutional credit sources in India is a serious concern, especially in rural India [1]. The availability of institutional credit at the right time and in adequate quantity has a crucial role in the advancement of the agriculture sector. It determines the level of productivity in the agriculture sector and the living standard of the rural communities. With sufficient credit availability, the farmers can use it to adopt new

*Corresponding author: priyanka.yadav@nfsu.ac.in

Kuldeep Singh and Prasanna Kolar (eds.) *Digital Agricultural Ecosystem: Revolutionary Advancements in Agriculture,* (321–338) © 2024 Scrivener Publishing LLC

technologies and modern inputs/machinery to enhance farm production. Credit is a major indirect input required in agriculture. The credit needs of farmers have multiplied due to increased commercialization of agriculture, changes in cropping patterns from subsistence cropping to cash cropping, and the use of modern technologies in production diversification. Besides being an important constituent of priority sector lending in India, the demand for credit remains unmet by its present supply. The majority of peasant communities remain deprived of adequate and timely availability of funds needed in the production process. Among those excluded, most peasants are marginal and small possessing limited resources at their end. Furthermore, huge disparities have been observed across several states in the country by several past studies [2, 3]. Agriculture is exposed to several risks such as the risk of crop loss due to crop failure, pests, drought, floods, and several other weather vagaries. Besides the risks from nature, farmers are exposed to several other risks such as a fall in the market price of crops, a rise in the price of inputs, illness, and other personal problems. Farmer suicides in India are very common and are at a startling rate which has raised serious concerns on the sustainability of agriculture not only in India but across the globe. The policy of providing cheap credit to vulnerable farming communities has not worked well in India. In fact, the study by Bose [4] argues that the policy of offering affordable loans within the official financial sector could negatively affect interest rates in the informal market, thus deteriorating the situation of rural households even more by way of increased interest burden on debt. Similar arguments are put forth by Gupta and Chaudhuri [5]. In a developing nation, banks can play a vital role in financial development since they are specialized financial institutions that can serve the financial needs of rural communities and, at the same time, contribute toward the reduction of poverty, help in generating employment opportunities, and help in the empowerment of marginalized communities, thereby ensuring sustainable development by not only creating social equalities but also by encouraging the development of new businesses. With the nationalization of major banks and the establishment of NABARD, regional rural banks have played a constructive role in fostering economic progress and reducing poverty in India, but there was a reversal after the major economic reforms of the 1990s which resulted in higher profitability of commercial banks but adversely impacted the rural poor [6]. Identifying barriers/constraints responsible for the non-availability of adequate and timely credit to vulnerable farmers in India makes the foundation of this study.

18.2   Literature Review

Saving farmers from the clutches of informal moneylenders in India has been a principal objective of the Indian rural credit delivery mechanism. Still, lending to the agriculture sector in India is far from satisfactory. Of the total indebted households in rural India, 40% are indebted to the informal sector [7]. Nonetheless, with the sharp growth in credit delivery in the rural areas following the multi-agency approach to credit delivery, a majority of farmers have either inadequate or zero access to institutional credit [1]. The unavailability of financial services in adequate quantity and at the right time leads to a sizeable loss in the country's GDP [8, 22]. The current supply of institutional credit in India falls short of meeting the existing demand [9]. In the past few decades, several major changes occurred in India's financial sector with special reference to lending to peasant communities. However, there is a discernible concern that a series of actions aimed at improving farmer's situation in the rural parts of India could not improve the situation up to the desired level. Hence, it becomes imperative to analyze the barriers that constrain access to credit from institutional sources in rural India (see Table 18.1).

Table 18.1 Barriers to institutional credit.

S. no.	Barrier	Meaning	References
1	Large distance from the bank	A significant spatial separation between the individual and the nearest financial institution	Toporowski [11]; Bhanot *et al.* 2012 [12]
2	Illiteracy	The inability to read and write proficiently	Ghosh [3]
3	Land records not upgraded	The existing land records have not been updated or modernized to reflect current information or changes	Panagariya [14]
4	Lack of product knowledge	An individual or group has insufficient understanding or familiarity with a particular product or its features	Mattthew and Uchechukwu [15]
5	Lack of collateral	A situation where an individual or entity does not possess sufficient assets or property that can be used as security or guarantee for obtaining a loan or credit	Conning and Udry [16]; Bardhan [17]
6	Fragmented landholdings	A condition where land is divided into numerous small and disconnected plots, typically owned by different individuals or entities	Singh [18]; Desai and Namboodiri [19]
7	Bank employees not supportive	The employees working at a bank are unhelpful or uncooperative in assisting customers with their banking needs or addressing their concerns	Yadav and Sharma [20]; Yadav and Sharma [21]
8	Complicated documentation	The required paperwork or paperwork processes involved in a particular context, such as obtaining a loan or completing a transaction, are complex, intricate, or difficult to understand	Pal and Laha [22]

(Continued)

Table 18.1 Barriers to institutional credit. (*Continued*)

S. no.	Barrier	Meaning	References
9	High transaction costs	The significant expenses or charges incurred when conducting financial transactions, such as fees, commissions, or other related costs that can be relatively expensive in comparison to the transaction value	Sarap [23]
10	Fear of action	A state of apprehension or reluctance to take the necessary steps or engage in certain activities due to concerns about potential consequences, risks, or negative outcomes	Boucher and Guirkinger [25]
11	Procedural delays	The slowdown or hindrance in the progress of a process or procedure due to extended waiting times, administrative bottlenecks, or inefficiencies in the established protocols or workflows	Chaudhuri and Gupta [26]

18.3   Data and Research Methodology

18.3.1   Data

Several studies in India as well as outside India were reviewed to identify the barriers to access credit from institutional sources. After carefully reviewing the literature, 11 barriers to use institutional credit in rural areas were identified as prime barriers. To analyze the relevance of barriers, the list of barriers was presented before a panel of experts. The panel included 20 members with five from academia, seven researchers, five social activists, and three experts from agriculture departments. The experts were asked to rank the relevance of all identified barriers on a Likert scale of seven points, where 7 meant "strongly agree" and 1 meant "strongly disagree," and the intermediate values show high/low agreement. To check for internal consistency, Cronbach's coefficient (α) has been used whose value was 0.763 which shows high internal consistency of the variables (barriers) used in the questionnaire. Table 18.2 presents the descriptive statistics including maximum values, minimum values, means, and standard deviations. The barriers have been ranked based on mean values. Furthermore, to test the presence of multicollinearity, Pearson's bivariate test was used. The results are presented in Table 18.3. The results show no problematic multicollinearity since all correlation values are less than 0.80 [25].

Table 18.2 Descriptive statistics of the barriers.

Barrier	N	Minimum	Maximum	Mean	St. dev.	Rank
1	20	1	7	3.000	1.556	11
2	20	2	7	4.151	1.424	8
3	20	2	7	3.750	1.333	9
4	20	2	7	3.600	1.188	10
5	20	1	7	4.150	1.348	7
6	20	2	7	4.600	1.095	6
7	20	3	7	5.000	1.124	4
8	20	2	7	5.350	1.137	2
9	20	3	7	5.400	0.940	1
10	20	2	7	4.650	1.663	5
11	20	2	7	5.250	1.970	3

Table 18.3 Correlation among barriers.

Barrier	1	2	3	4	5	6	7	8	9	10	11
1	1										
2	.594**	1									
3	.533*	.603**	1								
4	.313	.255	.233	1							
5	.627**	.262	.286	.500*	1						
6	.710**	.513*	.505*	.477*	.791**	1					
7	.361	.427	.141	.000	.278	.470*	1				
8	.238	.193	.234	.031	.239	.499*	.742**	1			
9	.072	−.008	.420	-.132	−.174	.061	.398	.551*	1		
10	−.244	−.021	.077	.298	−.140	−.110	−.282	−.210	−.108	1	
11	−.069	.267	.466*	.337	−.074	.098	−.024	.170	.199	.671**	1

*Note: *p-value 5%; **p-value 1%.*

18.3.2   Research Methodology

To deal with complex issues, the interpretive structural modeling (ISM) methodology was first put forward by Chaudhuri and Gupta [26]. A complex issue may be viewed by several experts in different ways. ISM helps to identify and structure complex relationships among variables in a simple way and suggests the future course of action in problem solving [27, 28]. In ISM, the mental unclear relationships are well defined, and group judgments are integrated to present a hierarchical model with a clear direction of the relationships among elements [29]. The detailed stepwise procedure for ISM is as follows:

1. Identifying elements/barriers that appear relevant to the problem under study either by the survey method or review of the literature or both.
2. Defining contextual relationships among elements with the help of expert's advice and building a structural self-interaction matrix representing pairwise relationships/associations among the elements under study.
3. Developing the initial reachability matrix by substituting relationships defined in step 2 into binary numbers 0 or 1.
4. Removing any transitivity among elements of the initial reachability matrix to get the final reachability matrix. A transitive relation is such that if an element A is related to B and B is related to another element C in the system, then A is also related/associated with C.
5. From the final reachability matrix, determining the number of levels in the hierarchical ISM model. This is based on iterations which continue until all elements have been assigned their respective levels in the hierarchy.
6. Checking the model for any conceptual inconsistency or variability if any and making the necessary modifications.
7. Classifying barriers into four different clusters based on their dependence and driving power. This is also known as MICMAC analysis.

18.3.2.1   Building the Structural Self-Interaction Matrix (SSIM)

After identifying the barriers, the next step is to define the contextual and circumstantial relationships between variables. In this study, to determine the level of relationships among barriers, the list of barriers was presented before the expert panel for discussion. After brainstorming, the relationships among variables were defined as presented in Table 18.4. These relationships may be any of the following four types: influensive, comparative, temporal, or neutral [26]. To define the nature of the relationship among variables, the symbols V, A, X, and O have been used in this study as follows:

V—if barrier "i" leads to barrier "j"
A—if barrier "j" leads to barrier "i"
X—if both "i" and "j" affect each other
O—if none of the barriers are related to each other

18.3.2.2   Reachability Matrix

18.3.2.2.1   Initial Reachability Matrix

To develop the initial reachability matrix, the SSIM matrix obtained in the previous step has been transformed into a binary number matrix as shown in Table 18.5 where all the cells take any one of the two values—either 0 or 1—based on the following rules:

If the value in (i, j) in the SSIM matrix is

V—the entry of the (i, j) matrix will be 1 and the entry of (j, i) will be 0.
A—the entry of the (i, j) matrix will be 0 and the entry of (j, i) will be 1.
X—the entry of both (i, j) and (j, i) will be 1.
O—the entry of both (i, j) and (j, i) will be 0.

18.3.2.2.2   Final Reachability Matrix

Any transitivity identified in the initial reachability matrix is removed to get the final reachability matrix. A transitive relationship is such that if element A is found to be related to element B and element B is found to be related to element C, then element A is also assumed to be related to element C. The sum of elements in the row and column shows the driving power and dependence, respectively. The same has been shown in Table 18.6.

18.3.2.3   Level Partitioning

The subsequent phase involves determining the levels within the hierarchical ISM model. This can be accomplished by estimating the reachability set and antecedent set from the final reachability matrix. The reachability set of a parameter comprises the parameter itself and other parameters that may be influenced by it. Similarly, the antecedent set includes the parameter itself and those parameters that may impact it. The intersection set encompasses the elements that are common to both the reachability set and the antecedent set. Parameters that share the same reachability and intersection sets in the initial iteration are assigned the top/highest order level in the hierarchy. After the parameter(s) has been assigned a level in the hierarchy, it is separated from other parameters since it will not lead to other parameters further. This iteration is repeated time and again until all the parameters obtain their respective levels in the hierarchy. These levels are helpful in determining the hierarchy of the ISM model.

As shown in Table 18.7, barriers 9 and 10 have the same set of reachability and intersection and, therefore, are assigned to level I. They have been dropped from the list of variables for further iteration to determine the next levels.

As shown in Table 18.8, barrier 11 has the same set of reachability and intersection and is assigned to level I in the hierarchy. This has been dropped from further iteration.

As shown in Table 18.9, barriers 7 and 8 have the same set of reachability and intersection and are assigned to level III. They have been dropped from further iteration.

As shown in Table 18.10, barriers 3, 4, and 5 have the same set of reachability and intersection and are assigned to level IV. They have been dropped from further iteration.

Table 18.4 The structural self-interaction matrix.

Barrier	11	10	9	8	7	6	5	4	3	2	1
1. Large distance from the bank	V	O	V	O	V	O	O	V	O	O	I
2. Illiteracy		V	V	V	V	V	O	O	V	O	I
3. Land records not upgraded	V	O	O	O	V	O	X	O	I		
4. Lack of product knowledge		O	V	V	O	V	O	O	I		
5. Lack of collateral		V	V	O	O	V	X	I			
6. Fragmented landholdings		O	O	O	O	V	I				
7. Bank employees not supportive	V	V	V	X	I						
8. Complicated documentation		V	O	V	I						
9. High transaction cost		A	O	I							
10. Fear of action		O	I								
11. Procedural delay	I										

Table 18.5 The initial reachability matrix.

Barrier	1	2	3	4	5	6	7	8	9	10	11
1	1	0	0	1	0	0	1	0	1	0	1
2	0	1	0	1	0	0	1	1	1	1	1
3	0	0	1	0	1	0	1	0	0	0	1
4	0	0	0	1	0	0	1	0	1	1	0
5	0	0	1	0	1	1	1	0	0	1	1
6	0	0	0	0	1	1	1	0	0	0	0
7	0	0	0	0	0	0	1	1	1	1	1
8	0	0	0	0	0	0	1	1	1	0	1
9	0	0	0	0	0	0	0	0	1	0	0
10	0	0	0	0	0	0	0	0	0	1	0
11	0	0	0	0	0	0	0	0	1	0	1

Table 18.6 The final reachability matrix.

Barrier	1	2	3	4	5	6	7	8	9	10	11	Driving power
1	1	0	0	1	0	0	1	1	1	1	1	7
2	0	1	0	1	0	0	1	1	1	1	1	7
3	0	0	1	0	1	1	1	1	1	1	1	8
4	0	0	0	1	0	0	1	1	1	1	1	6
5	0	0	1	0	1	1	1	1	1	1	1	8
6	0	0	1	0	1	1	1	1	1	1	1	8
7	0	0	0	0	0	0	1	1	1	1	1	5
8	0	0	0	0	0	0	1	1	1	1	1	5
9	0	0	0	0	0	0	0	0	1	0	0	1
10	0	0	0	0	0	0	0	0	0	1	0	1
11	0	0	0	0	0	0	0	0	1	0	1	2
Dependence	1	1	3	3	3	3	8	8	10	9	9	

Table 18.7 First iteration for level partitioning.

Barrier	Reachability set	Antecedent set	Intersection	Level
1	1,4,7,8,9,10,11	1	1	
2	2,4,7,8,9,10,11	2	2	
3	3,5,6,7,8,9,10,11	3,5,6	3,5,6	
4	4,7,8,9,10,11	1,2,4	4	
5	3,5,6,7,8,9,10,11	3,5,6	3,5,6	
6	3,5,6,7,8,9,10,11	3,5,6	5,6	
7	7,8,9,10,11	1,2,3,4,5,6,7,8	7,8	
8	7,8,9,10,11	1,2,3,4,5,6,7,8	7,8	
9	9	1,2,3,4,5,6,7,8,9	9	I
10	10	1,2,3,4,5,6,7,8	10	I
11	9,11	1,2,3,4,5,6,7,8,11	11	

Table 18.8 Second iteration for level partitioning.

Barrier	Reachability set	Antecedent set	Intersection	Level
1	1,4,7,8,11	1	1	
2	2,4,7,8,11	2	2	
3	3,5,6,7,8,11	3,5,6	3,5,6	
4	4,7,8,11	1,2,4	4	
5	3,5,6,7,8,11	3,5,6	3,5,6	
6	3,5,6,7,8,11	3,5,6	5,6	
7	7,8,11	1,2,3,4,5,6,7,8	7,8	
8	7,8,11	1,2,3,4,5,6,7,8	7,8	
11	11	1,2,3,4,5,6,7,8,11	11	II

Table 18.9 Third iteration for level partitioning.

Barrier	Reachability set	Antecedent set	Intersection	Level
1	1,4,7,8,	1	1	
2	2,4,7,8,	2	2	
3	3,5,6,7,8,	3,5,6	3,5,6	
4	4,7,8	1,2,4	4	
5	3,5,6,7,8	3,5,6	3,5,6	
6	3,5,6,7,8	3,5,6	5,6	
7	7,8	1,2,3,4,5,6,7,8	7,8	III
8	7,8	1,2,3,4,5,6,7,8	7,8	III

As shown in Table 18.11, barriers 1, 2, and 6 have the same set of reachability and intersection, and hence, they are assigned to level V. Since there are no more barriers left, therefore, the iteration stops at this level. With five levels identified, the hierarchical model is presented in the next step.

Table 18.10 Fourth iteration for level partitioning.

Barrier	Reachability set	Antecedent set	Intersection	Level
1	1,4	1	1	
2	2,4	2	2	
3	3,5,6	3,5,6	3,5,6	IV
4	4	1,2,4	4	IV
5	3,5,6	3,5,6	3,5,6	IV
6	3,5,6	3,5,6	5,6	

Table 18.11 Fifth iteration for level partitioning.

Barrier	Reachability set	Antecedent set	Intersection	Level
1	1	1	1	V
2	2	2	2	V
6	5,6	3,5,6	5,6	V

18.3.2.4 Development of the ISM Model

After determining the level for each barrier in the model, the following step is to develop the hierarchical ISM model. Based on the final reachability matrix, this model exhibits the contextual relationships among variables. After removing the transitive relationships, the hierarchical model called diagraph is developed with the help of vertices and edges (Figure 18.1). On the basis of iterations, five levels have been identified so far for this structure. Out of 11 barriers proposed in the model, two barriers—high transaction costs and fear of action—are at the pinnacle of the ISM model. The barriers lying at the bottom level are illiteracy, large distance from the bank, and fragmented landholdings. The rest of the other barriers lie between the top and bottom levels.

18.3.2.5 MICMAC Analysis

Here, a hierarchy of barriers that have been categorized into four groups based on their driving power and dependence is shown using the MICMAC analysis. These categories include autonomous, linkage, dependent, and independent barriers. Figure 18.2 shows the driving power and dependence of each barrier. By comparing this hierarchy with the one used in the ISM model, we can better understand the model's interpretation. The classification and analysis of each barrier's spread is conducted through the use of the MICMAC analysis, which considers its driving power and dependence and is shown as follows:

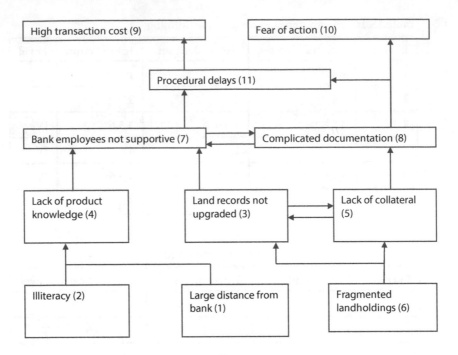

Figure 18.1 Diagraph of the contextual relationships.

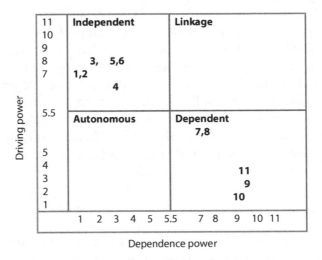

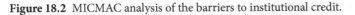

Figure 18.2 MICMAC analysis of the barriers to institutional credit.

18.3.2.5.1 Autonomous Barriers

Such barriers have a weak driving power, i.e., they cannot influence others and their dependence on others is weak as well. In other words, such barriers are less influential and are less affected by other barriers. In this study, no barrier falls under this quadrant.

18.3.2.5.2   Dependent Barriers

Such barriers have a strong dependence on other barriers, but they are weak on driving power. It means that any change in other barriers will affect them significantly while the reverse is not possible. In this study, barriers 7, 8, 9, 10, 11, and 12 fall under this quadrant.

18.3.2.5.3   Linkage Barriers

Barriers lying in this category have a strong driving power and strong dependence on others which makes them highly unstable/unbalanced in nature. Any change in these barriers leads to a feedback effect on themselves and others as well.

18.3.2.5.4   Independent Barriers

Barriers that are strong on driving power and low on dependence are covered in this category. In this study, barriers 1, 2, 3, 4, 5, and 6 fall under this quadrant. They are "key factors" and are of crucial importance [30].

18.4   Results and Discussion

Barriers to access credit from institutional sources have been identified and analyzed to determine their interrelationships in this study. Using the ISM technique, the barriers have been modeled to classify them into different hierarchical levels. Based on dependence and driving power, barriers are categorized into four distinct clusters. The first cluster corresponds to independent barriers characterized by minimal driving power and low dependence. In this study, no barriers have been categorized within this group of variables. The second cluster, situated in the southeast, encompasses dependent barriers exhibiting low driving power yet high dependence. Barriers that fall into this category are fragmented landholdings, bank employees not supportive, complicated documentation, high transaction costs, fear of action, and procedural delays. As these barriers possess limited driving power, they are susceptible to the influence of variables categorized as independent variables. Any alteration in independent variables results in a substantial impact on these variables as well. The third cluster contains barriers that are high on dependence as well as driving power. In this study, no barrier is classified in this category. The fourth cluster located in the northwest contains independent barriers that are high on driving power in terms of being influential but low on dependence. These are the "key" factors that are the most significant in bringing the desired results, i.e., any change in these barriers will have an impact on variables in the second cluster. According to the results of this study, variables classified in this category are distance from the bank, illiteracy, land records not upgraded, lack of product knowledge, lack of collateral, and fragmented landholdings. The diagraph presented in Figure 18.1 indicates how these barriers interact with each other. Knowing such interrelationships among barriers may be of crucial importance for strategic policymakers. The ISM model reveals that three barriers—illiteracy, fragmented land, and large bank distance—have a high driving power and are highly influential in impacting dependent variables. Therefore, working on these barriers will have a feedback effect on these and will automatically remove/reduce barriers of procedural delays, high transaction costs, and complicated documentation among others. The government should focus on eliminating these barriers in policy framing to make the rural credit delivery mechanism successful. The model also shows how the barrier of lack of product knowledge is driven by illiteracy. Furthermore, the barriers of high transaction costs and fear of action are affected by the lack of support from bank staff. Similar findings have been previously reported by several previous studies [5, 31, 32].

18.5   Implications of the Research

This study has many policy implications to offer. It may help the policymakers in better decision-making and designing key policies in order to improve access and usage of financial products and services in rural India. They can develop better products suited to the needs of the poor sections of society and can ensure better access to their products by all sections of the society on an equitable basis.

Besides numerous efforts to promote access to institutional credit in India in the past several decades, the prevalence of informal credit markets is an issue of deep disquiet among policymakers. In this context, this study has made a unique attempt to identify how interactions exist among barriers to access credit from institutional sources in rural India. On the basis of expert opinion, the interrelationships among barriers have been defined and presented in a hierarchical model. Most of the time, one or two barriers remain the focal point of most of the strategic decision-makers. However, it is quite possible that working on one barrier may simultaneously increase the influence of the rest of the barriers. The ISM model proposed in this study has shown how barriers interact with each other and has defined several interrelationships among barriers. The model has classified illiteracy, large distance from the bank, fragmented landholdings, lack of product knowledge, unupgraded land records, and lack of collateral as "key barriers." Such barriers are more strategy-oriented in nature, which also means that the removal of these barriers will result in the removal/reduction of the other remaining barriers also. This study will surely help in the strategic decision-making of policymakers in understanding the interrelationships among barriers and frame policies keeping in view such relations so that policies may be framed more effectively for rural India.

18.6   Conclusions

Access to finance by one and all is one of the most critical problems faced by transition economies, and India is no exception to it. The problem is more evident in the rural parts of India as disclosed by several studies/surveys in the past, and several factors contribute to poor access to finance by rural households since they have either limited or no assets to offer as security or collateral for loans, have limited product knowledge, and so on. This study has proposed a conceptual model for the analysis of barriers to access credit from institutional sources in rural India. Employing 11 parameters (barriers), contextual relationships have been defined, and a hierarchical model based on the power to influence other variables (driving power) and to get influenced by other variables (dependence power) is presented. The contextual relationships among barriers have been defined with experts' suggestions to present a hypothetical model that may incorporate the element of personal bias. The interrelationships among barriers may/may not be present in real situations which may affect the generalization and usability of the results of this study. To test whether such relationships exist in real-life situations may be a new direction for future researchers. In other words, the validity of the ISM model presented in this study may be checked and verified for linkages among variables in real-world situations. The list of barriers is not exhaustive since several other barriers are present in the literature which may be identified and modeled using ISM. Although including more such variables may enrich the results, the technique of ISM may become tedious as more and more variables are included in the model. Furthermore, this study attempts to identify the nature and direction of the relationship among several barriers in accessing credit from institutional sources in rural India, and quantifying the strength of the relationships is outside the scope of this study. Furthermore, multicriteria decision-making (MCDM) techniques like the analytical hierarchical process (AHP) and structural equation modeling (SEM) can be used by future researchers to determine the strength/extent of relationships among the barriers. Given the complexity of contextual relations, there is a need for unity of knowledge in determining the cause and effect relationships among variables [33].

References

1. Karmakar, K.G., Banerjee, G.D., Mohapatra, N.P., *Towards Financial Inclusion in India*, Sage Publications, New Delhi, 2011.
2. Kumar, N., Financial inclusion and its determinants: evidence from India. *J. Financ. Econ. Policy*, 5, 1, 4–19, 2013.
3. Ghosh, S., Determinants of banking outreach: An empirical assessment of Indian states. *J. Dev. Areas*, 46, 2, 269–295, 2012, http://dx.doi.org/10.1353/jda.2012.0034.
4. Bose, P., Formal–informal sector interaction in rural credit markets. *J. Dev. Econ.*, 56, 2, 265–280, 1998, http://dx.doi.org/10.1016/S0304-3878(98)00066-2.
5. Gupta, M.R. and Chaudhuri, S., Formal Credit, Corruption and the Informal Credit Market in Agriculture: A Theoretical Analysis. *Economica*, 64, 254, 331–343, 1997.
6. Akoijam, S.L.S., Rural credit: a source of sustainable livelihood of rural India. *Int. J. Soc. Econ.*, 40, 1, 83–97, 2012.
7. NSSO, Key Indicators of Situation of Agricultural Households in India, All India debt and investment survey. *NSS 70th Round, Ministry of Statistics and Programme Implementation*, Government of India, New Delhi, 2014.
8. Beck, T. and De La Torre, A., The basic analytics of access to financial services. *Financ. Mark. Inst. Instrum.*, 16, 2, 79–117, 2007.
9. Chattopadhyay, S.K., *Financial inclusion in India: a case study of West Bengal*. (Working Paper No. 8/2011), Department of Economic and Policy Research, Reserve bank of India, Kolkata, 2011, https://mpra.ub.uni-muenchen.de/34269/1/MPRA_ paper_34269.pdf.
10. Biradar, R.R., Trends and patterns of institutional credit flow for agriculture in India. *J. Asia Bus. Stud.*, 7, 1, 44–56, 2013, doi: 10.1108/15587891311301016.
11. Toporowski, J., Beyond banking: financial institutions and the poor, in: *Excluding the Poor*, P. Golding, (Ed.), pp. 55–69, Child Poverty Action Group, London, 1987.
12. Bhanot, D., Bapat, V., Bera, S., Studying financial inclusion in north-east India. *Int. J. Bank Mark.*, 30, 6, 465–484, 2012, Doi: 10.1108/02652321211262221.

13. Ghosh, S., Determinants of banking outreach: An empirical assessment of Indian states. *J. Dev. Areas*, 46, 2, 269–295, 2012, http://dx.doi.org/10.1353/jda.2012.0034.

14. Panagariya, A., *India: the emerging giant*, 1st ed., Oxford University Press, New York, 2008.

15. Mattthew, O. and Uchechukwu, A.A., Rural Farmers Sources and Use of Credit in Nsukka Local Government Area of Enugu State, Nigeria. *Asian J. Agric. Res.*, 8, 4, 195–203, 2014, doi: 10.3923/ajar.2014.195.203.

16. Conning, J. and Udry, C., Rural financial markets in developing countries, in: *Handbook of agricultural economics*, vol. 3, pp. 2857–2908, 2007, https://doi.org/10.1016/S1574-0072(06)03056-8.

17. Bardhan, P.K., Size, Productivity, and Returns to Scale: An Analysis of Farm-Level Data in Indian Agriculture. *J. Political Econ.*, 81, 6, 1370–1386, 1973, Doi: 10.1086/260 132.

18. Singh, J.P., Changing Agrarian Relationships in Rural India. *Indian J. Agric. Econ.*, 61, 1, 36–64, 2006.

19. Desai, M. and Namboodiri, N.V., Determinants of total factor productivity in Indian agriculture. *Econ. Political Wkly.*, 32, 52, 165–171, 1997, https://www.jstor.org/stable/4406231.

20. Yadav, P. and Sharma, A.K., An Investigation Into Factors Affecting Access to Financial Services in Farmers' Suicide Prone Bundelkhand Region of India. *Indian J. Finance*, 12, 6, 46–62, 2018, http://dx.doi.org/10.17010/ijf%2F2018%2Fv 12i6%2F128135.

21. Yadav, P. and Sharma, A.K., Financial inclusion in India: an application of TOPSIS. *Humanomics*, 32, 3, 328–351, 2016, https://doi.org/10.1108/H-09-2015-0061.

22. Pal, and Laha, A., Credit off-take from formal financial institutions in rural India: quantile regression results. *Agric. Food Econ.*, 2, 9, 1–20, 2014, doi: 10.1186/s40100-014-0009-y.

23. Sarap, K., Factors affecting small farmers' access to institutional credit in rural Orissa. *Dev. Change*, 21, 2, 281–307, 1990, doi: 10.1111/j.1467-7660.1990.tb00378.x.

24. Basu, P., *Improving access to finance for India's rural poor*, World Bank Publications, Washington DC, 2006, doi: 10.1596/978-0-8213-6146-7.

25. Boucher, S. and Guirkinger, C., Risk, wealth, and sectoral choice in rural credit markets. *Am. J. Agric. Econ.*, 89, 4, 991–1004, 2007, doi: 10.1111/j.1467-8 276.2007.01009.x.

26. Chaudhuri, S. and Gupta, M.R., Delayed formal credit, bribing and the informal credit market in agriculture: A theoretical analysis. *J. Dev. Econ.*, 51, 2, 433–449, 1996, https://doi.org/10.1016/S0304-3878(96)00407-5.

27. Gujarati, N., *Basic Econometrics*, Tata McGraw-Hill Publishing Company Ltd., New Delhi, 2006.

28. Warfield, J.W., Developing interconnected metrics in structural modeling. *IEEE Trans. Syst. Man. Cybern.*, 4, 1, 51–81, 1973.

29. Sushil, P., Interpreting the interpretive structural model. *Global J. Flexible Syst. Manage.*, 13, 2, 87–106, 2012, http://dx.doi.org/10.1007/s40171-012-0008-3.

30. Sohani, N. and Sohani, N., Developing interpretive structural model for quality framework in higher education: Indian context. *J. Eng. Sci. Manage. Educ.*, 5, 2, 495–501, 2012.

31. Chander, M., Jain, S.K., Shankar, R., Modeling of information security management parameters in Indian organizations using ISM and MICMAC approach. *J. Modell. Manage.*, 8, 2, 171–189, 2013, https://doi.org/10.1108/JM2-10-2011-0054.

32. Warfield, J.W., Developing interconnected metrics in structural modeling. *IEEE Trans. Syst. Man. Cybern. B Cybern.*, 4, 1, 51–81, 1973.
33. Nguyen, C.H., *International Conference on Rural Finance Research: Moving Results into Policies and Practice*, FAO, Access to credit and borrowing behavior of rural households in a Transition Economy, Rome, 2010.

19

Modeling the Water Consumption Process with the Linear Model and a Local Interpolation Cubic Spline

Varlamova Lyudmila P.[1]*, Seytov Aybek J.[1], Bahromov Sayfiddin A.[1], Berdiyorov Shokhjakhon Sh.[1] and Mirzaolimov Akhmadjon K.[2]

[1]Department Computational Mathematics and Information Systems, National University of Uzbekistan, Tashkent, Uzbekistan
[2]Military Institute of Communications and Information Communication Technologies, Tashkent, Uzbekistan

Abstract

The problem of water consumption is acute in all countries of the South-eastern region, in Central Asia. Special attention is given to water use issues in the Republic of Uzbekistan. In Uzbekistan, only 11.5 km³ of surface runoff of internal rivers and 9.5 km³ of return and groundwater are formed, and 60–67 km³ of water resources come from the Amu-Darya and Syr-Darya rivers. Water supply may fluctuate from year to year. The paper presents an analysis of water consumption in various industries based on the use of water. Since three types of mathematical models were used to predict water consumption, the result is very different from the actual water consumption. The population of the Republic of Uzbekistan and water consumption are growing at a high rate (2,000 people a day). To provide agriculture and the population with water, it is necessary to create a mathematical model of water consumption and make a forecast. The paper presents the results of studies on the calculation and forecasting of water consumption from 1992 to 2030. Based on the least squares method for linear and parabolic schemes, mathematical models are constructed, comparative analysis and forecasting using the constructed models provided.

Keywords: Mathematical model, water resources, distribution processes, waterways, agriculture, consumption, parabolic scheme, cubic spline

19.1 Background

The problem of water consumption is acute in all countries of the South-eastern region, in Central Asia. Special attention is given to water use issues in the Republic of Uzbekistan. In Uzbekistan, only 11.5 km³ of surface runoff of internal rivers and 9.5 km³ of return and groundwater are formed, and 60–67 km³ of water resources come from the Amu-Darya and Syr-Darya rivers. These rivers are transboundary. This means that most of Uzbekistan's water resources come from neighboring countries, and the provision of water resources is

---

*Corresponding author: dimirel@gmail.com

Kuldeep Singh and Prasanna Kolar (eds.) *Digital Agricultural Ecosystem: Revolutionary Advancements in Agriculture*, (339–368) © 2024 Scrivener Publishing LLC

always under the threat of decline, which requires economical water consumption and forecasting of water use. It should be noted that the population of the Republic of Uzbekistan has an annual increase of 1.5–2%[1], which in turn leads to an increase in water consumption.

Since water management systems and facilities have a large spatial extent, a lot of technological parameters, quantitative and qualitative changes in all characteristics can be obtained using only with the help of mathematical modeling methods [1–3].

Up to the present time, there is no unified systematic approach to the issue of modeling the dynamics of water management objects. There is a wide class of mathematical models of individual objects with different degrees of complexity. That is why the choice of mathematical models that will describe complex water distribution processes in water management systems with the required degree of accuracy is a very problematic task. Analyzing the mathematical models used in solving the problems of simulating the management of canals of irrigation systems, they can be divided into three main groups: static models, dynamic models with lumped parameters, and dynamic models with distributed parameters [2–8].

Analyzing data on the use of water resources of the republic by sectors of the country's economy for the period 1991–2020, it can noted that the largest consumer of the water resources of the republic is the irrigation industry, which provides water for irrigated agriculture in the country (Table 19.1). According to the results of calculations of the consumption of water resources to the total volume, the irrigation industry consumes over 84% of all water (Table 19.2) [9].

In some sectors of the country's economy, water consumption and water use vary depending on the water content of the year, while in others, they do not change. The sectors where water consumption and water use vary depending on the water content of the year include irrigation, electric power, fisheries, environmental releases in the Aral Sea region and the needs of the Aral Sea, and others. Industries where water consumption and water use do not change depending on the water content of the year include housing and utility services and industry.

The irrigation industry consumes 84.6% of the total water resources of the republic since agriculture plays a leading role in the country's economy and about 25 million rural residents of the republic are directly dependent on it, their level of livelihood, income, and well-being, so adequate water supply of the industry is extremely important.

During the 30-year observation, it was found that there were high-water years, and fluctuations in the amount of water were observed. As a result, the irrigation industry worked in accordance with the amount of water received [10].

The analysis and assessment of trends in water consumption and water consumption by sectors of the country's economy shows that water consumption and water use in some sectors of the economy (irrigation, energy, fisheries, environmental releases in the Aral Sea region and the needs of the Aral Sea, etc.) change due to changes in the water content of the year. In high-water years, they increase, and in low-water years, they decrease, and only in the industry and housing and utility services, water consumption does not depend on the water content of the year.

---

[1]https://countrymeters.info/en/privacy

Table 19.1 Data on the use of water resources in the Republic of Uzbekistan by sectors of the economy for the period 1991–2020 (million cubic meters).[2]

Years	Total water used	Including		Industry	Energy industry		Fisheries	Other
		Irrigation	Department of Housing and Utilities		Total	Dead losses		
1	2	3	4	5	6	7	8	9
1991	61,681	55,395	2,334	1,982	–	–	713	1,257
1992	61,510	55,658	2,133	1,784	–	–	536	1,399
1993	62,131	55,773	2,052	2,273	–	–	543	1,490
1994	58,445	53,381	2,392	1,002	–	–	530	1,140
1995	52,960	47,614	2,298	1,021	–	–	536	1,143
1996	53,525	49,485	2,263	801	4,317	203	501	272
1997	56,158	52,091	2,317	790	4,184	198	417	345
1998	56,697	52,871	2,082	779	4,364	246	402	318
1999	60,705	56,661	2,317	874	4,213	128	409	316
2000	48,070	44,406	2,182	735	3,947	76	372	299
2001	44,012	40,366	2,160	757	3,956	78	361	291
2002	50,259	46,296	2,336	688	3,953	91	430	418
2003	56,501	52,443	2,164	823	4,265	195	508	367
2004	58,457	52,219	2,150	851	4,068	203	524	548
2005	59,476	53,265	2,158	776	4,387	209	721	473
2006	58,616	52,509	2,283	814	4,446	217	520	523
2007	53,006	47,528	2,304	798	4,737	251	484	528
2008	43,870	38,589	2,325	804	4,735	273	463	435
2009	50,225	44,719	2,357	834	4,557	255	765	561
2010	57,169	51,645	2,385	839	4,870	246	694	548
2011	48,751	43,389	2,387	838	4,916	256	569	576
2012	56,096	50,906	2,362	744	4,729	255	662	554
2013	53,977	48,912	2,357	675	4,554	250	621	582
2014	51,794	46,857	2,335	691	4,561	256	562	582
2015	55,138	49,970	2,407	667	4,487	252	803	593
2016	56,241	50,123	2,512	701	4,621	260	804	473
2017	57,145	51,241	2,564	712	4,734	263	812	523
2018	53,412	48,324	2,364	682	4,212	241	684	528
2019	58,627	52,812	2,611	735	4,765	243	628	435
2020	57,169	51,645	2,385	839	4,870	246	694	548
Average value	55,060.77	49,903.1	2,309.2	910.3	4,457.92	215.64	575.6	602.1667

[2]Data from the Ministry of Water Resources in the Republic of Uzbekistan, 2020 [10].

Table 19.2 Consumption of water resources by sectors of the country's economy [average data for 30 years (1991–2020)].

#	Branches of the economy	Consumed water resources, km³	As a percentage of the total volume, %
1.	**Irrigation**	49,703	84.6
2.	**Energy industry**	4,191	7.1
		223 (**dead losses**)	0.4
3.	Department of Housing and Utilities	2,280	3.9
4.	**Industry**	936	1.6
5.	**Fisheries**	547	0.9
6.	Ecological needs of the Aral Sea	Determined by the Cabinet of Ministers depending on the water content of the year	–
7.	**Others**	621	1.1
Total		58,724	100

19.1.1 Application of Correlation and Regression Methods to Analyze Patterns of Changes in Water Consumption and Water Use in the Republic of Uzbekistan

Consider a regression model in which the variables x and y depend linearly on each other and on a number of factors. Disturbing factors include random causes, as well as measurement errors. There is no strong relationship between the variables. Deviations from the assumed form of connection, of course, can also arise due to an incorrect specification of the equation, i.e., an incorrect choice of the type of the equation itself that describes this dependence [11–14]. In what follows, we will assume that the specification was fulfilled correctly. Taking into account possible deviations, the linear equation of the connection of two variables (pair regression) can represent as

$$y = \alpha + \beta x + \varepsilon, \tag{19.1}$$

where α and β are unknown regression parameters (coefficients); ε is a random variable that characterizes the deviation from the theoretically expected regression—perturbation.

Thus, in Equation (19.1), the value of y is represented as the sum of two parts: systematic (x) and random (ε). In turn, the systematic part can represented as an equation

$$\hat{y} = \alpha + \beta x, \tag{19.2}$$

where $\acute{y}$ characterizes some average value of y for a given value of x [3, 7].

We make the following assumptions about the perturbation ε:

1) The perturbation ε is a normally distributed random variable.
2) The mathematical expectation ε is equal to zero: $M(\varepsilon) = 0$.
3) The dispersion of perturbations is constant: $\sigma^2_\varepsilon = \text{const}$.
4) Successive values of ε do not depend on each other.

Now, to build a linear pair regression for each observation i, the following relationship is valid

$$y_i = \alpha + \beta x_i + \varepsilon_i \qquad (19.3)$$

Since the independent variable x is interconnected with the dependent variable y, based on observations, we obtain a number of characteristics from Equation (19.3). It is required to determine the parameters α and β. It is impossible to obtain true values; we use a sample of a limited size. Hence, the values of the parameters α and β are statistical estimates of the true parameters. Let us denote the corresponding estimates as a and b. Thus, the linear pair regression equation has the form

$$\acute{y} = \alpha + bx \text{(on the model } y = \alpha + \beta x + \varepsilon). \qquad (19.4)$$

We accept a simple linear relationship between the variables x and y and some hypotheses about the shape of the curve, and we cannot uniquely select the parameters of the equation. That is, it is practically impossible to solve it by the analytical method, and a correlation approach to the solution is needed. The parameters are based on the selection criteria. Here, we have estimated parameters in the region of the correlation field. Different methods of parameter estimation rely on different selection criteria and, of course, give different values of parameter estimates for the same set of observations. It turns out that the resulting estimates have different statistical properties.

Most often, the estimation of regression parameters is carried out based on the least squares method (LSM), which was developed by K. Gauss and P. Laplace. LSM initially had a rather narrow scope—mainly in the processing of observational results in astronomical and geodetic calculations. This method received a new and wide area of application in economic and statistical calculations after the creation of the theory of regression. According to the LSM, the parameters of the regression equation are selected so that the sum of the squared deviations of observations from the regression line is minimal. The graph (Figure 19.1) shows the results of observations of the values of the variables x and y. A straight line $\acute{y} = \alpha + \beta x$ is drawn through the area occupied by the points. Deviation (disturbance) of any point with coordinates x_i, y_i will be e_i.

$$e_i = y_i - \acute{y}_i = y_i - (\alpha + bx), \qquad (19.5)$$

Likewise, a function of these parameters is the generalized point scatter index around the line, namely Σe_i^2. Hence, it is logical to accept the criterion according to which the regression coefficients a and b must be chosen so that the sum of the squares of the values of e_i is minimal, i.e., $\Sigma e_i^2 = min$.

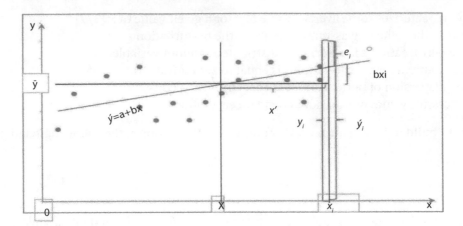

Figure 19.1 Pair linear regression.

A necessary condition for the existence of a minimum of a function is the equality to zero of the partial derivatives with respect to the unknown parameters a and b. So, let us find for the function

$$Q = \Sigma 5_i^2 = \sum_i (y_i - \overline{y}_i)^2 = \sum_i (y_i - a - bx_i)^2 \qquad (19.6)$$

partial derivatives with respect to a and b and equate them to zero.
Get

$$\begin{cases} \dfrac{\partial Q}{\partial a} = -2\Sigma_i(y_i - a - bx_i) = 0 \\[3mm] \dfrac{\partial Q}{\partial b} = -2\Sigma_i(y_i - a - bx_i)x_i = 0 \end{cases} \qquad (19.7)$$

Transforming the system, we obtain the standard form of normal equations

$$\begin{cases} \Sigma G_i = na + b\Sigma x_i \\ \Sigma x_i G_i = a\Sigma x_i + b\Sigma x_i^2 \end{cases} \qquad (19.8)$$

Dividing the first equation of System (8) by n, we obtain

$$\overline{Y} = a + b\overline{X} \qquad (19.9)$$

Thus, the least squares method gives such estimates for a and b, and the found line passes through the point with coordinates $\overline{Y}, \overline{X}$.

The values of the variables x_i and y_i can be measured in deviations from the mean, i.e., as $x_i - \bar{X}; y_i - \bar{Y}$.

We denote these differences as x_i' and y_i', respectively. In this case, the origin of coordinates will move to the point $\bar{Y}, \bar{X}$, and the system of normal equations will be simplified to

$$\Sigma x_i' \, y_i' = b\Sigma(x')^2,$$

Because $\Sigma y_i'$ and $\Sigma x_i'$ are equal to zero. Solving this equation for b gives

$$b = \frac{\Sigma x_i' \, y_i'}{\Sigma(x_i')^2}. \qquad (19.10)$$

From Equation (19.7), we get

$$a = \bar{Y} - b\bar{X} \qquad (19.11)$$

The sums required to calculate the parameter b can be obtained using the following formulas (subscripts i are omitted)

$$\Sigma(x')^2 = \Sigma x^2 - \frac{(\Sigma x)^2}{n} = \Sigma x^2 - n\bar{X}^2; \qquad (19.12)$$

$$\Sigma x'y' = \Sigma xy - \frac{\Sigma x \Sigma y}{n} = \Sigma xy - n\bar{X}\bar{Y} \qquad (19.13)$$

As follows from the above, the method for estimating parameters a and b does not depend on whether X has fixed or sample values.

The problem of statistical estimation can be divided into two parts: what value calculated from the sample should be taken as an approximate value of the characteristic of the general distribution (point estimate) and in what interval around this value the desired characteristic will be enclosed with a given reliability (interval estimate).

Based on the foregoing, there are requirements for statistical estimates. The choice of statistics as an estimate of parameter $\hat{\theta}_j$ (the amount of water for water consumption and water use in the country) was made taking into account the satisfaction of its following requirements:

- viability,
- unbiasedness, and
- efficiency.

Consistency. A natural requirement for a point estimate of a parameter is its convergence in probability to the estimated parameter, i.e., fulfillment of the conditions $lim\{|\theta - \xi| \langle \xi\} = 1$ or $\theta \overset{P}{\longrightarrow} \xi$, where P is the probability of the estimated parameter; ξ—permissible error.

An estimate that satisfies this condition is called consistent.

Unbiased. In practice, since it is necessary to use an estimate for a fixed $n = 29$ years, it is advisable to take care that the estimation error does not contain a systematic component, i.e., that the estimate is on average equal to the estimated parameter. This is expressed in the equality of its mathematical expectation to the estimated parameter: $M(\theta) = \xi$, where $M(\theta)$ is the mathematical expectation.

An estimate that satisfies this equality is called unbiased.

Efficiency. The consistency and unbiasedness of the estimate do not, of course, exclude the estimation error, which can reach a larger value for each specific implementation of the sample, the greater the variance of the estimate $D(\theta)$.

Of the two consistency and unbiased, we will consider the one that has less dispersion to be more efficient. It turns out that under certain conditions for each finite n, there is a non-zero lower bound on the values of the variance $D(\theta)n$. If the variance of the estimate θ_n has this boundary value, then the estimate is efficient.

The formation and use of water resources are greatly influenced by the power of solar radiation [12]; therefore, to determine their relationships, we used the equation

$$Q = A + BP \pm \varepsilon, \tag{19.14}$$

where Q —total water intake of the republic;
P —solar radiation power;
A, B —constant parameters of the relationship equation; and
ε —allowable interval.

Using the above Table 19.1, including it in the calculations of the solar radiation power P and the hydrothermal coefficient K, Table 19.3 was obtained.

We used the standard statistical application program [15] and the parameters of the equation for the relationship determined between various sectors of the country's economy. The calculation results are shown in Table 19.4 [16–20].

As can be seen from Table 19.4, R has negative and positive values. Negative values mean a decrease in water consumption and water usage in the republic, and positive values mean an increase. It can be seen from this that due to the influence of the solar radiation power, the total water intake in the republic and water use in irrigation are decreasing, while in the other sectors of the country's economy, they are increasing. To further refine these data, it is necessary to constantly organize accurate measurement of consumed water resources in all rivers, reservoirs, and other water intakes that provide water resources to the country's economic sectors [21, 22].

Table 19.3 Data on the consumption of water resources in the republic by sectors of the country's economy for the period 1991–2020 (million m³) with calculations of solar power and hydrothermal coefficient.

Years	Solar radiation power $P = Wm^2$	Hydrothermal coefficient $K = \dfrac{\Sigma Q}{\Sigma r °C}$	Total water consumed	Irrigation	Department of Housing and Utilities	Industry	Energy industry Total	Energy industry Dead losses	Fisheries	Others
1	2	3	4	5	6	7	8	9	10	11
1991	1,368.7	0.095	61,681	55,395	2,334	1,982			713	1,257
1992	1,364.3	0.048	61,510	55,658	2,133	1,784			536	1,399
1993	1,367.3	0.073	62,131	55,773	2,052	2,273			543	1,490
1994	1,367.7	0.055	58,445	53,381	2,392	1,002			530	1,140
1995	1,367.5	0.058	52,960	47,614	2,298	1,021			536	1,143
1996	1,368.9	0.05	53,525	49,485	2,263	801	4,317	203	501	272
1997	1,366.3	0.046	56,158	52,091	2,317	790	4,184	198	417	345
1998	1,367.9	0.067	56,697	52,871	2,082	779	4,364	246	402	318
1999	1,367.1	0.046	60,705	56,661	2,317	874	4,213	128	409	316
2000	1,367.1	0.043	48,070	44,406	2,182	735	3,947	76	372	299
2001	1,367.1	0.095	44,012	40,366	2,160	757	3,956	78	361	291
2002	1,366.9	0.048	50,259	46,296	2,336	688	3,953	91	430	418

(*Continued*)

Table 19.3 Data on the consumption of water resources in the republic by sectors of the country's economy for the period 1991–2020 (million m³) with calculations of solar power and hydrothermal coefficient. (*Continued*)

Years	Solar radiation power $P = Wm^2$	Hydrothermal coefficient $K = \dfrac{\Sigma Q}{\Sigma t°C}$	Total water consumed	Irrigation	Department of Housing and Utilities	Industry	Energy industry		Fisheries	Others
							Total	Dead losses		
2003	1,368.3	0.073	56,501	52,443	2,164	823	4,265	195	508	367
2004	1,366.3	0.055	58,457	52,219	2,150	851	4,068	203	524	548
2005	1,368.5	0.058	59,475	53,265	2,158	776	4,387	209	721	473
2006	1,367.5	0.05	58,616	52,509	2,283	814	4,446	217	520	523
2007	1,368.5	0.043	53,006	47,528	2,304	798	4,737	250	484	528
2008	1,369.1	0.095	43,870	38,589	2,325	804	4,735	273	463	435
2009	1,369.5	0.048	50,225	44,719	2,357	834	4,557	255	765	561
2010	1,368.7	0.073	57,169	51,645	2,385	839	4,870	246	694	548
2011	1,367	0.085	48,751	43,389	2,387	838	4,916	256	569	576
2012	1,370.1	0.071	56,096	50,906	2,362	744	4,729	255	662	554
2013	1,368.9	0.046	53,977	48,912	2,357	675	4,554	250	621	582
2014	0.043	0.066	51,794	46,857	2,338	776	4,561	256	562	582
2015	0.095	0.055	59,475	53,265	2,158	814	4,484	252	803	593
2016	0.048	0.058	58,616	52,509	2,283	798	4,446	217	520	523

(*Continued*)

Table 19.3 Data on the consumption of water resources in the republic by sectors of the country's economy for the period 1991–2020 (million m³) with calculations of solar power and hydrothermal coefficient. (*Continued*)

Years	Solar radiation power $P = Wm^2$	Hydrothermal coefficient $K = \dfrac{\Sigma Q}{\Sigma t^\circ C}$	Total water consumed	Irrigation	Department of Housing and Utilities	Industry	Energy industry Total	Dead losses	Fisheries	Others
2017	0.073	0.05	53,006	47,528	2,304	804	4,737	250	484	528
2018	0.043	0.043	43,870	38,589	2,325	834	4,735	273	463	435
2019	0.095	0.095	50,225	44,719	2,357	839	4,557	255	765	561
2020	1,368.7	0.073	57,169	51,645	2,385	814	4,870	246	694	548

Table 19.4 The results of calculating the effect of the relationship between the power of solar radiation on water consumption and water use of the sectors of the country's economy.

No.	Name of water consumers	The tightness of the relationship (correlation coefficient), R	Relationship equations	Note
1.	Total water intake	−0.860	$Q = 5,998,566.9 - 4,342.5\,P \pm 3,398.1$	*
		−0.905	$Q = 4,763,068.4 - 3,446\,P \pm 5,384.4$	*
2.	Irrigation	−0.931	$Q = 2,381,277 - 1,851.15\,P \pm 3,202.0$	*
		−0.926	$Q = 1,072,743.6 - 745.55\,P \pm 1,321.9$	*
3.	Department of Housing and Utilities	0.795	$Q = 37.143\,P - 48,523.5 \pm 78.17$	
4.	Industry	0.931	$Q = 53.77\,P - 72,788.8 \pm 55$	
5.	Energy	0.771	$Q = 148\,P - 198,064.7 \pm 219$	
6.	Fisheries	0.909	$Q = 110.6P - 150,714.2 \pm 144.0$	
7.	Others	0.99	$Q = 97.83P - 133,462.4 \pm 103.23$	

Note: * - —the dimension of the last member of the relationship equation, in million m³.

19.2   Establishment of the Patterns of Formation of Volumes of Water Resources in Areas of Their Usage

Exponential distribution. One of the distributions most frequently encountered in reliability theory [6, 8, 12] is the one-parameter exponential distribution given by the probability density

$$f(x;\theta) = \begin{cases} \dfrac{1}{\theta}e^{-x/\theta}, & x \geq 0 \\ 0, & x < 0, \end{cases} \tag{19.15}$$

$$F(x) = \begin{cases} \dfrac{1}{\theta} \int\limits_0^x e^{-x/\theta} dx = 1 - e^{-x/\theta}, & x \geq 0, \\ 0, & x < 0. \end{cases}$$

(19.16)

Reliability features

$$R(t) = \begin{cases} \int\limits_t^\infty \dfrac{1}{\theta} e^{--x/\theta} dx = e^{-t/\theta}, & t \geq 0, \\ 1, & t < 0, \end{cases}$$

(19.17)

$$h(t) = \frac{1}{\theta} \frac{e^{-t/\theta}}{e^{-t/\theta}} = \frac{1}{\theta}.$$

(19.18)

Table 19.5 shows the values of the exponential distribution in the formation of volumes of water resources in the areas of their use. The form of functions $f(t)$, $R(t)$ and $h(t)$ for exponential distribution is shown in Figure 19.2.

Table 19.5 Properties of the exponential distribution.

Characteristic function	$M_X(t) = (1 - \theta t)^{-1}, \quad t < 1/\theta$
Average	$\mu = 0$
Dispersion	$\sigma^2 = \theta^2$
Third central moment	$\mu_3 = 2\theta^3$
Fourth central moment	$\mu_4 = 9\theta^4$
The coefficient of variation	$\eta = 1$
Asymmetry coefficient	$\alpha_3 = 2$
Kurtosis coefficient	$\alpha_4 = 9$

Notes:
1. The exponential distribution is a special case of both the gamma distribution and the Weibull distribution [17–20].
2. This distribution is characterized by a constant intensity of water consumption, which also serves as a distribution parameter. The constant intensity of water consumption means that the probability of water consumption does not depend on how long it has worked before the considered time point.

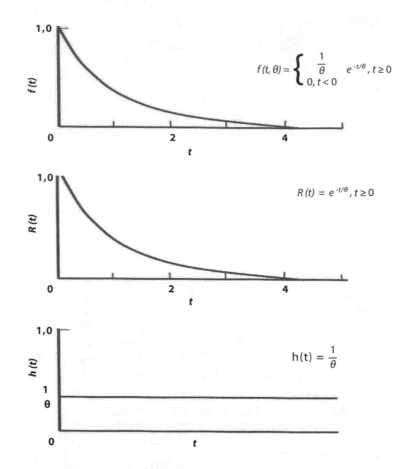

Figure 19.2 Functions $f(t)$, $R(t)$, and $h(t)$ for exponential distribution.

The average data on the use of water resources in the sectors of the Uzbekistan's economy for the period 1991–2020, as well as the results of calculations of the consumption of water resources as a percentage of their total volume (based on data from Table 19.6) diagram built (Figure 19.3). From this table, it can be seen that the bulk of water (85.0%) is used for irrigation in the agricultural sector of crops, vegetables and melons, vineyards, orchards, household plots, and villages. The remaining 15% of water resources are used in other sectors of the economy of the republic: housing and utility services (3.98%), industry (1.64%), energy (7.75%, irretrievable 0.36%), fisheries (0.45%), agricultural water supply (0.45%), and others (0.37%).

The current consumption of water resources in the sectors of the country's economy is subject to an exponential distribution law, which can be seen from the circular diagram of water consumption in the sectors of the economy of the republic.

The Poisson distribution is a useful approximation of the binomial and hypergeometric distributions. Table 19.7 shows the properties of the Poisson distribution.

Table 19.6 Using of water resources by sectors of the economy of the Republic of Uzbekistan [averaged data for 30 years (1991–2020 million m³)].

1.	**Irrigation (agricultural sector)**	48,694	85.0%
2.	**Housing and utility services**	2,278	3.98%
3.	**Industry**	940	1.64%
4.	**Energy**	4,430	7.75%
		206	0.36%
5.	**Fisheries**	259	0.45%
6.	**Agricultural water supply**	260	0.45%
7.	**Ecological needs of the Aral Sea**	–	–
8.	**Others**	210	0.37%
Total		57,187	100%

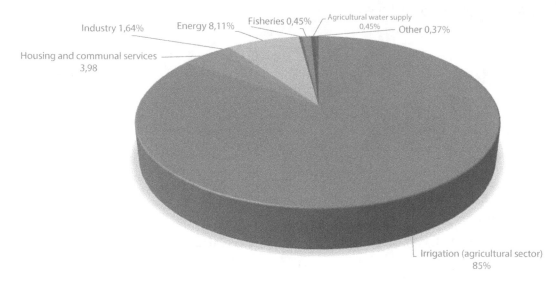

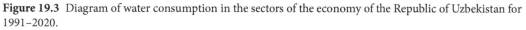

Figure 19.3 Diagram of water consumption in the sectors of the economy of the Republic of Uzbekistan for 1991–2020.

Table 19.7 Properties of the Poisson distribution.

Characteristic function	$M_X(t) = e^{\lambda\left(e^t - 1\right)}$
Average	$\mu = \lambda$
Dispersion	$\sigma^2 = \lambda$
Third central moment	$\mu_3 = \lambda$
Fourth central moment	$\mu_4 = \lambda\left(3\lambda + 1\right)$
The coefficient of variation	$\eta = 1\!\!\Big/\!\sqrt{\lambda}$
Asymmetry coefficient	$\alpha_3 = 1\!\!\Big/\!\sqrt{\lambda}$
Kurtosis coefficient	$\alpha_4 = 3 + 1\!\!\Big/\!\lambda$

It takes place in those cases when, on a certain interval or area, an event with probability appears a large number of times.

$$f(x,\lambda) = \begin{cases} \dfrac{\lambda^x e^{-\lambda}}{x!}, & x = 0,1,2\ldots\ldots, \ \lambda > 0 \\ 0, & invotherconditions, \end{cases} \tag{19.19}$$

$$F(x) = \sum_{i=0}^{x} \frac{\lambda^i e^{-\lambda}}{i!}, \tag{19.20}$$

where $f(x,\lambda)$ is the distribution function, and $F(x)$ is the distribution density.
In Figure 19.4, the Poisson distribution is shown for various values of the λ parameter.

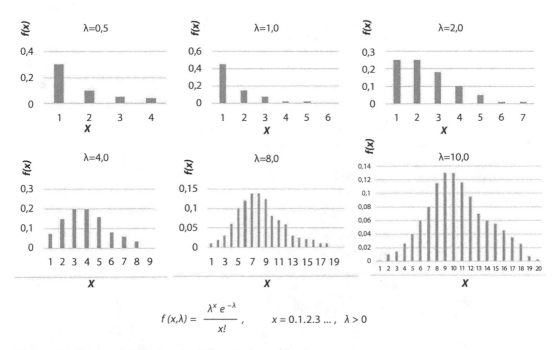

$$f(x,\lambda) = \frac{\lambda^x e^{-\lambda}}{x!}, \qquad x = 0.1.2.3 \dots, \quad \lambda > 0$$

Figure 19.4 Poisson distribution for different values of the λ parameter.

Notes:
1. $f(x,\lambda)$ is maximum for $x \leq [\lambda]$ (largest integer equal to or less than λ).
2. For small values λ, the distribution is concentrated near the origin. With growth λ, the distribution acquires an asymmetric bell-shaped shape. For large values $\lambda (\lambda > 9)$, the Poisson distribution can be approximately replaced by a normal distribution with parameters $\mu = \lambda$ и $\sigma^2 = \lambda$.
3. In our case, $\lambda = K$, where K is the coefficient of water consumption of crop species.

Figure 19.5 shows a diagram of the coefficient of water consumption K of the types of crops in the Republic of Uzbekistan, distributed according to the Poisson law.

The obtained research results show that the coefficients of water consumption K of agricultural crops correspond to the distribution according to the Poisson law.

The uniform distribution is determined by the functions

$$f(x) = \begin{cases} 1/(b-a), & a < x < b, \\ 0 \end{cases} \tag{19.21}$$

$$F(x) = \begin{cases} 0, & x \leq a, \\ (x-a)/(b-a), & a < x < b, \\ 1, & x \geq b. \end{cases} \tag{19.22}$$

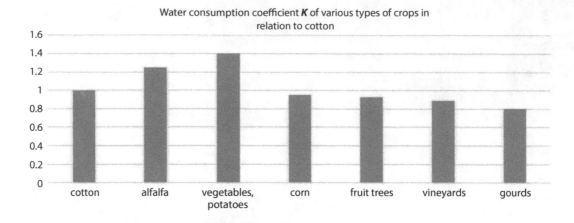

Figure 19.5 Diagram of water consumption coefficient K of crop types in relation to cotton in the Republic of Uzbekistan.

Reliability functions. Since $t \geq 0$, we believe

$$R(t) = \begin{cases} 1, & 0 \leq t \leq a, \\ \dfrac{b-t}{b-a}, & a < t < b, \\ 0 & t \geq b. \end{cases} \tag{19.23}$$

$$h(t) = \begin{cases} 0, & 0 \leq t \leq a, \\ \dfrac{1}{b-t}, & a < t < b. \end{cases} \tag{19.24}$$

The properties of uniform distribution are given in Table 19.8.

Functions $f(x)$, $R(t)$, and $h(t)$ for uniform distribution are shown in Figure 19.6.

Since housing and communal services, industry and energy mostly have closed water supply systems, they therefore have no losses due to filtration and evaporation. In the equations of water consumption in individual sectors of the country's national economy, the solar radiation power has an influence. Based on correlation analysis [6], the solar radiation power divides into two values according to their dimension: 1360–1364 W/m² and 1364–1368 W/m². Therefore, because of this, in calculating water consumption by housing and communal services and energy, we have two equations (patterns).

The water intake equation in housing and communal services has the following form:

$$Q_{\kappa x1} = 29.58P - 38{,}002.178 \pm 55.31, \tag{19.25}$$

Table 19.8 Uniform distribution properties.

Characteristic function	$M_X(t) = \dfrac{e^{bt} - e^{at}}{(b-a)t}$
Average	$\mu = \dfrac{b+a}{2}$
Dispersion	$\sigma^2 = \dfrac{(b-a)^2}{12}$
Third central moment	$\mu_3 = 0$
Fourth central moment	$\mu_4 = \dfrac{(b-a)^4}{80}$
The coefficient of variation	$\eta = \dfrac{b-a}{\sqrt{3}(b+a)}$
Asymmetry coefficient	$\alpha_3 = 0$
Kurtosis coefficient	$\alpha_4 = 1{,}8$

$$Q_{\kappa x2} = 39.38P - 51{,}499.52 \pm 79.26, \tag{19.26}$$

$Q_{\kappa x1}$, $Q_{\kappa x2}$ are the water intake by the housing and utility services (million m³ year), and P is the solar radiation power: in the first case, P changes from 1,360 W/m² to 1,364 W/m²; in the second case, from 1,365 W/m² to 1,368 W/m²; $R_1 = 0.8011$ and $R_2 = 0.9414$ are the correlation coefficients, respectively.

The dependence of the actual water resources with drawn by the housing and utility services of the republic on solar radiation power is shown in Figures 19.7 and 19.8.

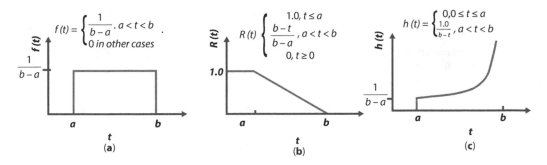

Figure 19.6 (a, b, c) Functions for uniform distribution.

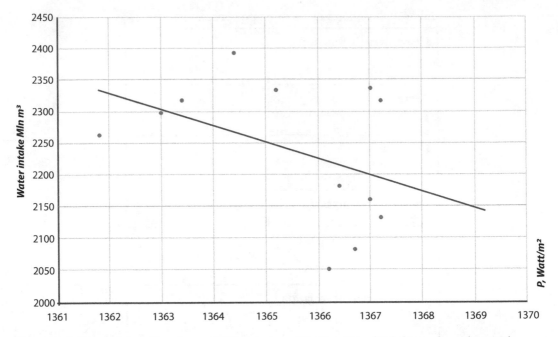

Figure 19.7 Water intake of housing and utility services of the Republic of Uzbekistan depending on the power of solar radiation.

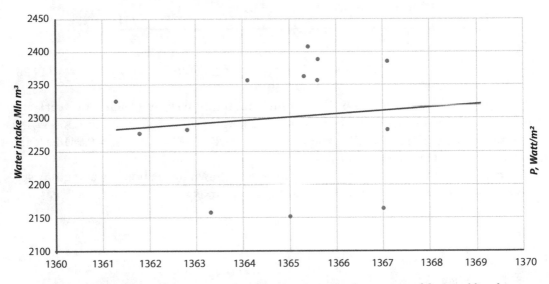

Figure 19.8 Solar radiation power. Water intake of the housing and utility services of the Republic of Uzbekistan depending on the power of solar radiation.

The water intake equation in the industry of the republic has the following types:

$$Q_{np1} = 357.8P - 486,729.0, \tag{19.27}$$

$$Q_{np2} = 82.143P - 111{,}499.0, \tag{19.28}$$

where Q_{np} is the water intake by the industry of the republic (million m³ year); P is the power of solar radiation behind the ionosphere (W/m²); 357.8, 486,729.0, 82.143, and 111,499.0 are the constant terms in the equations of solar–terrestrial relationships; $R^1 = 0.8774$ and $R^2 = 0.9433$ industrial water consumption depends on the power of solar radiation. The dependence of used water resources from solar radiation power shows Figure 19.9.

From Figure 19.10, it can be seen that the dependence on the actual withdrawn water resources of agricultural water supply corresponds to the law of uniform distribution.

Figure 19.9 Water intake of the industry of the Republic of Uzbekistan depending on the solar radiation power.

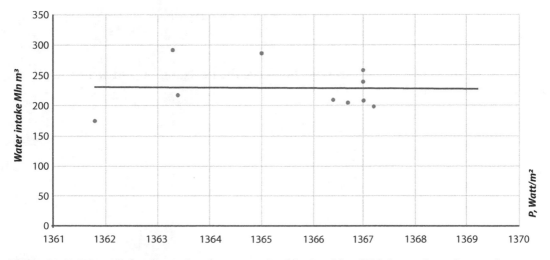

Figure 19.10 Water intake of agricultural water supply of the Republic of Uzbekistan depending on the power of solar radiation.

19.3   Forecasting Water Use Based on Mathematical Models of Water Management of Distributed Irrigation Systems

The President of the Republic of Uzbekistan approved the water resources strategy in the Decree of the President of the Republic of Uzbekistan No. PF-60 of 28.01.2022. In many regions of the country, the issue of eliminating the shortage of clean, freshwater, that is, the lack of drinking water, is considered one of the urgent issues at the state level [16–18]. The issue of solving the problem of water shortage in our country is one of the urgent issues in the development of science and technology. The occurrence of water scarcity mainly depends on the following characteristics of water resources [19–21]:

- due to water quality pollution and
- factors of natural absorption of water.

The issue of reduction of water pollution and natural absorption issues as the factors of emergence of the water problem is still important in the development of science and technology [21, 23–27].

19.3.1   Based on the Given Information, See the Model of Water Distribution Based on the Least Square Method

One of the widely used methods for solving this problem is the method of least squares [21]. This method consists of the following: we look at the sum of the squares of the differences between the values obtained in the experiment and the values of the empirical function at the corresponding points found theoretically:

$$\delta_i = y_i - Y_i = y_i - (ax_i + b) \tag{19.29}$$

$$S(a,b) = \sum_{i=1}^{n} [y_i - Y_i]^2 = \sum_{i=1}^{n} [y_i - (ax_i + b)]^2. \tag{19.30}$$

$\delta_i = y_i - Y_i = y_i - (ax_i + b)$, we call the difference the deviation x_i and write the differences for all values of δ_i:

$$\begin{cases} \delta_1 = y_1 - Y_1 = y_1 - (ax_1 + b), \\ \delta_2 = y_2 - Y_2 = y_2 - (ax_2 + b), \\ \dots\dots\dots\dots\dots\dots\dots\dots \\ \delta_n = y_n - Y_n = y_n - (ax_n + b). \end{cases}$$

$Y_i = ax_i + b$ the sum $\sum\limits_{i=1}^{n} \delta_i$ must be as small as possible so that the straight line is very close to the experimental points. Experimental points are located on both sides of the drawn straight line. Therefore, some values will be positive and some will be negative. Therefore, even if the distance δ_i between the experimental points and the straight line is large, the value of the sum $\sum\limits_{i=1}^{n} \delta_i$ can be small. In order δ_i to remove the influence of the signs of the values of on the sum $\sum\limits_{i=1}^{n} \delta_i$, it is convenient to take the sum of the squares of the differences instead of the sum $(\sum\limits_{i=1}^{n} \delta_i^2)$. We denote by $S(a,b)$ this sum. (2) We can choose the sum of the parameters a and b in such a way that this sum takes the smallest value:

$$S(a,b) = \sum_{i=1}^{n} [\gamma_i - (ax_i + b)]^2 = \min.$$

This is the essence of the method of least squares.

So, for example a and b, it is brought to find the values of the parameters that make the function $S(a,b)$ a minimum.

Theorem. If a function $Z = f(X;Y)$ has an extremum at $X = X_y$, $Y = Y_x$, then every Z first-order particular derivative is equal to 0 at these values of the arguments.

Based on this, the values of the parameters are the following system of equations:

$$\begin{cases} \partial Z / \partial X = 0 \\ \partial Z / \partial Y = 0 \end{cases}$$

must satisfy.

View the water distribution model based on the least squares method using the given data (Tables 19.1–19.4).

The distribution of water on the territory of the Republic of Uzbekistan is analyzed based on the data obtained between 1992 and 2020, and a mathematical model based on the method of least squares is created using these data [23, 28, 29].

First, we build the model in the form $Y_i = ax_i + b$:

$$S(a,b) = \sum_{i=1}^{6} [y_i - (ax_i + b)]^2 = \min.$$

$$\begin{cases} \dfrac{\partial S}{\partial b} = 2 \sum_{i=1}^{6} [y_i - (ax_i + b)] * 1 = 0 \\[2em] \dfrac{\partial S}{\partial a} = 2 \sum_{i=1}^{6} [y_i - (ax_i + b)] * x_i = 0 \end{cases}$$

$$\begin{cases} \sum_{i=1}^{6} b + (\sum_{i=1}^{6} x_i) * a = \sum_{i=1}^{6} y_i \\[2em] (\sum_{i=1}^{6} x_i) * b + (\sum_{i=1}^{6} x_i^2) * a = \sum_{i=1}^{6} x_i * y_i \end{cases}$$

(19.31)

Let's substitute numerical values into equations (19.31), the system of equations will look like this:

$$\begin{cases} 6b + 82a = 4093.4 \\ 82b + 1664a = 54621.2 \end{cases}$$

$$\begin{cases} 492b + 6724a = 335658.8 \\ 492b + 9984a = 327727.2 \end{cases}$$

We solve this system of equations and find the value of a, and b construct a function $Y_i = ax_i + b$ in accordance with Table 19.4 [30, 31].

$$a = -2.43306135$$
$$b = 715.484417$$
$$y(x) = 715.484417 - 2.43306135x$$

From the built model, we can calculate the value at the point we need.

$$y(31) = 715.484417 - 2.43306135 * 31$$
$$y(31) = 640.06$$
$$y(32) = 715.484417 - 2.43306135 * 32$$
$$y(32) = 637.626$$

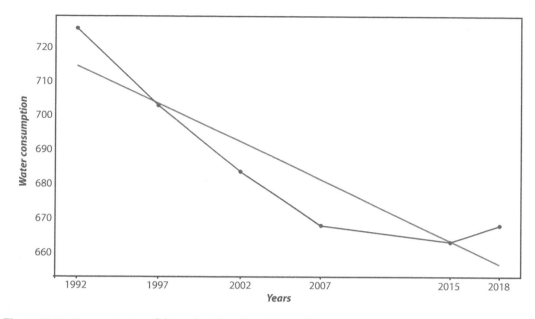

Figure 19.11 Representation of the analysis based on this model.

The graphical representation of the analysis based on this model is as follows (Figure 19.11):

___ A graph of the linear model of the device based on experimental data.
___ Graph drawn based on experimental data.

Based on the model built above, the water distribution processes in 2021, 2024, 2027, and 2030 were obtained based on predictions (Table 19.9).

Based on the built model, the graph created because of forecasting water distribution in 2021, 2024, 2027, and 2030 is presented below (Figure 19.12).

___ Plot of the linear model of the device based on experimental data.
___ Graph drawn based on experimental data.

It is important to see the patterns of distribution of water scarcity in the following years based on the forecast of water distribution in the following years based on the constructed model. In this work, the water distribution processes in 2021, 2024, 2027, and 2030 were analyzed on the basis of the built model [17, 23].

Table 19.9 Water consumption.

Years	1992	1997	2002	2007	2015	2018	2021	2024	2027	2030
Water consumption	726.0	703.3	683.9	668.3	663.6	668.3	652.5	645.8	639.2	632.5

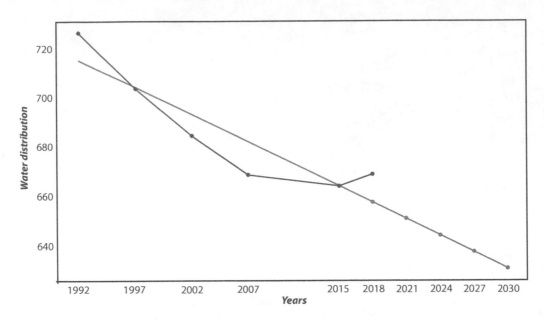

Figure 19.12 Water distribution in 2021, 2024, 2027, and 2030.

19.3.2   Building a Model Using a Local Cubic Spline

Using the local interpolation cubic spline model, which has the following form:

$$S_3(f,x) = \sum_{j=0}^{3} \varphi_{i+1}(t) f(x_{i+j-1}) \tag{19.32}$$

where

$$\varphi_1(t) = -\frac{1}{4}t(1 - 3t + 2t^2);$$

$$\varphi_2(t) = \frac{1}{4}(4 - 3t - 7t^2 + 6t^3);$$

$$\varphi_3(t) = \frac{1}{4}t(5 + 5t - 6t^2);$$

$$\varphi_4(t) = -\frac{1}{4}t(1 + t - 2t^2);$$

$$t = \frac{x - x_i}{h}; \quad h = x_{i+1} - x_i; \quad x \in [x_i, x_{i+1}]. \quad t \in [0,1].$$

We have the following

$$\sum_{k=1}^{4} \varphi_k(t) = 1 \tag{19.33}$$

Based on the data in Tables 19.1–19.4, a water consumption model was made (Figure 19.13).
-- Data-driven.
-- Based on the spline model.
Next, we will build a forecast model based on a cubic interpolation spline (Table 19.10, Figure 19.14).

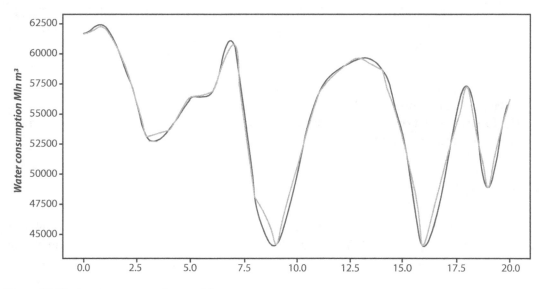

Figure 19.13 A water consumption model.

Table 19.10 Total water use forecast.

Years	Total water used (million m³)
2020	57,169
2022	57,738
2024	58,541
2026	57,145

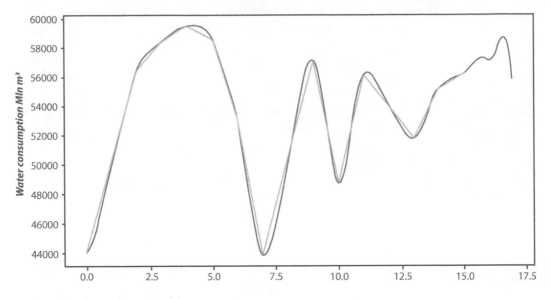

Figure 19.14 The predictive model.

-- Data-driven.
-- Based on the spline model.
The forecast based on the interpolation spline model shows that there will be a decrease in water consumption by 2030.

Conclusion

The use of the least squares method does not provide such accuracy of the model and requires further improvement. The prediction built based on a cubic interpolation spline model gives highly accurate results.

References

1. Khaydar, D., Chen, X., Huang, Y. *et al.*, Investigation of crop evapotranspiration and irrigation water requirement in the lower Amu Darya River Basin, Central Asia. *J. Arid Land*, 13, 23–39, 2021, https://doi.org/10.1007/s40333-021-0054-9.
2. Karshiev, R. *et al.*, Hydraulic calculation of reliability and safety parameters of the irrigation network and its hydraulic facilities. *E3S Web of Conferences*, EDP Sciences, p. T. 264, 2021.
3. Kabulov, A.V., Seytov, A.J., Kudaybergenov, A.A., Classification of mathematical models of unsteady water movement in the main canals of irrigation systems. *Int. J. Adv. Res. Sci. Eng. Technol.*, 7, 4, 13392–13401, April 2020, ISSN:2350-0328, India. (№ 5, Web of science, IF=3,98).
4. Rakhimov, Sh.Kh., Seytov, A.J., Kudaybergenov, A.A., Optimal control of unsteady water movement in the main canals. *Int. J. Adv. Res. Sci. Eng. Technol.*, 7, 4, 13380–13391, April 2020, India, ISSN: 2350-0328. (№ 6, Web of science, IF=3,98).

5. Narziev, J.J., Maxmudov, I.E., Paluanov, D.T., Ernazarov, A.I., Assessment of Probability Reliability of Hydro technical Structures during Operation Period, http://openaccessjournals. eu/index.php/ijiaet/article/view/949.

6. Narziev, J., Nikam, B., Gapparov, F., Infrastructure mapping and performance assessment of irrigation system using GIS and remote sensing. *International Scientific Conference "Construction Mechanics, Hydraulics and Water Resources Engineering" (CONMECHYDRO - 2021)*. Hydraulics of Structures, Hydraulic Engineering and Land Reclamation Construction. E3S Web of Conferences, vol. 264, 2021, https://doi.org/10.1051/ e3sconf/202126403005.

7. Rakhimov, Sh.Kh., Gafforov, Kh.Sh., Seytov, A.Zh., Mathematical models of channels of irrigation systems taking into account the discreteness of water supply. *International scientific and practical conference "Scientific support as a factor in the sustainable development of water management."* Report - Taraz, pp. S. 239–245, 2016.

8. Varlamova, L.P., Yakubov, M.S., Elmuradova, B.E., Water Resource Management in Distributed Irrigation Systems, in: *The Digital Agricultural Revolution: Innovations and Challenges in Agriculture through Technology Disruptions*, R. Bhatnagar, N.K. Tripathi, N. Bhatnagar, C.K. Panda (Eds.), p. 496, Scrivener Publishing LLC, 2022, Chapter 16. ISBN: 978-1-119-82345-2 April 2022.–Pp. 359-378 https://www.wiley.com/en-sg/The+Digital+Agricultural+Revo lution%3A+Innovations+and+Challenges+in+Agriculture+through+Technology+Disrupti ons-p-9781119823452#permission-section.

9. Shtengelov, R.S. and Filimonova, E.A., *UDC 556.182 Combined water intake systems as a method of optimal water resources management*, vol. 6, no. 11, pp. 21–24, ResearchGate, 2012, https://mivh.editorum.ru/ru/nauka/.

10. Levent Kavvas, M., Ercan, A., Polsinelli, J., Governing equations of transient soil water flow and soil water flux in multidimensional fractional anisotropic media and fractional time. *Hydrol. Earth Syst. Sci.*, Special Issue: Modeling hydrological processes and changes. 21, 3, 1547–1557, https://hess.copernicus.org/articles/21/1547/2017/hess-21-1547-2017-metrics.html.

11. Worm, G.I.M., Mesman, G.A.M., van Schagen, K.M., Borger, K.J., Rietveld, L.C., Hydraulic modelling of drinking water treatment plant operations, *Drink. Water Eng. Sci.*, 2, 15–20, 2009, www.drink-water-eng-sci.net/2/15/2009/.

12. Urbanowicz, K. and Firkowski, M., Modelling Water Hammer with Quasi-Steady and Unsteady Friction in Viscoelastic Pipelines, https://link.springer.com/chapter/10.1007/978-3-319-96601-4_35.

13. Abbas, A., Massoumi, F., Afshar, A., Marino, M.A., State of the Art Review of Ant Colony Optimization. *Appl. Water Resour. Manage., Water Resour. Manage.*, 29, 3891–3904, 2015. Published online: 1 July 2015 # Springer Science+Business Media Dordrecht.

14. Kartvelishvili, N.A., *Stochastic hydrology*, p. 163, Hydrometeorological publishing house, Leningrad, 1975.

15. *Irrigation of Uzbekistan*, vol. 3, p. 358, Fan, Tashkent, 1979.

16. Report of the Ministry of Water Resources for the period 1991-2020.

17. Grushevsky, M.S., *Unsteady movement of water in rivers and canals*, p. S. 288, Gidrometeoizdat, L, 1982.

18. Denisov, Yu.M., Mathematical modeling of the runoff process in mountain rivers // Collection of scientific. tr. Tashkent: SANIIRI, No. 39, pp. S. 30–36.

19. Kalinin, G.P. and Milyukov, P.P., Approximate calculation of the unsteady movement of water masses // *Proceedings of the TsIP*, vol. 66, 72 p., 1958.

20. Kunzh, Zh.A., Holly, F.M., Vervey, A., *Numerical methods in problems of river hydraulics*, p. 253, Energoatomizdat, M., 1985.

21. Rakhimov, Sh.Kh. and Begimov, I., Development of the theory of optimal distribution of water in irrigation systems under discrete water supply to consumers. Research report (interim), NIIIVP at TIIM, Tashkent, 2013.

22. Decree of the President of the Republic of Uzbekistan No. PF-60 dated 28.01.2022 https://lex.uz/docs/5841063.

23. Bahromov, S. and other, Local interpolation bicubic spline method in digital processing of geophysical signals. *Adv. Sci. Technol. Eng. Syst.*, 6, 1, 487–492, 2021.

24. Rakhimov, S., Seytov, A., Nazarov, B., Buvabekov, B., Optimal control of unstable water movement in channels of irrigation systems under conditions of discontinuity of water delivery to consumers. *IOP Conf. Ser.: Mater. Sci. Eng.*, 883, 012065, 2020, Dagestan, 2020, IOP Publishing DOI:10.1088/1757-899X/883/1/012065 (№5, Scopus, IF=4,652).

25. Kabulov, A., Normatov, I., Seytov, A., Kudaybergenov, A., Optimal Management of Water Resources in Large Main Canals with Cascade Pumping Stations. *2020 IEEE International IOT, Electronics and Mechatronics Conference (IEMTRONICS)*, Vancouver, BC, Canada, pp. 1–4, 2020, doi: DOI: 10.1109/IEMTRONICS51293.2020.9216402 (№ 5, Scopus, IF= 9.936.

26. Rakhimov, S., Seytov, A., Rakhimova, N., Xonimqulov, B., Mathematical models of optimal distribution of water in main channels. *2020 IEEE 14th International Conference on Application of Information and Communication Technologies (AICT)*, INSPEC Accession Number: 20413548, IEEE Access, Tashkent, Uzbekistan, pp. 1–4, doi: DOI:10.1109/AICT50176.2020.9368798 (AICT), (№ 5, Scopus, IF=3,557).

27. Kabulov, A.V., Seytov, A.J., Kudaybergenov, A.A., Classification of mathematical models of unsteady water movement in the main canals of irrigation systems. *Int. J. Adv. Res. Sci. Eng. Technol.*, 7, 4, 13392–13401, April 2020, ISSN:2350-0328, India, (№ 5, Web of science, IF=3,98).

28. Rakhimov, Sh.Kh., Seytov, A.J., Kudaybergenov, A.A., Optimal control of unsteady water movement in the main canals. *Int. J. Adv. Res. Sci. Eng. Technol.*, 7, 4, 13380–13391, April 2020, India, ISSN: 2350-0328. (№ 6, Web of science, IF=3,98).

29. J. J., N., I. E., M., D. T., P., A. I., E., Assessment of probability reliability of hydro technical structures during operation period. *Int. J. Innov. Anal. Emerg. Technol.*, 2, 1, 59–62, 2022. Retrieved from https://openaccessjournals.eu/index.php/ijiaet/article/view/949

30. Narziev, J., Nikam, B., Gapparov, F., Infrastructure mapping and performance assessment of irrigation system using GIS and remote sensing. *International Scientific Conference "Construction Mechanics, Hydraulics and Water Resources Engineering" (CONMECHYDRO - 2021)*. Hydraulics of Structures, Hydraulic Engineering and Land Reclamation Construction. E3S Web of Conferences, vol. 264, p. 03005, 2021, https://doi.org/10.1051/e3sconf/202126403005.

31. Kazakov, E., Jovliev, U., Yakubov, G., Extension of tubular water discharge limitations with water flow extinguishers. *Int. J. Sci. Technol. Res.*, 8, 12, 2080–2082, december 2019, ISSN 2277-8616, https://www.ijstr.org/final-print/dec2019/Extension-Of-Tubular-Water-Discharge-Limitations-With-Water-Flow-Extinguishers.pdf.

20

The Role of Electric Vehicles in the Agriculture Industry Using IoT: Turning Electricity into Food

Parul Asati[1]*, Sandeep Raghuwanshi[1], Arif Hasan[1] and Aadil Zeffer[2]

[1]Amity University, Madhya Pradesh, India
[2]DAMES, The University of North Carolina, United States

Abstract

The significance of agriculture in India gains new meaning as it intersects with the emerging concept of electric vehicles. The development patterns and prospects for off-road electric vehicles powered by green energy and agricultural robots are discussed in this study. The evolution of hybrid electric, robotic, and autonomous vehicles is increasing and enhancing work quality, as are other green fuels, energy-efficient technology, and electric automobiles. To better comprehend the difficulties and prospects in business and research, relevant digital technologies are also covered, including enhanced network communication, AI methods, and blockchain. This research paper explores the transformative potential of agricultural electric vehicles in addressing sustainability challenges within the agri sector while focusing on the role of achievement of environmentally conscious and productive food systems.

Keywords: Electric vehicle, modern agriculture, Internet of Things, renewable energy technologies, sustainability

20.1 Introduction

The agricultural sector is currently faced with significant obstacles like population expansion, energy calamity, weather change, labor scarcity, and the possibility of pandemic diseases. Between 2022 and 2050, the number of citizens is estimated to climb from 7.9 billion to 10 billion, while agricultural output is anticipated to increase [1]. Global warming and major health hazards are being created by the increasing number of cars and other fossil fuel-powered modes of transportation that are being used [2]. The combative evolution of secure, good, and more fuel well-organized automobiles is being encouraged by progressively stricter emissions and fuel efficiency criteria. The growing human population is driving up the order for food and more agricultural fruits worldwide; hence, energy consumption needs productivity, and electric vehicles help agriculture in production. Around the world, agriculture is known as the root or foundation of India where farmers are the

---

**Corresponding author*: nitinagarwal714.na@gmail.com

Kuldeep Singh and Prasanna Kolar (eds.) Digital Agricultural Ecosystem: Revolutionary Advancements in Agriculture, (369–380) © 2024 Scrivener Publishing LLC

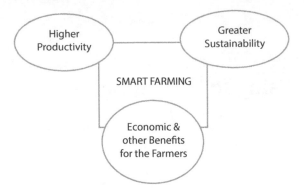

Figure 20.1 Evidence of smart farming technology (Dankan Gowda *et al.*, 2021) [29].

backbone of agriculture. Farmers are under increasing pressure to enhance production, and this pressure is decreasing the productivity of agriculture where the electric vehicle is the boon for the society. This includes the use of IoT, digital technology, and advanced agricultural equipment powered by renewable energy to improve the efficiency and profitability of farming.

Electric tractors have several benefits which enhance smart farming, and their use leads to producing large harvests of crops for Indian farmers. It is pertinent to mention here that electric vehicles also play a significant role in agriculture in terms of sustainable and modern technologies [3].

Currently, electric and hybrid mechanisms are seen as potential technologies for promoting the use of electric vehicles with the possibility to lower greenhouse and other waste gas emissions from the transportation sector [4]. The advantages include the fact that full electric propulsion produces no exhaust emissions and electric engine designs use less energy than traditional combustion engines powered by petroleum or diesel [5].

20.1.1 Electric Vehicles in Agriculture

In the present time, agricultural industries encounter significant challenges, including population growth, energy crises, climate change, scarcity of manpower, and the threat of pandemic diseases. However, a concerning trend involves the migration of agricultural employees to other sectors, coupled with the rising average age of the farmers [6].

This increases the demand for farm employees. To satisfy the demands of the projected population, agricultural scientists, farmers, and breeders must produce more food from small farmland areas in a sustainable manner. When combined with the decrease in rural labor, this illustrates the unavoidable necessity to boost efficiency by using more automated technologies on farms [7, 8].

20.1.2 Smart Agriculture and Smart Farming Using IoT Technology

The advancement of technology and research has enhanced the promotion of smart farming using electric tractors. More accurate information about the crop, soil, and environment may be acquired via IoT-based computer applications. The phrase "Internet of Things" initially emerged in a published study in 2006, explaining the paradigm of evolution notion brought about by the availability of Internet technology [9], which is extremely relevant in today's situations. Previous researchers examined 26,420 publications on Internet of Things (IoT) research from 2006 to 2018, beginning with the first appearance of the IoT keyword in 2006.

Weather, soil, and water are all drying up as agricultural land diminishes, making it increasingly difficult to produce food. Agriculturalists will gain from the use of IoT technology, which will allow them to reduce wastelands while increasing productivity. Agriculture will benefit from deploying the IoT in addition to the benefits stated above. We provide many novel, natural, and widely accessible energy sources, as well as the primary techniques for harvesting them [10].

20.1.3   Off-Road Vehicle Technology

The use of eco-friendly automobiles, such as battery-generated electric vehicles (BEVs), plug-in hybrid electric vehicles (PHEVs), and fuel cell vehicles (FCVs), is subsidized by the government in some countries to replace traditional internal combustion engines (ICEs). Electric agricultural vehicles are a type of habitual and electrical combination of vehicles [11]. The 1973 oil prohibition introduced a new age of life awareness in the United States. Since then, continuously rising energy prices and periodic countrywide petroleum scarcity have put energy prices and obtainability at the center of economic design in both the commercial and general locality [12].

20.2   Department of Energy

Fossil fuel tractors used in agricultural lands are contributing more to pollution, while electric vehicles are sustainable and environmentally friendly [9]. The benefits which we can avail from electric tractors are as follows:

- I.   Engine: low price, small size, and heaviness.
- II.   Regulator: low price, more power-holding ability, and large effectiveness.
- III. Transmissions: minimal mass, perpetually variable, and miscellaneous ratio.
- IV.   Vehicle mass: bottommost heaviness, less material price, and superior fabrication ideas.
- V.   Batteries: big energy thickness, low price, and large cycle living.
- VI.   Auxiliary devices: greater/warmer, air conditioners, chargers, state of demand index, and defense gadgets [9, 10].

Sonalika, Cellestial, and HAV manufacture electric tractors in India. Sonalika Tractors produced its technological marvel—the Sonalika Tiger Electric, Cellestial Tractors produced the Cellestial(55) HP Electric tractor, and Hybrid Agricultural Vehicle (HAV) produced the HAV(55)S1 to help farmers tackle all types of farm applications cheaply and responsibly with India's first field-ready electric tractor. Depending on the type and power take-off attachments used, these tractors run on conventional lead-acid batteries. Eco-effectiveness and green products have energized the great interest in the studies of the evolution and appeal of the LCA procedure [13]. The offroad plug-in hybrid electric tractor is designed for farming activities. Because of the rising popularity of vehicle electrification, agricultural tractor manufacturers are introducing hybrid powertrains with an emphasis on energy management strategy (EMS) [14].

Some of the hybrid electric tractors are operated on batteries with lead acid, use biogas as fuel, and have an electric power of 21 kW and a high speed of 25 km/h. A tractor is often built to haul several pieces of equipment for carrying and for agriculture area labor. In transport, a tractor is typically used to tow a caravan across rural highways or fields. In contrast, in fieldwork, such as sprayers and seed spreaders, the system may be employed concurrently to drive the implementation. There were two basic options discussed: automating regular vehicles and building specialized mobile platforms. As the world's population grows in the future decades, new manufacturing procedures that are more efficient, safer, and less harmful to the environment will be required [15].

20.2.1   Unmanned Ground Vehicles (UGVs) for Agriculture

Ground mobile robots with superior location and direction, wayfinding, groundwork, and pick-up technologies have previously proven their worth in open-air applications in manufacturing such as agriculture and agroforestry. Smart manufacturing is built on the tightly linked ideas of IoT, large data, and spectre computing. UGVs for advanced agriculture need to be built on the matching concept to avoid potential problems in applying twisted technology to manufacturing and agriculture. From 2017 through 2025, moving robots are a subset of agricultural robots and are anticipated to rise at a price of more than 15% each year. As a result, researchers and commercial enterprises devise novel solutions.

20.2.2   India a Growing Market for Tractors

Through food production, various upward and downward linkages contribute significantly to India's output, employment, and demand generation. Agriculture added nearly INR Rs. 1,604,044 crores toward the country's GVA in the year 2016, accounting for 15.4% of the total GVA. Farm mechanization in India is presently 40%–45% only, so it is very little when compared to other countries like the USA, Brazil, and China. The agricultural tractor retail is one of the main portions in the field of agriculture machinery in the country, with a yearly turnover of 6–7 lakh units. The biggest participants in the Indian tractor profession are Mahindra & Mahindra, Tractor and Farm Equipment Limited, Escorts, and John Deere, with Mahindra & Mahindra's existence being huge [16].

20.2.3   Electric Tractors

Agriculture accounts for a significant percentage of world pollution due to the usage of petroleum- and diesel-powered engine machines. However, this industry is also advancing toward a sustainable environment. Photovoltaic power might be an environmentally friendly approach to producing electricity for agriculture [17].

20.2.4   Green Technology for Agricultural Vehicles

Electric mini-vehicles are driven by domestically produced green power for small-scale family agriculture [18]. Considering the increasing price of petrol, the automotive sector's desire for electric vehicles is rapidly expanding, resulting in large profits for automakers [19]. The science and technology of autonomous agricultural off-road vehicles is driven by renewable energy systems [20]. Farming electric vehicles involve features such as precise steering, shifting speeds, and load ability. Self and Grabowski [21] demonstrated that agricultural electric vehicles equipped with internal combustion engines (ICEs) considerably contribute to the overall pollution caused by emissions. Electrical energy is utilized in many agricultural complicated parts, such as farm buildings, watering mechanisms, crop treatment, commodities processing, and storage space.

20.2.5   Agriculture Tractors Electrification

To switch off-road electric vehicles for improved agricultural applications, both supplies of electricity and energy are necessary for both road and off-road [22]. Electric vehicle technology has increased in recent years. To minimize emissions, numerous methods have been developed and adopted in the automobile market, including fully electric and hybrid vehicles.

20.2.6   Multipurpose Electric Vehicle for Farmers

Photovoltaic (PV) energy looks to be one of the more advantageous options for agriculture, particularly for countries with significant exposure to the sun. Several aspects, including equipment prices, ultimate applications, and connectivity to the electrical grid, contribute to higher fossil fuel costs and must be considered [23]. The electric vehicle's target is renewable energy for agricultural multipurpose systems (RAMseS) for farmers. Electric vehicles give a quicker and more useful technology than standard, hybrid, and hydrogen fuel cell automobiles in agriculture. Energy sources required to store solar generated electrical

Figure 20.2 Evidence of electric vehicle driving efficiency in agriculture (Rosales, J.C. *et al.*, 2022) (Asati, P. *et al.*, 2024) [34, 43].

energy for multifunctional agricultural EVs. The benefits of this situation for agribusiness are not being discussed or overlooked, as more precise, efficient, and ecologically friendly solutions are emerging [24].

20.2.7   Organic Farming with Electric Vehicles

A change in food, farming, and mode of transportation would be an option for organic farming [25]. Digitization could result in industrialized agriculture, using technologically advanced vertical gardening techniques and artificial intelligence-powered robots, or the lack of it could lead to a rebirth of labor-intensive farming. Organic farming is based on the fact that there is not sufficient demand for organic products, and food is going to get too expensive and scarce to feed the entire globe. Lower productivity would necessitate the use of more agricultural land, resulting in fewer trees and less biodiversity. We could consume only healthy foods and power our automobiles with renewable energy batteries.

20.3   Electric Vehicles and Robots in the Agricultural Sector

The agriculture industry is currently dealing with several issues, including population expansion, rising energy needs, shortages of workers, and global warming [26]. Electric vehicles are needed in agriculture to improve work efficiency and worker comfort. Nearly 400 electric vehicle tractors were invented from 1954 till the present.

When combined with the loss in rural labor, this illustrates the unavoidable necessity to boost efficiency on farms by implementing more automated technologies. Furthermore, electric cars in agricultural areas might improve operating safety, soil health, and productivity. In agriculture, switching large machines with smaller remote or electric motor-operated machines can help to lessen the issues related to soil settling. Electric vehicles offer several benefits, including the development of precision agriculture, better conditions for workers, a smaller ecological footprint, and increased crop revenue.

20.3.1   Internet of Things (IoT) for a Sustainable Future

Digitalization has made agriculture "smart," emerging as the epicenter of the already occurring technical innovation, and it has tremendous potential for development and practical advantages to the people. The Internet of Things (IoT) methods are now recognized among the primary foundations of the next generation of factories. IoT-based innovations provide an entirely new viewpoint on the future advancement of numerous professions, such as a career in engineering agriculture and medicine, as well as other fields that are still being investigated [27].

Over 28% of accessible land for agriculture is accounted for wasted food although over 800,000 people are currently hungry. Using the Internet of Things in agriculture would surely help to satisfy food demand while also enhancing the overall efficiency of agricultural manufacturing processes. Installing IoT devices in urban or industrial settings has no significant energy challenges because electricity and chemically powered batteries are readily available nearly anywhere [28].

20.3.2   IoT Technology for Smart Agriculture and Farming

Agriculture data have become more accessible due to the technological breakdown of IoT devices [29]. Because of enhanced water utilization and supply and disposal optimization, the technologies may be utilized to raise production by farming food more environmentally friendly while simultaneously safeguarding the natural world. The IoT makes it possible to create agricultural process-supporting tools. Remote surveillance systems, tools for supporting decision-making, robotic agriculture systems, and fertilization systems are all terms for the same thing.

20.3.3   Electric Robotics and Machines in Agriculture

Automation methods, intelligent sensors, and farming robots (automated machinery) have experienced amazing success in farm operations and piqued the curiosity of many, leading to the creation of more logical and adaptive gear [30]. Automation studies and development are continually expanding and changing as a result of continuing sensor discoveries, lower equipment prices, and the emergence of innovative control techniques. It is concerning far more than the installation of robots, cameras, or innovative technologies; additionally, it is about accelerating the digitization of industrial sectors [31]. Modern advances in technology and modernization are driving such a shift in the business model, altering the structuring and interface for greater business agility [32, 33]. Under the quicker acceptance and production of hybrid and electric vehicles by the FAME initiative, the Indian government is promoting ecologically friendly vehicles [34].

20.4   Blockchain-Based IoT Systems

In the case of electrically powered vehicles, it is still to be set how to anticipate the use of energy and power demand for an arrangement of route issues to ensure that the automobile will be able to perform the task [35]. The current IoT structures are establishing the path for a transformed world where the high mass of our everyday technology will be networked [36]. Blockchain has the potential to play a significant role in agriculture. Traditional IoT systems save collected data to organized servers for later use. Blockchain technology provides an innovative framework for decentralized preservation and data control based on the concept of an exchanged, safe, and distributed journal that stores and manages data without a requirement for a centralized organization or a trusted outsider.

20.4.1   Turning Electricity into Food

As the world grows increasingly technologically advanced and industrialized, the phrase of the era is development, or, more precisely, progress [37]. Change is a recurring topic in humanity as we currently know it. Every country strives for both resources and progress. Every accomplishment comes at a price, so there is constantly an opportunity expense. The sources of energy in earlier times must give way to those in the future. Solar energy is the power of tomorrow for many enterprises and applications, and that era is now. With solar-charged electric cars using an environmentally friendly, lower form of energy, the possibilities of using solar power are endless. Solar energy is renewable and infinite in supply. Solar power growth in industries such as agriculture is unaffected by EVs and is expected to continue. As the population rises and food suppliers seek better solutions, we are witnessing more innovative companies utilizing solar power as an innovative way to efficiently supply the food people need.

Modern agriculture relies heavily on energy obtained mostly from petroleum and coal. It may be described as an innovation that turns petroleum and coal into food in this manner. However, the availability of petroleum and coal is limited, and climate change necessitates a reduction in usage. As a consequence, it is not too early to look at how agriculture might be modified to employ renewable energy sources that do not contribute to climate change [38]. There is both a problem and a desire for machines that can transform energy into food. Agriculture receives around US $600 billion per year worldwide in government support [39]. Agriculture is responsible for 8% to 10.8% of the total global greenhouse gas (GHG) emissions. Global average temperatures rose to 0.74°C [40]. Agriculture is accountable for a notable fraction of man-made emissions, which is up to 30% based on the report of the Intergovernmental Panel on Climate Change (IPCC) [41]. Agricultural pollution and regulation must be taken into consideration when subsidizing agriculture [42].

Conclusion

The article discusses the various aspects of farmers and the technology they adopted to make the environment sustainable, where the government also tries to make changes in the updating through which the farmers can consume energy and save money. As discussed in the article, many reviews of the literature explain how IoT and ICT are very important for agriculture because agriculture is the foundation of India and also the primary income for the farmers. Technical feasibility or replacing conventional tractors with electric vehicles is necessary. We conclude that renewable energy on the farm should be observed as part of a great transition that will entail notable modifications and converting to live agricultural operations to ensure a truly sustainable agriculture. The Internet of Things has helped agriculture to clear the way by implementing current technical responses to time-explored understanding. This permits the interval between manufacture and satisfying production and aggregate to be synthesized. Hence, we can say that electric vehicle is a boon for society.

References

1. Maja, M.M. and Ayano, S.F., The Impact of Population Growth on Natural Resources and Farmers' Capacity to Adapt to Climate Change in Low-Income Countries. *Earth Syst. Environ.*, 5, 2, 271–283, Mar. 2021, doi: 10.1007/S41748-021-00209-6.
2. Parker, J.D., Akinbami, L.J., Woodruff, T.J., Air Pollution and Childhood Respiratory Allergies in the United States. *Environ. Health Perspect.*, 117, 1, 140–147, 2009, doi: 10.1289/EHP.11497.
3. Binswanger, H. P., *The economics of tractors in South Asia*. International Crops Research Institute for the Semi-Arid Tropics, 1978.
4. Nemry, F. and Brons, M., Plug-in Hybrid and Battery Electric Vehicles. Market penetration scenarios of electric drive vehicles, 2010.

5. Sadek, N., Urban electric vehicles: A contemporary business case. *Eur. Transport Res. Rev.*, 4, 1, 27–37, Mar. 2012, doi: 10.1007/S12544-011-0061-6/TABLES/4.

6. Miyake, Y., Kimoto, S., Uchiyama, Y., Kohsaka, R., Income change and inter-farmer relations through conservation agriculture in Ishikawa Prefecture, Japan: Empirical analysis of economic and behavioral factors. *Land*, 11, 2, 245, 2022.

7. Christiaensen, L., Rutledge, Z., Taylor, J. E., The future of work in agri-food. *Food Policy*, 99, 101963, 2021.

8. Maja, M.M. and Ayano, S.F., The Impact of Population Growth on Natural Resources and Farmers' Capacity to Adapt to Climate Change in Low-Income Countries. *Earth Syst. Environ.*, 5, 2, 271–283, Jun. 2021, doi: 10.1007/S41748-021-00209-6.

9. Vermesan, O. and Friess, P., *Building the Hyperconnected Society-Internet of Things Research and Innovation Value Chains, Ecosystems and Markets*, p. 332, Taylor & Francis, 2015.

10. Agricultural Biotechnology, doi: 10.22271/ed.book.1026.

11. Choi, W. S., Pratama, P. S., Supeno, D., Jeong, S. W., Byun, J. Y., Woo, J. H., ... Park, C. S., Characteristics of reduction gear in electric agricultural vehicle. In *IOP Conf. Ser.: Mater. Sci. Eng.*, vol. 324, no. 1, p. 012036, IOP Publishing, 2018, March.

12. Resen, M.M., Electric Vehicle Feasibility for Farms in Eastern South Dakota, 1981, [Online]. Available: https://openprairie.sdstate.edu/etd/4051.

13. de Souza, L.L.P., Lora, E.E.S., Palacio, J.C.E., Rocha, M.H., Renó, M.L.G., Venturini, O.J., Comparative environmental life cycle assessment of conventional vehicles with different fuel options, plug-in hybrid and electric vehicles for a sustainable transportation system in Brazil. *J. Cleaner Prod.*, 203, 444–468, Dec. 2018, doi: 10.1016/j.jclepro.2018.08.236.

14. Ghobadpour, A., Mousazadeh, H., Kelouwani, S., Zioui, N., Kandidayeni, M., Boulon, L., An intelligent energy management strategy for an off-road plug-in hybrid electric tractor based on farm operation recognition. *IET Electr. Syst. Transp.*, 11, 4, 333–347, Dec. 2021, doi: 10.1049/els2.12029.

15. Gonzalez-De-Santos, P., Fernández, R., Sepúlveda, D., Navas, E., Armada, M., Unmanned ground vehicles for smart farms. *Agron.-Clim. Chang. Food Secur.*, 6, 73, 2020.

16. Malik, A. and Kohli, S., Electric tractors: Survey of challenges and opportunities in India. *Mater. Today: Proc.*, 28, 2318–2324, 2020.

17. Lombardi, G. V. and Berni, R., Renewable energy in agriculture: Farmers willingness-to-pay for a photovoltaic electric farm tractor. *J. Clean. Prod.*, 313, 127520, 2021.

18. Vogt, H.H., Albiero, D., Schmuelling, B., Electric tractor propelled by renewable energy for small-scale family farming. *2018 13th International Conference on Ecological Vehicles and Renewable Energies, EVER 2018*, May 2018, pp. 1–4, doi: 10.1109/EVER.2018.8362344.

19. Flint, J., Zhang, D., Xu, P., Preliminary Market Analysis for a New Hybrid Electric Farm Tractor, 2014.

20. Ghobadpour, A., Boulon, L., Mousazadeh, H., Malvajerdi, A. S., Rafiee, S., State of the art of autonomous agricultural off-road vehicles driven by renewable energy systems. *Energy Procedia*, 162, 4–13, 2019.

21. Self, S. and Grabowski, R., Economic development and the role of agricultural technology. *Agric. Econ.*, 36, 3, 395–404, May 2007, doi: 10.1111/J.1574-0862.2007.00215.X.

22. IEEE Power Electronics Society, IEEE Power & Energy Society, IEEE Industry Applications Society, and Institute of Electrical and Electronics Engineers, *ITEC2019 : 2019 IEEE Transportation Electrification Conference and Expo : Suburban Collection Showplace*, Novi, Michigan, USA, June 19-21, 2019.

23. Mousazadeh, H., Keyhani, A., Mobli, H., Bardi, U., Lombardi, G., el Asmar, T., Technical and economical assessment of a multipurpose electric vehicle for farmers. *J. Cleaner Prod.*, 17, 17, 1556–1562, Nov. 2009, doi: 10.1016/j.jclepro.2009.05.009.

24. Loukatos, D., Petrongonas, E., Manes, K., Kyrtopoulos, I. V., Dimou, V., Arvanitis, K. G., A synergy of innovative technologies towards implementing an autonomous diy electric vehicle for harvester-assisting purposes. *Machines*, 9, 4, 82, 2021.

25. Neumann, K., Wrong memes : Organic farming and battery electric vehicles, in: *Sustainable Development and Resource Productivity*, pp. 114–121, Nov. 2020, doi: 10.4324/9781003000365-12.

26. Ghobadpour, A., Monsalve, G., Cardenas, A., Mousazadeh, H., Off-Road Electric Vehicles and Autonomous Robots in Agricultural Sector: Trends, Challenges, and Opportunities. *Vehicles*, MDPI, 4, 3, 843–864, Sep. 01, 2022, doi: 10.3390/vehicles4030047.

27. Nižetić, S., Šolić, P., Gonzalez-De, D. L. D. I., Patrono, L., Internet of Things (IoT): Opportunities, issues and challenges towards a smart and sustainable future. *J. Clean. Prod.*, 274, 122877, 2020.

28. de Souza, C. P. and Baiocchi, O., Energy resources in agriculture and forestry: How to be prepared for the Internet of Things (IoT) Revolution. In *Energy Systems and Environment*, InTechOpen, 2018.

29. Gowda, V. D., Prabhu, M. S., Ramesha, M., Kudari, J. M., Samal, A., Smart agriculture and smart farming using IoT technology. In *Journal of Physics: Conference Series*, vol. 2089, no. 1, p. 012038, IOP Publishing, 2021, November.

30. Gorjian, S., Minaei, S., MalehMirchegini, L., Trommsdorff, M., Shamshiri, R. R., Applications of solar PV systems in agricultural automation and robotics. In *Photovoltaic Solar Energy Conversion*, pp. 191–235, Academic Press, 2020.

31. Tabaa, M., Monteiro, F., Bensag, H., Dandache, A., Green Industrial Internet of Things from a smart industry perspectives. *Energy Rep.*, 6, 430–446, Nov. 2020, doi: 10.1016/j.egyr.2020.09.022.

32. Nordelöf, A., Messagie, M., Tillman, A.M., Ljunggren Söderman, M., Van Mierlo, J., Environmental impacts of hybrid, plug-in hybrid, and battery electric vehicles—what can we learn from life cycle assessment? *Int. J. Life Cycle Assess.*, Springer Verlag, 19, 11, 1866–1890, Oct. 14, 2014, doi: 10.1007/s11367-014-0788-0.

33. Malik, A. and Kohli, S., Electric tractors: Survey of challenges and opportunities in India. *Mater. Today: Proc.*, 28, 2318–2324, 2020.

34. Rosales, J. C., Machado, R. L., Machado, A. L., Andrade, H. G., Kroessin, L., Design specifications of an autonomous electric vehicle for use in family farm units. *Engenharia Agrícola*, 42, 2022.

35. Schmidt, J. R. and Cheein, F. A., Assessment of power consumption of electric machinery in agricultural tasks for enhancing the route planning problem. *Comput. Electron. Agric.*, 163, 104868, 2019.

36. Hassan, M.U., Rehmani, M.H., Chen, J., Privacy preservation in blockchain based IoT systems: Integration issues, prospects, challenges, and future research directions. *Future Gener. Comput. Syst.*, 97, 512–529, Aug. 2019, doi: 10.1016/j.future.2019.02.060.

37. Emard, A., Turning the power of the sun into food. *Renew. Energy Focus*, Elsevier Ltd, 16, 5–6, 111–112, Dec. 01, 2015, doi: 10.1016/j.ref.2015.10.001.

38. Bardi, U., El Asmar, T., Lavacchi, A., Turning electricity into food: The role of renewable energy in the future of agriculture. *J. Cleaner Prod.*, 53, 224–231, Aug. 2013, doi: 10.1016/j.jclepro.2013.04.014.

39. Laborde, D., Mamun, A., Martin, W., Piñeiro, V., Vos, R., Agricultural subsidies and global greenhouse gas emissions. *Nat. Commun.*, 12, 1, 1–9, May 2021, doi: 10.1038/s41467-021-22703-1.

40. Liu, D., Guo, X., Xiao, B., What causes growth of global greenhouse gas emissions? Evidence from 40 countries. *Sci. Total Environ.*, 661, 750–766, Apr. 2019, doi: 10.1016/J.SCITOTENV.2019.01.197.

41. Tubiello, F.N., Salvatore, M., Rossi, S., Ferrara, A., Fitton, N., Smith, P., The FAOSTAT database of greenhouse gas emissions from agriculture. *Environ. Res. Lett.*, 8, 1, 015009, Feb. 2013, doi: 10.1088/1748-9326/8/1/015009.

42. Chen, Y.H., Wen, X.W., Wang, B., Yan Nie, P., Agricultural pollution and regulation: How to subsidize agriculture? *J. Cleaner Prod.*, 164, 258–264, Oct. 2017, doi: 10.1016/J.JCLEPRO.2017.06.216.

43. Asati, P., Raghuwanshi, S., Vashisht, A., Vyas, R., Singh, P. R., Factors influencing health & environmental intentions to adopt electric vehicles from the perspective of business school students. *Int. J. Religion*, 5, 1, 743–750, 2024.

Index

Activities, 161-167, 169-172
Adulteration, 161
Advancements, 162
Agri market, 153
Agricultural ecosystem, 212
Agricultural finance, 201
Agricultural Produce Marketing Committees
    (APMCs), 57
Agricultural revolutions 4.0 and 5.0, 147
Agricultural value chain, 146, 155
Agriculture, 35-46, 71, 73, 75-77, 83-86,
    161-172, 292, 293, 294, 307-316, 321, 340
Agriculture 5.0, 160
Agriculture infrastructure, 214-216
Agriculture skill council of India (ASCI),
    213
Agriculture transformation index, 216
Agriculture value chain, 212-213
Agri-food sector, 71, 79, 81
Agritech investment, 219
Artificial intelligence (AI), 145, 161-163,
    167-172, 260, 273, 275-276, 284, 286-287
Analysis of imports and exports,
    132-134
    import–export gap, 134
    increasing trend, 134
    potential for export expansion, 134
    steady export growth, 134
    trade balance, 134
Analytics, 35, 39
Application, 342
    analyze patterns, 344
    correlation, 343
    regression methods, 343
ATMEGA328, 243
Augmented reality (AR), 11
Auto-driver, 161
Automated, 263

Bank, 322, 323, 328, 331-324
BharatNet, 153
Bibliometric analysis, 21
Big data, 145, 147, 150, 157, 158
Biotechnology, 145
Blockchain, 161, 273, 275-276, 280, 284, 286
    blockchain-features, 113-114
    blockchain-concepts, 113
    blockchain-introduction, 111
    proposed model, 115
Britannia, 217

Carrot2, 20
Certification, 72-75, 86
Citation gecko, 20
Climate change, 162, 172
Climate-smart farming methods, 154
Components of precision irrigation
    management, 183
    precise communication, 183
    precise control, 183
        flow control devices, 183
        positioning systems, 183
        variable rate sprinklers/emitters, 183
    precise information, 183
        moisture measuring unit, 183
        weather monitoring unit, 183
    precise response, 184
        data management and decision support
            systems, 184
Consumers, 71-74, 77, 80-82, 86
Consumption, 341, 349
    modeling, 341
    process, 341
Corporate sustainability reporting, 71, 89
Crop, 161-168
Crop monitoring, 165, 168
Cropin, 218

Data acquisition, 131
  chemical-specific sensors, 132
  close-range sensing, 131-132
  GPS-DGPS, 132
  remote sensing, 131
Data analysis, 269
Data analytics, 307, 308, 310-316
Data analytics and modeling, 181
  data integration, 181
  geostatistics, 181
  machine learning, 182
  modeling of soil processes, 182
  soil health indices, 181
  statistical analysis, 181
Data management tools, 129
  geographic information system (GIS), 130
  variable rate treatment (VRT), 129
Data security, 162
Data utilization, 130-131
  drones, 131
  global positioning system (GPS) and
    geographic information system (GIS), 131
  internet of things (IoT), 130
  radio frequency identification, 131
  robotics, 130
DEA model, 127-128
Decentralized financial insurance, 203
DeHaat, 218
Department of Energy, 371
Diagram, 353
Digital, 263, 264, 265, 266, 267
Digital agricultural ecosystem, 5
Digital agriculture, 145-147, 151, 152, 159
Digital agriculture mission 2021–2025, 152
Digital ecosystem, 35, 37
Digital farming ecosystem, 17
Digital finance, 167, 172
Digital infrastructure, 308, 312, 313
Digital optimization, 71, 81, 82, 89
Digital platform, 71, 82, 84, 86, 89
Digital processes, 73, 74
Digital technology, 36-38
Digital transformation, 175, 176
Digital trends, 72
Digital value chain, 148
Digitization, 85, 87, 88
Diode, 242

Direct-to-consumer (DTC), 9
Distributed ledger, 194
Distribution, 352
Doubling farmers' income (DFI), 213
Drone-based, 161

Early sensing, 162
Ecologically safe production, 71-78, 81, 82
Economy, 81, 88, 89, 161-164, 172
e-Governance initiatives, 153
Electric vehicles and robots in agriculture
    sector, 374
Electronic national agriculture market
    (e-NAM), 57
Engagement, 35, 38, 49
Enterprise resource management, 199
Environmental, 293, 294
Environmental impact, 147, 151, 157
Environmentally safe production, 71-75, 81, 83,
    87
ESP32, 243
Evidence of electric vehicles driving efficiency
    in agriculture, 373
Evidence of smart farming technology, 370

Farm, farmland, 259, 260, 263, 264, 269
Farmer, 291, 294, 295, 296, 297, 298, 299, 303,
    304, 305, 321, 322
Farmer producer organization, 212, 214
Farming, 307-316
Farming data, 207
Farming industry, 307-316
Fertiliser consumption, 292
Fertiliser sprayer, 291, 292, 295, 296, 298, 299,
    304
Fertilizer, 291, 292, 293, 294, 295, 296, 297, 298,
    299, 300, 301, 303
Fertilizer spraying, 162
Fertilizer usage, 292
Field-programmable gate arrays (FPGAs),
    10
Financial services, 322
Finolex, 217
Food grains, 291, 292
Food safety, 162, 172, 195
Food Safety and Standards Authority of India
    (FSSAI), 154

Food security, 145-148, 151, 155, 156-158, 160
Food systems, 145, 148, 155, 158
Function, 344
    requirements, 345, 346

G20 nations, 156, 157
Geo-tagged, 163
Global farmer insights, 221
Global food security, 156, 160
Global open data for agriculture and nutrition |
    GODAN, 12
Goods, 71-75, 79, 81, 82
Greenhouse gas (GHG), 221
Gross value addition, 276
Growth drivers, 214

Harvesting, 161-163

I2C, 250
Impact of globalization on Indian agriculture, 127
Implications, 138
    managerial implications, 138
    theoretical implications, 139
India digital ecosystem of agriculture (IDEA),
    154, 212
Industry, 4, 76, 78, 79, 83, 84, 193
Innovation in agriculture, 149, 150, 158
Innovative, 161-165, 169
Institution, 169-172
Institutional credit, 321-324, 334
Internet of Things (IoT), 3, 145
Internet technology, 154
Introduction, 91
ISM, 326-327, 331, 333-334
ITC, 217
ITC's e-Choupal ecosystem, 149

Jain irrigations systems, 217
Jio Krishi, 154
John Deere, 218

Kisan Sampada Yojana, 154
Knowledge sharing, 36-39, 49
Krishi Yantra App, 154

Laser land leveling, 276-277, 289-290
Linear pair regression, 343
Livestock, 75, 82, 83, 85

Marico, 217
Market, 71, 73-75, 80-82, 84-87, 89, 71
Mega food park, 216
Methodology, 135-137
MICMAC, 326, 331
Mobile applications, 165-169
Model, 360
    consumption, 365, 366
    local cubic spline, 364-366
    mathematical, 360
    patterns, 363
    square method, 360-362

National economic strategy, 74, 75, 76, 80, 81
National Food Security Act (NFSA), 146
National Mission for Sustainable Agriculture
    (NMSA), 216
National mission of agricultural extension and
    technology, 153
Nestle, 218
Nutrition, 146, 148, 151, 155, 156, 159, 160

Open network for digital commerce (ONDC),
    213, 225
Organic agricultural product, 71, 73, 74
Organic animal husbandry, 72
Organic crop, 72
Organic feed, 72
Organic fish, 72
Organic lands, 76, 78
Organic mushroom, 72
Organic product, 71-74, 76-80, 82, 86
Organic production, 72-78
Organic seaweed, 72

Precision agriculture, 163, 273-274, 276,
    287-289
PRISMA flow diagram, 19
PRISMA protocol, 19
Properties, 357
    poisson distribution, 354-355

Radiator water temperature, 234
Regression, 165-171
Remote sensing and imaging techniques, 180
    aerial imagery, 180
    electromagnetic induction (EMI), 180
    ground penetrating radar (GPR), 180

hyperspectral imaging, 181
light detection and ranging (LiDAR), 179
satellite imagery, 180
thermal imaging, 179
Renewable energy, 197
Reverse polarity circuit, 241
Revolutionize, 172
Robotics, 145, 150, 151, 153, 158, 159, 162, 259, 263
Rural development, 321

Safe storage, 205
SDG, 307-316
Sectors of the economy, 353
Seed quality, 204
Sensagri, 154
Shark tank, 296, 297
Smart, 260, 261, 262, 263
Smart agriculture, 18
Smart contract, 200
Smart farming, 147, 149, 154, 157, 159,
    273-276, 279, 285-286, 288, 290
Social media, 35-37, 164, 167-171
Soil ecosystem services, 177
    human health advancement, 176
    sustainable plant production, 177
    water quality control, 176
Soil health, 176, 293, 294
Soil quality, 176
Soil sensors, 179
    IoT-enabled soil monitoring systems, 179
    soil compaction sensors, 178
    soil erosion sensors, 178
    soil moisture sensors, 178
    soil nutrient sensors, 179
    soil organic matter (SOM) sensors, 179
    soil pest/insect sensors, 178
    soil pH sensors, 179
    soil pollutant sensors, 178
    soil temperature sensors, 177
Solar radiation, 350, 358
Special economic zones (SEZs), 215
Start-ups, 217-219
STM2CubeIDE, 247
STM32, 242
Subsidy, 292, 304
Supply chain, 198
Supply chain - sericulture
    bed cleaning - sericulture, 104
    chawki rearing, 105-107

cocoon harvesting, 105
collective moth egg preparation, 99
copulation in silkworm, 98
diseases in silkworm, 107-110
embryogenesis - the life history of the
    silkworm, 97
grainages - the silkworm rearing farms in
    India, 103
hygiene conditions for egg rearing in
    grainages, 102-103
mounting - sericulture, 104-105
mulberry - the fodder of Bombyx Mori,
    92
platation techniques of Mulberry, 93-96
predator in silkworm, 110-111
pupa to cocoon stage, 106
rearing of silkworm - an art by itself, 97
segregated method of egg preparation, 98
silkworm egg preparation, 98
silkworm egg rearing, 98-102
traits of silkworm, 107
Sustainability, 273, 277, 290
Sustainable, 162-163
Sustainable development goal 2 (SDG 2), 211
Sustainable development goals, 146
Sustainable farming, 307, 309, 316
Systematic literature review, 19

Technology, technologies, 162, 163, 164, 166,
    168, 169, 262, 263, 264
The Directorate of Marketing and Inspection
    (DMI), 58
Thevenin's theorem, 239
TLS (total link strength), 25
TouchGFX designer, 245
Transorb, 241
Turning electricity into food, 375

Unified farmer services interface, 154
Uniform, 354-356
    distribution properties, 357-359
Unmanned systems, 81, 83

Value-based food supply chains, 148
Venture capital investments, 220
Virtual reality (VR), 11
Visualisation of similarity, 25
Voltage divider, 233
VosViewer, 25

Water, 339
    intake, 347, 359
    management objects, 340
    management systems, 340
    resources, 351
Water management, 206

Weather forecasting, 162, 163, 165, 167
Weather station, 202

Yield, 162-163
Yield gap, 214
YouTube, 35-39, 43-44, 48-50

Printed in the USA/Agawam, MA
May 31, 2024

867067.006